Libraries
AND THE
Internet/NREN

Libraries
AND THE
Internet/NREN

Perspectives, Issues, and Challenges

CHARLES R. McCLURE
WILLIAM E. MOEN
JOE RYAN

Mecklermedia
Westport • London

Library of Congress Cataloging-in-Publication Data

Libraries and the Internet/NREN : perspectives, issues, and challenges
/ Charles R. McClure, William E. Moen, Joe Ryan.
   p.   cm.
  Includes bibliographical references (p.) and index.
  ISBN 0-88736-824-7 (alk. paper) : $
  1. Internet (Computer network) 2. National Research and
Education Network (Computer network) 3. Library information
networks–United States. I. McClure, Charles R. II. Moen, William E.
III. Ryan, Joe, 1951- .
Z674.82.I59L48 1994
021.6'5'0973–dc20   93-29297
                                             CIP

British Library Cataloguing-in-Publication Data is available

Mecklermedia Corporation, 11 Ferry Lane West, Westport, CT 06880.
Mecklermedia Ltd., Artillery House, Artillery Row, London SW1P 1RT, UK.

Printed on acid free paper.
Printed in the United States of America.

Contents

List of Figures and Tables

Acknowledgments

This research study could not have been completed without the assistance and involvement of a number of organizations and individuals. We appreciate funding by OCLC and Mecklermedia Corporation for the project. We thank OCLC's Martin Dillon and Erik Jul for their interest in this project. Additional support provided by Syracuse University contributed to the successful completion of the study. School of Information Studies' students who participated in the project include the following: Bonnie Gratch conducted one of the site visits, and contributed to analysis and write-up of the site visits and survey analysis; Tracey Lemon assisted in survey data entry and analysis; and Diana Lauterbach participated in the research and literature review for the public library section. Beth Mahoney, at the School of Information Studies, provided editorial, graphics, and word processing assistance.

We are especially indebted to those who participated in the focus group sessions and responded to the survey. The high response rate to the survey instrument was indicative of the interest engendered by the study.

But the focus group sessions could not have been completed successfully without the advice and assistance of such individuals as Donna Mancini, Dekalb County Library System, Decatur, Georgia; Jean Polly, Liverpool Public Library, Liverpool, New York; Steve Cisler, Apple, Inc., Cupertino, California; Pat Moholt, Columbia University, New York; and Charles Farley, Gaylord Bros., Liverpool, New York. The assistance of the Public Library Association in providing a mailing list for the survey was also essential, and we gratefully acknowledge their assistance.

A special note of thanks goes to Howard McGinn and Diana Young of the North Carolina State Library, Peter Lyman and John Waiblinger of the University of Southern California, and William Arms and Barbara Richards of Carnegie Mellon University. They unselfishly gave of their time and energy helping to organize and participating in the site visits. In addition, their staffs, other members of their communities, and numerous other individuals gave freely of their time and expertise during the site visits for which we are very grateful.

Finally, a number of individuals offered suggestions, comments, and ideas regarding the study that helped the study team design the data-collection instruments and analyze the data. Comments from and discussions with Paul Peters, Clifford Lynch, Steve Cisler, Donna Mancini and the strategic planning committee at DeKalb County Public Library, Laura Isenstein, Pamela McLaughlin, and Jean Polly greatly assisted our work on this study.

Preface

The impacts of the evolving Internet/National Research and Education Network (NREN) on libraries are likely to be monumental in both scope and practice. As the Internet/NREN develops, as connectivity to the network becomes ubiquitous, and as individuals and organizations learn how to exploit the network, the very nature of the networked electronic information resources will uproot and redefine many of the previously held assumptions that librarians and information specialists have traditionally taken as gospel.

What these impacts are, how they will affect libraries, and how libraries might best respond to them will be some of the most critical issues facing libraries as they enter the electronic networked environment. Indeed, the context of these debates may need to move from how might the library community best respond to the impacts, to how the library community can best shape networking developments and the environment in which they will deliver networked-based services and products.

To shape events and not just respond to them, the library community must be better informed about the Internet/NREN. Libraries must recognize the importance and pervasiveness of the changes that will result from internetworking and working in "cyberspace." They must recognize that virtual, digital libraries are emerging—regardless of whether traditional libraries want them to or not.

Thus, the purpose of this book is to explore issues, topics, and impacts related to the role of libraries in the Internet/NREN. The book is not a tutorial on how to use the Internet/NREN or a description of specific information services and resources available on the network—other works are available that accomplish those objectives. Moreover, the book focuses on academic, public, special, and school libraries and not all types of libraries and information centers. Such is due, in part, to the lack of knowledge and research about these other areas of library involvement in the Internet/NREN as of 1992.

A number of themes resonate throughout this book, regardless of the library setting or issue area being discussed. For example, all types of libraries are concerned about how to get connected to the Internet/NREN and how they will pay for Internet/NREN information resources and services. These and similar themes can be identified in each of the first six chapters. Other issues and topics tend to be unique to particular library contexts.

More specifically, this book:

- reports exploratory research findings related to libraries' efforts to move into the Internet/NREN environment;
- identifies key issues and topics that will require additional attention, discussion, and research related to libraries and the Internet/NREN;
- expands the existing knowledge base regarding libraries and their role in the Internet/NREN;
- proposes recommendations and strategies for how libraries might best flourish in the Internet/NREN; and
- encourages the library community to take a proactive stance in shaping national policy initiatives to enhance the role of libraries in the Internet/NREN.

The book captures the developments and status of library involvement in the Internet/NREN as of late 1992. Clearly, developments are continuing rapidly, but the book will have served its purpose if it helps encourage discussion, analysis, pilot projects, and issue resolution that promote the role of libraries in the Internet/NREN.

Although this work is intended primarily for librarians and information specialists, it will be of interest to educators, government officials, and the broader range of information professionals. The impacts of the Internet/NREN will likely blur the roles and responsibilities of all members of society. As electronic information over the network becomes pervasive, all of us will become "electronic librarians."

This book brings together a range of information and research work that has been done by researchers at Syracuse University as well as writings by others. The first four chapters offer a summary of research conducted at the School of Information Studies related to the role of academic libraries (Chapters 1 through 3) and public libraries (Chapter 4) in the Internet/NREN. The authors gratefully acknowledge the funding from Meckler Corporation and OCLC, Inc. that supported the completion of these two studies. Portions of these chapters have appeared in other publications. This book, however, provides an opportunity for the material to be presented together in one source.

Chapters 5 and 6 discuss the evolving role of library media programs and special libraries in the Internet/NREN. For special libraries and library media programs, a number of unique factors will pose new challenges and opportunities for these librarians. Chapter 7 reviews and assesses key issues related to the Government Printing Office's Depository Library Program and how depository libraries might move into the Internet/NREN environment. The importance and role of library education and training is explored in Chapter 8, offering a number of specific recommendations for how library educators might use the Internet/NREN.

Chapter 9 provides an essay on the economics of library involvement with the Internet/NREN, suggesting that significant changes are needed in the manner in which libraries are funded if they are to survive in an electronic environment. Chapter 10 concludes with an overview of critical success factors affecting libraries in an Internet environment and offers recommendations for next steps as librarians move into this networked setting.

A recent policy statement, "Technology for America's Economic Growth: A New Direction to Build Economic Strength," issued by the Clinton administration on February 22, 1993, stated that the administration would:

> Create an information infrastructure technology program to assist industry in the development of the hardware and software needed to fully apply advanced computing and networking technology in manufacturing, in health care, in life-long learning, and in libraries.
>
> [In addition,] access to the Internet and developing NREN will be expanded to connect university campuses, community colleges, and K–12 schools to a high-speed communications network providing a broad range of information resources. Support will be provided for equipment allowing local networks in these learning institutions access to the network along with support for development of high-performance software capable of taking advantage of the emerging hardware capabilities.

The policy statement goes on to support a range of initiatives that will connect the library and education community to the Internet/NREN, will support their use of the network, and will provide seed monies for pilot and demonstration projects in using the network.

Our crystal ball cannot determine how this initiative, or a range of other initiatives, will eventually evolve over the next several years. What is clear, however, is that the world is moving toward an electronically connected information network in which virtual libraries and electronic multimedia information resources will be the norm. We hope that this volume will encourage librarians and information specialists to reassess the role of libraries in this new world. We hope this work will help them move successfully into new roles to support and enhance the public's use of the Internet/NREN.

Charles R. McClure,
William E. Moen,
and Joe Ryan

Academic Libraries and the NREN: The Perpetual Work-in-Progress Towards the Virtual Library[1]

In any case, the network of computers and communications will become the characteristic infrastructure of the postmodern world. It will consist of roughly four parts. The first is composed of the network's links. . . . The second will consist of the sensors and monitors that connect the network to the world. . . . The third part will be comprised of databases including encyclopedic information, musical and theatrical performances, and records of all kinds. Finally, there will be information processors both for the purpose of keeping the network itself in order and to provide expert services of particular kinds. . . . The information links are like the nerves that pervade and help to animate the human organism. The sensors and monitors are analogous to the human senses that put us in touch with the world. Databases correspond to memory; the information processors perform the function of human reasoning and comprehension. Once the postmodern infrastructure is reasonably integrated it will greatly exceed human intelligence in reach, acuity, capacity, and precision.

Albert Borgmann, *Crossing the Postmodern Divide*

Academic institutions, and their libraries, were early beneficiaries of national electronic networking initiatives. Since the mid-1980s, increasing numbers of academic libraries connected to the Internet experienced firsthand the possibilities and problems, the opportunities and threats, of the emerging networked environment. There has been, however, little empirical research concerning the effects on and implications for academic libraries in this environment. To examine and understand the impact of networking on academic libraries, a study team at the School of Information Studies,

Syracuse University, conducted a year-long, multipart research project to investigate how academic libraries are responding to the Internet and the evolving National Research and Education Network (NREN). Chapters 1, 2, and 3 report the study's findings and analysis. Appendix A describes the study methodology.

This chapter provides background information about academic libraries and networking. This information guided the preliminary data collection. Ongoing monitoring of the literature informed the data analysis and the study team's understanding of the issues throughout the project. Chapter 1 is not meant as a comprehensive and exhaustive literature review. Instead, it introduces a selection of major issues uncovered by a review of the literature.

A literature review of such a dynamically evolving area as academic libraries and networking could never be complete. This is all the more true because so many ideas and issues are being discussed in electronic forums on the network. In fact, traditional literature reviews may be called into question—another unforeseen impact of the networked environment. Given this, it would be a herculean task to accomplish exhaustivity.

Chapter 2 reports the results from the study team's site visits to two academic libraries. The site visits provided a focused and detailed look at how particular academic libraries are actively preparing themselves for and meeting the challenges of the networked environment.

Chapter 3 discusses a wide range of key issues affecting the development of academic libraries in the networked environment that emerged from the focus group sessions held with people knowledgeable about academic and research libraries. These issues provide a sense of the tone, concerns, and perspectives of the various individuals who participated in the data-collection process.

THE ACADEMIC LIBRARY CONTEXT

The academic library, the traditional center of scholarly research and instructional materials for an academic community, is on an evolutionary path, a path that may lead to its demise or its metamorphosis and re-creation. There is little likelihood that it can remain in its current form given the converging forces acting on it. As one of several life forms in an academic community, its essential task has been "to arrange the objects to favor the metabolic processes of thought," a vehicle to support the life of the mind (Weiskel, 1986, p. 562).

The library does not exist in isolation and will be affected by the changing information flows within the academic community.

These changes will result in long-term structural changes within the academy. Understanding the library, not in terms of buildings nor even the books contained within the buildings, but rather an idea, a set of functions, and an interaction of people reveals the library primarily as a process. And as a process, the library has the capability of evolving or coevolving alongside the academic community in which it resides.

The forces shaping the evolution of the library from its traditional concerns and activities threaten as well as nurture the future of the library. A primary force is that of technology. Electronic computer networks, powerful "scholar workstations," digitized information in the forms of full-text and multimedia documents, sophisticated searching and retrieval or other data manipulation software, and other emerging information technologies open up new vistas for information creation, information access, and information processing. Yet other forces—social, behavioral, economic, and political, are influencing the choices available to libraries.

The library is not without force and influence itself. It has had in the past, and continues to have, a centrality in the information environment of the academic community. Lynch (1992b, p. 34) restates the traditional library functions that have successfully defined its mission:

- select and acquire information;
- house and preserve information;
- organize information; and
- provide access to information.

The primacy of print-based materials will likely continue to absorb much of the library's efforts, but the traditional functions increasingly will be called into question as the networked environment evolves.

Lynch (1992b, p. 34) suggests further that librarians will need to confront, live with, and reconcile competing demands that include:

- continuing to acquire "traditional" paper-based information;
- acquiring or providing (subsidizing) access to electronic versions of the existing paper-based reference works, journal subscriptions, and similar materials;
- acquiring or providing (subsidizing) access to A&I [abstracting and indexing] databases that provide

access to the journal literature—materials held by the library as well as those available through interlibrary loan or document supply services, and existing both in paper and electronic forms;

- acquiring or providing (subsidizing) access to new electronic-only forms of information (e.g., listservs, netnews, multimedia publications, numeric databases, weather information, factual databases); and
- acquiring, developing, or providing (subsidizing) access to the information refinery services—evaluative, correlative, and filtering services—to control the flood of information generated by the first four demands.

Librarians' skills and knowledge relevant to the traditional functions are critical resources in confronting the new information environment evolving in the academic community. In addition, the librarians' service orientation and capacity to teach users information skills may be the two characteristics that will assist them in maintaining a central role for the electronic library of the future.

Three contexts are relevant as a framework for examining the issues academic libraries face given the growth of the networked environment: technology, access, and economics. While technology and economic issues are common to other libraries in this new information environment, academic libraries are facing challenges to their unique role in the process of scholarly communication. The advent of electronic networking and digital information is dramatically affecting how scholars and students access and disseminate information. Thus, the access issue has a special cast for academic libraries given their traditional responsibilities in the area of scholarly information.

TECHNOLOGY CONTEXT

The current situation of academic libraries can be understood in several technological contexts. One is the context of library automation that has evolved over the past thirty years. Another is the separate contexts of networking technologies that accompanied library automation efforts and the networking technologies developed by computer scientists and others that have resulted in the Internet/NREN. A third technological context is the digitization of information such as full-text and multimedia documents and the whole arena of electronic publishing.

Library Automation

Library automation passed through a number of stages in arriving at the point now where library information systems provide online access to a wide range of electronic information sources and services (Arms, 1989a). Early implementation of computerized systems in libraries converted manual backroom processes such as acquisitions, circulation, and cataloging into automated activities. The existence of the machine-readable cataloging record (MARC) developed at the Library of Congress in the late 1960s was fundamental to the rapid spread of library automation through the academic library community. "It is hard to overemphasize the importance of the existence of this standard to the progress of library automation" (Arms, 1989a, p. 41). The standardized MARC record enabled the emergence of bibliographic utilities such as the Online Computer Library Center (OCLC), the Research Libraries Information Network (RLIN), and the Western Library Network (WLN). These utilities pioneered the use of telecommunications networks for library applications.

Early automation systems were often developed in-house, but by the mid- to late-1970s, commercial vendors began marketing library automation products such as circulation systems, cataloging systems, and acquisition systems. Integrated library systems, where circulation, acquisitions, cataloging functions were handled by the same computer systems, appeared as turnkey systems in the early 1980s (Reynolds, 1985).

For users of libraries, the fundamental reorientation to bibliographic information came with the availability of that information through the online public access catalog (OPAC). OPACs appeared in the early 1980s and provided users with entirely new ways to search bibliographic records representing a library's holdings. By the mid- to late-1980s, libraries began to mount locally bibliographic, abstracting and indexing (A&I), and other databases. Users could search these databases at the same terminal, and in some cases, with the same interface, that they used to search the online public access catalog. These access mechanisms enabled users to search citation and abstract databases of journal literature, locally produced data files containing campus information, as well as the library catalog. As the 1990s opened, libraries began offering access via computer networks (campus-wide and national networks) to remotely held electronic information through their library information systems.

Networking Technologies

Two different networking technologies and cultures have affected the current status of the academic library. Early in the development of library automation systems, bibliographic utilities emerged to serve the growing need to share bibliographic records in machine-readable format. Bibliographic utilities created shared cataloging systems, and these systems used telecommunications links established by the utilities to connect individual libraries to a central bibliographic database housed at the utility. The systems of shared cataloging (and other resource-sharing activities provided by the utilities) was a natural outgrowth of the long history of library cooperation and resource sharing through operations such as inter-library loan.

For libraries "networking" has meant cooperative activities, such as resources sharing, cataloging, etc., whether or not those activities were based in telecommunications and computer systems. In particular, "networking" as provided by the utilities had less to do with a communications facility than as a means to receive and provide services. "Library networks are organizations that provide high-level services, such as shared cataloging or interlibrary loan; these services are usually based on a computer network of some sort, but the justification for a network is the service it provides, not the communication facility itself" (Arms, 1989b, p. 40).

While these library networks were developing in the 1970s, computer scientists had already put in place the ARPANET, an experimental packet-switching network sponsored by the Defense Advanced Research Projects Agency (DARPA). DARPA funded the early developments in new electronic networking technologies beginning in the 1960s. By 1969, the ARPANET was functioning as a prototype packet-switched network serving researchers and scientists. Although DARPA established ARPANET as an experimental network, it soon became a production-oriented operation. Scientists and researchers working on Federal contracts, primarily with the Department of Defense, used the network for the exchange of electronic mail messages, transfer of files (using the File Transfer Protocol), and remote logon (using the Telnet function) to other computers (Gould, 1990).

In the 1970s, several Federal government agencies established other similar packet-switched networks. A suite of protocols known as TCP/IP (Transmission Control Protocol/Internet Protocol) provided the basis for exchanging data across different networks. Protocols enabled different kinds of computers to communicate and computers on separate electronic networks to exchange data. "Called the 'Internet protocols,' these rules and procedures provided a universal language allowing electronic messages to be sent across multiple interconnected networks" (Gould, 1990, p. 4). The network of networks, the Internet, was born. Lynch and Preston (1990) provide additional background information on the Internet.

The management and organization of the ARPANET underwent changes in the early 1980s, and in 1985 the National Science Foundation (NSF) took the lead in continuing the development and deployment of an electronic research network based on the established ARPANET (Aupperle, 1993). Specifically, NSF had the goal of creating a high-speed backbone network that would connect supercomputer sites around the country. The next step in the development was pivotal. NSF, now having established its NSFNET backbone, began to organize a number of regional networks that would serve two purposes. First the regional or mid-level networks would provide the link between individual researchers and their academic institutions (or research laboratories) and the NSFNET backbone. Second, the mid-level networks would provide a decentralized, organizational foundation for network services, administered at the regional level, funded in part by NSF.

During the last half of the 1980s, many of the educational institutions (at which researchers, scientists, scholars, and others were using the Internet to communicate with colleagues, share data, use supercomputer resources, and access databases) began installing local area and wide area networks on their campuses. As additional computers were connected to these local networks, the number of potential users of the Internet increased dramatically.

The Internet is not only a U.S. computer network but a truly global network. Vinton Cerf, one of the pioneers of the Internet and president of the Internet Society, testified in congressional hearings on the national information infrastructure (NII) that in 1993 the Internet comprised over 1.5 million computers linked through more than 10,000 networks in approximately fifty countries. Although it is difficult to specify exact numbers of users, Cerf estimates that there are well over 5 million. Given the interconnection of the Internet to other public and private electronic messaging systems, Cerf suggests that as many 15 million users are exchanging electronic mail (Cerf, 1993). The user community in the United States is estimated at 1 to 2 million and accounts for 80 percent of the host computers of the global Internet (Office of

Science and Technology Policy, 1992). In recent years, the Internet has shown tremendous growth in number of users, networks connected, and traffic (Lottor, 1992). Cerf testified that the Internet system is doubling annually in users, networks, hosts, and traffic. While such growth may not continue indefinitely, Cerf projects a user population of 100 million by 1998.

The other computer networking initiative directly affecting academic communities was BITNET. Established in 1981 under the auspices of EDUCOM, a higher education association concerned with the effective use of information technology, BITNET connects approximately 570 colleges, universities, and industrial laboratories and more than 2,000 hosts (CREN GROWTH, 1993). The network operates under different protocols than the Internet and primarily uses electronic mail and message services for the exchange of information (Network Advisory Committee, 1989a; Quarterman, 1990, Britten, 1990). Electronic mail moves between the Internet and BITNET through network gateway mechanisms.

Library Automation and Networking

With the library online public access catalog residing on a computer, the logical next step was to provide access via the campus network to the catalog and any other information resources available through the library information system. Lynch (1989a) describes problems and solutions in developing appropriate telecommunications and network structures to provide remote access to library resources such as the OPAC. Remote access to the library information system enabled faculty, students, and staff to search the system from offices, dormitories, and homes. The library's information system had now become a "networked information resource," raising an entirely new set of issues and concerns related to networking and academic libraries.

Online catalogs and library information systems were some of the earliest publicly accessible Internet resources. Beginning with MELVYL, the University of California's online catalog, numerous institutions developed the catalog to be publicly accessed by Internet users (Lynch and Preston, 1990). Well over 200 online catalogs and library information systems are accessible via the Internet. Lynch (1989c) details many of the technical and policy questions that such Internet access created. Kibirige (1991) discusses a number of problems with existing online catalogs, especially some vendor-supplied turnkey systems, which were not designed for the wide-ranging and complex networking environment of the Internet.

Bailey (1989, p. 2) argues that the new library-based integrated information systems can "synergistically combine traditional collections and services with new computer-based information resources and services." Building integrated access to the online catalog, locally mounted citation databases, and network access to remote resources and services will be long-term undertakings, and as Bailey says, these integrated access systems will "increasingly become the 'heart' of the evolving electronic university; however, the lifeblood of information that flows through this heart will be in both print and electronic form" (p. 29).

National Networking Policies and Libraries

Now in the early 1990s, the Internet, like academic libraries, is in a transitional stage. The NSF has been reducing its subsidies to the regional networks in recent years and is guiding the Internet towards privatization and commercialization. Privatization means that the Federal government will no longer subsidize directly network services and connections. Commercialization will allow the lifting of current restrictions on traffic flowing over the network and acceptable use of the network will not be limited to network traffic supporting research and education (National Science Foundation, 1992). The direction and character of the moves towards privatization and commercialization have sparked widespread debate within the networking community (Eldred and McGill, 1992; Estrada, 1992; Weiss, 1992).

Federal policy concerning national networking has been developing for several years. A number of key pieces of legislation focus on the emerging networked environment.

The High Performance Computing Act of 1991 (P.L. 102-194) authorized the creation of a National Research and Education Network (NREN). After several years of legislative action, President Bush signed the act into law in December 1991. McClure et al. (1991), provide a comprehensive legislative history and assessment of the act and related legislative initiatives. In the act, the NREN is one of several components in a high-performance computing and communications program. Other components of the program are (Committee on Physical, Mathematical, and Engineering Sciences, 1992, p. 20):

- high-performance computing systems;
- advanced software technology and algorithms; and
- basic research and human resources.

In the FY 1993 proposed budget for the high-performance computing program by the Office of Science and Technology, only 15 percent of the funds are allocated to the NREN. The majority of the funds are targeted at the high-performance computing systems and the advanced software technology and algorithms components (McClure, 1992).

The NREN, as authorized by the High Performance Computing Act of 1991 (P.L. 102-194), however, is not intended to be a general purpose communications network. Like the effort of DARPA in the 1960s and 1970s, Federal funding for the NREN is intended to move networking technology forward and serve as an experimental environment that will result in technologies and products to enable a national information infrastructure (NII). "The primary purpose of NREN is to establish a gigabit communications infrastructure that would revolutionize the ability to collaborate among members of the research and education community" (Office of Science and Technology Policy, 1992, p. 4). The NREN project consists of an operational federation of Federally funded networks to serve the research and education community (the Interagency Interim NREN, IINREN), and a research and development component for high-speed networking technologies.

As a Federally funded, multiagency initiative, the principal goals of the NREN program are: establishing a gigabit network for the research and education community and fostering its use; developing advanced networking technologies and accelerating their deployment; stimulating the availability, at a reasonable cost, of the required services from the private sector; and catalyzing the early deployment of a high-speed, general purpose digital communications infrastructure for the nation (Office of Science and Technology Policy, 1992).

The research and education community obviously includes a wide variety of library types, and one can expect that academic libraries will be a component of the NREN. Yet the Office of Science and Technology Policy (1992, p. 27) in its first report to Congress (and then under the Bush administration) as mandated by P.L. 102-194 provided a cautionary note:

> The library community is concerned that it as a whole be interconnected, and that many diverse information sources be

available at low (or no) cost. Nearly all research libraries, and several public library systems, are already connected, but no NREN funding has been targeted specifically for library connectivity, and the magnitude of the task clearly precludes a Federal approach. *Achieving widespread library connectivity will depend inevitably on creative ideas introduced at the local level.* [emphasis added]

A recent Clinton administration technology policy statement (Clinton and Gore, 1993) appears to change the policy context for the development of the Internet/NREN to a more proactive position.

The NREN, however, means different things to different people. Expectations are high for library inclusion in NREN planning and use. Whether or not these expectations are realized will depend on how the library community presents its interests to Federal policymakers. The NREN of the High Performance Computing Act, however, may not be the vehicle of widespread connectivity. The policy debates will continue, and the library community can influence the shape of these deliberations and choices of Federal policymakers.

In other policy initiatives, then-Senator Albert Gore, a main proponent of the High Performance Computing Act, sponsored the Information Infrastructure Technology Act of 1992 (S. 2937). The legislation introduced the idea of "grand applications" to parallel the "grand challenges" of the High Performance Computing Act of 1991. Grand applications focus on applications of high-performance computing and high-speed networking that will provide large economic and social benefits to the nation. These include tools for teaching, digital libraries of electronic information, computer systems to improve the delivery of health care, and computing and networking technology to promote U.S. competitiveness. The purpose of this act is to ensure that the technology developed by the 1991 High Performance Computing Act offers applications for K–12 education, libraries, and other areas. The bill did not pass the 102nd Congress.

In January 1993, the National Competitiveness Act (S. 4) was introduced in the U.S. Senate. This act incorporates most of the components of the Information Infrastructure Act of 1992, as well as the Manufacturing Strategy Act (S. 1330) and the Wind Engineering Act (S. 3273), both considered in the 102nd Congress. Representative Boucher introduced a more extensive version of this bill in April 1993, entitled the High Performance Computing and High Speed Networking Applications Act of 1993 (H.R. 1757).

The Government Printing Office (GPO) Wide Information Network for Data Online Act of 1991 (WINDO) [H.R. 2772; S. 2813, Senate version titled GPO Gateway to Government Act] would authorize GPO to provide online access, through the Internet, to a range of Federal information systems and electronic databases. The service would be free to depository libraries. The act was replaced in September 1992 by another bill, Government Printing Office (GPO) Electronic Information Access Enhancement Act of 1992 (H.R. 5983). The replacement bill reduced the coverage of Federal information required by the earlier legislation, did not require access through the Internet, and provided no appropriations to fund the service. This bill did not survive the 1992 session.

In March 1993, new GPO legislation was introduced in the House and Senate. The Government Printing Office Electronic Information Access Enhancement Act of 1993 (S. 564; H.R. 1328) requires the Superintendent of Documents to provide online access to the *Congressional Record* and *Federal Register* and, as determined by the Superintendent of Documents, other "appropriate" documents. Depository libraries will have free access to these documents, and others will pay incremental costs of distribution. The legislation was passed by Congress and signed into law (P.L. 103-40) in June 1993.

The Federal information policy arena, a rich mix of legislation, agency guidelines and directives, court decisions, and other documents (Hernon and McClure, 1991; 1987), encompasses a range of issues stimulated by Federal involvement in networking and the potential of network-accessible Federal information resources. Whether lobbying for legislation to fund the connection of K–12 schools and libraries to national networks or conducting policy analysis to develop a government-wide information locator (McClure et al., 1992), opportunities and needs exist for librarians to help shape the networked environment, its resources, and its availability.

The Clinton administration has expressed its commitment to advancing the NII and increasing the deployment of information technology in the cause of education, research, and national competitiveness, and passage of this legislation could be the beginning of new Federal initiatives. The recent technology policy statement issued by the Clinton administration (Clinton and Gore, 1993, p. 14) includes a number of networking initiatives, such as:

> Access to the Internet and developing NREN will be expanded
> to connect university campuses, community colleges, and K–12
> schools to a high-speed communications network providing a

broad range of information resources. Support will be provided for equipment allowing local networks in these learning institutions access to the network along with support for development of high-performance software capable of taking advantage of the emerging hardware capabilities.

The policy statement also recommends funding networking pilot projects through the National Telecommunications and Information Administration (NTIA).

NTIA will provide matching grants to states, school districts, libraries, and other non-profit entities so that they can purchase the computers and networking connections needed for distance learning and for hooking into computer networks like the Internet. These pilot projects will demonstrate the benefits of networking to the educational and *library* communities [p. 17, (emphasis added)].

Policymakers are developing networking and information policy that will have long-term effects on academic libraries. The eventual shape of the networked environment, however, can serve the academic library community, if and only if, librarians actively participate in the policy process.

ACCESS TO INFORMATION CONTEXT

An expanding array of information exists in electronic form, and increasingly these information resources reside on the Internet/NREN. Network-accessible OPACs and other bibliographic and citation databases are available. The bulk of the information referred to by these resources, however, are in paper-based formats. Access to information in the networked environment gains new meaning and creates new pressures for libraries.

While electronic networks give new meaning to "access," they are not simply about digitized information. They also are opening up new horizons for communication. The opportunities for communication among scholars and researchers, and opportunities for new forms of publications and authorship will also challenge the traditional roles of libraries in the process of scholarly communication.

The Process of Scholarly Communication

Historically, the academic library, and particularly the research library, has played important roles in the process of scholarly communication (Cummings et al., 1992). One of the responsibilities of universities has been the creation and communication of new knowledge. Whether the knowledge created is theoretical or practical, the researcher or scholar is responsible for communicating that knowledge, and the library facilitates that communication. Most often the communication is in a documented form (i.e., recorded in some way). This communication or transmission of knowledge is critical to the teaching and research functions of the university. The scholarly journal has been an integral element in this communication process for over three centuries (Osburn, 1984).

Osburn (1989) suggests that the process of scholarly communication involves the researchers and scholars who initiate the communication, publishers and libraries that disseminate, organize, and preserve the documented communication, and other scholars and researchers who receive the communication. One can also add students as another group which participates in the communication. Peer review, publication, and the scientific model are essential elements in this process. Libraries, as one of the structures involved in the process, play at least two functions: to collect and preserve the documents containing scholarly communication, and to provide access mechanisms by affecting some bibliographic control over the documents.

The sheer amount of information created and published in recent decades, as well as the specialization of this knowledge, has put increasing strains upon the scholarly communication system. Faculty and students expect the library to acquire the increasing numbers of specialized journals. The dramatic cost increases for scholarly journals in recent years show little signs of abating. Yet, the process of scholarly communication (i.e., creation, communication, publication, acquisition, organization, preservation, and dissemination) has changed little. There are signs, however, that scholars and researchers are employing the networked environment in novel ways for creating, communicating, and publishing information. Okerson, Strangelove, and Kovacs (1992) document the proliferation of electronic journals, newsletters, and academic discussion lists that scholars and researchers are using.

The digitization of information, communication via electronic networks, and remote access to information—components of the networked environment, are opening up the process of scholarly communication to a reevaluation and possibly to fundamental changes. Rogers and Hurt (1990) explore one future vision of scholarly communication. Cummings et al. (1992), in a comprehensive report on university libraries and scholarly communication, recognize threats as well as opportunities for academic libraries.

Michelson and Rothenberg (1992), while focusing on archival collections, generally examine the interaction between information technology and scholarly communication. They describe the modern research process as including:

- identification of sources;
- communication with colleagues;
- interpretation and analysis of data;
- dissemination of research findings; and
- curriculum development and instruction for preparing the next generation of scholars.

They conclude that the "impact of information technology on these processes is resulting in unprecedented transformations in scholarly communication" (p. 241).

Universities also see opportunities for reclaiming the results of their researchers and participating in the process by publishing and disseminating information (Boyce, 1993). Traditional print-based publishers of scholarly journals are anticipating new electronic markets for their products. For example, Elsevier Science Publishers' experimental project—the University Licensing Program (TULIP)—makes a selection of its scholarly journals available over the Internet (Wilson, 1992). Vendors and information brokers such as OCLC, Colorado Alliance of Research Libraries (CARL), Research Libraries Group (RLG), and Faxon have entered the process and provide information retrieval services and document delivery services for journal articles (Ensor, 1992). And the academic library is attempting to find a new role for itself in this electronic publishing environment while carrying out its traditional responsibilities for the bulk of scholarly communication that still appears in print-based documents.

User Expectations and Realities

Library users received a taste, sometimes bitter, of the potential of information technology through their use of OPACs in the 1980s. One of the results of the increasing use of information technology in libraries has been to increase user expectations about information access and information delivery. Electronic access to "information about information" in the OPACs provided potentially new ways to accomplish the objectives of a library catalog. One of objectives, as stated by Charles Cutter, in the late nineteenth century (Cutter, 1985) was to show what a library has. A library that had not completely converted all its bibliographic records to machine-readable form, however, meant the user could not rely on the OPAC to show what the library has and received only a partial view of the library's holdings. Yet searching OPACs for information about information has become the dominant method for most users in identifying library holdings.

Libraries incorporated CD-ROM–based technologies for citation databases and some mounted A&I databases on their mainframe and offered access through the OPAC. The information about information available in these databases did not always match the holdings of the library. The speed at which users could find pointers to articles and books was accompanied by a growing expectation that the library should be able to provide the actual information, not just pointers to it. Users wanted as quick access to the actual information as they had to the information about information.

Network-accessible library information systems (i.e., OPACs and other databases and information resources offered through a single point of access available through either dial-up or direct network connections through campus-wide networks) provided another opportunity for users' expectations to increase. If the remote user, from his/her office, dormitory, or home, could find the information needed, then why not expect the library to deliver the information, electronically or otherwise, to wherever the user is. Users are taking "access to information" seriously. Access means not just knowing that the item of information exists, but getting the actual information into the users' hands.

Users began to utilize the network connection not only to connect to local library resources, but also to connect with remote sites at which they had no official affiliation. Library OPACs accessible via the Internet/NREN provided new veins to mine in the search for information. Geographical considerations are generally meaningless in the networked environment; however, political, social, behavioral, institutional, and organizational considerations are enormously meaningful. Libraries also recognized the importance of these remote information resources, and some libraries began providing, through their own library information system, access to other libraries' OPACs and a host of other resources.

Libraries are now experimenting with networked resource discovery tools such as wide area information systems (WAIS), Gopher,

Archie, and others (Brett, 1992). Developed specifically for the networked environment, these tools enable users to access full-text information databases and other resources residing on the network and retrieve information from those resources to their local machines. Access is closely tied to the delivery of desired information.

Integrated library information systems, combining network-accessible OPACs, locally mounted databases, remote log-on and file transfer (e.g., Telnet and FTP) capabilities, and resource discovery tools lay the foundation for the virtual library—seamless access to information resources regardless of geographic location.

Since users incurred no direct charges connecting to these remote information resources—whether through the library, from their offices, or their homes—the virtual library was an extension of the "information commons" that individual libraries had always provided, that is, "a place which subsidizes access to information so that it appears to readers to be free . . ." (Lyman, 1992a, p. 76). Information, or at least information about information, appeared to be free. Actual information, if it was acquired by one's own library, also appeared to be free. Information acquired by other libraries might be available without direct charge through interlibrary loan. However, it is the current economic context of academic libraries that may change dramatically the image and reality of an information commons.

ECONOMIC CONTEXT

Nowhere in the literature are there glowing and optimistic projections of funding for academic libraries or for their parent institutions. Instead, one reads of cutbacks, retrenchment, and doing more with less. Yet the need for adequate campus information infrastructures must be met if the potential for meaningful access to and use of network information is to be accomplished. This issue is explored in more detail in Chapter 9.

Structural changes in the U.S. economy have moved information to a privileged position as an economic commodity. Information has always had value, but in recent decades the economic value of information has become preeminent. Universities traffic in information. It is the currency of scholarly communication. Therefore, one might assume that universities, and academic libraries in particular, might enjoy a golden age as central players in the so-called information age. Yet debt, recession, the ever-increasing costs of information, and taxpayer attitudes are reflected by public and elected officials who tend "to see higher education more like the fatted calf than the sacred cow, more something to be sacrificed at the altar of fiscal prudence than something to be protected in the face of economic downturn" (Heterick, 1991, p. 2).

In the emerging electronic information environment where networks—campus, regional, national, and international—offer exciting new opportunities for information access, dissemination, and communication, academic libraries must balance limited resources between new initiatives and traditional activities. The information technology necessary for the creation, storage, communication, and dissemination of information requires infusions of funds, yet universities and their libraries have few new monies to allocate to electronic resources and information technology.

The economic constraints are real and ongoing, and it is unlikely that the library can continue to be all things to all people but will have to choose between what it will do, and do well, and those activities and services it will have to discontinue. Some see that electronic formats of information, such as electronic journals, may offer cost avoidance strategies for libraries since they will not have to process, bind, and store back issues of paper journals (Drake, 1992a). Marcum (1992) suggests, however, that the outcome of electronic access to information will be decreased access to published serials and monographs. Shreeves (1992, p. 581) concludes that "taking the cost of electronic information from current resources is not a pleasant prospect, but it may be the only strategy available for many."

Libraries are spending more money and adding less to their collections. Between 1986 and 1990, median price per subscription for serials increased 51% in the Association of Research Libraries (ARL). Serials expenditures in those libraries rose 52 percent, and the median number of subscriptions decreased by 1 percent. Expenditures for monographs increased by 19 percent, but the number of monographs purchased decreased by 16 percent (Runkle, 1992). Another perspective on this situation is offered by the most recent ARL statistics (Association of Research Libraries, 1993, p. 9):

- ARL members paid $15.7 million more for serials in 1992 than in 1991, but had an average of about 600 fewer subscriptions per library, or around 60,000 fewer serials among all ARL academic libraries
- The libraries purchased some 100,000 fewer monographs than in 1991, but paid over $300,000 more for them.

Such numbers challenge the basic mission of an academic library to collect and preserve the record of the human intellect. Lyman (1992a, p. 75) raises the possibility "that higher education can no longer afford, or is no longer willing to support, traditional research libraries." This financial crisis may "force a fundamental reshaping of the mission of research libraries" (Nicklin, 1992, p. 19). Heterick (1991) suggests that already faculty are asking university funding sources whether some library funding would not be better used by individual departments to purchase information they need, for example, from online database services.

The constrained fiscal situations of colleges and universities affect more than the materials and acquisitions budgets. Libraries need adequate information technology to operate in the networked environment. For example, users' expectations for downloading information to their personal disks mean that dumb terminals used to search the local OPAC are not sufficient. Library staff members need to be informed and experienced with network resources and navigation and therefore must have adequate equipment at their disposal. If librarians are to have the skills needed to perform new tasks, staff training and development are necessary. And on it goes.

The library's privileged position as the intellectual storehouse of the academy is no longer secure. The network not only offers librarians access to new information resources, but faculty and students can also get to those resources independently of the librarian. A competitive market is developing, a market in which the library must compete. Funders of university libraries, even sympathetic ones, counsel the library to prepare to move into a position of accountability that may be difficult to achieve. Evaluation of service provision by libraries will doubtless be on the agenda for budget analysts and administrators. Dickeson (1991, p. 140) suggests that "assessment of higher education has materially shifted from inputs to outcomes. From items on the shelves to uses of the information. From degrees held by staff to quality of services rendered. From usable computer storage capacity to results of processing."

The economic context presents these and other issues that academic libraries must address. Solutions are available, but they are not always easy for some to accept, nor do they come without tradeoffs. Yet the economic realities of university funding, new requirements for accountability, and other economic considerations external to the library will condition what choices will be available to libraries as they prepare for and enter the networked future.

These three contexts, technology, access, and economic, provide the backdrop for academic libraries as they move into the twenty-first century. Computer networks and new generations of computers and sophisticated software will likely provide technical solutions for information processing. These technical solutions, however, may confound the problems associated with academic libraries' roles in the process of scholarly communication and in the access, organization, storage, and dissemination of information. Technical solutions will not answer policy, organizational, and behavioral issues but instead may exacerbate them. Finally, the economic context of fiscal constraints will continue for the foreseeable future. It is against this backdrop of technological innovation, cultural norms, and economic realities that the issues facing academic libraries stand in stark relief.

IMPLEMENTING THE VIRTUAL LIBRARY

Academic library leaders, staff, university administrators, campus computing centers, and others are working, discussing, strategizing and planning, writing, and thinking—all in an attempt to identify and respond to the issues of the networked environment. The term virtual library appears in articles and books to describe the emerging information environment in which existing libraries may participate. Gapen (1993, p. 1) offers one definition of the virtual library:

> . . . the concept of remote access to the contents and services of libraries and other information resources, combining an on-site collection of current and heavily used materials in both print and electronic form, with an electronic network which provides access to, and delivery from, external worldwide library and commercial information and knowledge sources. In essence, the user is provided the effect of a library which is a synergy created by bringing together technologically the resources of many, many libraries and information services.

The network is the enabling technology to link together in a seamless manner the heterogenous information resources, services, and people of the virtual library.

In reviewing the literature of the past several years, there is no shortage of views of the future electronic university or electronic library. Kenneth M. King (King, 1989), former president of EDUCOM, articulated a vision of the networked environment that resonates with possibilities:

- to connect every scholar in the world to every other scholar and thus reduce the barriers to scholarly interaction of space, time, and culture;
- to connect to the network all important information sources, specialized instruments, and computing resources worth sharing;
- to build databases that are collaboratively and dynamically maintained that contain all that is known on a particular subject; and
- to create a knowledge management system on the network that will enable scholars to navigate through these resources in a standard, intuitive, and consistent way.

King also acknowledges a central role for libraries in this vision:

- collecting, preserving, organizing, presenting, and managing scholarly information regardless of format;
- designing the network management systems which permits scholars to access information resources in a standard, consistent, and intuitive manner;
- connecting libraries to the network and managing interlibrary interaction, and bibliographic resources on the network; and
- supporting scholarly access to network information resources.

Nor, in more recent writings, is there a shortage of more realistic, and sometimes pessimistic, reactions to the pressures academic libraries are facing. Optimistic views seem to give way to realism as planning for the future takes over merely envisioning it and as actual prototypes of new services are implemented.

One of the assumed technologies in most visions of the networked future, in addition to a robust and adequate network infrastructure, is the "scholar's workstation." The universal workstation environment was one of the "preferred futures" resulting from a series of workshops with university provosts and library directors sponsored by RLG in 1991 (Dougherty and Hughes, 1991). This environment incorporates the notion of a "wired campus, with workstations universally accessible. . . ." The descriptions included: "an integrated library/computer facility, transparent to the user; comprehensive access to national databases in all formats; information 'virtually' accessible in one place; workstations for everyone for all the information needed; a universal terminal that can handle multimedia in all formats; workstation access to all media—in many locations; universal access to databases, regardless of users and resource location" (p. 11).

Few visions of the networked future, however, have the library as the central or focal point. Instead, the library is offered any number of roles, functions, and responsibilities on a continuum from being bypassed to being an important stakeholder in the networked environment. Larsen (1991, p. 44) describes one likely scenario in which the library exists as a "network-based information server." He offers four steps libraries can take to contribute to King's vision and objectives:

- A library can build local primary-content databases accessible network-wide.
- Libraries can expand their interoperability with information providers on the network, using such protocols as Z39.50.
- Library reference staff need to know how to find materials on the network and how to utilize those resources.
- Improved mechanisms for online collaboration are needed, including tools to assist in finding collaborators.

Larsen (1990, p. 37) also proposes that an appropriate image for the future is that of a "colibratory" in which a comprehensive information architecture links "information servers (e.g., libraries) over a high-performance network (e.g., the NREN) with information customers (end-users) in a manner encouraging the collaborative exploration of advanced techniques for information access and delivery."

The logical or virtual library of the networked environment (or rather as Kibbey and Evans [1989] suggest, the network is the virtual library) may not comprise the operating metaphor. Instead, a virtual information marketplace, not the virtual library, more accurately depicts the networked environment. Information will be available at the scholar's workstation from a wide variety of sources. Some of the information may be "free" while other information will be available on a pay-per-use basis. A networked "information commons" is unlikely. Yet even these suggestions utilize the past to talk about the future.

Some writers are cautioning against the idea of the virtual electronic library. Shaughnessy (1992, p. 123) states that the virtual library is "one of the most dangerous ideas to confront research librarianship in recent years." The danger in this metaphor is that campus administrators might question the need to build local collections, maintain paper-based materials, or do the necessary bibliographic and collection maintenance work involved in the traditional collections. Resource sharing is important, but it is not a substitute for basic, up-to-date collections located on campus.

Lynch (1992c, p. 111) suggests that information technology is changing how the activities of universities are carried out and that the technology can be used to modernize, innovate, and finally transform. "Transformation is a form of revolution. . . . but another characteristic of revolutions is the emergence, apparently from nowhere, of new forces. . . . when and if these new forces do emerge, they may change our assumptions in important ways." Imagining transformation is often limited by focusing on extrapolation from the past or present. Those "new forces" will likely make any of our visions of the logical library, the virtual information marketplace, or whatever we call it, slightly or largely out of touch with what actually comes to pass.

ISSUE AREAS IN RECENT LITERATURE

Libraries face a range of issues as they confront the networked environment. Many of these issues are linked with others. Each of these areas contain a number of specific issues. Issue areas identified through the literature review are:

- electronic publishing and networked information resources;
- access and ownership of information;
- costs and funding of electronic resources;
- copyright and intellectual property;
- organizing networked information resource;
- planning for technology change;
- the library within broader university administrative concerns;
- the library and the computing center—new partners?;
- a new information delivery paradigm;
- creating evaluation methods for network services;
- regrowing staff; and
- research for the future.

Based on literature (through early 1993), the following sections review current and perceived future issues and problems libraries must address as the transformative power of information technology proceeds.

Electronic Publishing and Networked Information Resources

The networked environment of electronic, digital information enables the automated distribution of print products, but it also enables "new ways of representing and creating knowledge" (Lyman, 1992b, p. 99). Understanding these two different functions of the networked environment is essential if libraries are to choose appropriate responses. Can libraries play roles in both of these processes?

Electronic publishing does not require the existence of the Internet/NREN. Publishers have been producing information in electronic formats (e.g., CD-ROM, magnetic tape, etc.), and libraries have been using these information resources for many years. Libraries are also familiar with online database searching services such as DIALOG. To some extent, libraries were instrumental in developing the current market for these information products and services. One can only speculate on how these services and products would have developed without libraries. Yet the networked environment of the Internet/NREN provides new service options for the producers of electronic information, options that do not necessarily include the libraries.

There is also a growing phenomenon of electronic publishing that is occurring because of the Internet/NREN. In what could be considered a stage of "innovation" rather than "modernization," network technologies are being used to produce electronic products in the form of electronic journals and newsletters. These electronic products on the network provide an early test case for libraries in developing processes and procedures in response to networked resources. Ensor (1993) reports on various network-based electronic journals as well as efforts by more traditional publishers, distributors, and online information services to provide full-text materials in electronic formats.

Stoller (1992) provides an overview of electronic journals as well as indicating several critical issues for libraries in dealing with electronic journals. Since electronic journals can be individually subscribed to at no direct cost, Stoller suggests that libraries will need to play a role in acquiring, providing access, and preserving electronic journals if these information resources are to become important and acceptable elements in the world of scholarly communication. Libraries must decide if they will play an intermediary role with electronic journals as they do for paper-based journals. How will they be received? How will users access them? What bibliographic control must be accomplished? How will they be archived?

Bailey (1992b, p. 32) enumerates twelve problems related to network-based electronic serials that will need to be solved to ensure that a "significant non-profit serial publication system will emerge from the efforts of network-based electronic serials publishers. . . . characterized by low or no subscription fees and the retention of intellectual property rights by authors." He also suggests that librarians have important roles in bringing about the future of electronic serials including the development of tools to help users locate and access these serials; collecting, preserving, and providing local access to them; promoting the development of standards to improve storage, distribution, display, and printing; and to publish or help their academic units to publish electronic serials. Bailey (1992a) also offers a selected bibliography on network-based electronic publishing.

Electronic journals are one incarnation of publishing in the networked environment. Experimentation with these publications offers libraries an opportunity to identify and solve some of the emerging issues of networked-based publishing. Yet simply finding ways to provide access to electronic journals is only one aspect of a complex set of legal, policy, and technology concerns related to electronic publishing. Librarians need to be aware of the trends in electronic publishing. In part, this means working with print-based publishers, some of whom are already testing the waters of network access to their products. Hawkins et al. (1992), provides an overview of the electronic publishing industry. Lynch (1991) discusses electronic publishing and networked-based digital libraries.

The bulk of scholarly information is still paper-based. For the network to offer a stable, effective, and productive environment for scholarly communication, research, and instruction, new models for the distribution and provision of information are needed. Solutions will need to address the fundamental economic issues of publishing, whether paper- or network-based. The Coalition for Networked Information (CNI) sponsored a meeting on economic issues involved in migrating publishing from paper to digital forms of information. Serials Review (Grycz, 1992) devotes a special issue to the economic models for networked information discussed at that meeting. Contributors offer articles on economic models, copyright, acquisition-on-demand proposals, and other relevant topics.

Peters (1992, p. 19) explains the Rights for Electronic Access to and Delivery of Information (READI) program CNI is designing in response to the need for balancing attention "to each of the major factors that shape the production and utilization of knowledge in society: value, rights, cost, price, and protection as well as mechanism [sic]." Peters acknowledges that such a program can help accelerate progress during this phase in the evolution of networked information, namely the modernization of information delivery.

Dougherty (1992, p. B3) sees the need for a transitional strategy from the paper-based publishing of today to the electronic information environment that is still over the horizon. The Universal Journal Factory would be a cooperative effort of universities "whose principal mission would be publishing and distributing scholarly journals in printed form." He proposes an aggressive intervention by universities as a response to the unceasing cost inflation of scholarly information. While its initial products would be printed journals, the factory "would be building the capacity, by storing the printed information electronically, to produce and distribute products in electronic format—when the conditions exist that justify the expense."

Another vision incorporates the idea that universities should regain control of the scholarly communication process by recognizing that they are "part of a perfect, vertically integrated enterprise . . . and must take an enterprise-wide perspective on the resources and challenges" (Yavarkovsky, 1990, p. 20). A university-based electronic publishing network would provide access to scholarly papers located on computer facilities at participating institutions. In addition, such an initiative could help bring order to some electronic publishing occurring on the networks and bring increased legitimacy to electronic publishing for tenure and promotion decisions. In addition, Yavarkovsky suggests that research libraries might have archival responsibility in this vision. Yet, because scholars and students can access such networked information independent of libraries, "frankly, the role of librarians is not entirely clear in the electronic library of the future" (p. 17).

The electronic publication and distribution of information is at the heart of the networked environment. Tools for access and technologies to store and retrieve are essential ingredients (see Cleveland, 1991), but it is the actual information on the network—what is available, how it got there, who controls it, how much it costs, who can use it—that will be the linchpin to successful exploitation of new technologies.

An increasing amount of information is available on the network; the bulk of the information, however, does not originate with traditional print-based publishers. At present, publishers are concerned that there is not a critical mass of users to justify a commitment to networked provision of their information (Hoffert, 1992). Some users claim, however, that there is not enough appropriate information on the network to attract more scholars and researchers. If large numbers of scholars and researchers perceive the network as only marginally useful for scholarly research and production, institutions may delay investments in the technology infrastructure.

Publishers are waiting for users to create enough demand. Users are waiting for enough appropriate research material on the network before investing even more in technologies to exploit electronic information. And in this quandary are the librarians who are attempting to deal with current electronic information access, and taking on the new roles and responsibilities the networked environment is creating. Academic libraries can address the supply/demand dilemma by demonstrating to scholars the value of existing electronic resources (e.g., developing discipline-based pathfinders to relevant materials) and by working with and encouraging publishers to offer research-oriented electronic materials (e.g., Elesevier's TULIP).

Access and Ownership of Information

The library debate over access v. ownership of information is not new, yet the networked environment changes the parameters of that debate. In the past, interlibrary loan was a needed supplement to owning materials. Libraries recognized that they could not afford, nor would have the space to house, all materials that users might need. Still, the warehouse, "just-in-case" model was the basis for most library collection development policies. In part, this is an aspect of the value that libraries add to information—they build collections of materials, gathering appropriate and relevant information together in one place for researchers, scholars, and students. At a time when stagnant or decreasing materials budgets have threatened this model, the networked environment offers new possibilities to move to a "just-in-time" model of acquisitions.

Marcum (1992) asks a set of questions that academic librarians must address when balancing access and ownership:

- What will library users have access to once libraries begin to invest most of their resources in access systems rather than collections?
- Is it feasible for librarians to substitute "access" for "collections"?
- What are the implications of this new system—the networked-based technologies used in writing, editing, storing, and disseminating intellectual works—for scholars and publishers?
- What adaptations are required of libraries?

Marcum suggests that access v. ownership is not an either/or question. Electronic access must be incorporated into overall collection development; it can complement and become part of traditional collection development. Yet balancing access and ownership is particularly difficult because of budget cuts, and she notes that the "practical effect [of budget cuts] is that access to electronic information has been expanded while access to published monographs and serials has decreased . . ." (p. 66).

From the perspective of a university administrator (Louis, 1992, p. 121), cooperation and resource sharing among libraries is essential in resolving the access and ownership questions, and this cooperation must be greater than it has been in the past. Because of the continuing fiscal crisis, he states flatly that "ownership . . . must be abandoned in favor of access" to pooled resources.

Leach and Tribble (1993, p. 359) examine the "just-in-time" model and describe several existing document delivery services. They recognize that the combination of network access to bibliographic information and timely document delivery service will "enable and encourage librarians and academic faculty to rethink their approach to collection development." While this can be phrased in the argument of "ownership v. access," it also cuts to the heart of a value-added process of the traditional library function of bringing together relevant material into a "collection."

Network connections can provide a new model for information access and document delivery where the library acquires only those items at the time they are requested by users. The network also provides individual researchers, scholars, and students with that capability. The "just-in-time" model will have major impacts on the traditional collection-building efforts, and it raises new questions about funding information delivery and equity of information access.

Costs and Funding of Electronic Resources

Academic end-users of the Internet environment incur few, if any, direct charges for network use. Access to the network and its resources appears free to most academic end-users. Parent institutions or the library absorb costs of the network connection. Similarly, the library absorbs the costs of locally mounting bibliographic citation and A&I databases. As academic libraries consider providing information in electronic form, they need to choose if and how they will recover costs. Libraries must also deal with the issue of who can access local electronic information resources. Since geographical boundaries no longer limit access to a library's collection, academic libraries can find themselves providing (i.e., subsidizing) local electronic resources to a global constituency.

If the library chooses to provide access rather than own materials, an acquisition-on-demand model raises questions of who pays and how much. Bailey (1992c, p. 80) suggests several pricing schemes for electronic journals in the networked environment, including:

- traditional annual subscriptions, with file distribution and access limited to subscribers;
- site licenses for unlimited or "block" (i.e., a fixed number of file retrievals) access by institutional users;
- block access charged for individual users;
- per-use charged for all users; and
- free access.

Similar schemes may be developed for other networked resources. Chapter 9 offers additional insight on the economic dimension of electronic resources.

A site license requires a library to pay a single, flat fee for an information resource available to specified users associated or affiliated with an institution. Hunter (1992) explores site licenses from the perspective of a publisher and comments on the advantages and problems for libraries with such an arrangement.

Paper-based distribution of journals entails the library acquiring the entire journal. In addition to the cost of the journal, other "hidden costs" to libraries include processing, binding, shelf space, photocopy, etc. Electronic distribution offers the possibility of "unbundling" the journal so that users can obtain only the information (e.g., article, chapter, etc.) they need. Drake (1992b) examines this model of acquisition-on-demand as an alternative to the costs associated with acquiring journals. This model assumes that people will buy individual articles and that these are available in electronic form for access on a "just-in-time" basis.

As noted previously, such access-oriented approaches to information provision have significant implications for the long-term quality of collections. In addition, issues of equity become quickly apparent. Who pays in an acquisition-on-demand model? The library as an "information commons" acquired and provided access to material for all students, faculty, and staff with no direct charge for use. In the acquisition-on-demand model, will all users be charged directly for the information they need? This may impose new financial burdens on certain sectors of the student body and faculty and may restrict access to information previously available in the information commons.

Copyright and Intellectual Property

Networked information resources share characteristics (e.g., digital format, transferability, malleability, etc.) that differentiate them from other traditional information resources. These characteristics, however, cast a long shadow over policymakers, networking technologists, publishers, and librarians as they discuss the impacts on copyright and intellectual property in a networked environment.

Copyright is one mechanism for dealing with intellectual property, and as Kost suggests, "copyright is the pure invention of the printing press" (Kost, 1992, p. 67). Garcia (1987, p. 15) agrees "that the printing press gave rise to the need for a copyright system because it was printing that made the widespread reproduction of works financially possible and that created an economic market for intellectual works, and with it an incentive to copy. Copyright prevented the pirating of works because the publisher acted as a bottleneck."

In a networked environment where copying information is simply done by downloading a file from a host to a local hard disk, and where cutting and pasting can easily change the text of the file, and where one can redistribute copies of the edited work under one's own name through the variety of dissemination channels available through the network (e.g., listservs, FTP sites, etc.), the constraints that made copyright work reasonably well are missing.

Oakley (1988) identifies some of the problems that modern information technology, particularly information networks, has created for the intellectual property system in the United States. He provides background to the issues and suggests a number of approaches for resolving the problems. The range of solutions include amending the Copyright Act of 1976 (P.L. 94-553), overall revision of the act, the use of compulsory licenses, new legislation, contract arrangements, and others.

In the years since the Library of Congress Network Advisory Committee sponsored meetings (Network Advisory Committee, 1987; Network Advisory Committee, 1989b) that discussed intellectual property in the context of electronic information and networks, no widespread agreement has yet emerged for resolving the issues Oakley identified. Grycz (1992) includes proponents of various solutions to protecting intellectual property in the networked environment (see Jensen, 1992; Kost, 1992; Hunter, 1992; and Lyons, 1992).

The producers and users of networked resources, however, are not waiting for the legal air to clear. Publishers are distributing electronic journals and experimenting with other electronic information resources. Users download information from the network for research and other purposes. Quotes and passages from listserv postings turn into citations in subsequent publications. Still, Oakley (1991, pp. 23-24) suggests:

> Authors and publishers want to protect their work. Ordinary users wonder what they can do with information they find online. And librarians seek new ways to use technology to delivery information to their clients and to preserve information sources for succeeding generations.

Libraries and universities have vested interests in any decisions concerning intellectual property and copyright. Libraries have vast stores of paper-based information that they "own," but will they be able to migrate this information to electronic form without undue copyright burden? What would be the result on scholarly publication and access to information if universities institutionally claim copyright on faculty publications?

The policy issues involved in copyright and intellectual property are evolving based on changes in the technology. Technological solutions may emerge to protect the electronic property of authors, editors, and publishers (Corporation for National Research Initiatives,

1989), yet it appears that comprehensive solutions to the issues will be decided in the public policy arena. Libraries and universities must be involved in the policy debates and discussions to ensure their interests, and the interests of their constituents, are represented.

Organizing Networked Information Resources

The network can be compared to a library with the lights turned off and all the books randomly dumped into rooms that are not listed in the building's directory. Identifying or even determining whether resources exist on the network is a daunting task. After that, the user must locate and be able to access them. Traditional activities of libraries have included the functions that help users in accomplishing those tasks, and the question now is how can librarians perform similar functions in the networked environment. First and foremost, librarians will need education and training to gain the requisite knowledge and network skills to function in the networked environment.

Nielsen (1990, p. 105) suggests that librarians are in a position to take on responsibilities for information organization and retrieval in the networked environment, but cautions that "we may not be as well-prepared as we should be" to take on this task. In the area of organizing networked resources, Nielsen senses that a "reinvention" of librarianship may be necessary to deal with the complex knowledge organization issues inherent in network resources. These issues include the unique characteristics of networked resources, the mass and scope of the resources, and the relevance of current cataloging practices to these resources.

In describing and classifying networked information resources, libraries need to take into account the special characteristics of these resources (Moen, 1992). Unlike traditional library materials, networked resources are dynamic and volatile. The relative stability of a book or a sheet of microfiche is absent. Instead, changes in content to networked resources occur frequently (e.g., files available at a FTP site, data in a weather database, etc.). Yet identifying and describing are two essential elements in organizing these resources for effective use.

Lynch and Preston (1992) explore a "user" perspective in deploying databases of descriptive information to navigate and access networked information resources. They call for the development of large-scale prototypes to examine technical and user behavioral questions. A primary concern in developing navigational tools is ensuring these systems will "scale up" and effectively support users navigating through an ever-increasing mass and variety of networked resources.

Dillon et al. (1993), report findings from a project that investigated both the nature of electronic textual information available through the Internet and the practical and theoretical problems associated with using current cataloging rules and record formats for creating MARC records for those resources. Based on the results of the study, they offer three recommendations (pp. 35–36):

- implement the creation of machine-readable cataloging records (MARC) for remotely accessible electronic information objects;
- monitor the use effectiveness of records created for providing description and access information; and
- extend cataloging rules and formats to include interactive network systems and services.

In addition, they propose modifications to the USMARC computer files format and offer guidelines to assist catalogers with the application of existing cataloging rules for describing networked resources.

Developing the organizational principles and practices for networked resources is one challenge. Developing appropriate and effective navigational and resource discovery tools is another (see the special issue of *Electronic Networking,* [Brett, 1992]). One concern is whether the library and networking communities can collaborate on the tools, practices, and processes for organizing networked information resources. The Coalition for Networked Information (CNI) has brought together representatives of these communities to discuss data elements to describe the resources and how the description can be accomplished. Librarians can take a leadership role, based on their professional experience in organizing information, in bringing networked resources under some form of bibliographic control. They can also collaborate with networking technologists to arrive at new technical solutions to the organizational problems of networked resources.

Planning for Technology Change

The use of information technology in libraries continues to evolve. One can suggest that the changes have been incremental—

from the earliest uses of computers in libraries to the present where network accessible integrated library systems provide access to a wide range of information resources. At each incremental change, librarians and patrons employed the technology to enhance their access to and retrieval of information. And at each step, new demands and responsibilities accrued to library staff in mediating and training users of the new technology.

The development of the University of California's MELVYL system is well-documented in a three-part series appearing in Information Technology and Libraries, (Special Section: Happy Birthday to MELVYL, 1992a, 1992b, 1992c) as well as other writings by staff involved in MELVYL's development (Lynch, 1992a, 1989a, 1989b). The multiple perspectives on this one system show that the technology road travelled by MELVYL—a library information system as well prepared as any for the networked environment—has not always been a smooth one. The case of MELVYL shows the importance of planning for technology change. MELVYL was a key part of a plan the University of California developed and adopted to enhance the value of its libraries to research and education. Another planning document is guiding MELVYL development through the next five years.

Planning for technology change is essential if organizations are to direct their use of information technology rather than having the technology direct organizational goals. McClure (1991) suggests that a user perspective provides a robust framework for planning the use of technology. A user perspective assumes that information technologies should not be designed or implemented according to technical criteria alone but must account for particular communication behaviors, information use patterns, and work environments of potential users.

Focusing on social, behavioral, and organizational concerns can counteract the technological imperative that results from attending only to the technology (i.e., the technology can do it, therefore we have to use it!). While overall goals can be expressed in vision statements and planning documents, the new technologies in the networked environment open up a space for potential innovation and transformation. Organizational plans should be flexible to exploit new opportunities and services the technology offers.

Planning for technology change does not only address the implementation of the technology—the hardware, software, retrieval systems, resources discovery tools, etc. Planning must accommodate the impact on staff, including new duties and responsibilities that result from the technology, and the stress of working in a dynamic environment where technology changes rapidly. In addition, planning needs to address how the technology will impact library services, roles, and relationships with other campus units. Ultimately, planning for technology change should specify service goals and objectives that focus on the information needs of the users.

The Library Within Broader University Administrative Concerns

Even those libraries that have strategically envisioned themselves as central to the provision of networked information on campus face constrained resources and university administrators who may view campus-wide priorities much differently than library leaders. Hughes (1992) reports the findings from a survey of chief academic officers (CAOs) and library directors at ninety-six major U.S. universities to compare their perceptions of campus-wide priorities. The survey asked respondents to rank priorities including: undergraduate education, diversity, budget, electronic information, national network, and others.

The research hypotheses suggested that CAOs and library directors at the same campus would give similar rankings. The results were, however, quite the opposite. In particular, marked differences were evident in the rankings given by CAOs and library directors from the same campus on two priorities fundamental to the development of the virtual library.

> The CAOs' low ranking of an NREN-like network and the medium position given to developing greater access to electronic information resources seem to indicate that the vision of the logical library will be achieved much more slowly than most of the information profession's rhetoric suggests. Within an environment of serious budget constraints, these two initiatives, which could require a significant new and continuing investment in equipment and infrastructure, are not viewed as high resource expenditures among CAOs (p. 144).

Such differences in perspectives on the development of library services could be based on the fact that the library has not yet made the case for its role in the networked future and the importance of preparing now for that future. This situation would argue for strategic planning and strategic partnerships with other campus units who are envisioning the new ways information can and should be provided on campus, and then communicating their case to the university administration.

Dougherty and Dougherty (1993, p. 324) suggest that traditional library activities "will have to be reassessed and probably reconfigured to accommodate new information resources." They recognize that academic administrators have "limited knowledge about how the campus information environment really operates or, more specifically, about the nature and traditions of libraries and academic computing centers." At the same time as the administrators want their campuses to take advantage of the new technologies, "they also want to put a lid on expenditures." The question remains, how does the library (possibly in strategic partnership with the computing center and the faculty) make the case that the investment will need to be made—at the infrastructure level as well as at the applications and services level—to serve the information needs of campus users?

In a report issued by the Higher Education Information Resources Alliance (HEIRAlliance, 1992; DeLoughry, 1992), five university presidents and library directors provided perspectives on the investment and use of information technologies on their campuses. Directing their remarks to other university presidents, these spokespeople suggest the importance of promoting these technologies by integrating them with the mission and core values of the institution. Acknowledging a range of priorities, they claim that the "key to all of them is the development of organizational, instructional, and informational infrastructures. . . ." The contributors to this report see a critical need for leadership from the very top of the academic organization in creating the climate for innovative solutions through a robust informational infrastructure that is integrated, efficient, and functional.

The report contains an eleven-point checklist of items that university presidents should do to prepare their campuses for the future including these selected key concerns:

- support librarians in efforts to focus on knowledge access and management as well as the traditional acquisition, organization, and preservation of information;
- focus overall coordination of information resources at a high administrative level to create an intersection point for traditionally independent lines of authority;

- develop motivation and support mechanisms to encourage uses of information-rich databases and new modes of interaction in the teaching/learning process; and
- require cost-benefit analyses and assessment mechanisms of technology investments, with attention given to innovative ways of recouping some of the investments through the benefits they will yield.

While such checklists are useful, institutions will still need well-trained, knowledgeable, and visionary leaders.

The library's role in the larger campus information environment may be expanded. Moholt (1990, p. 43) suggests that as "libraries lose their walls," focusing more on the "idea" of the library rather than it as a "place," the skills and practices of librarians can be applied to other information-based activities. She notes the broad range of administrative and other activities on campus that are information intensive. Since librarians have "a global perspective on information and a set of skills important to addressing information issues beyond the library," they can be new players in the campus information resources management environment. This, of course, requires a rethinking of what business the library is in—the warehousing of books and other materials or the provision of a wide range of information services—and rethinking its relations with other campus units.

The Library and the Computing Center—New Partners?

The networked environment, along with the less than bright budget picture for most academic institutions, have brought together the library and computing center in ways that would have been difficult to envision as little as ten years ago. Different historical contexts, cultures, and missions defined these separate organizational units. Yet, the distributed computing environment, the rise in amount and importance of electronic information, and the types and ranges of skills necessary for the provision of networked-based information have encouraged new collaborations between the library and the computing center. Quinlan (1991, p. 103) explores the historical differences, identifies the similarities, and discusses the emerging relationships. She suggests that emphasis needs to be placed not on "who shall report to whom, but organizationally . . . on ensuring the right mix of staff is brought together so that the user community can be served as efficiently and effectively as possible."

Didier (1990) describes how the Michigan Business School combined its library and computing units into a single organization called Information Resources. This was not merely an organizational rearrangement for reporting purposes. Department managers in library and computing areas in Information Resources routinely work together, and individual staff from each area are paired to address issues of mutual responsibility. The "converging nature of these information-based operations" motivated the reorganization. Since neither unit could provide all the information or assistance a user might need, collaboration allows them to focus on a single point of service for the user: unified access to information. This affirms Quinlan's imperative to have a staff, whether librarians or computer specialists, with the appropriate skills for the benefit of the user community.

University administrations have questioned the separate organizational arrangements of the library and the computing center. Some universities have initiated changes in reporting structures of these units, others have merged the units. Martin (1992, p. 78), while reviewing the organizational models, suggests that regardless of the organizational structure on a particular campus, the question comes down to "Who's in charge?" of campus information. Should librarians, with their service-oriented perspective on information provision direct the campus information environment? Or should the responsibility reside with computing center staff and their technological expertise?

The new campus information environment (i.e., telecommunications-based, distributed processing, and networked information) forces the issue of library and the computing center collaboration. Many issues surrounding the provision of information on campus require cooperative and collaborative solutions. (See the discussions in Chapters 2 and 3.) One major focal point is user training. New levels of computer and network literacy will be needed by users in the networked environment. While the library may attempt to train users as another facet of library instruction, "computing center staff have an overlapping concern with user training and can be partners in the process" (Saunders, 1992, p. 69). Another major overlapping area is user support—which unit is responsible for what aspect of network information retrieval?

The lines drawn by the historical differences between the library and computing center are shifting and blurring.

Technological expertise is no longer limited to computing center staff; librarians have become more technically literate in the realm of networks, computers, and telecommunications. The service ethic—a hallmark of the librarian—is adopted by computing center staff in response to users' demands in the distributed computing environment. Dougherty (1987, p. 296) sees that the partnering between these units is between "natural allies," and they have complementary skills and knowledge to share. The differences between the library and the computing center do not have to be barriers to cooperation. Project-based collaborations are a basis for developing and providing services that neither the library nor the computing center have been able to do on their own.

A New Information Delivery Paradigm

New information delivery paradigms can grow out of the current and ongoing efforts of academic libraries that are experimenting with new ways of serving the information needs of campus users. The importance of these trials and experiments, and the sharing of experiences and results, cannot be overstated. The literature is expanding with reports of these attempts. This section, while not meant to be comprehensive nor exhaustive, explores the range of efforts currently underway.

Technology can assist in providing access to information traditionally held as reserve reading material. Bosseau (1993, p. 366) reports on an Electronic Reserve Book Room, which is a step toward electronic document provision for and enhanced access to a high-use core collection of print materials. "This strategy is driven not only by the opportunity to exploit new computer and communication technology, but also by the need to resolve problems being generated by the increasingly difficult fiscal environment."

The library at Indiana University has been providing reference service via electronic mail since 1987 as part of an electronic Academic Information Environment (Bristow, 1992). The library's experience suggests that to be useful this type of service should be part of a broader framework for electronic services and that the service will be used most frequently by people who have integrated computing into all aspects of their work and communication. These observations point to a likely evolutionary nature of these services as users become more network and computer literate. Still and Alexander (1993) discuss the policy issues of integrating the use of the Internet and Internet resources documentation in reference activities.

At Earlham College (Beth and Farber, 1992), the library in collaboration with DIALOG Information Services provided unlimited online searching access for faculty and students in an attempt to understand how such activities might affect the teaching/learning process. In addition, the experiment highlighted impacts of providing online access to electronic information in areas such as reference services, bibliographic instruction, and interlibrary loan.

Electronically delivering the information a user wants to a desktop workstation requires large repositories of electronic materials and standards for electronic document storage, processing, and transmission (Cleveland, 1991). Carnegie Mellon University (see Appendix B) and others have ongoing projects to investigate the digitization of text and images for document delivery. In a joint research and demonstration project, the National Agricultural Library (NAL) and the North Carolina State University (NCSU) Libraries and the NCSU Computing Center developed an Internet-based document delivery system for library materials (North Carolina State University, n.d.).

Collaboration to enhance resource sharing has been a feature of traditional library information provision. Collaboration is likely to play a central role in the networked environment as well. Organizations will combine their efforts to provide access to electronic information as they have with paper-based library materials. One example is the collaboration of Cornell, Stanford, and Carnegie Mellon Universities, the Massachusetts Institute of Technology, and the University of California to "create a joint online collection of current documents in computer science and to develop an index to the collection" (Watkins, 1992, p. A20).

Libraries are experimenting with different models for accommodating electronic journals. In one project, the University Libraries at Virginia Polytechnic Institute have developed a "message-based automated system for electronic journal management" (Kriz, 1993). This system provides completely automated receipt, indexing, and storage of CHIPS, an electronic journal published by the Chile Information Project. It provides users with full-screen search and display interface through which they can retrieve and read articles online.

Columbia University Law Library recently initiated a five-year project to create a virtual library, a library of the future that solves three critical issues. "The library of the future will alleviate storage problems in overcrowded libraries, provide easy access to fragile materials, and allow storage and access to materials increasingly available only in electronic form" ("Library of the Future," 1993). Project JANUS combines digital conversion and storage of documents (text and graphics), massively parallel supercomputing, and advanced search-and-retrieval software for natural language queries against full-text documents.

This small sample of pilot projects, demonstration projects, and experiments herald some of the networked-based services and products libraries can offer. By taking a leadership role in developing these ideas, academic libraries are readying themselves for the future, not just responding to it. These activities help to uncover problems and issues as well as solutions, and they provide guidance to others.

Creating Evaluation Methods for Network Services

While there is much attention in the literature to the technical possibilities of networks, electronic data storage, transmission, and access via the scholar's workstation, few people are discussing how to evaluate the services that an electronic library will offer. Those writers who suggest this is an issue of importance are less specific about the details of evaluation techniques. The general sense is that libraries must move beyond the traditional measures of inputs, collection size, acquisitions, and outputs to measures of outcomes and impacts. Dickeson (1991) notes the changing assumptions about evaluation in academic organizations. Library administrators have yet to translate those concerns into ways of thinking about evaluations of services that are only beginning or have yet to emerge.

Hernon and McClure (1990) suggest that evaluation is a decision-making tool intended primarily to (1) ensure that the highest quality services are provided to intended users, and (2) assist decision-makers in resource allocation for those services that best facilitate the accomplishment of organizational goals and objectives. Evaluation is tied closely with planning, and McClure (1991, p. 36) argues for a user-based perspective for strategic planning and performance measures to understand the "role, importance, and impact of networked information services in the academic setting." As indicators of the quality with which some service or process accomplishes, performance measures relating to academic networks will assist academic, computing, and library administrators to (p. 36):

- determine the appropriateness of goals and objectives;
- assess the degree to which stated objectives are accomplished;

- determine the appropriateness of resource allocations;
- monitor the status of specific networked services and operations;
- demonstrate accountability and/or justify services;
- assist institutional staff in professional development;
- determine if networked services should be continued, modified, or discontinued;
- fine-tune existing services and activities to better meet user information needs;
- compare the relative costs and benefits among various networked programs and services; and
- provide objective evidence in support of decision making.

McClure also suggests that performance measures typically examine a service in terms of extensiveness, efficiency, effectiveness, and impact. Without such measures, "we can only guess at what seems to work well and why" (p. 37).

Although it may be difficult for some to entertain the possible services the library can offer in the networked environment, those who are already implementing networked-based services (e.g., electronic reference services, document delivery, etc.) will need to establish suitable methods for evaluating their success. Such evaluation should be built into project design and not be added as an afterthought. Evaluation must combine with a strategic planning process to address two key questions: How successful are the existing networked information services we provide, and what services should we provide in the future?

Regrowing Staff

Regrowing staff "means more than developing essential on-the-job staff skills; it requires reconceptualizing the role of the university library and the role of the client, and then regrowing staff who will shape the new directions for the library and the new information behavior of clients" (Jennings, 1992, p. 5). To accomplish this regrowing, the staff need to take upon themselves some of the responsibility for changing, but library leadership is required to foster the conditions for such growth, change, and involvement by the staff. A major challenge facing academic libraries is determining the roles and the services they will offer in the new networked environment. Jennings suggests that the library's own staff can offer important perspectives when library administrators begin asking strategic questions about the future of the library and its role in the university.

Specifically, Jennings recommends that the library must move away from a "production mode of service" that focuses on selection, acquisition, cataloging, storage, and lending to a "facilitator mode." "The library's increasingly important new roles will be to provide clients with advice about electronic information and to help them develop skills in accessing, using, and managing this information" (p. 11). These new service roles will require a change in staff profiles based on principles including: collaboration with others, repackaging information, providing on-demand access via document delivery services, information filtering, and others.

Cargill (1992, p. 83) reaffirms this change in service roles and suggests for reference services an "emphasis on focused proactive service to the user rather than passive or reactive service by the organization." Such proactive service will be directed to students, researchers, and for curriculum support. Reference services in the electronic environment require a client-centered concentration on information management and access, and less emphasis on collection development and bibliographic control that have often in the past served the needs of librarians rather than the needs of users.

Public services staff will need to understand "the hardware, software, networking situations, or lack thereof, for each full-text database, to be able to switch adroitly among different software, networks, and hardware, and to be able to explain this to users who are in the library, who are calling from their offices, homes, or dorm rooms, or have left messages on the library's electronic bulletin board" (Racine, 1992, p. 102). Training staff in a range of technical skills and competencies is essential if the library is to develop and deliver successful networked-based services.

New skills and competencies will also be required of technical services staff in the electronic environment (Corbin, 1992). These include:

- computer literacy;
- network literacy;
- knowledge of electronic transaction processing systems (for acquisitions, claiming, fund transfer, etc.);
- database management skills;
- project management;
- systems analysis, design, evaluation, and support; and
- fiscal planning and management.

Corbin suggests that while technical services functions for the paper-based library will continue (e.g., acquisitions, selection, bibliographic control, etc.), many of these will be automated or assisted by automation. The reliance on information technology will require diverse technical skills such as computer programming and operation, hardware and software installation, and system maintenance to handle the automated traditional functions and new responsibilities in the electronic library.

From reconceptualizing the library in the networked environment to acquiring the skills necessary for service delivery, library staff play a crucial role in determining the success of the future academic library. Preparing staff to participate effectively in the development and delivery of networked-based services should be the priority of library administrators. Yet, there is a disturbing lack of staff training programs geared to the emerging service roles of the electronic library evident in the literature.

Research for the Future

Issues can be defined as topics or possible decision areas where there is conflict among different stakeholders. Resolving, or at least addressing, the issues is necessary for effective decisions to be made. Research on these issues can contribute to the process of issue resolution and decision making. And from the literature review, there is clearly a wide range of topics requiring investigation.

A research program can guide the questions and prioritize the topics for individual researchers. Penniman (1992) describes four areas that the Council on Library Resources has identified for research to help guide libraries in redesigning themselves as information delivery systems—and moving away from the idea of library-as-warehouse. Reconceptualizing the library away from the library-as-warehouse model focuses attention and emphasis less on assets than on output, outcomes, and impacts. The four general areas are: (1) human resource issues; (2) economic issues; (3) infrastructure questions; and (4) processing and access issues.

Adapting these four areas to identify research questions for academic libraries in the networked environment provides another view of the issues this chapter presents.

Human Resource Issues. The academic library in the next decade will require staff who are competent in both paper-based and electronic-based information processing. Books will not suddenly disappear, and electronic information services will develop along-side some of the traditional functions. Staff are more likely to need new competencies in addition to the traditional skills and knowledge relevant to librarianship. Also, the library may attract new specializations (Corbin, 1992) such as computer programmers, systems analysts, and other technology professionals who will work collaboratively with information specialists.

The following research questions begin probing the human resource issues of the networked library:

- What is the impact of electronic-mediated information services on staff who are drawn to the face-to-face service-oriented nature of librarianship?
- What effective training and education programs can be developed for current staff to ensure computer and network literacy?
- How can staff be regrown (i.e., informed, enthused, and encouraged) to assist in reconceptualizing the library?
- What changes are required of library and information science education to prepare professionals for the new library information environment?

Although some networked-based library services are emerging, other services will likely evolve as the new environment unfolds. Research is needed now to identify the range of skills, attitudes, and values of staff for the library of the future so administrators and library leaders can develop appropriate programs of training and education.

Economic Issues. Libraries have learned that information technology does not automatically generate cost savings, and it would be unwise for libraries to think that the networked environment and electronic information will bring reduced operating and materials expenditures. Instead, economic constraints will force academic libraries to make difficult choices about the services they will and will not be able to provide. To make informed decisions, an understanding of the costs and benefits of the various services is needed.

Confounding the economic situation is the lack of information on the real costs of networked-based services and operations. The campus networking infrastructures to which the libraries connect have shielded the libraries from the true costs of network connections. Changes in subsidies to regional networks, privatization and commercialization of network services, and other changes in the external environment will likely bring increased costs to libraries for the use of networks and networked services and products. Research is needed to identify a variety of network costs and benefits, and the following questions point to other important economic concerns for the library:

- What will be the economic impacts on users when libraries rely on acquisition-on-demand and document delivery models?
- What are appropriate cost/benefit analyses for evaluating networked-based library services and products?
- To what extent should economic considerations guide decisions concerning information provision on campus?
- Can the library afford an information commons model in the networked environment (i.e., subsidizing access to networked information to make it appear to be "free")?

Adequate planning for the networked library should include an examination of potential economic impacts from staffing to the provision of electronic information. Empirical research and economic modelling can assist decision-makers as they plan for the library's future.

Infrastructure Questions. Aligned closely with economic considerations are a range of issues concerning infrastructure investment and development. Library automation projects of the 1970s and 1980s occurred during times of relative prosperity for libraries. The need for increased infrastructure expenditures to prepare for the networked environment face the stark economic reality of library budget cuts and retrenchment. If academic libraries are to provide high-quality networked-based services and products, an adequate information infrastructure must be in place.

An information infrastructure is the foundation on which organizations can develop appropriate applications for the provision of information. A campus information infrastructure will include the people who produce and use the information, the information resources such as documents and databases, the information processes, and the technology for manipulating and accessing the information. While many campuses are wired now with local and wide area networks, Wilson (1991) reports that higher education may have to spend billions of dollars on local campuses to take advantage of emerging national networked environment.

Research in this area needs to examine such questions as:

- What models exist in other sectors for examining and redesigning business processes prior to determining the appropriate infrastructure to support those processes?
- What are the elements of and how can a library define and describe an adequate infrastructure for the networked environment?
- What is the relationship between the library's infrastructure and the campus infrastructure?
- What are the impacts (i.e., cost shifting) of an inadequate infrastructure on service delivery and user support?

Understanding costs, benefits, and impacts of an adequate information infrastructure as well as rethinking the services, products, and applications the infrastructure can support will assist library administrators in making the case for needed investments.

Processing and Access Issues. Processing materials for use in the library (e.g., acquisition, cataloging, binding, etc.) should serve the goal of access. Often, though, the focus is more on processing—the internal functions of the library—and less on user services and access. One model for library service in the networked environment suggests customized information packaging for users. Processing information in this model is directly connected to user information needs.

The roles of libraries in processing and providing access to information in the networked environment are emerging. Often the networked-based library services evolve from traditional services (e.g., electronic mail reference queries). Other services are new departures for libraries (e.g., providing a listserv). Research in this area can identify appropriate roles and services for libraries, and the following questions point to several relevant issues:

- What processing activities of networked resources should libraries provide (e.g., cataloging resources, printing and binding electronic journals, SDI services, etc.)?

- How do people currently use the network for information gathering and how can the library develop services to assist them?
- What value-added services and products can libraries offer that enhance users' access to networked resources?
- Is knowledge management and information filtering the new mode of processing for the electronic library?

A user-based approach in developing appropriate library services is essential if the library is to play a central role in the networked environment.

The research areas listed above are illustrative of topics and issues that need investigating. They also are not the only way to group the issues uncovered in the literature review. Another grouping could include issues related to:

- technology;
- organizational structure;
- behavioral perspectives;
- legal concerns; and
- planning and evaluation.

If the library community is to reconceptualize the library, research should assist that process by systematically investigating the emerging networked environment and examining the broad range of issues that confront the transition of the library from the present to the unformed future.

THE ONGOING TRANSITION

Academic libraries are in a special position regarding networking activity since in many cases, connections to the Internet for individual campuses were put in place at the institutional level, and the libraries did not have to pick up the full cost of establishing and maintaining a connection. Instead, the wired campus was in place (or being built), and by connecting to the campus network, the library could enjoy the benefits of Internet access. This ease of network connection enabled the early participation, at a relatively low cost, of academic libraries in the Internet. In addition, academic libraries have had the opportunity to experiment with network use and develop new information services and products. Much of the leadership and participation of academic libraries (compared to public, K–12, and special libraries) in networking activity is the result of the special position of the academic library in the networked environment.

Being on the early frontline of network use, however, brought burdens as well as benefits to academic libraries. Their "bleeding-edge" participation has resulted in a more realistic appraisal of problems and issues, as well as opportunities, involved with the networked environment. Compare, for example, the differences between public and academic librarian responses to the research study's survey reported in Chapters 3 and 4. Early optimistic visions are now tempered by the barriers, constraints, and problems academic libraries experienced firsthand. Still, academic libraries see the promises of the networked environment for serving the information needs of campus communities and continue their exploration of network technologies and network resources.

Evolution, transition, reconceptualization, and other metaphors capture the fluid state in which academic libraries currently exist. For some, the movement represents a change in the academic library paradigm. Young (1991, p. 8) suggests that the following trends are symptomatic of the library's transitional environment:

- increasing involvement of digital electronic systems in library and scholarly information organizations;
- movement towards networked information systems and a shift away from resource ownership towards access to shared resources from diverse collection sources;
- shift towards a more fluid format where information is available in a multiple array of formats, both graphic and digital;
- shift towards greater user choice and control of the form and content of information and away from system constraints;
- rapid changes towards a global perspective on information issues, especially in acquiring scholarly information resources from non-domestic sources of supply;
- increasing proliferation of information production that necessitates an increase in the ability to process and manage information at an ever-increasing level of efficiency;
- concern about the social and economic impact of information illiteracy and electronic illiteracy;

- growing concern over the economic consequences and property ownership implications of a transition from a graphic/print-based information society to a culture dependent on electronic communication as a means of information transfer and exchange;
- increasing concern about individual privacy and confidentiality, especially in relation to personal information and to issues involving individual information selection and choice;
- increasing involvement of different teams or groups of individuals engaged in collaborative work using information technology which bridges time and geographic distance allowing cooperative group intellectual research and problem solving; and
- a growing awareness that the transition to a new library paradigm requires a careful examination of the values underlying the information creation, exchange, and sharing process.

For many academic libraries, realistic assessments based on their networking experience in this transitional phase now inform their visions of the networked future. For most libraries, though, this transition has just begun. And for all libraries, the virtual library is likely to be a perpetual work-in-progress. Intimations of evolution can be found in examples of libraries already deeply involved in the networked environment. Technological innovations continue to expand the service horizon. Services that could not be implemented ten years ago (e.g., desktop electronic delivery of journal articles) are now available. As more librarians gain network skills and competence, they begin to imagine even more service possibilities for their users.

It is not enough, however, to imagine potential uses of the networked environment. We must develop strategies and determine the next steps to move academic libraries and the campus information environment forward in their transition and reconceptualization. We need to focus not only on a "preferred future" for the library but also on what the library "needs" to be doing to build that future. RLG sponsored a June 1992 workshop, "Preferred Library Futures: Charting the Path," (Dougherty and Hughes, 1993) that brought together representatives of six stakeholder groups (publishers, research consortium/foundation directors, university administrators, faculty, campus information technology managers, and library directors) to "consider what an effective university library must be like in the future and what strategies might be pursued in order to transform the library and other components of the current campus information environment" (p. 3). Participants developed ideas for specific pilot projects that would lay the groundwork for the campus information environment in the next century (p. 14). Their concepts included:

- devise a prototype that will help interested stakeholders understand better the factors that are limiting universities's ability to act;
- bring the national discussion of library futures to the local campus and develop collaborative models for problem solving within the university;
- develop network access for everyone from a personal workstation;
- develop a clear strategy for information sharing across institutions;
- start with an upheaval; give no money for materials to the library for a year; invest the funds in developing a new campus information infrastructure; and
- devise a project to ensure preservation of electronic information.

Pilot projects can move the stakeholders on campus from talk to action, thus establishing the credibility and demonstrating the value of information provision in the networked environment.

In summary comments about the workshop, one participant (James Michalko, President, RLG) noted that there is the "necessary goodwill for a productive partnership among the stakeholders. . . . What is more, the urge to change among all stakeholders was evident" (p. 23). Yet differences in their perceived importance of issues and trends will work against trouble-free collaborations. "All this said to me that the organized anarchy of the university is not going to produce a revolution in electronic information provision for the humanities and social sciences any time soon" (p. 24).

Academic libraries must take a leadership role in identifying, addressing, and resolving the issues confronting them in the networked environment. They must collaborate with other campus stakeholders to create the conditions for networked information provision. They must explore strategic partnerships with publishers and other information providers. Only they can chart a path to the transformation of the library that maintains the library's critical function in campus information environment. Others will not do the hard work for them.

Sympathetic observers of libraries cast the future in a positive light, yet they recognize necessary changes if libraries are to take advantage of the opportunity the networked world offers (Browning, 1993, p. 62).

> Realizing this vision will transform libraries from guardians of tradition to catalysts of a vast change. By breaking down the walls that separate libraries from each other and from their users, librarians dissolve the barriers that separate libraries from publishers. This will change the economics of publishing, and with that, the way in which ideas are disseminated and culture is made.

Thoughts such as these demand more than simple incrementalism from the present to the future. This is the talk of reconceptualization and transformation.

Notwithstanding the challenges—from the dynamic, fast-changing nature of the networked environment to copyright dilemmas and from budgetary constraints to staffing, academic libraries are acting. They are moving toward the world of the virtual library. Because of their efforts, these libraries provide important sources of information for research on the current and anticipated impacts of networks on libraries. The next two chapters explore the findings from the empirical data collected during this research project. These findings suggest that much work and rethinking of the role of academic libraries in the networked environment are needed.

NOTES

1. The phrase "perpetual work-in-progress" is taken from Dougherty and Hughes (1991, p. 17) where they report that realizing one of the visions of the preferred future "will be a perpetual work-in-progress."

REFERENCES

Arms, Caroline. (Summer, 1989a). Libraries and electronic information: The technological context, part one. *Educom Review* 24(2): 38–43.

Arms, Caroline. (Fall, 1989b). Libraries and electronic information: The technological context, part two. *Educom Review* 24(3): 34–43.

Association of Research Libraries. (1993). *ARL Statistics, 1991–1992.* Washington, DC: Association of Research Libraries.

Aupperle, Eric M. (Winter, 1993). Changing eras: Evolution of the NFSNET. *Internet Society News* 1(4): 3.

Bailey, Charles W. Jr. (1992a). Electronic publishing on networks: A selective bibliography of recent works. *The Public-Access Computer Systems Review* 3(2): 13–20. Available from: LISTSERV@UHUPVM1; send message: GET BAILEY PRV3N2.

Bailey, Charles W. Jr. (March, 1992b). Network-based electronic serials. *Information Technology and Libraries* 11(1): 29–35.

Bailey, Charles W. Jr. (Spring/Summer, 1992c). The Coalition for Networked Information's acquisition-on-demand model: An exploration and critique. *Serials Review* 18(1–2): 78–81.

Bailey, Charles W. Jr. (1989). Integrated public-access computer systems: The heart of the electronic university. In Joe A. Hewitt, ed., *Advances in Library Automation and Networking*, vol. 3. (pp. 1–33). Greenwich, CT: JAI Press, Inc.

Beth, Amy and Farber, Evan I. (September 15, 1992). Lessons from DIALOG: Technology impacts teaching/learning. *Library Journal* 117(15): 26–30.

Borgmann, Albert. (1992). *Crossing the Postmodern Divide.* Chicago: University of Chicago Press.

Bosseau, Don L. (January, 1993). Anatomy of a small step forward: The electronic reserve book room at San Diego State University. *The Journal of Academic Librarianship* 18(6): 366–368.

Boyce, Bert R. (March, 1993). Meeting the serials cost problem: A supply-side proposal. *American Libraries* 24(3): 272–273.

Brett, George H. (Ed.). (Spring, 1992). Accessing information on the Internet. [Special Issue]. *Electronic Networking: Research, Applications and Policy* 2(1).

Bristow, Ann. (November, 1992). Academic reference service over electronic mail. *College & Research Libraries News* 53(10): 631–632+.

Britten, William A. (February, 1990). BITNET and the Internet: Scholarly networks for librarians. *College & Research Libraries News* 51 (2): 103–107.

Browning, John. (Premier Issue, 1993). Libraries without walls for books without pages. *Wired* 1.1: 62–65+.

Cargill, Jennnifer. (Spring, 1992). The electronic reference desk: Reference service in an electronic world. *Library Administration and Management* 6(2): 82–85.

Cerf, Vinton G. (March 23, 1993). National information infrastructure. Written testimony to the U.S. House, Committee on Science, Space and Technology, Subcommittee on Technology, Environment and Aviation. (E-mail message posted April 13, 1993 by vcerf@cnri.reston.va.us.).

Cleveland, Gary. (1991). *Electronic Document Delivery: Converging Standards and Technologies.* (UDT Series on Data Communication Technologies and Standards for Libraries, Report #2). Ottawa, Canada: IFLA International Office for Universal Dataflow and Telecommunications.

Clinton, President William J. and Gore, Vice President Albert, Jr. (February 23, 1993). *Technology for America's Economic Growth: A New Direction to Build Economic Strength.* Washington, DC: Executive Office of the President.

Committee on Physical, Mathematical, and Engineering Sciences, Federal Coordinating Council for Science, Engineering, and Technology, and Office of Science and Technology Policy. (1992). *Grand Challenges 1993: High Performance Computing and Communications.* Washington, DC: National Science Foundation.

Corbin, John. (Spring, 1992). Technical services for the electronic library. *Library Administration and Management* 6(2): 86–90.

Corporation for National Research Initiatives. (1989). *Knowbots in the Real World: Workshop on the Protection of Intellectual Property Rights in a Digital Library System,* May 18–19, 1989. Reston, VA: Corporation for National Research Initiatives.

CREN GROWTH. (1993). This electronic file contains statistics on BITNET connections since 1981. It is available from LISTSERV@BITNIC.BITNET.

Cummings, Anthony M., Witte, Marcia L., Bowen, William G., Lazarus, Laura O. and Ekman, Richard H. (1992). *University Libraries and Scholarly Communication: A Study Prepared for the Andrew W. Mellon Foundation.* Washington, DC: Association of Research Libraries.

Cutter, Charles A. (1985). Rules for a dictionary catalog: Selections. In Michael Carpenter and Elaine Svenonius, eds., *Foundations of Cataloging: A Sourcebook* (pp. 62–71). Littleton, CO: Libraries Unlimited, Inc.

DeLoughry, Thomas J. (October 14, 1992). Presidents urged to help expand use of technology on campuses. *The Chronicle of Higher Education,* A19–A20.

Dickeson, Robert C. (1991). Reactions from a university president. In Gary M. Pitkin, ed., *The Evolution of Library Automation:*

Management Issues and Future Perspectives (pp. 133–142). Westport, CT: Meckler.

Didier, Elaine K. (February, 1990). A synergistic approach to defining a new information environment. *Academic Computing* 4(5): 24–41.

Dillon, Martin, Jul, Erik, Burge, Mark and Hickey, Carol. (1993). *Assessing Information on the Internet: Toward Providing Library Services for Computer-Mediated Communication* (Research report). Dublin, OH: OCLC Online Computer Library Center, Inc.

Dougherty, Richard M. (June 17, 1992). A "factory" for scholarly journals. *The Chronicle of Higher Education*: B1, B3.

Dougherty, Richard M. (July, 1987). Libraries and computing centers: A blueprint for collaboration. *College & Research Libraries*, 48(4), 289–296.

Dougherty, Richard M. and Dougherty, Ann P. (January, 1993). The academic library: A time of crisis, change, and opportunity. *The Journal of Academic Librarianship* 18(6): 342–346.

Dougherty, Richard M. and Hughes, Carol. (1993). *Preferred Library Futures II: Charting the Paths.* Mountain View, CA: Research Libraries Group, Inc.

Dougherty, Richard M. and Hughes, Carol. (1991). *Preferred Futures for Libraries: A Summary of Six Workshops with University Provosts and Library Directors.* Mountain View, CA: Research Libraries Group, Inc.

Drake, Miriam A. (1992a). Side roads and electronic highways. *Library Hi Tech* 10(3) Issue 39: 67–70.

Drake, Miriam A. (1992b, Spring/Summer). Buying articles in the future. *Serials Review* 18(1–2): 75–77.

Eldred, Susan M. and McGill, Michael J. (Fall, 1992). Commercialization of the Internet/NREN: Introduction. *Electronic Networking: Research, Applications and Policy* 2(3): 2–4.

Ensor, Pat. (January/February, 1993). E-journals and full-text access. *Campus-Wide Information Systems* 10(1): 25–35.

Ensor, Pat. (December, 1992). Automating document delivery: A conference report. *Computers in Libraries* 12(11): 34–35.

Estrada, Susan. (Fall, 1992). Commercialization and the Commercial Internet Exchange: How the CIX can help further the commercialization of the Internet. *Electronic Networking: Research, Applications and Policy* 2(3): 24–28.

Gapen, D. Kaye. (1993). The virtual library: Knowledge, society, and the librarian. In Laverna M. Saunders, ed., *The Virtual Library: Visions and Realities* (pp. 1–14). Westport, CT: Meckler.

Garcia, D. Linda. (1987). The OTA report on intellectual property rights. In *Intellectual Property Rights in an Electronic Age: Proceedings of the Library of Congress Network Advisory Committee Meeting* (Network Planning Paper No. 16, pp. 9–18). Washington, DC: Library of Congress, Network Development and MARC Standards Office.

Gould, Stephen B. (1990). *The Federal Research Internet and the National Research and Education Network: Prospects for the 1990s.* CRS Report for Congress. Washington DC: Congressional Research Service, Library of Congress.

Grycz, Czeslaw Jan. (Ed.). (Spring/Summer, 1992). Economic models for networked information [Special issue]. *Serials Review* 18(1–2).

Hawkins, Donald T., Smith Frank J., Dietlein, Bruce C., Joseph, Eugene J., and Rindfuss, Robert D. (Winter, 1992). Forces shaping the electronic publishing industry of the 1990s. *Electronic Networking: Research, Applications and Policy* 2(4): 38–60.

HEIRAlliance. (September, 1992). What presidents need to know . . . about the integration of information technologies on campus. HEIRAlliance Executive Strategies Report #1. Boulder, CO: CAUSE. Available electronically. Send the electronic mail message:GET HEIRA.ES1 to HEIRAES@CAUSE.COLORADO.EDU.

Hernon, Peter and McClure, Charles R. (1991). United States information policies. In Wendy Schipper and Ann Marie Cunningham, eds., *National and International Information Policies* (pp. 3–48). Philadelphia, PA: National Federation of Abstracting and Information Services.

Hernon, Peter and McClure, Charles R. (1990). *Evaluation and Library Decision Making.* Norwood, NJ: Ablex Publishing Corporation.

Hernon, Peter and McClure, Charles R. (1987). *Federal Information Policies in the 1980s.* Norwood, NJ: Ablex Publishing Corporation.

Heterick, Robert C. Jr. (1991). The institutional perspective. In Gary M. Pitkin, ed., *The Evolution of Library Automation: Management Issues and Future Perspectives* (pp. 1–18). Westport, CT: Meckler.

Hoffert, Barbara. (September 1, 1992). Books into bytes. Library *Journal* 117(14): 130–135.

Hughes, Carol A. (July, 1992). A comparison of perceptions of campus priorities: The 'logical' library in an organized anarchy. *The Journal of Academic Librarianship* 18(3): 140–145.

Hunter, Karen. (Spring/Summer, 1992). The national site license model. *Serials Review* 18(1–2): 71–72+.

Jennings, Lois. (1992). Regrowing staff: Managerial priority for the future of university libraries. *The Public-Access Computer Systems Review* 3(3): 4–15. To retrieve this article, send the following e-mail message to LISTSERV@UHUPVM1.BITNET or LISTSERV@UHUPVM1.UH.EDU: GET JENNINGS PRV3N3 F=MAIL

Jensen, Mary Brandt. (Spring/Summer, 1992). Making copyright work in electronic publishing models. *Serials Review* 18(1–2): 62–65.

Kibbey, Mark and Evans, Nancy H. (Fall, 1989). The network is the library. *EDUCOM Review* 24(3): 15–20.

Kibirige, Harry M. (September, 1991). Information communication highways in the 1990s: An analysis of their potential impact on library automation. *Information Technology and Libraries* 10(3): 172–184.

King, Kenneth M. (1989). National networks and higher education. In *Connecting the Networks: Proceedings of the Joint Library of Congress Network Advisory Committee and EDUCOM Meeting* (Network Planning Paper No. 18, pp. 15–17). Washington, DC: Library of Congress, Network Development and MARC Standards Office.

Kost, Robert. (Spring/Summer, 1992). Technology giveth. . . . *Serials Review* 18(1–2): 67–70.

Kriz, Harry M. (March 3, 1993). Electronic journal system. [Posted electronic message] *Public Access Computer Systems Forum (PACS-L)*. Available from: PACS-L@UHUPVM1.BITNET.

Larsen, Ronald L. (Fall/Winter, 1991). The library as a network-based information server. *EDUCOM Review* 26(3/4): 38–44.

Larsen, Ronald L. (February, 1990). The colibratory: The network as testbed for a distributed electronic library. *Academic Computing* 4(5): 22–37.

Leach, Ronald G. and Tribble, Judith E. (January, 1993). Electronic document delivery: New options for libraries. *The Journal of Academic Librarianship* 18(6): 359–364.

"Library of the future" takes shape at Columbia University Law Library. (February 1, 1993). Press release.

Lottor, M. (1992). *Internet Growth (1981–1991)*. Menlo Park, CA: SRI International.

Louis, Kenneth R.R. Gros. (1992). The real costs and financial challenges of library networking: Part 1. In Brett Sutton and

Charles H. Davis, eds., *Networks, Open Access, and Virtual Libraries: Implications for the Research Library* (pp. 118–122) Urbana-Champaign, IL: University of Illinois at Urbana-Champaign, Graduate School of Library and Information Science.

Lyman, Peter. (1992a). Can higher education afford research libraries? *Library Hi Tech* 10(3) Issue 39: 75–78.

Lyman, Peter. (Spring/Summer, 1992b). Can the network reduce the cost of scholarly information? *Serials Review* 18(1–2): 98–99.

Lynch, Clifford A. (November/December, 1992a). Beyond the ordinary card catalog: MELVYL learns from years of experience. *EDUCOM Review* 27(3/4): 20–23.

Lynch, Clifford A. (1992b). Networked information: A revolution in progress. In Brett Sutton and Charles H. Davis, eds., *Networks, Open Access, and Virtual Libraries: Implications for The Research Library* (pp. 12–39). Urbana-Champaign, IL: University of Illinois at Urbana-Champaign, Graduate School of Library and Information Science.

Lynch, Clifford A. (Spring/Summer, 1992c). Reaction, response, and realization: From the crisis in scholarly communication to the age of networked information. *Serials Review* 18(1–2): 107–112.

Lynch, Clifford A. (Winter, 1991). The development of electronic publishing and digital library collections on the NREN. *Electronic Networking: Research, Applications and Policy* 1(2): 6–22.

Lynch, Clifford A. (1989a). From telecommunications to networking: The MELVYL online union catalog and the development of intercampus networks at the University of California. *Library Hi Tech* 7(2) Issue 26: 61–83.

Lynch, Clifford A. (Fall, 1989b). Library automation and the national research network. *EDUCOM Review* 24(3): 21–26.

Lynch, Clifford A. (1989c). Linking library automation systems in the internet: Functional requirements, planning, and policy issues. *Library Hi-Tech* 7(4) Issue 28: 7–18.

Lynch, Clifford A. and Preston, Cecilia M. (Spring, 1992). Describing and classifying networked information resources. *Electronic Networking: Research, Applications and Policy* 2(1): 13–23.

Lynch, Clifford A. and Preston, Cecilia M. (1990). Internet access to information resources. In Martha E. Williams, ed., *Annual Review of Information Science and Technology*, vol. 25 (pp. 263–312). NY: Elsevier Publishers.

Lyons, Patrice A. (Spring/Summer, 1992). Knowledge-based systems and copyright. *Serials Review* 18(1–2): 88–91.

Marcum, Deanna B. (1992). New realities, old values. *Library Hi Tech*, 10(3) Issue 39: 62–67.

Martin, Marilyn J. (Spring, 1992). Academic libraries and computing centers: Opportunities for leadership. *Library Administration and Management* 6(2): 77–81.

McClure, Charles R. (Spring, 1992). From the editor. *Electronic Networking: Research, Applications and Policy* 2(1): 4.

McClure, Charles R. (Fall/Winter, 1991). Planning and evaluation for the networked environment. *EDUCOM Review* 26(3/4): 34–37.

McClure, Charles R., Bishop, Ann P., Doty, Philip, and Rosenbaum, Howard. (1991). *The National Research and Education Network (NREN): Research and Policy Perspectives.* Norwood, NJ: Ablex Publishing Corporation.

McClure, Charles R., Ryan, Joe and Moen, William E. Moen. (1992). *Identifying and Describing Federal Information Inventory/Locator Systems: Design for Networked-Based Locators, vol. 1 of Final Report.* Bethesda, MD: National Audio Visual Center. (ERIC Document Reproduction Service ED 349 031).

Michelson, Avra and Rothenberg, Jeff. (Spring, 1992). Scholarly communication and information technology: Exploring the impact of changes in the research process on archives. *American Archivist* 55: 236–315. (Also available electronically via FTP from the Coalition for Networked Resources file server at FTP.CNI.ORG in /pub/docs: GET SCITA.TXT for an ASCII text version; GET SCITA.PS for the Postscript file. References to the article are in SCITAEND.TXT and SCITAEND.PS respectively.)

Moen, William E. (1992). Organizing networked resources for effective use: Classification and other issues in developing navigational tools. *Proceedings of the American Society for Information Science 1992 Mid-year Meeting* (pp. 10–21). Silver Spring, MD: American Society for Information Science.

Moholt, Pat. (February, 1990). Libraries and campus information: Redrawing the boundaries. *Academic Computing* 4(5): 20–21+.

National Science Foundation. (Fall, 1992). National Science Foundation Acceptable Use Policy, June 1992. *Electronic Networking: Research, Applications and Policy* 2(3): 16.

Network Advisory Committee. (1989a). *Connecting the Networks: Proceedings of the Joint Library of Congress Network Advisory*

Committee and EDUCOM Meeting. (Network Planning Paper, No. 18). Washington, DC: Library of Congress.

Network Advisory Committee. (1989b). *Intellectual Property issues in the Library Network Context: Proceedings of the Library of Congress Network Advisory Committee Meeting* (Network Planning Paper No. 17). Washington, DC: Library of Congress, Network Development and MARC Standards Office.

Network Advisory Committee. (1987). *Intellectual Property Rights in an Electronic Age: Proceedings of the Library of Congress Network Advisory Committee Meeting* (Network Planning Paper No. 16) Washington, DC: Library of Congress, Network Development and MARC Standards Office.

Nicklin, Julie L. (February 19, 1992). Rising costs and dwindling budgets force libraries to make damaging cuts in collections and services. *The Chronicle of Higher Education:* A1, A28–A30.

Nielsen, Brian. (October, 1990). Finding it on the Internet: The next challenge for librarianship. *Database* 13(5): 105–107.

North Carolina State University. (n.d.). The North Carolina State University Libraries and the National Agricultural Library Joint Project on Transmission of Digitized Images: Improving Access to Agricultural Information. [Press release]. In *Linking Researchers and Resources: The Emerging Information Infrastructure and the NREN Proposal* (ARL Briefing Package No. 4). Washington, DC: Association of Research Libraries.

Oakley, Robert L. (Fall, 1991). Copyright issues for the creators and users of information in the electronic environment. *Electronic Networking: Research, Applications and Policy* 1(1): 23–30.

Oakley, Robert L. (1988). Intellectual property issues and information networks: A background paper. In *Intellectual Property Issues in the Library Network Context: Proceedings of the Library of Congress Network Advisory Committee Meeting* (Network Planning Paper No. 17, pp. 5–54). Washington, DC: Library of Congress, Network Development and MARC Standards Office.

Office of Science and Technology Policy. (December, 1992). *National Research and Education Network: A Report to Congress* [DRAFT]. Washington, DC: Office of Science and Technology Policy.

Okerson, Ann, Strangelove, Michael and Kovacs, Diane. (1992) *Directory of Electronic Journals, Newsletters, and Academic Discussion Lists,* 2nd ed. Washington, DC: Association of Research Libraries, Office of Scientific and Academic Publishing.

Osburn, Charles B. (October/December, 1984). The place of the journal in the scholarly communication system. *Library Resources and Technical Services* 28(4): 315–324.

Osburn, Charles B. (May, 1989). The structuring of the scholarly communication system. *College & Research Libraries* 50(3): 277–286.

Penniman, W. David. (October 15, 1992). Shaping the future: The Council on Library Resources helps to fund change. *Library Journal* 117(17): 40–44.

Peters, Paul Evan. (Spring/Summer, 1992). Making the market for networked information: An introduction to a proposed program for licensing electronic uses. *Serials Review* 18(1–2): 19–24 .

Quarterman, John S. (1990). *The Matrix: Computer Networks and Conferencing Systems Worldwide.* Bedford, MA: Digital Press.

Quinlan, Catherine A. (1991). Libraries and computing centers. In Gary M. Pitkin, ed., *The Evolution of Library Automation: Management Issues and Future Perspectives* (pp. 91–106). Westport, CT: Meckler.

Racine, Drew. (Spring, 1992). Access to full-text journal articles: Some practical considerations. *Library Administration and Management* 6(2): 100–104.

Reynolds, Dennis. (1985). *Library Automation: Issues and Applications.* New York: R.R. Bowker Company.

Rogers, Sharon J. and Hurt, Charlene S. (January, 1990). How scholarly communication should work in the 21st century. *College & Research Libraries* 5(1): 5–8.

Runkle, Martin. (1992). The changing economics of research libraries. In Brett Sutton and Charles H. Davis, eds., *Networks, Open Access, and Virtual Libraries: Implications for the Research Library* (pp. 104–117) Urbana-Champaign, IL: University of Illinois at Urbana-Champaign, Graduate School of Library and Information Science.

Saunders, Laverna M. (Spring, 1992). The virtual library today. *Library Administration and Management* 6(2): 66–70.

Shaughnessy, Thomas W. (1992). The real costs and financial challenges of library networking: Part 2. In Brett Sutton and Charles H. Davis, eds., *Networks, Open Access, and Virtual Libraries: Implications for the Research Library* (pp. 123–127) Urbana-Champaign, IL: University of Illinois at Urbana-Champaign, Graduate School of Library and Information Science.

Shreeves, Edward. (Spring, 1992). Between the visionaries and the Luddites: Collection development and electronic resources in the humanities. *Library Trends* 40(4): 579–595.

Special section: Happy birthday to MELVYL (Part 1). (June, 1992a). *Information Technology and Libraries* 11(2): 146–181.

Special section: Happy birthday to MELVYL (Part 2). (September, 1992b). *Information Technology and Libraries* 11(3): 271–303.

Special section: Happy birthday to MELVYL (Part 3). (December, 1992c). *Information Technology and Libraries* 11(4): 405–419.

Still, Julie and Alexander, Jan. (March, 1993). Integrating Internet into reference: Policy issues. *College & Research Libraries* 54(3): 139–140.

Stoller, Michael E. (Spring, 1992). Electronic journals in the humanities: A survey and critique. *Library Trends* 40(4): 647–666.

Watkins, Beverly T. (September 2, 1992). Many campuses start building tomorrow's electronic library. *The Chronicle of Higher Education*, A19–A21.

Weiskel, Timothy C. (November, 1986). Libraries as life-systems: Information, entropy, and coevolution on campus. *College & Research Libraries* 47(6): 545–563.

Weiss, Allan H. (Fall, 1992). Commercialization of the Internet. *Electronic Networking: Research, Applications and Policy* 2(3): 7–15.

Wilson, David L. (June 3, 1992). Major scholarly publisher to test electronic transmission of journals. *The Chronicle of Higher Education*, A17, A20.

Wilson, David L. (December 4, 1991). High cost could deny big computer advance to some colleges. *The Chronicle of Higher Education*, A1, A32.

Yavarkovsky, Jerome. (Fall, 1990). A university-based electronic publishing network. *EDUCOM Review* 25(3): 14–20.

Young, Peter R. (October 11, 1991). *Knowledge Communities and Information Network Policies* (12th Yuri Nakata Lecture). Chicago: The University of Illinois at Chicago, The University Library.

Academic Library Innovators:
A Report from Two Site Visits

An increasing number of innovative academic libraries are connecting to electronic networks, providing access to networked information resources, and developing network-based services and products. This chapter presents a discussion based on site visits to two of these libraries. These sites, Carnegie Mellon University and the University of Southern California, have received national attention for their organizational and technological initiatives which are preparing their libraries to serve future academic information needs in a networked world.

The literature reported in Chapter 1 identifies a range of issues that libraries are or will be facing in the networked environment and also points to a number of important projects and efforts at universities across the country. Through such projects, academic libraries are building the future—readying themselves in a variety of ways to deliver information services in the networked environment. The process of readying themselves involves experimentation with information technology in the organization, storage, access and retrieval, and dissemination of information. More importantly, this process includes a re-examination of organizational and structural arrangements, staff and management responsibilities, and service roles and opportunities that the networked environment enables.

The study team determined that, in conjunction with other data-collection techniques, a case study approach would provide a focused and detailed look at how two leading-edge academic libraries are meeting the challenges of the electronically networked environment (see Appendix A for a description of the study methodology, and in particular, the site visit methodology). The site visits would be exploratory investigations and attempt to uncover and understand the circumstances and forces shaping the library's roles in campus networking activities and the provision of networked services.

Site visits to libraries of excellence and innovation would offer the study team another perspective (in addition to the literature review and the focus groups) from which to investigate the impacts of networking on academic libraries. The findings from the site visits could shed new light and corroborate (or refute) claims made by focus group participants or discussed in the literature. By choosing sites that are network connected and actively exploring information technology in the provision of information, the study team expected to find (and did) staff and managers who were knowledgeable about issues, problems, and solutions based on their firsthand experience with the emerging networked environment—local and national.

The University of Southern California (USC) provided a site at which the library offers substantial leadership in campus-wide use of networking for the delivery of information. The library, through its vast traditional holdings and its new campus information service, USCInfo, has staked out a place as the focal point for electronic information resources on campus. The Center for Scholarly Technology (CST), a collaborative project between the library and the academic computing unit, has served as an "incubator" for the development of innovative information technologies and the exploration of the active interdependencies of the library and computing services in the networked environment. The library's leadership role and the new approaches to organizational arrangements convinced the study team that USC would be a rich source for a site visit.

Carnegie Mellon University has gained national prominence as an innovator and pioneer in developing an "electronic library" in conjunction with its Project Mercury. The project has three major thrusts: software and architecture for an electronic library in a distributed computing environment; a library information system; and electronic publication in partnership with publishers. Carnegie Mellon was also one of the first institutions to undergo a major reorganization of information technology providers, placing the libraries and computing departments within one division reporting to a vice-president for academic affairs.

In both cases, the site visits were exploratory studies to identify and describe the evolution, development, and current use of electronic networks and networked information resources. The rationale for the studies was to provide a description of how these libraries arrived at their current position and how they are actively preparing themselves for the evolving national networked environment. A major objective of the site visits was to learn how the libraries' leadership got involved, how it influenced the campus vision and initiatives in the areas of networking and use of networked information resources, and how, organizationally the leaders positioned their libraries to play such a central role. An examination and understanding of these libraries' actions would contribute to the ongoing discussions within the academic library community concerning the changing roles and responsibilities of the library in the campus environment.

The literature review reported in Chapter 1 guided the researchers in their site visit investigations, yet the issues identified in the literature review took on new meaning through conversations, discussions, and demonstrations at Carnegie Mellon University and the University of Southern California. These people—the risk-takers who are charting new directions, the staff who are living through a time of uncertainty and change, the administrators who are moving the library forward under difficult budget situations—are clearly central to the successes of these libraries in preparing themselves for the future.

The following sections summarize findings and analysis from the site visits. An initial section describes general themes and critical factors the researchers identified through the site visits. This is followed by a discussion of key findings based on the data analysis. The concluding section presents some final comments on what the researchers learned from the visits and what it may mean generally for academic libraries.

An important component to understanding the circumstances at both institutions is detailed background information for each site. Appendix B contains specific details and information about each site: a general description of each site, a description of the development and current local networking environment on each campus, and an examination of the organizational relationships and structures of key campus units.

There is a commonality among the issues identified in the site visits and those reported in the literature review (see Chapter 1) and the focus groups (see Chapter 3). The study team's original intention for this exploratory study was to identify and describe the paramount issues facing academic libraries as they confront the challenges of a new information production and use environment. The emergence of common issues and concerns through the study's multiple data collection strategies provides credibility and hopefully increases the utility of the findings. Also, by providing a view of the issues in the context of two libraries, the study team hopes to contribute to the ongoing discussions within the library community and to provide other libraries with relevant information so they might benefit from the experiences of these two organizations.

The University of Southern California and Carnegie Mellon University are dynamic institutions. Through the site visits the researchers were able to document changes in organizational structures, in personnel, in technology infrastructure, and in other areas of campus life. The site visits occurred in 1992, and these sites have continued to change—in some cases, major reorganizations within the universities have occurred. Thus, throughout this chapter, it is important to remember that the data was collected in 1992 and represents the institutions at that time. This report, then, is a snapshot of two very dynamic institutions at one point in time.

THEMES AND CRITICAL FACTORS

The site visits produced a wealth of descriptive information, including many insightful comments by the participants. During the data analysis, a number of critical success factors emerged—key ideas that could propel the organization into the future. These factors (vision, leadership, entrepreneurship, partnering, technology, planning, and people) were important elements enabling these sites to move into the future, a future where the library will provide services and products in a networked environment. Figure 2-1 summarizes these thematic areas and critical factors. These themes and critical factors create a foundation from which the subsequent issues can be appreciated and successfully addressed. They serve as a guide to understanding how these organizations are readying themselves for the networked future.

Vision

Library and institutional leadership developed a vision of the library in the networked environment, are committed to the vision, and provide the plans, organizational structures, and support to bring the vision to fruition. Library leaders are positioned to articulate a vision of the library's future. Moving towards the vision requires library managers and staff to translate the vision into goals, objectives, and activities. The support of university administrators is helpful, but often a lack of understanding at the highest levels of the institution means that needed resources are not available to the library. Yet the library leaders, with an entrepreneurial spirit and an understanding

Vision
• Library and institutional leadership developed a vision of the library in the networked environment, are committed to the vision, and provide the plans, organizational structures, and support to bring the vision to fruition.
• These libraries recognized that information delivery, not access to high-performance computer resources, would be the primary focus and activity of the network.

Leadership
• These libraries offer important information resources useful to the university community, and they have talented and computer-literate staff to lead campus use of networked resources and services.
• These libraries recognize their user communities want improved access to networked information resources, and they are initiating services for these users.
• Library management recognizes the need for and is committed to training staff and providing opportunities for professional development for the networked environment; structured, group training can be most efficient.

Entrepreneurship
• The parent organizations of these libraries support and engender an entrepreneurial spirit among campus units.
• These libraries took advantage of being the first to negotiate with database vendors and to begin realizing the vision of online access to information.
• Limited resources increased these libraries' motivation to invest in creating enhanced access to their research resources.

Partnering
• Computing services units are very helpful, supportive, and open to collaborative work with the library.
• Early partnering of the library and computing services units provided the foundation for an effective relationship to meet the challenges of the Internet/NREN environment.
• Commitment to collaboration and partnering is a strategic choice, and it includes partnering with academic faculty, with other campus units, and with external organizations and companies.
• A number of organizational forms for collaboration and partnering exist, but the point is to provide opportunities for people at various levels of the campus units to work together.

Figure 2-1. Critical success factors.

of the power of collaboration and partnering, can move towards realizing their vision. The vision guides the library in creating appropriate organizational structures and allocating resources. The lack of vision threatens the library's transition into the networked environment.

Technology
• A sophisticated campus computing/networking environment benefits the library enormously.
• These libraries focused on improving access to locally mounted
  large bibliographic databases, as well as acquiring new databases
  of bibliographic and full-text reference information.
• These libraries integrated the library automation issues into the
  broader campus networked environment.
• Integrated information systems provide coherent access and ease of
  use.

Planning
• The need for planning in advance of the demand is essential.
• Library staff participate in articulating a strategic mission statement
  in terms of the roles they want to define for themselves and action
  plans to carry it through.

People
• Individuals "synched very well together" and were able to build
  and maintain bridges across units.
• Tenacity of those involved move the vision forward.
• Serendipity and entrepreneurial attitudes exist among some of the
  key players and organizations.

Figure 2-1. Critical success factors, *continued*

*These libraries recognized that information delivery, not access to
high-performance computer resources, would be the primary focus and
activity of the network.* For these library leaders, the networked environment is more than just a collection of interconnected computers. Their vision recognizes the potential of the network to deliver a
wide variety of information to users. Network users communicate
with one another and interact with information resources. By fram-
ing the network focus in terms of information, the library has a
central role in the networked environment.

Leadership

*These libraries offer important information resources useful to the
university community, and they have talented and computer-literate staff
to lead campus use of networked resources and services.* These libraries
see the networked environment offering new, if at times problemat-
ical, opportunities to serve the academic community. The experience that library staff gained in automation activities over the years
means they have a familiarity with a range of information technologies (e.g., OPACs, CD-ROM resources, electronic networking with

bibliographic utilities). This experience is being translated into the networked environment. Librarians are exploring the network, discovering existing resources, and anticipating uses of the network in which the library can serve a central role. There is a conscious awareness that the library's future is being able to tap, organize, or in other ways offer networked resources to the academic community.

These libraries recognize their user communities want improved access to networked information resources, and they are initiating services for these users. Carnegie Mellon, with its focus on computer science and engineering, has a relatively computer literate campus. One challenge to the library was to identify and develop the best ways to bring improved access to networked information to the users. By developing projects that serve those users, the library shows its responsiveness. At USC, segments of the user community have shown tremendous interest in how the network can improve their research, teaching, and collaboration with colleagues. Library-sponsored Internet presentations for faculty members have been "standing room only," one indication of the interest in the user community.

Increasing the visibility of the library in the networked environment has meant reaching out to the users, informing them of the what's available and what's coming. Like other experiences with automation, however, the expectations of the user community may grow faster than the resources of the library to fulfill them. Yet the libraries are taking an active role in responding to the users' needs and interests by assuming responsibility for providing services and exploring new opportunities to shape future demand.

Library management recognizes the need for and is committed to training staff and providing opportunities for professional development for the networked environment; structured, group training can be most efficient. Library managers acknowledge that the networked environment requires new skills and responsibilities, and these libraries are acting responsibly to bring training to the staff. Investing now in staff training and professional development pays off handsomely in several ways. Library staff learn about the opportunities and difficulties of delivering electronic services. Training provides a foundation for all staff, so that differences in existing skills and computer literacy can be ameliorated. With a basis of understanding, both hands-on technical skills and the broader understanding of networking issues, staff can participate knowledgeably in planning and implementing the networked library. Staff are an invaluable resource for solving problems resulting from the new technologies. Managers also recognize that one-time training is not sufficient and that work schedules must accommodate staff needs to increase skills and understanding of the networked environment, how to navigate in it, and discovering the resources that are available.

Entrepreneurship

The parent organizations of these libraries support and engender an entrepreneurial spirit among campus units. While both Carnegie Mellon and USC are private universities and may not be subject to some of the bureaucracy of state universities, the more important point is that the universities have provided a space, whether by design or omission, that allow people to experiment, try out new ways of doing things, and in general have supported an entrepreneurial spirit. There is accountability, but it is after the fact.

As one respondent said, if he wanted to take a large part of the materials budget and move it into purchasing electronic information, he could do it. He would not be told he could not do it beforehand. But, he would be held accountable for the success of the resulting service. Flexibility, innovation, and risk taking are, in part, a reaction to the dismal budget situations. The libraries had to consider new ways of doing things since they are and will continue to be asked to do more with less. Yet the entrepreneurial spirit, nurtured at administrative and staff levels, enables people to see opportunities for acting on new ideas, taking on new responsibilities, and engaging in problem solving.

These libraries took advantage of being the first to negotiate with database vendors and to begin realizing the vision of online access to information. At both sites, and as part of the entrepreneurial environment, library leaders took the initiative early on to discuss arrangements with database vendors to mount locally citation and other bibliographic databases. This was a outgrowth of the early vision of online access to information. Although these activities happened in the mid-1980s, an entrepreneurial spirit continues to motivate them to search out new opportunities now—in the case of USC's involvement with the *Chronicle of Higher Education,* and Carnegie Mellon's collaboration with journal publishers to provide full-text journal articles.

Limited resources increased these libraries' motivation to invest in creating enhanced access to their research resources. This is another way of responding to the "doing-more-with-less" situation driven by the constraining budgetary climate. Entrepreneurship is about managing and organizing the resources of an enterprise, and responds to the question of "what can we do with the skills, resources, etc., that we have" as well as seeing new opportunities to reallocate and supplement those resources through partnering and collaboration.

Partnering

Computing services units are very helpful, supportive, and open to collaborative work with the library. The library, even with its experience with automation efforts in the past, does not have all the technical skills required to thrive in a networked environment. At both sites, the computing services units have entered into collaborative projects with the library. There is healthy communication at various levels, from top administrators on down, between the library and computing services. This has not occurred without some wrinkles. The differences in cultures between the two organizations are real, but the computing services staff see the library as an ally in attempting to serve the technology and information needs of the campus. While each site has chosen to structure the relations between the two units organizationally differently, the important point is that a conscious organizational strategy has enabled and enhanced cooperative and collaborative work.

Early partnering of the library and computing services units provided the foundation for an effective relationship to meet the challenges of the Internet/NREN environment. A history of cooperative relations between the library and computing services enhanced the abilities of these two units to forge new alliances and participate collaboratively in developing networked services and products. In the evolving networked environment, these units are more closely tied together than previously. The trust and understanding established by previous joint efforts allow a running start on the necessary collaborations. The ongoing collaboration recognizes distinct differences in the organizational cultures, yet also recognizes the complementary skills and understanding each partner can contribute to improved campus-wide services.

Commitment to collaboration and partnering is a strategic choice, and it includes partnering with academic faculty, with other campus units, and with external organizations and companies. Library managers pursue joint activities with other campus units and off-campus businesses and organizations to realize visions and goals of the electronic library. These strategic partnerships allow one organization, often the library, to leverage its limited resources and technical skills to engage in projects and activities it could not do on its own. These libraries recognize the potential for the academic faculty to become collaborators and partners in training and creating awareness among all campus citizens.

A number of organizational forms for collaboration and partnering exist, but the point is to provide opportunities for people at various levels of the campus units to work together. There is not one correct "form" of collaboration, but rather a range of forms that enable joint goals to be reached. The highest levels of administration (i.e., university, library, computing services, etc.) recognize the importance of cooperation and encourage joint activities. The focus is not on how the organizational chart represents the collaboration. Instead, the collaborations focus on projects, deliverables, and outcomes. Of prime importance is the opportunity for staff at all levels to work with their counterparts from the collaborating organization. The collaborations succeed when top administration acts collaboratively and enables staff to work collaboratively.

Technology

A sophisticated campus computing/networking environment benefits the library enormously. Both universities have invested heavily in networking technologies that allow for connectivity of students, staff, and faculty to computer and information resources. Not only is the local networked environment continually growing, there is also an awareness that the network will serve primarily as a vehicle for the transmission of information. The library, as a central resource for information, has been an important early network resource on campus. At USC, the library established library satellites that provided an example of its early leadership in distributed computing.

These libraries focused on improving access to locally mounted large bibliographic databases, as well as acquiring new databases of bibliographic and full-text reference information. Providing online access to citation databases created a user base for the libraries in the local networked environment. Citation and bibliographic databases enabled new access to important journal literature. These resources and the local networked environment created an awareness of electronic information in the user community and assisted users in developing online searching skills. Providing a single user interface to the locally mounted databases gives users improved access to the information in the databases, which, in turn, results in better access to the information they need.

At USC, users are able to download search results and move them via electronic mail or file transfer to their computer accounts. These services assist users in accessing and using the information they discover online. The increased expectations for delivery of full-text information v. "information about information" puts additional pressures on the libraries "to deliver." But as shown at Carnegie Mellon, there is a commitment to doing just that—the bitmapped page images databases or other full-text database resources assist in delivering the information to the desktop.

These libraries integrated the library automation issues into the broader campus networked environment. The technology that provided enhanced access to bibliographic information no longer stands alone within the library. Developing new access mechanisms for library materials must take account of the remote users—people in their offices, dormitories, homes, etc., rather than focusing on the people who physically visit the library. The library must focus less on information technology as a way of accomplishing backroom processes and focus more on network *service* delivery. What will be visible to network users in the future will not be the library as a place or a collection but the services and information the library can deliver.

Integrated information systems provide coherent access and ease of use. These libraries have a variety of information systems—online public access catalogs, integrated information systems, locally mounted commercial databases, CD-ROM–based systems, and others. The technology challenge is to integrate access to these various systems for the ease of users. Developing a campus-wide common interface can provide users with a more coherent view of information. Yet, a single user interface for all information may not be functional. The costs of maintaining such an interface across many platforms is resource intensive. Libraries can pursue the goal of integrating information systems through the use of client/server architecture and standards-based solutions such as Z39.50 for information retrieval in a networked environment.

Planning

The need for planning in advance of the demand is essential. As the networked environment evolves, as the technology, information resources, and services evolve, so too will user demands evolve. The library faces a very critical, yet subtle, planning problem. They must anticipate where the faculty and students will be two or three years from now in their use of networks and networked resources. Planning in advance of the need can be accomplished if the library is taking a leadership role in the development of networked information on campus. It can shape services to respond to the evolving information use by faculty and students and possibly begin shaping the demands rather than only reacting.

Library staff participate in articulating a strategic mission statement in terms of the roles they want to define for themselves and action plans to carry it through. Library staff are the most important resource the library has in anticipating new and evolving uses of the network. Staff work with a variety of users, communicate with faculty about research needs, and guide students to information resources. They can serve as constant environmental scanners for indications of changes in users' information behaviors, expectations, and uses brought by the networks. They must be brought into the planning processes within the library and in the larger information environment of the university. These library managers recognize the importance of staff and facilitate their understanding and professional development so that they can participate in defining the roles for the library and staff in the networked environment. The staff will assist in generating the action plans necessary to fulfill the vision and mission of the electronic library.

People

Individuals "synched very well together" and were able to build and maintain bridges across units. The people are central to the success of the projects that are moving the library into the networked environment. These individuals could envision the future library and value the importance of collaboration. The entrepreneurial atmosphere allowed and encouraged them to take risks, and they are courageously taking the risks and assuming the responsibilities for their successes and mistakes.

Tenacity of those involved move the vision forward. People—librarians, academic faculty, computing services staff—persevere in building their vision of the electronic library because "it's the right thing to do." Even if all the details are not yet worked out, or even known, these people feel challenged by the opportunities and are moving ahead by doing things. There is no sense of paralysis because of the uncertainty. Instead, good people work hard in moving forward on their vision.

Serendipity and entrepreneurial attitudes exist among some of the key players and organizations. The electronic library corresponds closely to a vision shared by many people, both inside and outside the library. Technical computing services staff and librarians shared an understanding of what the network enables. They made a decision that the network would be the means to distribute information on campus, provide access to remote information resources, and promote and enhance communication among colleagues. While computing services staff might be more oriented toward the technical, hardware, and software aspects of the network, and librarians oriented toward services and the information content of network accessible resources, they agreed on the essential nature of the network as a vehicle for information delivery and access. The key people also shared an entrepreneurial spirit that allowed them to recognize and act on opportunities both on campus and with external organizations.

Summary of Themes and Critical Factors

Some of these factors have similar characteristics and serve to reinforce each other. Some may be more or less likely to be present at other institutions. These two sites, however, demonstrated attention to most of these in their research, planning, development, and implementation phases in preparing for the electronic library. Because of this attention to these factors, they are in a better position to exploit the coming networked future. This is not to suggest, however, that all issues and concerns have been resolved. Rather, the advances these sites have made provide a new context in which to address old and emerging issues.

FINDINGS FROM THE SITE VISITS

This section focuses on the multifaceted relationship between the library and the networked environment, local and national. It discusses the major issues of concern within the libraries on staff, services, collections, and organizational structure. The evolving electronic library, networked information resources, and networked environment also raise issues for the library in relation to the broader campus community and external organizations. An issue is a topic or possible decision area where there is conflict among different stakeholders (where the stakeholders might be library staff, university administrators, publishers, document delivery services, etc.). Generally, an issue will need to be resolved—or at least addressed—before a decision is made.

The range of issues that surfaced during the site visits and subsequent data analysis is very broad, in part because the impacts of the networked environment result from the variety of ways in which networks are being used and the groups involved in the maintenance or use of the networks and networked resources. For example, librarians use the network to search remote OPACs, students use the network for e-mail exchange, faculty use the network to connect to computer resources, full-text information is delivered to desktop workstations, and people are producing electronic journals.

By focusing on the library in the networked environment as the unit of analysis, however, the researchers were able to analyze the data collected during the site visits (e.g., interview transcripts, field notes, documents, demonstrations, etc.) and group the issues into categories. These key issue areas are summarized below.

- library leadership and the library's visibility on campus;
- organizational structure;
- collaboration and partnerships;
- two cultures—the library and the computer center;
- expansion of duties—new skills requirement;
- new roles for the library staff;
- training, continuing education, and time to learn;
- new service demands;
- training and educating users;
- fast pace of technology change and development;
- organizing network resources;
- impact on collection development;
- electronic journals and the problems of scholarly communication;
- listening to and learning from users;
- limits to service in the networked environment;
- infrastructure needs;

- user interface designs;
- planning process and communication; and
- reconceptualizing the library

Library managers at both sites have been aware of potential impacts of the evolving networked environment on the library, even if the managers did not always know exactly what shape those impacts might take. Through a conscious strategy of planning for training, communicating with staff, upgrading technology, etc., library managers have attempted to work with the library staff to bring the networked environment into their lives and the life of the campus community. In effect, they are attempting to address some of the issues that are identified in this section.

From the site visits, it is clear that the effects brought about by the development of networked-based information services and products have been and will continue to be significant. Further, because of the evolving character of the networked environment, new issues will emerge and older issues will be recast and reappear. It is in the library's interest as a central campus information provider to identify and address, if not resolve, local issues. The broader academic library community has a vested interest in participating in issue identification and resolution. This can be considered one of the components of leadership the library can offer.

Library Leadership and the Library's Visibility on Campus

Ideally, the library is well positioned to lead the campus into the networked information world. Its function, more than any other campus unit, is connecting users to information, and the library community has developed principles, practices, and procedures to accomplish this function. Yet the library must act if it is to lead. By acting as a campus leader, the library's visibility and centrality in the networked environment can be enhanced.

The library can lead by spearheading the initiatives that bring the benefits of the network to students, faculty, and staff. Leadership is evident when the library plays the role of a catalyst in developing campus-wide visions and goals for the local networked environment. Leading means identifying and acting on opportunities, and assembling or deploying the necessary resources so opportunities are not missed. Leaders take responsibility for shaping the future, communicate their goals, and help others to share and work toward a vision of the future.

The University of Southern California library has pursued a conscious strategy to provide leadership on campus in the realm of networked and electronic information service. The library established library satellites early in the distributed computing experience at USC. The library also took the lead in developing the campus-wide information system, USCInfo. While primarily offering users access to HOMER (USC's online catalog) and commercial bibliographic databases, it also includes the campus phonebook/directory. There are plans to incorporate other sources of campus information in USCInfo.

Another area in which the USC library has acted, thereby increasing its visibility in the local networked environment, is in the outreach seminars it has organized collaboratively with the Center for Scholarly Technology (CST) and computing services. These faculty-to-faculty seminars provided opportunities for faculty peers to discuss, demonstrate, and encourage use of the network connection for communication, research, and information gathering. The use of "technology champions" to provide information relieved the library, computing services, and CST of the appearance of "internal technology persuaders and presenters." Instead, faculty peers could demonstrate how they were using the technology right now to solve information and communication needs related to their research and teaching. The library's involvement in such seminars allows it to play a leadership role in bringing the technology to the academic community and to continue to explore its responsibilities to the community for providing access and information about networked resources.

The network provides new opportunities for the library to reassert its centrality in the provision of information on campus. There are no guarantees, however, that simply providing access to networked resources will highlight the library. Further, the library is in a delicate balancing act by presenting itself as a central player in the networked environment even as it is attempting to bring its own staff up to a functional level of competence in this environment and providing the staff with adequate tools and training.

If the library takes a leadership role in increasing faculty awareness about the network, it then has the opportunity to assume new responsibilities to meet the needs of these users by developing appropriate new services. It may, in fact, be able to shape user demands by leading rather than reacting. The network offers individuals new mechanisms for resource gathering and resource sharing outside of the library. The library must capitalize on the new visibility by asserting itself as a service provider—it must acknowledge that in the networked environment the library must move beyond defining itself as a "place" or a "collection," and focus on information services.

Organizational Structure

The organizational arrangements of the library and other campus units, in particular computing services, are important factors in the design of the networked campus. USC and Carnegie Mellon experiences suggest that no one model will hold the answer for all libraries. The important lesson is that both sites recognized that innovative changes in organizational structure were needed to move towards the visions of electronic information services.

According to one respondent, the approach taken by USC (e.g., not merging the library and computing services, creating the CST) has been successful in terms of building relationships because it is less threatening and less disruptive than some of the merger models that have attempted to bring libraries and computing services under a single organizational structure. This model also offered opportunities for people at the middle level of management and operations to work together and understand each other's cultures. CST is staffed by people from the two organizations. Further, other opportunities exist for library and computing services staff to work together and communicate with each other.

The benefits of USC's organizational arrangement, however, are not without some costs. One respondent pointed out that the stability of the organizationally interdependent arrangement during the first two years between the library and computing services occurred because of persuasion, in particular by the director of CST acting as an intermediary. The budget also affects the relationships and the responsibility for working collaboratively. For example, some activities such as interface design, tape loading, and user support exist on the boundaries of the organizations—each do some of these things. In the early years, with a relatively stable economic environment, a momentum was built based on the best efforts at persuasion: "people on the library side should be interested because . . ." and "people on the computer side should be interested because. . . ." But when the resources are declining, when budget cuts threaten operations and activities, collaborative efforts can be undermined. The library is re-examining the existing organizational arrangement with computing services.

A closer look at the USC experience shows that even with a decision to pursue one organizational structure for campus-wide information networking, changing circumstances may mean that the structure must change as well. The dynamic nature of the networked environment may mean that structural arrangements between units need to evolve as new service roles and responsibilities evolve for libraries and computing centers.

Collaboration and Partnerships

Academic libraries have never been islands unto themselves. They have been central to the mission of the university and have participated with faculty, students, and other campus units in education and research. In the networked environment, its roles and relationships are changing in dramatic ways. At USC, the relationship between the library and computing services provides an example of a most fundamental realignment of collaboration.

The library satellite development is an example of how the library and computing services have evolved in terms of their respective roles for campus computing, networking, and information access (Johnson, Lyman, and Tompkins, 1990, p. 186):

> The library had been a pioneer in the use of microcomputers, databases, and networks and, as a result, considered itself a partner of Academic Computing in the development of campus computing resources. It became dependent on the resources of Academic Computing at about the time that Academic Computing began to redefine its philosophy away from the provision of computer cycles for expert users and toward a philosophy based on networking and reaching out to new computer users.

This relationship has been an evolving, and at times, worrisome, interaction/interdependency. Yet the fact that the library and computing services are entering into the phase where computing services will operate and maintain the library's production-level computer systems for backroom processing is an important and challenging departure in the established partnership. Computing services and the library are each taking on interdependent roles in the provision, production, and maintenance of library-based bibliographic information.

Such collaboration is not without risks. Library management realizes that it is turning over the most critical library systems to an organization over which it has no direct authority. The maintenance, support, and operation of these "library systems" will depend on a group of people who do not report to the university librarian. "It's a dependency without authority." One respondent suggested, however, that the end product of this further step in collaboration will be something better than the library could have done on its own.

Collaboration and partnering between campus units and other off-campus organizations and businesses have been essential to the innovative developments at both sites. At Carnegie Mellon, active partnerships provided the means to carry out Project Andrew and Project Mercury. USC's work with the *Chronicle of Higher Education* and Carnegie Mellon's participation in Elsevier's TULIP (the University Licensing Program) offer real world experience for partners in the delivery of full-text information. The success of these efforts has depended, in part, on the culture of the parent organization, which allowed and encouraged an entrepreneurial and risk taking attitude, and the internalization of that culture on the part of campus units.

Two Cultures—The Library and the Computer Center

The networked environment has brought the library and computer services units together in ways unimaginable ten years ago. Each unit had developed to serve different purposes while sharing the goal of supporting the instructional and research needs of the academic community. The development of each unit also included the establishment of different organizational cultures (i.e., the underlying values, behaviors, and attitudes of the unit). According to Spradley (1979, p. 5), culture refers to "the acquired knowledge that people use to interpret experience and generate social behavior." He goes on to describe culture as a "cognitive map. In the recurrent activities that make up everyday life, we refer to this map. It serves as a guide for acting and for interpreting our experience. . . ."

Given the interaction between the library and computing services, a primary organizational challenge has been to foster cooperation and collaboration between two units with distinct cultures. The culture of computing services places a high value on technology for its own sake and has, in the past, minimized computing services' role in providing end-user support. The "techie" or "hacker" label represents a particular orientation of computer services staff. Library staff, on the other hand, value highly the one-to-one personal service they give users who are trying to solve information problems. The technology, for librarians, is a means to the end, not an end in itself. Other differences in the cultures include a focus on process for librarians and a focus on getting the job done and the product out the door for computing services staff.

Many respondents during the site visits discussed the effects of the two different cultures of the library and computing services on staff relations and working relationships as a result of collaborative projects. Their comments revolved around differences of role perceptions and professional styles. The following comments illustrate some of their perceptions:

- "It's very tricky to have such a marriage of two different cultures. 'Computer folks' and 'library folks' dress differently, have different planning styles and concepts about scheduling things. I had to spend quite a bit of effort building respect among the staff for these two respective cultures. For example, computer folks didn't always appreciate the richness of library science knowledge about user behavior or information access needs, and library folks were not always aware of all the technical problems nor the complexity of those problems."
- "The computer people seem to define themselves as project-oriented and the librarians are more process-oriented. The computer folks' structure is too informal and their style of management is different from the librarian's style."
- "One clear difference is the practical concern of the librarians for how something can be used and how users may react v. the theoretical view of the programmer of what can be done. Computer services personnel don't care that much about organizational structures; librarians, however, prefer to have planned and structured operations. Possibly there's a gender difference too. Males as the 'explorer' are possibly more comfortable with hacking and experimenting. It's the user support v. software engineer distinction. The concept of librarianship is managed information, but the networks are unmanaged. Librarians want to catalog what's over the network. This unmanaged information poses a problem for librarians."

Library staff are service oriented. That is part of the historical culture of libraries. They focus on the library's "hardware and software" (i.e., the collections and the finding tools) from the perspective of librarians serving as intermediaries to the materials and as teachers in the use of library tools. A user service orientation is relatively new to computing services and is brought into sharper relief because of the distributed computing environment. Computing services now must serve a much broader campus community rather than the more self-selected and computer-literate users of the previously dominant mainframe computing environment.

Beginning with the automation of library processes in the early 1980s, some members of the library staff began developing skills that resembled skills of the computer center staff—programming, systems operation and maintenance, and so on. The evolving networked environment has brought library and computer center staff into increasingly collaborative work. Yet aspects of the two cultures continue to inform the collaborations. Sometimes this results in tensions between staff from the computer center and staff from the library.

Most respondents spoke positively of the effects of collaboration, and the two cultures seemed to act as points of reference, not as points of conflict. Computing services staff have developed sensitivities to the needs of users. Library staff have incorporated new understandings of the technology and thereby have assuaged some of their fears of the fast-paced changes that come with information technology. This movement toward a common cultural ground is essential for successful collaboration.

Expansion of Duties—New Skills Requirement

Many library staff expressed a worry that new job demands resulting from the networked environment are not being accompanied by cutbacks in other responsibilities. For example, training sessions introduced them to resources and tools they need to incorporate into their professional work. But becoming competent network users requires a commitment of time beyond the training sessions. This led to a renewed sense that they would be juggling more work activities.

Another person stated that in preparation for the National Research and Education Network (NREN), librarians must come to understand the technical aspects of networks and networking, whether or not their roles required this knowledge. A director of library automation saw a need for new skills by traditional library systems/automation positions. He explained:

> Library systems people are used to running bounded systems with strong vendor support, limited functionality, and a user group of peers. With more Internet use, all this is gone. No vendor; it's a different environment; leave one level of comfort for controlled chaos. The technical skills are needed for the systems/automation type of role, plus the mentality and service orientation of the reference librarian.

While technical knowledge about the networked environment may be specified, other duties and accompanying skills for this environment may evolve over time. Until the library identifies the network-based services it will offer, specific job descriptions are unlikely. In the meantime, library staff, and in particular those dealing with users, are feeling like they have entered into a new arena with unspecified duties, but duties nonetheless.

New Roles for the Library Staff

The impact of the electronic library and the networked environment on librarians' roles was a major topic in most interviews. Comments about librarians' roles were often put in the context of the differences in the two cultures of the library and the computing center, possibly because elements of each are seen as desirable for the emerging role of professional staff in the electronic library.

One individual stated that she really did not think a new type of librarian was needed to function effectively within the networked environment but rather an expansion of the traditional role. She suggested:

> We are always adding new aspects to the role as new technologies emerge . . . but the essential characteristics of the 'new' librarian would be self-motivation, spirit of inquiry, and initiative-taking. . . . Since there is so much networked information out there, our role is to funnel it and make it meaningful for users.

These essential characteristics may be necessary but not sufficient for librarians working in a reconceptualized networked library. Libraries will face increased competition in delivering information from a variety of new players in the networked environment. The traditional role of librarians focused on collections and the library as a place. The reconceptualized library must focus on services and adding value to information through filtering, organizing, and other forms of knowledge management.

During a group discussion with reference librarians, several respondents commented on how there may be two types of librarians—the more traditional type and others who will be more oriented to the technology. In part, this separation will occur because some librarians will not want to have the "faceless contact" that the network will bring. "I don't want to see the day when we don't have face-to-face contact with the patron; that's what I like!"

Library staff expressed a worry common to many librarians: users take away from the online systems only what is easily gotten, and they may not be finding the most relevant or complete information for their needs. The problem of users not knowing "what is in the database" may become even more pronounced when users access remote networked resources that are under very little quality control. As a result, an expanded role of librarian as information evaluator, filter, and manager may emerge. Further, the networked environment holds opportunities for librarians to expand teaching roles. Users need help in using the systems and more importantly in discovering, locating, and using networked resources.

Whatever the roles—new or expanded—library staff stated that these roles and duties need to be written into job descriptions. This, however, may be easier said than done at this point in time. The networked environment is evolving, as are the services and activities of libraries in this environment. It may be premature to write "network use" responsibilities into all appropriate job descriptions. Library staff may try to remove some of the uncertainty about this evolving environment through demands for written job descriptions. A more proactive stance by staff might be shaping their own roles and duties in the networked environment. By defining their roles and duties in terms of networked-based services and products the library will offer, they participate in reconceptualizing the library.

The description of the essential characteristics of the "new" librarian listed above may be a requirement for staff to comfortably operate in the networked environment for the near future. Self-motivated, inquiring, and initiative-taking librarians will see opportunities in the networked environment to carry out their traditional roles in new ways, adopt new service roles, and carry out the new functions with networked-based technology.

Training, Continuing Education, and Time To Learn

There are at least two aspects of issues related to training. First is the need to train the library staff in the use of the network. The other is the need to provide training to the users of the library and the network. In the first case, these libraries have taken steps to provide the staff with some hands-on training in network use as well as providing a broader context of the networked environment through professional development seminars. To the extent that people have participated, these efforts have been successful. Library managers acknowledged that while it is costly to provide training, the lack of the training is even more costly. Training is also a way to get the library staff to buy-in to the networked resources environment.

One respondent suggested that schools of library and information science must take on responsibilities for preparing new professionals for this environment, something they are not currently doing. "Electronic publishing and informal publishing are going to force librarians to learn a whole new set of skills in order to cope. It's not a staff training problem, but has to filter back to the schools—which it hasn't." (See Chapter 8 for a discussion of library education.)

The interviews and some of the written documentation at the sites identified the need for increasing awareness and improving staff and user training for the networked environment and the new technology applications developed locally. One site responded to this need by establishing several communications channels (e.g., newsletters, etc.) to keep staff informed and aware of new developments. The library also appointed a training task force, which targeted groups for training and organized procedures and materials. Clearly, a great deal of time was expended preparing information notices for staff and offering training sessions, not always with good results, however. "This experience with staff training during July and August 1991 confirmed suspicions that training would require tremendous effort over a long period of time" (Troll, 1992b, p. 69).

At one site, library management acknowledged that it is the library's responsibility to provide some level of training for the staff in the use of the Internet. There, a series of training sessions offered library staff an initial hands-on exposure to the Internet and the resources available through the network. They received Unix accounts from which they could connect to the Internet and experiment with Telnet and FTP. The classes lasted approximately four hours during which network trainers explained Telnet, FTP, USENET, and log on procedures.

Some respondents claimed that the actual tools used to connect to the Internet are relatively straightforward (although one believed that Telnet and FTP are still basically "hacker tools"). The main difficulty was in the lack of navigational and resource discovery tools to find out what is available via the network. In addition, the library staff thought the training class was too encapsulated—too much in too short of time. Library staff stated clearly that they want more classes and training sessions on network use and networked information resources.

Training is essential if staff are to stay a step ahead of their patrons. A sentiment expressed by more than one librarian was that they did not want to "look foolish" or "lacking in knowledge" when approached by the patron asking about networked resources.

Library staff also felt the need to develop competence and knowledge of what is available on the network, especially as it relates to their own areas of subject expertise. They understand their roles as information providers and as professionals who make the links between a wide variety of sources and literature for their users. With the advent of massive amounts of networked information, resources that have not yet been brought under any systematic control, the staff worried that they may not be doing their jobs as well as they should. Given their existing work schedules, they were concerned that they will not have the time (nor opportunity, given the technology availability) to master the chaos.

Several of the library staff respondents mentioned that they use their computers at home in the evenings and on weekends to explore the network and enhance their skills. Not all staff, however, had or desired this option. One respondent mentioned that she has a strict line drawn between her work life and her personal (i.e., home) life. This balance is important to her and she did not want others to expect that she learn this on her own time. In other cases, library staff do not have appropriate equipment (e.g., computer and modem) to do such learning at home.

At one site, the hands-on training sessions were not the librarians' first exposure to the Internet and electronic information. Library managers and staff had organized a series of professional development seminars for library staff on issues related to NREN, electronic journals, etc., to provide a broader context of the networked environment. At both sites, library managers and staff participate in national networking activities, and thus become a conduit for communicating current information about the evolving networked environment to the library staff.

The training and education issues are fundamental to helping library staff become knowledgeable about the networked environment—in both practical skills and about the larger issues. Training sessions cannot be a one-time activity. The library must commit the resources to an ongoing process of training and retraining and incorporate time in the librarians' schedule to gain experience and competence on the job.

New Service Demands

Library staff and management recognize that network connections and access to network resources will bring increased service demands. The nature of these demands, however, is unclear. For example, providing improved retrieval and twenty-four-hour network access to a growing number of bibliographic and full-text databases make it easier and more convenient for users to receive online library services. Yet library managers need to schedule maintenance and operations staff on a twenty-four-hour basis in addition to providing up-to-date documentation, electronic reference services, trouble-shooting and other user support such as training for remote users and document delivery options.

The new environment not only creates new service demands, but can also offer new ways for responding to the demands. For example, supporting different interfaces for different platforms plus the fast pace of technology change have increased demands on maintaining current documentation. Online help systems and electronic bulletin boards for user support are two mechanisms that take advantage of the technology to respond to user needs.

Science librarians at one site talked enthusiastically about the use of electronic mail on campus to receive reference questions and inquiries. They were also well aware of the implications of offering electronic reference services. Library staff must attend to their electronic mail on a regular basis and implies that time and easily accessible equipment must be available. Ignoring the broader implications of new services can easily result in staff and user frustration.

Another problematic service demand concerns the library staff's ability to serve as automation troubleshooters for the public terminals. A library respondent noted, "we have to be mechanics, along with all our other skills." Library staff are called upon increasingly to answer technical network and hardware questions, in addition to the more familiar questions about searching strategies, etc. Computing services staff may be "officially" responsible for computer and network problems; the library staff may be "officially" charged with aiding users in network searching and use of those resources. Yet in a distributed computing environment, the lines between these activities are not so clearly drawn.

Computing services staff also face new services demands. Previously they supported the high-end users in a mainframe environment. Staff expected an adequate level of computer literacy from the members of the academic community who used these computing facilities. Rather than having a service orientation, computer center staff saw their mission to provide the stable computing environment for users. The focus was on hardware and software and less on the users. This has changed in the distributed computing and networked environment. How the computer center responds to this change is tempered by the culture and sense of mission of the unit. Not previously responsible for dealing with the broad population of the campus, the computing center now must provide user support and training aimed at much less sophisticated users.

The networked environment also brings major resource demands on the library collection and interlibrary loan. According to one respondent, the interlibrary loan system and the document delivery system in this country cannot deal with current demands. Networked accessible OPACs are only going to increase this demand. Interlibrary loan staff directly feel the impact of networked information resources. Because so many of the databases are bibliographic, users have increased requests for interlibrary loan, which is a free service to faculty and students. In a single year, the number of borrowing requests at one site increased by over 70 percent (Arms and Michalak, 1990). Interlibrary loan and other resource-sharing arrangements will need to be reexamined, if not reinvented, along with many other library services in the networked environment.

Library staff at one site have anticipated this impact and are developing document delivery options such as electronic full-text document delivery to the desktop and use of commercial document delivery services. They are exploring new cooperative arrangements with other libraries for more timely resource sharing. A variety of document delivery services are planned including: a courier service delivering articles to a campus office; articles borrowed via interlibrary loan delivered to the branch library of choice; full text of articles on the UMI CD-ROM printed and held in the library for pickup; a book check out and hold for pickup service; and a service to get books from the collection to be put on reserve (Troll, Spring 1992a, p. 96).

Responses to anticipated service demands can take a number of forms. The Network Navigation Group at USC is attempting to create more demand for the network through its outreach and training efforts. Yet they are trying to minimize the one-on-one response to the service demands. This group organized and sponsored two faculty-to-faculty seminars to introduce Internet resources. They developed documentation for resources on the network and are compiling a "top-twenty" list of guides to networked resources. In addition, they are experimenting with ways to reach potential users of the network. One of their strategies has been to establish a network newsgroup aimed at having users help each other in learning about networked resources.

Confounding the service demand issue, library managers and staff are uncertain about the networked-based services the library will want to, will have to, or be capable of providing. Another aspect to developing library services is determining what the users will need or how to shape the demands when users do not know what they need. At this point in the development of the networked environment, experimenting with new services is important. But there is a sense that the service demands will evolve along with the environment, and these libraries are only beginning to think how they might actually shape these demands.

As library staff respond to new service demands emerging in the networked environment, it is not a matter *if* other tasks will be removed. It is now a matter of deciding what responsibilities can be removed to allow them adequate time to deal with new activities. Respondents, both library staff and managers, concluded that new service demands cannot simply be added to the existing workload. Yet the difficult decisions remain as to which staff tasks will be removed.

Training and Educating Users

A major issue, with no easy solutions, is how to train and educate members of the academic community (undergraduate and graduate students, faculty, and staff). Many members have little or no experience with using computers, much less with any sort of communications software or network use.

One respondent suggested that a new level of computer literacy—network literacy—must be integrated into the culture of the users. The technology is not going to be as simple as using a telephone, so a cultural change is necessary, and the responsibility for learning and understanding gets pushed onto the users. This, however, does not answer the question of who will provide the opportunities for learning.

From the perspective of computing services, there is a wide diversity of people needing new levels of support because of the networked environment on campus. A technological solution may be possible for some of these users (e.g., better interfaces). The decentralized nature of networked computing, however, brings with it the possibilities of decentralized support, (e.g., individual academic departments will be responsible for training their students and faculty). Centralizing the support for the network and better coordination of training, however, may gain some economies of scale.

Services provided by the library staff and computer center staff primarily relate to training and user support. At one site, computing services staff offer a variety of workshops, one of which includes the basic mechanics of using the library information system within the total computing environment, focusing on saving, printing, and other general applications. Library staff prepare documentation and offer training on the library information system in special workshops, as well as in course-related instructional sessions and with individual faculty and students.

However, a coordinator of database searching commented that there is a conflict between library staff perceptions of the need for better training and the assumptions by many of the faculty that students can learn to use the systems on their own. She stated that the workshops taught by computing services staff do not deal with search strategy and retrieval features, and when the library offered sessions, few people showed up. "The attitude around here seems to be 'I'll figure it out myself'."

Traditional bibliographic instruction methods may not offer the appropriate model for training for the networked environment. Instead, new training and education initiatives will be needed. The USC library, along with CST and computing services, targets particular audiences for disseminating information about the networked environment. These sessions use network-knowledgeable members of the academic faculty in faculty-to-faculty presentations and have gotten standing-room-only participation. Also, library staff who have responsibilities to specific academic departments have begun outreach efforts to explain and demonstrate network use and the electronic information available. The Network Navigation Group has established a campus online newsgroup on network resources to provide a forum to share information about using the network and networked resources.

Yet in general, training is based on a reactive model—waiting for the demand. In part, this is due to limited resources. The sense was that when the demand appears, when prospective users are clamoring at the door, the resources to respond to the demand will also appear. Leadership, however, requires a proactive, not reactive, stance.

Overall, there is still no clear statement or agreement on who will take responsibility to provide training in network use and networked resources nor what level of training will be needed. Nor is it clear what are the most effective means to help users gain the network and information skills to be successful in the networked environment. Many library respondents had already concluded that one-on-one training would not be feasible and new group training mechanisms will be needed. A computing services respondent suggested, however, that the training issue will be taken care of by software. "Window-based software means that you don't have to train them. If you are going to have to train people to use all this stuff, then you have lost." This faith in a technology fix to a human problem of training and education avoids the question of "what do we do now?"

Fast Pace of Technology Change and Development

The pace of change at both sites places demands on staff and managers. They have lived through the early library automation, online searching services, CD-ROM, and possibly one or two generations of online public access catalogs. The networked environment will likely bring the pace of technology change to a new level for library staff. Previously, the hardware and software were means to an end, and staff focus was still on the printed book or journal. In the networked environment, technology is fundamental to accessing and using information resources. Library deployment of information technology has been a mixed blessing from the vantage point of staff. The costs and problems associated with the technology have frequently been more apparent than the benefits. Thus, there is a mistrust and a hesitancy about the claims made on behalf of the network technologies and the networked information resources.

For staff, technology change can be ameliorated with sufficient training and education. Staff members felt strongly about being knowledgeable of the technology and resources available on the network in order to serve the users. Some of the librarians suggested that people will respond to this dynamic, volatile environment in very individual ways. Some librarians do not and will not use computers and are reluctant to change. Others embrace the new opportunities. One library respondent said bluntly, "I hate to be hard-nosed about this, but I think some people are going to have to come to terms with this thing. I like to think I am a librarian and not an archivist—I want to know what's going on now."

Computing services staff are familiar with the constant change of technology—it is part of their domain. Collaborations between librarians and computing services staff are increasing the librarians' exposure to new technologies and possibly increasing their comfort level with the pace of change.

An ambitious technology agenda, like that with Project Mercury, with its uncertainties of funding, tight timelines, and such, required project staff to move very quickly at times. One respondent referred to the fast pace and "enormous pressure that people here have had to live with." Even conscientious attempts at communicating to staff through electronic mail and newsletters were not always enough. "As a result one of the biggest problems was the feeling of mistrust among some of the library staff, especially the branch librarians, who felt like they were out of the communications flow."

Developing new applications is only one part of the service equation. Another part is implementing these new applications, and for that to be successful, staff on the front lines must be briefed, trained, prepared, and primed. Thus, the challenges are not only technological. Both sites are developing new networked-based technologies and applications of which the full impacts (e.g., organizational, personnel, resource) have yet to be identified and resolved. Managers face the challenge of managing the changes brought by the new applications and innovations.

Library staff, though, must learn from their colleagues in computing services how to become more comfortable with the type and rate of change that will accompany the networked environment.

Organizing Network Resources

Many library staff commented on the need to bring some order to the resources available on the network. Some talked about trying to do this on their own but also thought it was a larger problem than could be solved by one individual or one institution. Several people suggested that while they are willing to work on this organizational effort, a national strategy will be necessary to limit redundancy of effort. If librarians do not do this, according to one respondent, others will, and "librarians will be left in the dust." Yet the activity of identifying, organizing, and providing seamless access to these resources is a responsibility the librarians feel they must assume if they are to serve their patrons.

Most respondents had some internal or personal method to keep track of the resources they have encountered. These personal systems are almost entirely paper-based—notebooks, slips of paper, and so on. So when there is a need to use the resource, it means finding the reference to the resource that they might have encountered months ago. The finding function that is provided by library catalogs to local collections does not exist for networked resources. For library staff to exploit the networked resources, easy-to-use and well-organized finding tools are essential.

Impact on Collection Development

The electronic library and networked resources present new challenges for collection development. What collection policies are appropriate for networked resources? Collection policies previously have guided library acquisitions to serve the information needs of a local campus community. Yet networked libraries have an opportunity to serve electronic communities of users who may not be affiliated with the parent institution. Are such users to be considered in collection development? Even to think in terms of "collections," however, overlays a traditional "bricks and building" library perspective on the networked environment. More appropriate metaphors might be information development and knowledge management.

Also, networked bibliographic and abstracting and indexing (A&I) databases are putting an increased pressure on paper-based materials and collections. Users quickly find pointers to information sources, but library holdings do not always match journals indexed by the A&I resources. Strategies for dealing with this increased demand include: purchasing second copy and additional new journal titles on microform; acquiring the CD-ROM periodical collections that backup certain vendors' electronic bibliographic indexes; and attempting to cancel certain publications for which an electronic equivalent is available.

Respondents agreed that acquisition of and access to electronic information or networked resources should occur if they are in the realm of the library's normal collecting interests. As a collection development officer stated, "It's just another type of information." One can, however, point to the special characteristics of this "type of information" and begin to see the complexities for collection policies. Networked information resources are often dynamic and volatile. Files of information can and do change frequently. Even if a resource fits the "collecting interests" of the library, which version of the item do you collect? What the library collected yesterday may need to be "recollected" tomorrow because of dynamic changes in the contents of the resource.

For the immediate, if not foreseeable, future, libraries will collect both electronic and non-electronic (e.g., paper-based) information resources. One respondent suggested that "limited financial resources can result in competition, and we need to find a balance between acquiring electronic and non-electronic sources." Acquiring a full-text database that serves one discipline on campus may result in the cancellation of materials used by other disciplines. While competition between departments on campus for the library's acquisitions budget is not new, the networked environment adds new complications. Instead of a percentage of overhead charges on research grants supporting the library's acquisitions budget, departments or individual researchers may want to retain those funds to purchase information for their own use. The networked environment provides an opportunity for "just-in-time" acquisitions for individual scholars and researchers as well as the library.

There is a question, however, as to the appropriate model to choose for "acquiring" networked information. For example, are the electronic journals that fit the scope of the collection development policies printed out and stored for future access? Or is a bibliographic record for such journals created and stored with the other records for library holdings. This, of course, raises the ongoing concern of what the "library catalog" is supposed to contain. Catalogs, in the past, have contained surrogate documents representing the holdings of the library. If electronic information, not held by the library, is to be included in the catalog, the fundamental nature of the library catalog changes. New methods for alerting the users to this fact must be developed.

One respondent expressed concern with the issue of access v. ownership of information. Owning materials provides a local avenue for access. "Hypothetical access does you more harm than no access." What seems to be implied here, for example, is that providing access to A&I and other citation databases, which may point to materials the library does not collect, leaves users worse off than if they never knew about those sources. Delivering materials to users is the important issue—whether or not the library collects the materials or provides access to them through a document delivery service or interlibrary loan. The library's use of commercial document delivery services raises the question of who pays the price. Is the end-user charged for documents that are not collected by the library but must be acquired through the commercial channels such as CARL's UnCover? As one respondent suggested, "We can absorb anything into the materials budget, but it is a question of what do we quit doing to absorb it?"

Librarians are beginning to use the network in their daily work activities, and in the area of collection development, they are using the network for bibliographic verification and resource discovery. A respondent in charge of collection development brought to the attention of the selectors (those individuals within the library who select in specific disciplines) a list of electronic discussion groups relevant to their disciplines, and asked them to notify their faculty liaisons about these resources. Such discussion lists would then be subscribed to by individual faculty members, and the library would have served the purpose of pointing these information resources out. Yet as the faculty members become effective network users, they will likely not rely on the library to find out about network resources. Self-sufficient network users will use the library only if it provides them with information services they cannot easily provide for themselves.

At one site where grant money initially funded locally mounted commercial databases, library managers moved these database expenditures to the materials budget. According to a collection development officer, these resources do appropriately belong in the materials budget. With online databases included in the materials budget, deciding on what to mount and what to deselect will be made collaboratively as with other acquisitions and collection development decisions. Transaction statistics on some of the electronic resources are available for collection officials to use in making their decisions. Usage, however, for databases and paper-based materials is only one factor. Core resources in each discipline will be collected. Further, the competing interests will have to argue out how limited funds will be allocated for needed paper-based or electronic information resources when they are both considered in the materials budget. The access v. ownership issue will also be played out in the materials budget. If the library develops an acquisition-on-demand, or "just-in-time" collection policy, a key question is whether or not the costs for the "just-in-time" materials come from the materials budget.

Electronic Journals and the Problems of Scholarly Communication

One of the issues with which these libraries are attempting to deal, namely electronic journals, goes quickly beyond the realm of technological and library organizational solutions. The networked environment is providing new opportunities for the production and dissemination of scholarly communication. From the library's perspective, many other stakeholders are deciding the place of electronic information in the process of scholarly research and communication. The library's role in shaping these decisions is unclear.

More than one respondent claimed that the university has an opportunity to take back control over the intellectual production by its faculty. Some respondents suggested that it is time to rethink the whole issue of scholarly production given the effect that pressures on faculty to publish has had on libraries in terms of collection, inflated serials costs, and such.

Existing networked-based electronic journals offer libraries an opportunity to explore their role in providing access, adding value to the journals by providing local indexing, and determining collection policies for these materials. They are, however, only beginning to consider various alternatives for managing electronic journals. Libraries can print out paper copies of electronic journals to bind and put in the regular collection. They might simply include a record in the local catalog with information for the user to connect to the resource via the network. Another alternative is to store the electronic journal locally for access via the campus-wide information system. Each of these are ways to accomplish the library's participation in the process of scholarly communication, but which way (if any) offers the library an opportunity to add value to the information resource?

Listening to and Learning from Users

Project Mercury devoted serious attention to user studies and system performance evaluations. These user studies and concerns of different user groups are informing many of the efforts on user interface design and other LIS II features. In fact, focus group interviews conducted in late 1990 resulted in a long list of user needs and expectations, which supplied the Project Mercury staff with what became the high-priority features implemented in LIS II. Users tested these features in both the Motif and VT100 frameworks, and as a result, each user interface underwent substantial revision.

There was also a need to learn from these "listening and learning" experiences how and when system designers could better collect user information. As the following statements from two respondents suggest, communication strategies may need revision:

- "We should have gotten the faculty departmental computer liaison person more involved."
- "As a result of the process of conducting the focus groups at the beginning of planning for LIS II, we have discovered that user focus groups and surveys are good, but in our case we did not have sufficient representation from the everyday user. We made some assumptions about the level of computer sophistication that may not reflect the searching preferences/needs of other groups of users."

Understanding user information needs and behaviors can offer important insights for system and services design. This is a critical concern since many campus users are just learning about the networked environment—and learning what questions to ask. Therefore, library educational and outreach efforts can inform users as well as offer an opportunity for users to provide feedback to system and service planners.

In the collaborative arrangements between computing services and the library, network user support staff are learning from the library staff, who are network users themselves, what questions other "users" may have and can develop appropriate service responses to the questions and problems. The computer services unit is recognizing that there are many "user" populations on one campus. This is an important insight, especially for computing services, which may not be as familiar as the library in interacting with heterogenous user groups.

Limits to Service in the Networked Environment

A science librarian talked about her experience in monitoring a professionally oriented (engineering) listserv. Someone requested information on minority programs at academic institutions. She replied to the discussion group about a program offered by her institution to encourage minority enrollment in engineering. After the requests for additional information began arriving, she handed it off to the appropriate office on campus that works with the minority program.

There was a double-edged quality about this experience, and the respondents recognized it. They saw how they could be inundated with requests for information through their active participation in discussion groups. However, they also felt that when people asked questions for which they knew the answers, they should provide answers. They use the networks to gather information, and more than once, they have received information useful to their professional work in the library.

More broadly construed, this issue encompasses the questions: Who are your users? What users do the librarians on one campus serve? What about non-affiliated remote users? The implications of a global constituency for the library will require policy decisions that may result in *limiting* services to remote users. Already, the library at one site has carefully defined user groups to control access in order to protect the licensing agreements for network accessible databases.

Infrastructure Needs

The library, as well as the campus, needs an adequate information infrastructure to fulfill the visions of operating an electronic library. The infrastructure includes people, information resources, information processes, and the technology an organization has at its disposal for developing services and products. Effective network services and applications can be built only if the technology foundation exists. This is a non-trivial matter given the currently installed systems that must be upgraded, and even more importantly, the need for an adequate number of computers or workstations for library staff. In these tight budgetary times, the need for infrastructure investment challenges both university and library administrations to allocate sufficient resources or redeploy existing resources in the current period for long-term benefits.

One respondent, however, suggested that no vision exists at the highest levels of the university for information technology, networking, and networked resources. "The university administration doesn't have a vision about the networked environment as a competitive advantage. Their vision is faculty centered—hire star faculty who bring in grants." The faculty, however, is only one component of the information infrastructure. At other levels within the university, there is an appreciation and understanding that the library, computing services, and the network are strategic resources. While the university administration claims that technology can deliver information more cheaply than libraries can, they are neither interested in investing in the infrastructure, nor do they realize that these services do not yet exist. In such instances, strategic planning can provide a means to understand what is needed, what is possible, and what choices have to be made.

Infrastructure comprises the components listed above, but often the concern is expressed in terms of adequate information technology. At one site, lack of appropriate equipment for staff is a major problem. Some library staff have computers on their desks, but most do not have modems nor are they connected directly to the network. An unevenness of technology deployment among librarians can exacerbate already-existing differences in attitudes and skills they have toward the new technologies.

This lack of equipment can frustrate staff who want to use the network in their daily work. For example, to check their electronic mail accounts, staff must find the machines that offer connection to the campus hosts—either through dial-up or direct connection to the campus network. Several respondents expressed frustration at the time they spent going to the machine, logging on, and so on. Personal desktop machines with network access would enhance their effective and efficient use of time. In addition, ready access to equipment would offer staff more opportunities to practice what they had learned in the network training classes. Without such equipment, the librarians who have been introduced to the Internet will be frustrated in not having easy opportunities to explore and increase their skills. Ease of access to adequate equipment can reduce some of the pressures the librarians feel in taking on the new responsibilities for network competence.

Management is not oblivious to this problem. Plans are underway to get better network connection for the library staff. The restrictive budget situation, however, is a main impediment to wiring the buildings and providing appropriate equipment to all library faculty. Since there is little likelihood for a near-term improvement in resources, managers must examine how the existing budget can be reallocated for needed infrastructure investments.

Budgets for technology are quite different in the library and the computer center. The computer center budget is oriented towards the technology—"everyone there has the latest equipment and network connections on their desks, they work with the latest tools." The technology budget within the library is a small fraction of the total budget. The focus of the budget is in materials and personnel. For the library staff, this has led to some tensions and frustrations. Through the collaborative work with computer center staff, librarians have been exposed to a level of technology and understanding they would not have picked up on their own. Yet, library staff do not have the equipment to keep up with the fast pace of technological change.

One respondent gave an interesting perspective on computing services. He sensed that technology investment priorities will change as to placing good equipment (he had a NeXt machine on his desk) on the desktops of library staff and academic faculty. This change will occur only when there is enough material (relevant material such as a large number of electronic journals) available on the network. An adequate supply of electronic resources will drive not only the demand for network access, but also for the equipment to access and exploit the electronic resources.

User Interface Designs

With the range of platforms existing on campuses, a major consideration is to determine which and how many interfaces to support. The goals of providing multiple user interfaces for LIS II and responding to user feedback about the interfaces have challenged Project Mercury designers as they negotiate between building for the small-screen dumb terminal and building to exploit the power of the large-screen Macintosh or workstation. According to one respondent:

> I would have spent more time thinking about simpler machines (which are more common among the campus community) for the user interface and less time on the high-end machines. . . . About 80 percent of our user interface was carried away by the bells and whistles of functions that are included in the Motif interface for the high-end machines, using that as a model. But now we are struggling with how to make the Mac and PC interfaces similar and have the functionalities of Motif.

Much of what has been learned by the Carnegie Mellon libraries' and Project Mercury's staff resulted from experimentation, user studies, transaction log analysis, and library staff feedback. Interface design and redesign and development of new features are a response to such formal types of input and user studies.

The goal of accessing a range of information resources through a single user interface carries added resource expenditures when dealing with an environment containing many different hardware platforms. In addition, the single interface operates effectively only for those resources under local control (i.e., the databases mounted locally). When one enters the networked environment of the Internet, users are faced with a variety of interfaces. The standard for information search and retrieval, Z39.50, provides a possible solution to interface issues.

Planning Process and Communication

Library management sees the importance of involving the library staff in the intellectual activity of discussing the impact of the network in the library. At one site, a senior library manager drafted a white paper, "The Internet Challenge: Issues of Professional Concern and Responsibility," for circulation to library staff to engage them in a discussion on a variety of issues related to the networked environment.

> It is now time for us to begin articulating a formal strategy and philosophy on what role the library will play in "servicing" the Internet. The Academic Information Services Division will provide leadership in articulating necessary issues for us to address, provide support to the library faculty in developing the necessary technical skills, and foster the necessary dialogue between the library and University Computing Services with the goal of facilitating a common and collaborative program of development and support. It is, however, the library faculty as a whole that must come to a common understanding and articulation of our mission in this area.

The white paper delineates a number of issues that the library staff must address in order to arrive at the "formal strategy and philosophy" in response to the networked environment.

New organizational arrangements are also being used for planning purposes. At one site, an ad hoc group has been brought together to determine and choose new ways to provide information about networked resources. Without any official mandate, the Network Navigation Group addresses issues related to the existence of networks on campus—how to educate people to become of the network, to learn what is available, and to help them become users on the network.

How to involve and when to involve staff in the planning process are ongoing challenges for managers who need to communicate with staff, solicit their input, as well as meet deadlines. These responses illustrate the challenge:

- "The teams should have moved out of the computer services units and into the library sooner so that reporting relationships and communication flow could have been improved."
- "The library staff should have been encouraged to have taken a more active part in the project by having more incentives to actively participate."
- "The library staff would have liked to have been more involved in the decisions, but we had to move very fast. . . ."
- "We learned that although the key leaders had a meeting of minds and a shared vision, they need to invest more time in getting others to understand and share their visions and plans."

The need for staff involvement was apparent in discussions with library managers, but how that is accomplished is a major issue.

A respondent suggested that the most subtle planning problem the library faces is that new services take time to put into place, sometimes two or more years. This means that library managers and staff "must anticipate where the faculty will want to be in a couple of years." He acknowledged that most of the initiatives have been based on this anticipation. One challenge then, is correctly anticipating the needs of users who may not even know what the technology has to offer. Another major challenge is dramatically shortening the time to bring a new service "to market." A robust information infrastructure and skilled staff are two requirements for the flexibility and responsiveness the library will need to operate successfully in the networked environment.

Reconceptualizing the Library

More than one respondent suggested that the networked environment will bring fundamental changes in the delivery of library services. At one level, it is a reconceptualization of the library. "This campus will not go back to the warehouse model of libraries." Another respondent, however, thought that it is the "economics of libraries that are destroying 'the way things were always done,' not the technology. Technology is part of the solution that will return libraries to worrying about information content and not economics. It won't be easy though."

While one of the value-added activities the library offers to users is precisely the collection of relevant materials within the library, the combination of new networked information resources, the means to access those resources by members of the community, the continuing budget constraints, and other factors will put additional pressures on the library management to examine existing practices. The traditional research library with a central library and numerous branch libraries may not be appropriate for the future. Library managers are examining how to achieve some efficiencies by moving away from the branch library approach and providing more centralized library services.

One respondent stated that the traditional one-to-one service that libraries have been able to offer is "extraordinarily expensive and time consuming." Even more, such one-to-one service does not reach the majority of members of the community. Instead, the library management is discussing how to provide better tools and more group training as a means for utilizing resources better.

The research library may be threatened by competition from other information providers that users can access for their information needs. The network allows users to contact these providers directly, and have information faxed or delivered to the desktop electronically. A respondent suggested that the current support for the library that comes out of the overhead of research grants may be threatened as those researchers purchase the information they need, and the network makes that transaction easier to accomplish.

There are multiple forces and threats to the academic library, and libraries are actively engaging them on a number of fronts. Yet the question is whether or not libraries are willing to consider fundamental and strategic changes that will lead to a reconceptualization of the library. A sense emerges from the discussion with site visit participants that a transformation of the library is in the making. Incrementalism in response to the opportunities and threats the networked world presents will not be sufficient.

The academic library and the university face a future shaped by the world of electronic information and high-speed networks.

The uncertainty that exists in this transition from a paper-based, collection-oriented, bricks and mortar library paradigm to a future that is in the process of being created and defined can take a toll on staff and organizations. The issues discussed here need to be addressed by university and library policymakers, managers, and staff. More importantly, the library and the university should be aware that in such a dynamic arena, new issues will arise constantly, and changing circumstances will redefine existing issues. It is imperative that libraries have in place a process for ongoing environmental scanning. Knowledge and awareness of issues and potential solutions are essential. As one respondent suggested, "It's better to be frustrated by seeing what you can do, but not be able to, rather than be oblivious to the whole thing."

BUILDING FOR THE NETWORKED FUTURE

The study team selected the libraries at Carnegie Mellon University and the University of Southern California because they are actively involved in building the library to participate in the networked future. They build on a history of library services and library culture, which offer strengths and liabilities. Library services have focused on collecting and organizing materials to answer user information needs. The values, attitudes, and behaviors embodied in the culture have placed a premium on service to users and access to needed information. The visionary leadership at both sites recognize that these values and functions will still be essential in the networked environment. Further, they recognize that many, but not all, traditional library activities will continue in parallel as the new roles, services, and image of the electronic library evolves.

Earlier in this chapter, critical success factors based on data from the site visits were identified. Attention to these factors are enabling Carnegie Mellon and USC to prepare for networked-based services in the virtual library. From the discussion of the findings, a set of "building blocks" for preparing the campus networked environment can further be identified. Figure 2-2 illustrates these building blocks. Libraries must determine how they can provide leadership (cooperatively with other campus units or on their own) to ensure these building blocks are solidly in place.

One looks to sites such as Carnegie Mellon and USC for glimpses into the future. Neither site has a pre-existing road map to follow. Instead, through planning and vision, they are each blazing a trail to the future. And since the future is always one more day down the road, building this future will be a perpetual work-in-progress.

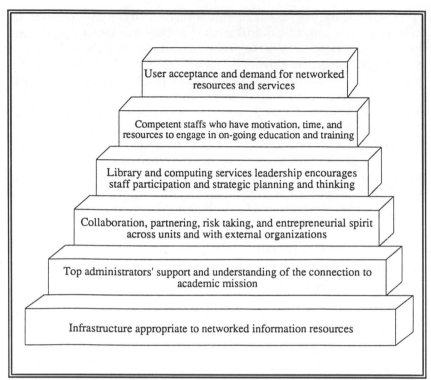

Figure 2-2. Building blocks for preparing the academic networked environment.

For the people who are guiding the evolution at these libraries, they are less likely to ask the question: When will we know if we are there? More likely, they will ask questions similar to those they have been asking these past years: What opportunities are there for the library and what can we do to create those opportunities?

Their vision of the electronic library providing access to a world (literally, given the global reach of the network) of information from the scholar's and student's desktop is not compromised by the current dismal budget situations, the lack of adequate infrastructure, or the fears and worries of overworked staff. The vision enables the library leadership to plan and guides their choices as they confront all the very real issues that develop *because* the library is evolving and is moving into an uncertain area.

Academic libraries will change, but the networked environment is accelerating the rate of change. This increase in "quantity" or rate of change will produce a qualitative change of such a magnitude that we are calling this the reconceptualization of the library. The fundamental question for libraries is whether they will shape the changes or continue in a reactive mode to pressures both internal and external to the academic environment.

One source of pressure is the lack of adequate resources to do all things and be all things to all users. "Doing more with less" may be an admirable goal, but in fact this slogan may disguise the need to make difficult choices about the allocation of existing budgets. There will not be the money nor the capacity of staff to continue all the traditional activities as well as take on new service roles appropriate to the networked environment. Further, new funds for needed infrastructure investment will likely not materialize. The question then is the power of the vision of the reconceptualized library to guide the redeployment of current budgets. The vision should suggest the core services, the required infrastructure, and the new services and roles needed.

Another pressure forcing changes in academic libraries is the users who have gotten a taste of the networked environment and whose expectations for information access includes timely information delivery. The library faces competition from new information providers such as document delivery services that utilize networks, fax machines, and other technologies to directly serve users. Those users in the past would have looked to the library and interlibrary loan services to procure needed information. The academic library no longer has a captive market.

Academic libraries today are likely to claim that they have a central role in information provision on their campuses. To make the assumption that their centrality on campus will continue could be a major strategic error. How should they respond if told that they will be one "information server" among many in the networked environment? What can they do to "differentiate" their information product or service from the competitors who are already providing alternatives for users. How will a library react when it finds that its competitor is actually an academic library across the country that has decided to "market" customized information services?

A comparison with concerns in the 1980s about information brokers competing with libraries is not warranted. Imagine instead a Dialog or BRS (or a Regional Bell Operating Company!) offering easy network access to gigabits of well organized information searchable through intuitively robust front ends (present versions of WAIS and Gopher will seem primitive by comparison). The information (e.g., a journal article, newspaper column, etc.) is shipped immediately over the network to the user's computer or fax machine. All this and at a cost low enough for the user to think it is worth the price—*given* the service, the timeliness of information delivery, and the low level of effort in getting the information. In fact, cable companies, telephone companies, online database vendors, and other networked-based information providers may not even care what happens to the library. A recent article in *Time* magazine (Elmer-Dewitt, 1993) on the "electronic superhighway" mentioned libraries only in passing, thereby highlighting the idea that libraries really have no role in the networked future.

What can distinguish the academic library's information service or product from competitors such as the one just described? (Remember, CARL's UnCover and other vendors' services already exist.) It will not be the fact that it "collects" or "owns" information. It may not even be the fact that the library "provides access" to information. To distinguish networked-based academic library services and products from its competitors requires the library to rethink how it adds value to information resources and how it recovers costs. The electronic journal? Let's store those relevant electronic journals locally, index their contents, and make them searchable from the scholar's workstation. Do faculty want a selective dissemination of information (SDI) program? Let's provide them electronically with tables of contents from journals relevant to their research and teaching, and subsidize the delivery of specific articles in formats that best suit their needs.

The academic library has an edge on its competitors, though, since it knows the specifics of the mission of the university—research and teaching. It is in a unique position to create, collate, and package information for curriculum support. Virtual reserve reading rooms can end the frustration of instructors and students by providing electronic storage and access for course materials. Examples as these point in directions for adding value to the information the user community needs.

Finally, the academic library faces few barriers in determining its users' information behaviors, needs, and competencies. Its market is right there on campus, and "market surveys" can inform the library about needed information services and products. The rapid expansion of the capabilities of information technology will likely be translated into rapid changes in how users perceive their needs and possibilities. The library must become a flexible and responsive organization to satisfy new user demands. More importantly, the library as the "expert in information and information technology" can work to shape the demands of users by providing services and products in anticipation of the need.

In the examples of Carnegie Mellon and USC, we see two institutions that, since the mid-1980s, have thought about and made changes in organizational structures as a way to respond to changing situations. Leaders at these two sites see, at times more clearly than others, the opportunities and problems along the way for the library to reinvent itself as a networked-based electronic library. They realize they do not have the opportunity to create this new library *ex nihilo*—that actually might be doable. Instead, they need to evolve the existing library, its practices, and activities into an energized source of information services and products. Library and campus leaders realize the library cannot go this one alone. The collaborative relationships and joint projects between the library, computing services, and other units show how these institutions are developing a basis for flexibility and responsiveness in the dynamic and volatile networked environment.

No longer will the academic library be only a place, a building, a collection. Instead it takes on new forms, possibly less tangible than books and bricks, but substantial in the core of what libraries have always been about—identifying, organizing, and making accessible information, and connecting real users with real information needs to that information. That substantial core of the library is also the core of the vision of the electronic, wired academic library. Properly deployed, the technology may provide new ways for librarians to carry out the library's substantive functions.

REFERENCES

Arms, William Y. and Michalak, Thomas J. (1990). Carnegie Mellon University. In Caroline R. Arms, ed., *Campus Strategies for Libraries and Electronic Information* (pp. 243–273). Bedford, MA: Digital Press.

Elmer-Dewitt, Philip. (April 12, 1993). Take a trip into the future on the electronic superhighway. *Time*, 50-58.

Johnson, Margaret L., Lyman, Peter and Tompkins, Philip. (1990). University of Southern California. In Caroline R. Arms, ed., *Campus Strategies for Libraries and Electronic Information* (pp. 176–192). Bedford, MA: Digital Press.

Spradley, James P. (1979). *The Ethnographic Interview*. Fort Worth, TX: Holt, Rinehart, and Winston, Inc.

Troll, Denise A. (Spring, 1992a). Information Technologies at Carnegie Mellon. *Library Administration and Management* 6(2): 91–99.
Troll, Denise A. (1992b). *Library Information System II: Progress and Plans.* Mercury Technical Report Series, No. 5. Pittsburgh, PA: Carnegie Mellon University.

Academic Librarians' Perspectives on the Internet/NREN: Key Issues

As suggested in Chapters 1 and 2, the literature and the site visits present an important perspective on the evolution of the networked environment and the response by academic libraries to that environment. Another approach to understand better how academic librarians perceive the development of the Internet/National Research and Education Network (NREN) is to report, largely in their own words, their perspectives. Although the participants in the academic study oftentimes had conflicting points of view, there were a number of topics where they had similar views, or there were common themes throughout their views.

The following key issues will affect the development of academic libraries in the networked environment and are based primarily on the results from the focus group sessions, follow-up interviews, and site visits. Appendix A describes the method for conducting these sessions, the selection and composition of the participants, and the process that guided data collection. It is important to remember that these views represent the thinking of academic librarians, and those familiar with academic libraries as of 1992.

During the data-collection activities, the academic librarians identified issues covering many topics. Thus, the information reported in this chapter is a snapshot of views held at that time. For purposes of discussion, the chapter groups the issues within a number of categories. These categories are:

- the academic library in the broader campus and networked environment;
- Internet/NREN impacts on the academic library;
- reconsidering academic library services; and
- transitioning to the future.

The issues discussed in this chapter are not intended to be a comprehensive list, but rather, are considered to be those most significant, interesting, and with the greatest potential impact on the future of academic libraries. Many of the issues are closely interrelated, and it is difficult to discuss one without referring to others. Nonetheless, this chapter provides the reader with a sense of the tone, concerns, and perspectives of the various individuals who participated in the data-collection process.

THE ACADEMIC LIBRARY IN THE BROADER CAMPUS AND NETWORKED ENVIRONMENT

Issues underlying this category are:

- reorganizing academic information resources management;
- sorting out new roles and relationships;
- relationship with academic computing services (ACS);
- what can libraries provide or contribute to the networked environment?;
- education and training;
- development of "national" academic libraries;
- market-based model for library services;
- the role of regional networks (regionals as libraries?, regionals inhibiting access?, selling only connectivity?); and
- affecting the broader policy framework.

A number of the issues relate to how the academic library will evolve in the broader campus and networked environment. Not only will the library have to reconsider specific services and activities within the library, but its roles and relationships with other campus units, and with organizations beyond the local campus must also be reconsidered. The issues discussed in this section suggest that some of these roles and relationships will require a fresh and new assessment as academic libraries enter the national electronic networked environment.

Reorganizing Academic Information Resources Management

If researchers are to exploit the electronic networked environment effectively, they must have service-oriented individuals operating the networked infrastructure. The key stakeholders are the faculty, students, the library, individual departments, information support services (audiovisual), administrative computing, and academic computing. Currently these key players typically lack coordination, planning, and leadership.

As long as these stakeholders continue to be disorganized and lack coordination, campus community members will be "on their own" in the electronic networked environment. In this context a few individuals may flourish, but many others will be frustrated and non-productive. Clearly there will be a need to partner responsibilities and roles both within the campus setting and with organizations outside the campus.The development of new organizational models for linking and coordinating academic information resources management will be critical to the success of the researcher in the electronic networked environment. When asked what these models might be, some offered the notion of a combined academic computing services and academic library, some mentioned the idea of a campus-wide "information czar," and others thought all information services might be coordinated under library operations. But in fact, there has been little research and visioning on what models might be most appropriate for what types of situations.

A number of the participants had a very positive and up-beat view of their situation and the challenges they faced. The comment was offered, and agreed to by others, that "If you don't look out for yourself and the library, no one else will." This view may be due, in part, to the fact that generally, these participants were from the larger, better supported academic libraries. But this attitude clearly carried through to other aspects of the discussion as well. There was a "can-do" and "give me a chance" perspective (mixed with a healthy service orientation and user perspective). Furthermore, the view was "if the library doesn't figure it [campus networking] out, no one will."

Sorting Out New Roles and Relationships

There are a number of key players and stakeholders in the development of the networked environment: librarians, publishers, government policymakers, network producers/managers, users, academic computing services, campus administrators, technology vendors, and others. A range of roles and responsibilities for each of these stakeholder groups in the networked environment is possible. Currently, the match between stakeholder groups and roles/responsibilities is unclear—in part because of the evolving, dynamic nature of the networked environment.

There was agreement that the Association of Research Libraries (ARL) and especially the Coalition for Networked Information (CNI) have taken a leadership stance in helping in the use of the network for libraries. But this leadership was primarily in terms of lobbying and being "cheerleaders." A number of the participants agreed that individual libraries, however, would have to develop strategies and techniques on their own and not to expect others—such as the associations—to do the hard work for them.

In terms of roles for other organizations, participants also agreed that the vendors and the mid-level regional networks should be more active in new services development, advancing Internet technological applications, and providing training. Indeed, a number of librarians believed that vendors and mid-levels had responsibilities for working with academic libraries in such areas but are not shouldering these responsibilities.

Relationship with Academic Computing Services (ACS)

Many of the study participants thought they had a good working relationship with their respective academic computer services group. A number of individuals commented that they had this relationship prior to the recent developments with the network and that they simply built on that relationship. It was unclear what was meant by "good working relationship," but most of the participants seemed to be satisfied by the current situation.

Some librarians commented that it was to the advantage of computing services to work with the library—indeed, "computing services has more to gain by working with the library than the library had in working with computing services." One rationale put forward to support this statement was that computing services gained credibility by working with the library and that they would be "credentialed" by being associated with the library since there was no credentialing agency for computing services. Another thought that it was the library that really knew about information services and meeting user needs and that most computing services desperately needed those skills.

The extent to which joint planning between the library and computing services has occurred is unclear. Some librarians indicated that they had worked together successfully with their computing services to develop a campus-wide information system (CWIS). A CWIS can be defined as a locally developed network, accessible by members of the academic community, that provides access to:

- Locally mounted information resources and services such as class schedules, the library OPAC, unique databases developed at that particular institution, and

other institutionally created information resources;
and

- Remote information resources and services to which
the CWIS serves as a gateway; the CWIS may link the
local user seamlessly to network gophers, wide area
information systems (WAIS) in remote locations, or
other distant information resources.

Some academic librarians, however, noted that computing services
had taken the lead in developing the CWIS with very little library
involvement.

The range of institutional configurations for academic computing and the library relationships with ACS appears to be quite
broad. One participant commented that there was just one person
at ACS that they really had to deal with, that they were a very small
unit, and that the library was able to pretty much do what it wanted.
In fact, one got the sense that in this particular setting, the library
was the driving force in networking development on that campus.

The discussion raised the issue whether the library *should be* the
driving force in planning and developing networked information services. To some extent, the library has been able to do this because,
they believed, there was more "slop" in the library budget, and it is
easier to move resources around (within the library) than at ACS.

Another factor that assists the library in taking a leadership
role in campus networking initiatives, some participants believed, is
that the faculty have a more natural affinity for the library than they
do for ACS. They are more familiar with the library, know more
people at the library, and appreciate the fact that the library "supports" their research directly. This relationship, since it already is in
place, is a positive factor contributing to the library's ability to provide leadership on campus.

But one library director commented that the only way he
could ensure a good relationship with ACS and to make certain
that the library's priorities were considered in terms of campus networking was to support half-time, a joint position between the
library and ACS. One had the sense that if this had not been done,
the library would have had a much more difficult time in "getting
connected."

There also was the sense that at some institutions, ACS
believed it was more to their advantage to have good relationships
with the library than in past years. "Two years ago, we [the library]
needed them more than they needed us; now it is the other way

around." With tight budgets, the notion that ACS "supports" the institution may leave it more vulnerable for cuts than other units who provide "direct" services. Thus, as one person stated, ACS wants to "tie their star to the library."

Another commented that the culture of the library was much more supportive and understanding for user services than that of ACS. While ACS may get along with the computer people and techies, they typically do not relate well with other members on the faculty. "ACS types don't work with the masses." The character of the distributed network environment, however, will require ACS to move more into services delivery (e.g., user support). This may cause some friction between the library and ACS.

Overall, however, there is still the sense that each institutional setting will have idiosyncratic differences and that it is difficult to generalize about relationships between the library and ACS, given such differences. The librarians agreed that it was important to nurture/develop linkages with ACS. Critical success factors for successfully integrated library/ACS activities include:

- high-level administrative coordination between the library and ACS;
- support from institutional administration for the library and ACS to cooperate/collaborate on information services development and management;
- joint programs and planning activities;
- good interpersonal relationships among library and ACS staff at middle management positions;
- library attitudes that embrace electronic information access;
- respect for ACS' and librarians' respective strengths;
- ability of both ACS and the library to experiment with ideas and some resources on new projects; and
- education and training for librarians about the technology and its applications; education and training for the ACS staff on providing user support.

These factors occur within a complex institutional environment which is likely to vary depending on organizational structures, personalities, and institutional history. But, the notion of critical success factors for the library and ACS to work together successfully as a team deserves additional research attention.

What Can Libraries Provide or Contribute to the Networked Environment?

This topic generated discussion both directly and indirectly on a number of different occasions. Generally, participants thought that the library, as currently operated, had little to contribute to the information services available on the network. Some noted that having access to bibliographic information through OPACS was an important contribution. Others, however, disagreed, noting that it would be more important to make available the actual information rather than bibliographic pointers to that information.

One comment suggested that the library's function in "preserving stuff," would become one of its primary roles in the future rather than an active disseminator of information resources. An implication of the library as a "preserver of stuff" is that fewer libraries might be needed to accomplish this task. Generally, the focus group participants were hard-pressed to identify specific, unique information services and products that would make the academic library an essential element in the networked environment.

One participant noted that usually one is struck with "techno-non-shock" upon using a library. That is, there is very little modern technology apparent to the user. Moreover, this same person commented, the lack of modern information technology in the library would limit the library's ability to innovate and create new and "exciting" information services and products for the Internet.

Education and Training

Many participants commented that there was no one "in charge" regarding education and instruction related to the Internet at their institution. There was no formal training available for new Internet users except some workshops offered at some ACS departments. The library, typically, was not involved in campus-wide instruction regarding the Internet. To those who initiated or stated a need, then perhaps someone would help. Moreover, there were no resources to do instruction on campus. Given tight budgets, many of the participants stated that they were not going to reallocate existing resource to deal with education and training issues.

A medical library director noted that there was some centralized instruction at his particular institution, done under the guise of "information management education." This incorporated aspects of bibliographic instruction (BI) with hands-on technology applications. This particular setting, however, is unique as the instruction comes from a combined effort of different institutions who all support the library.

There was some agreement that BI needed to take on a new role and that what currently is done as BI must be recast to better incorporate accessing and using networked information resources and products. One person thought it would be especially good to get the BI groups at the American Library Association working on this problem, and sooner would be better.

They recognized that there was an opportunity on campus for some unit to develop and implement courses/instruction in networked information resources. The right place for this to be done would likely vary from campus to campus. The current budget crunch made offering new services very difficult indeed. At one institution, for example, there are some 40,000 students. How could the library possibly be able to mount an effort to deal with all these people? On the other hand, as one person noted, there is yet to be a critical mass problem where people were demanding "someone" do something about this.

There was some sense that the library should concentrate first on graduate students—who were seen as the most supportive and knowledgeable about the library. The comment was also made that they should focus instruction on graduate students since there was "nothing" there for undergraduates [!]. Overall, while there was some concern with education and instruction issues, the topic did not excite the librarians as much as planning for new systems and discussing new ideas for what networked initiatives might be possible for their institution.

Another aspect of this issue was some recognition that their own staff may be inadequately prepared to deal with identifying and accessing Internet resources and information; but they had no plans to do much about it in the short term. One librarian commented: "Yep, this is a problem. Nope, we're not able to do much about it." Thus, an aspect of this issue is the degree to which the library, itself, invests in its own staff. There is a serious lack of attention being given to instruction both for students/faculty as well as library staff.

Development of "National" Academic Libraries

There were split opinions as to whether there would evolve "national" academic libraries that users would prefer to contact electronically rather than using their institutional library—thus, sending their business to those libraries that best met their needs. One person suggested that this is already happening in his library; others were not sure or did not think so. They thought a more likely scenario would be increased development of services such as those provided by CARL, state networks, or the Freenets—places that actually courted a large national/international constituency group to use their services.

There was some agreement that the "lead" academic libraries should move forward and provide an example of what can, in fact, be done in the networked environment. Not only do they need to provide an example, they also need to set a tone or an attitude of accomplishment and "we can do it." Indeed, a key concern is how to develop some "good examples of good examples" of academic libraries utilizing the network and integrating the network into the campus research and instruction effectively.

Currently there are a number of individual academic libraries where "neat" projects are being done, where, innovative uses of the network are being tried, and some networked products are delivered to users. Some of the participants, however, saw these examples as glitzy "add-on" services and not applications for day-to-day library services. As pointed out by one of the participants, the lead academic libraries also need to provide examples of using the network to accomplish traditional library services.

Market-Based Model for Library Services

A market-based model of demand for specialized services being provided by some libraries caused some consternation among the participants. In effect, as one person commented, there could evolve a "national playing field" for academic library services, and the market might determine which libraries provided the best services. This competitive model might, in fact, be welcomed by some libraries as a means of garnering additional income. CARL was offered as an example of a library consortium that had moved, successfully, from a local to a national playing field and was doing quite well.

In response to a possible scenario where some academic and research libraries become centers of excellence for specific types of services or products through use of the network, one library associate director responded: "They better not be providing national reference service out of *my* library." Others commented that in fact, such was already occurring, that is, some reference departments were getting the reputation for having outstanding services and were receiving electronic mail–based reference questions from outside their immediate constituency.

The development of the electronic networked environment allows libraries to have a global constituency. Clients from anywhere in the world may request services from a library. To some extent, this model may already be developing (e.g., reference librarians receiving questions via e-mail from a constituency outside the immediate campus setting). Some libraries may find it appropriate to develop information services and products for target audiences in a global rather than a local market. Such services and products could be priced to be a "cost-recovery" or a "profit-making" operation.

In a market-based library networked environment, clientele can select which OPAC, which reference service, and what databases might be queried—in some instances, the "best" information services may not be those provided by the local library. Indeed, the best information services may not come from what we now consider traditional academic libraries.

An implication of such an evolution, one participant commented, was that perhaps then, these national libraries would start charging for their services and products both as a means of supporting services to a broader constituency and as a means of supporting other library services. Some participants were disturbed by this possible model, but one senior academic library administrators said that her library, in effect, already used this model for some traditional services.

The Role of Regional Networks

Increasingly, it may be difficult to separate the roles of mid-levels, or the regional networks, and libraries. One person commented that some services and products being developed by the regionals look much like library services, or services that should be provided by libraries. There was some concern that libraries did not find this to be much of a problem. Key aspects of this issues are:

- What can libraries bring to the network?
- What can the networks provide for the libraries?
- To what degree are regional networks competing and/ or cooperating in the provision of electronic services?

Examining these questions may help to clarify roles and responsibilities, but increasingly, the lines between who provides what kind of networked information resources and services are blurred. As more service providers enter the networked market, this blurring will be exacerbated.

Regionals as Libraries? There was some sense that information services being provided by the regionals were fundamentally different than information services provided by libraries. Indeed, a number of the services on the networks did not require library involvement; thus, libraries are being by-passed in the chain of provision of information. An aspect of the issue is ownership of books v. ownership of digital information. It is the digital information that will prosper on the networks, not the books.

But one person asked: "If regionals mount a range of information resources available over a file server, provide gopher service to other databases, and provide electronic reference and referral services, isn't this what a library does?" The question clearly bothered some of the other participants.

One of the participants commented that the "library is not the network, the network is only the infrastructure." But separating the infrastructure from the services may be easier said than done. One person suggested that libraries should exist as "things on the networks" and not try to replace networks. On the other hand, another suggested that if libraries did not become more actively engaged in network development and services, they (the libraries) would find themselves at the "mercy of the networks."

Regionals Inhibiting Access? Some raised concerns about the future role of the mid-level networks. One concern was that the mid-levels might be less the "glue" that held national networking together and more the content controller that determined what would and would not be made available electronically, and who could access it. In fact, one person commented that the role and activities of some mid-level regionals was "already suspect." They showed little interest in getting libraries connected, their pricing structures eliminated the opportunity for many libraries to get connected, and they did not seem to understand that getting connected was only part of the problem—the problem also was providing basic services and value-added services.

One participant believed that some mid-levels had a strangle hold on a particular geographic area in terms of connectivity and services. Regionals as operating monopolies were not seen as conducive to the development of the network. More competition among the regionals and between regionals and national networks is needed, she thought. However, the continued subsidies given to the mid-levels by the National Science Foundation (NSF) mean that in the short term, regionals (1) will remain in place regardless of what they do and how well they do it, and (2) may have limited incentives to be competitive and identify/meet user information needs. Such may change, drastically, if future NSF funding for regionals is reduced or eliminated.

Selling Only Connectivity? There was general agreement that many of the regional networks thought that all they needed to do was get the libraries connected and then the library would figure out what to do with the connection. However, a number of participants commented that for a host of reasons, many of the regionals (with the specifically stated exception of New York and California) really had not made much effort to connect libraries, and the prices for connection eliminated the possibility of connecting. One participant commented that it was very difficult to get libraries in her region connected at all, let alone worry about what resources were available for them on the network.

But the concern about "so what do I do with the network after I'm connected" came up in a number of contexts. The sense of some was that good librarians would figure out what to do with the connection; others, "even after you give them the connection would not know what to do with it." Everyone agreed, however, that much more attention should be given to designing specific services and products that would be of use to libraries. On the other hand, one individual commented that by definition, many of the networked information services and products simply would not work in a library context because of librarian attitudes, lack of resources, and inability to change.

But in the context of providing specific services, or designing new information services for the networked environment, it was unclear who would do this, what services might be proposed, and how they would be implemented. The costs (or how the costs would be carried) for developing such services really were not discussed or considered in this context.

Affecting the Broader Policy Framework

One person commented that funding and getting money is critical. It will be very important to see who gets money as a result of the NREN legislation. Although the High Performance Computing Act of 1991 (P.L. 102-194) was passed by Congress and signed into law by the President, appropriations have yet to find their way to the library community. His view was that few government dollars would go to libraries.

Indeed, the history of the development of NREN thus far was that (1) research and high-performance computing received funding, and (2) networks and network technology received funding. He noted that libraries have not, as yet, been seriously in the pipeline. Unless libraries are in this resource pipeline, it would be quite unlikely that they would be players, thus, contributing to the likelihood that network development would by-pass most of the library community.

It was unclear how familiar the participants were with the language in the High Performance Computing Act of 1991 that established the NREN. In fact, it seemed that only one or two of them had actually read and considered the language. A number were surprised to learn that there was little mention of libraries in the bill and that the role of libraries and their possible responsibilities in NREN development received little attention.

When pressed as to what initiatives should be taken in the post-legislation period (i.e., we fought to get the bill passed, now what do we do?), specific ideas were not forthcoming. A response offered by a number of participants was that we must have meaningful "National Information Policy." Some of the participants felt that saying there was a need for National Information Policy ended the matter since specific policy initiatives for Federal policymakers was not forthcoming

When probed further on the matter and the interviewers put some possible initiatives on the table (e.g., provide Internet connections to all libraries or a set of libraries in each state, support pilot projects, encourage partnering, etc.), there was no agreement as to whether such initiatives were ones that should be supported. Generally, the sense of the discussion was that we needed National Information Policy, and that if we had this national policy, a number of the issues would be resolved. This discussion resulted in no specific policy proposals as critical for the post-P.L. 102-194 agenda.

Participants also generally agreed that the library community had no "clout" in policy development. Indeed, there was the sense that it was unlikely that this would change in the near future. One person commented that the political naïveté of the library community was another negative factor injuring its ability to be a player in the networked environment. He gave the example of not promoting the use of the library and network in the context of jobs, economic recovery, or economic development. The point being, he suggested, that libraries have to use whatever political opportunities there are to move themselves forward and get resources.

In effect, the sense of some of the participants was that the library community needed to find a "hook" to link into Internet funding and development. That hook might be economic development or something else. One other possible hook suggested was making Federal information more widely accessible via the network. Indeed, there is specific language in PL 102-194 directing Federal agencies to better disseminate electronic information via the Internet/NREN. These might form the basis of some policy initiatives from the library community to demonstrate their importance and roles in a national information infrastructure.

There was also the sense that libraries should not be complaining about receiving inadequate government resources for networking when, in fact, they have not done much to nurture relationships with policymakers in this arena. One person commented, "You can't go to governing bodies and whine about not receiving resources when you haven't done anything and don't have a plan for what it is you want to do." Nonetheless, there was general agreement that the library community, in general, had to do a better job of telling policymakers why libraries are an important component in the national networked environment.

INTERNET/NREN IMPACTS ON THE ACADEMIC LIBRARY

Issues included in this category are:

- infrastructure development;
- individual scholars as libraries;
- dependent or self-sufficient users;
- network education and training for library staff;
- barriers for exploiting the network in their organizations;
- need for planning;
- evaluation of networked services;
- identifying electronic networking costs;
- fee-based v. free services;
- staffing for the virtual library; and
- who *is* a librarian?

The development of national electronic networking raises a range of issues regarding how the library, itself, will be affected. Can business continue as usual? The issues discussed in this section suggest that what the library does, how it does it, and how it defines itself as an information collector, manager, and disseminator will need to change quickly in the immediate years ahead.

Infrastructure Development

Information infrastructure is an underlying foundation for organizations and includes a range of components:

- *people* include the information users and producers who direct, prioritize, interpret, and apply data and information to a range of daily decision-making and policy problems;
- *documents, databases, and other information entities* are those items that hold information;
- *information processes* include collection, storage, retrieval, dissemination, communication, and display of information; and
- *technology* is the machinery and the know-how for manipulating and accessing information.

Individuals commented that a number of libraries were "hopelessly out-of-date" with the deployment and use of information technologies. Clearly, it will be difficult for academic libraries to move into the networked environment with non-existent or outdated information infrastructures.

A significant commitment to infrastructure development and strategic planning will be needed to maintain an adequate technological infrastructure and develop new electronic services. This constant development and implementation, and trying to stay up to date (in the context of declining and tight budgets), appeared to combine excitement and stress at the same time. Most participants, however, expressed concern that their library would not be able to obtain the information infrastructure needed, or, if they were fortunate enough to obtain it, could not keep it up to date.

Librarians were also unsure of what, exactly, comprised an "acceptable" or "adequate" infrastructure in the electronic networked environment. Some librarians commented that they did not have individual workstations in their library. Others commented that they had not been able to move into the CD-ROM environment and still limited online database searching due to lack of resources and infrastructure. Librarians are likely to face significant challenges in the future as they try to deploy and maintain information infrastructures for their libraries.

Individual Scholars as Libraries

The network allows individuals to become publishers, distributors, and interlibrary resource lenders without involving the library. Examples of individuals that upload papers and databases on file servers are commonplace now. Individuals may soon mount files on FTP locations (rather than depositing them in libraries) as one way of making their personal "libraries" available to others.

For example, if an author has a paper in electronic format, it can be easily distributed to entire computer discussion lists without going through the library. Or, other members on the network can request copies of a paper directly from an author without involving the library—a new model of interlibrary loan! In addition, massive storage devices allow individuals to collect and maintain their own library—but in an electronic format.

An interesting aspect of this issue is the degree to which faculty want to become individual libraries—making their information available upon request, providing electronic copies of their publications, and developing and organizing personal electronic libraries which they have collected from the network. Some faculty members may wish to have the library manage their electronic information for them rather than become libraries themselves.

One person suggested that improved resource sharing among libraries via the Internet was only a short-term anomaly. Libraries share books and "things" whereas the network allows the sharing of data and information. In the future, sharing of "things" would have less importance and there would be less need for "things." Further, individuals will be more directly (and easily) involved in resource sharing rather than going through libraries. As increased amounts of library-like information was digitized and made available on the networks, there would be less need to go through libraries for resource sharing except for "archival" and historical material. In short, as one person stated, "there will be less and less 'stuff' that libraries will have that people will want."

In considering this point of view, librarians were unsure as to possible effects on the academic library. In the short term, they believed the academic and scholarly community would still need someone to organize material, index it, and otherwise provide access. The idea that individuals could now start acting as if they were "little libraries of their own" gave a number of participants pause. No clear conclusions were reached as to the implications of such a development or how the library might best respond. But in fact, such a development suggests a "replacement" process for individuals performing traditional library functions.

Dependent or Self-Sufficient Users

Some thought that an important challenge for the academic library of the future was to educate users to be self-sufficient in the use of the library—which, one assumes, includes various electronic information services and products. One participant commented: "Good Lord, we don't have the staff or time to be able to help everyone all the time, they [users] must learn how to take care of themselves."

This position is somewhat opposed to the notion where librarians are intermediaries who, with their special knowledge and skills, provide customized services and are the linkage between the information and the user. Indeed, there may be an inherent contradiction between the self-sufficiency strategy and the librarian as intermediary notion. Additional thinking is needed about the contradictory and compatible aspects of these two positions.

Network Education and Training for Library Staff

Although there is general agreement that training and education of librarians as electronic navigators are essential, there was less clarity about how to accomplish this task. When asked what specific strategies were currently being used in their libraries now, one library director responded, "We are giving the staff the wonderful opportunity to learn [the network] on their own." Others agreed, unfortunately, that such was about the best that they had been able to do thus far—although they all agreed formal programs were needed.

Indeed, the discussants believed that they not only need to train and educate their own staff, they needed to educate their users as well. One participant commented: "I guess we will need to educate our staff if we expect them to educate the users [in the use of the network]." The resources and level of effort needed for this effort, however, are significant and there was little evidence that any of the participants had thought about a long-range strategy (and budget) to do it.

Education for library staff in how to use the Internet to provide a range of services was only one side of the issue, however. A number of individuals were quite concerned that there was inadequate knowledge in the library about technical aspects of setting up local area networks, maintaining routers and servers, integrating a range of systems, and so forth. To what degree would librarians in the future have to become more technologically literate? A number of individuals were concerned that the profession, as a whole, could not face the challenge of garnering adequate technical literacy and networking proficiency in a short period of time.

Barriers for Exploiting the Network in Their Organizations

Participants identified a number of barriers that would limit the effectiveness with which they could access and use the network in their organizations:

- user attitudes and resistance (one participant said that attitudes would not change until some of the faculty retired and quit influencing students);
- lack of technical knowledge within the library and on campus;
- physical access (connectivity) to the network;
- training;
- knowledge of what is on the network and how to access it;
- degree to which library staff are "ready" for using the network;
- resource allocations made within the institution— administrators may not value the need for networked environment; and
- the sense that at some point in the future networked information resources will be much more expensive than they are now.

There was the sense that no formal library or institutional strategic planning exists to deal with these barriers, to develop specific objectives for flourishing in the networked environment, or developing a time schedule of activities that needed to occur over time for the library to be a "player" in the networked environment. Participants found it easier to identify barriers than to think strategically about what to do about minimizing the impact of the barriers.

Need for Planning

The librarians discussed the importance of strategic planning in a number of settings. Libraries need a plan, a vision, a perspective that will garner them resources. What exactly that plan or vision might be was not articulated by the participants. There was agreement, however, that planning how the library might evolve would be essential—less for the provision of information services, and as a mechanism for obtaining resources. Some thought that strategic planning was likely to have greater impact on developing effective services as opposed to securing better funding.

In the context of planning, some individuals raised the issue of the "library community" being perceived as isolated on campus and in the broader information community when trying to develop policy initiatives, etc. Librarians thought it would be extremely important for the library community to not be isolated, to identify key stakeholders and develop strategic alliances with these stakeholders. For example, strategic alliances between the library community and the mid-level regionals may be beneficial to both groups. More thinking about how to develop and nurture such strategic alliances is needed.

In discussing the nature of a strategic plan, participants identified these key components:

- vision statement;
- environmental scan;
- long-range goals, annual objectives;
- administrative/organizational structure (including the definition of roles and responsibilities among key stakeholder groups);
- identification of users and their information needs;
- information resources and services to be made available;
- hardware and software architecture;
- education and training programs;
- research and development programs;
- budget; and
- anticipated benefits for and impacts on stakeholders.

Part of the strategic plan, however, included scenario development and visioning a future electronic library.

A scenario is the process by which policymakers consider future conditions or states for the organization. A scenario includes a detailed description of these possible evolutions of the institution over the next three to five years. A key concern in scenario development is comparing and assessing a range of possibilities as a basis for the institution's vision to ensure the well-being of the organization.

A vision statement is a description of a possible future state or set of activities and services for the institution. Vision statement development requires institutions to make explicit their assumptions about the future and to envision a future state of the organization in light of these assumptions and in light of possible organizational goals and resources.

In the strategic planning process, vision statement development is a precursor to setting mission, goals, objectives, program development, and evaluation. Vision statements encourage planning participants to think in terms of new opportunities for the institution, and to define possible states of being that do not now currently exist. One person commented that existing strategic planning models were inadequate because they failed to link services planning, technology planning, and scenario development and visioning. There was some concern that new and innovative planning models suitable for a dynamic and ever-changing networked environment were not being developed.

Evaluation of Networked Services

Participants generally agreed that to date, no one (institutional administrators) had come to them and asked for an accounting or justification of the resources that had been used thus far on networking. Moreover, a number of the participants did not see it as their responsibility to provide information that demonstrated the effectiveness, efficiency, or impact of networked information services on traditional areas of teaching, research, and service. Indeed, one person commented that it more properly was the responsibility of the faculty and students to provide such data. They did think that at some point in the future they would need to provide such data, but it was not an issue now.

Some were unsure that even in the future, they might be asked to show data demonstrating the efficiency, effectiveness, or impact of the networked campus. There was the sense that this was becoming a "typical" library area of activity and that budget battles were fought for the library overall and less for particular services or operations.

This discussion of the relative lack of importance (currently) for ongoing evaluation and assessment of the library's role in the networked environment continues the existing attitudes and mentalities about evaluation for traditional library services and operations. One participant indicated that "selling sizzle" might be more effective and important than having data indicating overall effectiveness and impact, although, he also agreed that it would be nice to have such data.

Another comment was that such data may not assist them in obtaining extra resource allocations given the tight nature of campus budgets. The decision to spend money on networked services would largely be an internal, library-based one. Such reallocation decisions would be based on competing needs and demands within the library and less on institutional needs and demands.

The issue of evaluating the success of the networked information environment on campus did not receive much attention. One had the sense that the current priority was to stay up with the technology developments, worry about impacts on access and user services later, and then, if time allows, consider a process to assess the impact and changes that the networked environment has had on the library, the users, or the institution overall. Overall, there was little consideration of the issue: How will we know how well we have implemented the academic networked campus?

The discussion on evaluation demonstrates some of the problems that the academic library community may face in the future in terms of being a player in the networked campus. The key battles for resources need to be fought at the institutional level—not within the library budget. The lack of evidence that the library has made a difference in teaching, research, and service with its "networked services" will not assist the library to fight the institutional budget battles successfully. While anecdotal information may be useful and serve a useful role, longitudinal data, tracking the use, effectiveness, efficiency, and impact of networked services, and focusing on outputs and outcomes rather than inputs, are likely to have much greater credibility at budget time.

Identifying Electronic Networking Costs

Currently, there is little tangible data available that document the direct and indirect costs for supporting participation in the

electronic networked environment by either (1) academic computing, (2) the library, or (3) the academic community as a whole.
Cost categories for "start-up" v. "ongoing" participation are largely
unknown. Except in the sense that network participation would
require additional resources, participants had not analyzed the
types of costs associated with network participation.

Further, it is unclear what costs are associated with what type
or level of involvement, that is, typologies of levels of participation
(in terms of equipment and services) have not been developed. An
argument put forth by some library managers that "the network will
save us money," may not be accurate. Indeed, this issue related to
the one previously discussed. By and large, institutional officials
simply do not know whether the network "saves" the campus
money, if the network improves productivity, or if the academic
community "learns" better because of the presence of a network.

Without a clearer sense of the costs, and models of appropriate services and their corresponding costs, library managers may
find it difficult to estimate future costs, plan for networked services,
or demonstrate accountability for the services currently being provided if asked to do so. But similarly to the issues regarding evaluation, there was little enthusiasm to conduct the research needed to
explore these costs and assess the nature and types of costs for
establishing and operating a digital library.

Fee-based v. Free Services

The issue of fee v. free evolved in the context of the survival of
the library in the long term. There was some agreement among the
participants that two-tiered pricing schemes (different pricing
schemes for different user groups) were inevitable if libraries were
to be effective participants in the networked environment. Some
reached this conclusion that fees are a "necessary evil," and others
thought it was both appropriate and necessary. Indeed, fees might
simply be part of the Darwinian evolution of libraries into the networked environment.

In fact, some saw "market-driven" libraries as not necessarily a
bad thing. Some commented that a key problem with libraries is
that they have not responded to their markets and to their clientele. Market-driven libraries would be more responsive to clientele
information needs. One person, however, voiced concern about
those clientele groups that could not pay for services and access.
Moreover, some disenfranchised groups cannot articulate what

their information needs are. The response of participants was ambivalent, some suggesting that the surviving traditional libraries would "take care of them [the disenfranchised]."

Others noted that libraries were kidding themselves if they did not think there was a market for information services in the networked environment. The example of CARL was offered as a "national library" that, in effect, was competing with the more traditional libraries. The point being that some people are willing *now*, to pay for certain types of "library" services. One person suggested that the fact that libraries were now just considering this issue and its implications in the electronic networked environment was more evidence that many of them simply would not survive the future.

In fact, a number of participants believed that some members of society simply would not be able to cope with the networked environment—just as there would be some libraries that will not be able to cope. One person suggested that neither market-driven libraries nor traditional libraries could solve the problems related to disenfranchised groups in our society.

Staffing for the Virtual Library

Many discussants were concerned about where the library would get the staff they needed to operate in an Internet virtual library context. One person commented that his library has just been flat "lucky" to have obtained someone with a combination of technical, system, and user skills. He described the person's background and the process by which he was "discovered," and it clearly was very idiosyncratic. But others agreed that this had happened to them as well. The options appear to be:

- luck out and find someone with background and skills from some other line of work;
- hire someone away from another unit on campus;
- recruit out of library school;
- train them within the library (and then try to keep them!); and
- look for someone from the private sector.

The participants offered little hope that they would get the people they needed from library schools—except perhaps the electronic navigator reference librarian type. But certainly they would not get someone with the needed technical skills.

One person commented that the staffing problem would get better as time passed. He noted that the Fortune 500 companies do not expect to have one person with skills in multiple areas and have great user/bedside manners as well. His problem, he noted, was that he needed people that knew a lot about a *range* of different technical and service-related issues. In one sense, he knew this was unrealistic, yet because he could not hire two or three additional people, that is what was needed.

Later, the question was raised, "who are the true librarians, anyway?" Defining the librarian in the virtual library context will deserve careful thought—especially if we have been unable to define a librarian in a traditional context. It will be difficult to define the skills necessary for the electronic, virtual librarian until we can define the types of library services and products to be provided. On the other hand, maybe the library does not need to be defined *a priori* and it should just evolve. In such an evolutionary environment, librarians will constantly need to re-educate, and perhaps, reinvent themselves on a regular basis.

An interesting issue that arose was based on the fact that for many librarians the social interaction, the personal contact, was a key reward factor for working in this field. The more the networked environment evolved, and the more clientele relied on remote access to the library or other computer-mediated access to information, the less interpersonal contact there might be. One participant commented: "We would then have to split ourselves, again, to deal with both electronic and traditional information services"; the implication being that we would be forced to cover more service territory and spread ourselves more thinly yet! This raises the issue of the difficulty of retaining "traditional" librarians and/or re-educating those traditional librarians to work in a more electronic mode with *less* direct interpersonal interaction with patrons.

Who Is a Librarian?

There was some insecurity about how the networked environment might affect users' perceptions of who is a "librarian" and who should be asked for assistance. In response to an example describing the Cleveland Freenet where community members could obtain assistance from, for example, a garage mechanic about car repairs or a local gardener about growing plants, it was pointed out that users do not really care who gets them the information, just that they get the needed information. But another asked: "Doesn't an information professional do more than just provide information?"

One person largely discounted the possibility that librarians would be replaced because of quality of information issues (i.e., librarians were concerned about the quality of the information they provided, whereas non-librarian information providers may not be so concerned). Another participant responded that quality was not the key issue here, rather it was ease of access (e.g., Mooer's law: in acquiring information, the law of least effort is the single most important factor in determining the selection of an information source). One participant commented: "The paradox is that if you want to use libraries successfully, you must make a real effort to get the information you need."

In fact, in the future, it may become much easier (and with less effort) to obtain information over the network from whoever might be available—regardless of whether the person is a librarian. This concern returns to an earlier issue about librarians pointing to information rather than actually delivering the information. Some participants strongly believed that librarians better start moving toward information delivery rather than information pointing.

RECONSIDERING ACADEMIC LIBRARY SERVICES

Issues related to this category are:

- knowledge management;
- managing electronic journals;
- providing access to remote information resources;
- instructional support to faculty;
- network instruction;
- support for remote instruction;
- an internet room;
- organizing the network;
- digitizing information;
- using the Internet/local networks to support traditional library services;
- government information; and
- electronic collection development.

Many of the responses from project participants dealt with the evolution of academic library services within the evolving electronic networked environment. Being connected via the Internet/NREN to other libraries, remote and local constituency groups, and to an ever-expanding array of electronic resources significantly changes the existing notions of what constitutes "library services."

When discussing electronic services, the librarians often assumed the need for a demand-based organization that responded to *individual* electronic information needs and offered customized services. Secondly, they assumed the importance of providing users with information delivery rather than bibliographic citations or "pointers" to where the information might be obtained. As the findings and issues discussed in this section suggest, a range of innovative ideas for such services are brewing, but many of them also raise new issues and problems.

Knowledge Management

The notion of knowledge management appeared to be one that many of the participants thought would be appropriate for libraries to develop as a service concept. One participant noted that librarians manage "stuff" or "things," and what most users wanted was management of information resources in a broader context and in light of their information needs. The specifics of what knowledge management is, exactly, are somewhat unclear. However, the participants felt that these activities comprised, or would contribute to knowledge management:

- *Filtering information*: Given the overload of information on the network, there is a very real need for someone to filter, select, and synthesize the information into a context or presentation that meet specific user information needs. The filtering process would require the librarian to have specific knowledge about (1) particular subject areas or disciplines, (2) the needs of the individual being served, (3) making value judgments about what information would "best" meet user information needs, and (4) presenting the information in a format and with a style appropriate for the needs of specific individuals.
- *Locating and reorganizing information*: Many users do not know what information is available in electronic format. Knowledge management would locate the range of information sources related to a specific need, reorganize that information in light of specific objectives, and provide analysis and assessment of

what that information means vis-à-vis the user's information need.

- *Customizing software and developing new applications*:
  Access to and use of electronic information is oftentimes problematic because available software does not
  match user needs or equipment. Software could be
  developed to assist users in making sense out of electronic information in an easier and more user-friendly
  fashion.

- *Translating electronic information resources across different
  formats*: The *logistics* of getting information out of one
  format and into another are time consuming and
  require skills that many users simply do not have. Yet
  there is a very real need to be able to have a range of
  different electronic information services and products
  "talk to each other" or at least, be compatible with
  each other so that the user could get the information
  in the format he/she wanted.

It may be less important as to who does the knowledge management than that someone or something does this for electronic
information. The implication here, is that users may not care
whether the library or someone else does the knowledge management, just that someone (anyone) does it.

An example of knowledge management might be the development of Hytelnet—a hypertext program available on the Internet that
is a directory of Telnet-accessible locations. The software was developed in a library context, put out on the net, and further developed
and customized by the users of the software themselves—thus, the
software is always being improved. The library, however, only serves as
an organizational locus for managing this ongoing development.

Moving the library more into a knowledge management
stance probably would constitute a reconceptualization of the
library which may or may not be accepted by librarians. Again,
there was the concern on the part of some participants that librarians were not ready to be "knowledge managers" and that the role
and responsibilities would fall to others.

Managing Electronic Journals

Libraries can keep digital files of various electronic journals
(e-journals) and provide their users with access to them via a wide

area information server (WAIS). The approach is to archive files of the various e-journals locally and be able to search them through a WAIS server. Increasingly, more journals will be made available in electronic format. Many faculty do not want to subscribe to all the electronic journals, rather, they want the journals "unbundled" and to have access to those articles and features of most interest to them. The library could manage both the collection and dissemination of these electronic journals for the entire campus rather than people having to do so on their own.

Providing Access to Remote Information Resources

Facilitating public access to Internet resources and services will be essential in the academic networked environment. Access to network resources can be accomplished either by bringing the resources to the library or "taking" the users to the resources. The library can mount and index a range of local files either on its own server or through a campus-wide information system (CWIS).

For example there may be locally important files to mount or the library can download files, discussions from lists, or other electronic information, provide an index to these sources and make them available to users. Some libraries may wish to simply have programs embedded within their OPAC that drops users into the Internet. A key issue for the library is integrating the various access systems coherently for ease of use by library patrons.

Instructional Support to Faculty

Academic institutions will need to provide both an information infrastructure and applications/services support to faculty to assist them in a range of activities. One approach is to establish a service such as a networking instructional lab. Such a lab could assist faculty by:

- learning about the range of electronic instructional technologies;
- obtaining assistance in selecting the type of instructional technology that might be most appropriate for specific instructional objectives;
- receiving instruction from lab consultants on how to design and create the instructional technologies needed;

- digitizing instructional material to make them available over the network for remote access; and
- receiving instruction from lab consultants on how to use networked-based tools such as bulletin boards, listservs, file servers, e-mail, and so on, in support of instruction.

The library could establish a server of electronic instructional material that either (1) have been posted on the Internet/NREN, or (2) have been developed locally. Such material could include hypercard stacks, digitzed graphics, complete instructional programs or handouts for specific topics, or other similar material. The instructional material could then be accessed by faculty as needed, downloaded, and modified for specific instructional purposes.

Network Instruction

What might the library do to provide electronic instruction to faculty and students? Terminals used to access library resources will also need to inform patrons of information available on the CWIS and at remote sites. To exploit these information resources, electronic instruction could be made available over the network or maintained locally. Innovative approaches need to be developed for such instruction. These innovations could be individualized to specific learning needs; they could unbundle Internet resources and services to provide instruction on only those of interest to the user; and they might include multimedia approaches.

Support for Remote Instruction

Increasingly, reserve rooms might be electronic as a means of supporting "tele-learners" and students who want to use the library and a range of instructional materials remotely. Such initiatives will need to be carefully coordinated with faculty. But some librarians saw this as an important opportunity for the library to become more centrally involved in the instructional aspects of their university. A broad range of instructional materials to support curriculum could be created, managed, and made available through the library.

An Internet Room

Increasingly, public access terminals to the Internet will be essential components in the academic networked environment.

While such "Internet Rooms" might be located throughout the campus, primary attention could be given to having an Internet Room in the library. The shape of such initiatives is unclear. Some libraries may wish to simply have programs embedded within their OPAC that drop users into the Internet. Indeed, a key issue for the library is integrating the various systems coherently for ease of use by library patrons.

It will be essential that there are trained professional staff available to assist patrons as they use the terminals to access the Internet. Indeed, a range of instructional techniques (hypercard stacks, etc.) could be provided with the Internet terminals. For example, if someone is using the terminal and needs to use a specific network-based application, staff could assist the patron in how best to use the application.

Organizing the Network

Libraries need to work together to develop approaches for having bibliographic control over networked information. The current, volunteer-based approach, simply will not be workable in the future. Schemes might be developed where a consortia of selected libraries are responsible for developing WAIS or gophers for certain types of information. For example, one university might have responsibility for coordinating bibliographic control over and providing gopher access to government information.

Other organizing efforts might include:

- maintaining "white pages" and "yellow pages" directories, both locally and nationally;
- developing information inventory/locator systems of resources on the networks;
- establishing "bibliographic control" over network resources;
- managing bulletin boards or lists, or engaging in electronic publishing; and
- providing "reader's advisor" services to users, directing them to specific sources on the networks.

While some of these might be seen as "traditional" library services, they have yet to be successfully applied to the network environment.

Digitizing Information

Increasingly it will be necessary to digitize much of the existing print-based information. This digitizing process can be done by optical character recognition (OCR) as well as scanners for specific types of print materials such as photographs and 35mm slides. Clearly, there will be issues of copyright and licensing, but it is likely that these will be worked out among authors, publishers, and the libraries. One participant likened the process of digitizing information for the network as the move from Dewey to LC classification: "determine which were the most important items to change [put in a digital format] because the library could not afford to recatalog everything [digitize all the library holdings]."

Using the Internet/Local Networks To Support Traditional Library Services

A number of the librarians thought that it was essential to provide traditional services in the networked environment. They suggested the following types of electronic services:

- submitting reserve lists by faculty in electronic format;
- developing reserve materials that are mounted on servers; and
- participating in electronic class discussions to aid in the assessment of available information resources or in making selected information available to the class;
- providing materials to other libraries electronically;
- managing and making available local and remote software and scientific electronic instrumentation packages;
- selective dissemination of information by distributing tables of contents of selected journals to faculty; faculty review the tables, select those articles that they are especially interested in, and the library either (1) delivers the article in print form, (2) faxes a copy of the article to the faculty, or (3) if available in electronic form through CARL Uncover, etc., provides the faculty person with full text of the desired article;
- providing local, state, and national electronic reference and referral services; and
- maintaining a range of statistics describing services and operations over the network. These statistics

> might be organized and coordinated by a consortia of
> other libraries so that state, regional, or national statis-
> tics could be accessed electronically.

Other individuals in the data-collection activities discounted the
provision of "traditional" services electronically and argued, rather,
for a reconceptualization of what the library did and how it did it. s
One person stated: "We must do things differently, not just do
things electronically."

Government Information

Some of the participants noted that there was a need to get
government information out and available on the Internet. One
librarian commented that her library is loading Tiger data from the
Bureau of the Census. Some disparaging comments about the
efforts of the government to make its data available were made.
Someone else noted that the CD-ROMs issued by the GPO were
nothing better than orphans—since they often had inadequate or
no documentation. The main question to be addressed, one person
suggested, was who exactly provided user support for government
electronic information services and products?
The transition of the Depository Library Program (DLP) into
the networked environment was raised in passing but not much discussion occurred. The sense of the group was that the DLP would
need to develop a range of value-added services and products. How
this would be done was unclear. One good thing about the DLP was
that it did care about the user. But it was also clear from these individuals that they were afraid of being "overwhelmed" with networked government information and being unable to (1) identify
what government agencies were making what information available,
and (2) provide the necessary support within the library to access,
manage, and make available that information to their users.
One individual, with a background in documents librarianship, charged that many of her colleagues in the academic library
really did not "care" about government information and were
unwilling to support the documents department. She indicated that
electronic government information would likely be a "growth area"
and that libraries had better learn how to identify, manage, and disseminate government information. After all, she said, "if we are
unable to do this, who will provide the citizenry with access to government information?" No one responded to her question, and the
group moved on to other topics.

Electronic Collection Development

The moderator raised the process of collection development of electronic resources as a means of determining how traditional library activities might be changing. The participants initially stated that you just go about collection development of electronic resources as you would traditional resources. One person, however, suggested that there were implications for electronic collection development that made it different than traditional aspects of collection development:

- To what budget line would such an item be charged?
- What electronic format should the item be purchased in?
- Are there licensing considerations that must be resolved to provide access to the item?
- What kind of technical support would be needed for the item?
- What kind of public service support would be needed for the item? Would we need additional staff or staff training?
- How would the electronic information be archived and maintained?
- How many people would it support, or how many users could use it?

After she had raised these issues, the sense of the group was that she probably was right and that traditional service activities might change in an electronic context.

Some additional thought and analysis needs to be given to identifying a range of library services/activities to be provided in the networked environment and exploring how those services might change or evolve in an electronic context; what the implications of such changes would be in terms of organizing the library; and if such changes would constitute a "reconceptualization of the library."

TRANSITIONING TO THE FUTURE

Issues included in this category are:

- reconceptualize the library;
- moving to the virtual, digital library;

- survival of libraries in the networked environment; and
- need for further research.

The findings and issues discussed in the previous sections are linked by a number of common themes. These themes suggest a rapidly changing and dynamic context in which academic libraries must evolve if they are to continue to be key players in the provision of campus information services.

Reconceptualize the Library

One person commented that the library needed to be reconceptualized as a server for many sources of information. This notion of the library as server conjured up an image—supported by some of the other participants—for a "reconceptualized library." It would be useful to explore that image in greater detail—aspects of a server and how that would relate/expand the academic library. One envisions being able to "click-on" a host of icons of library resources and information opportunities, be connected directly (to real people, information, videos, multimedia, etc.), obtain the information and/or service needed, and do it all remotely.

Participants thought that the notion of a CWIS to be a transparent link to the Internet so that users could go anywhere and use a range of sources and tools was an especially good idea—linking to CARL, Freenets, electronic journals, and commercial providers. The library would determine what it was that the users needed and provide them with access to those sources since "the library could not provide access to everything." A two-tiered approach was needed: the library takes care of the masses in an expanded CWIS strategy and the Internet junkies could take care of themselves! When asked why such an approach was not already in place, one person responded, "we're working on it."

Some thought that new models, especially new visions, would be needed for the library. Some aspects of those visions would be:

- moving from reactive to proactive;
- from "just-in-case" "just-in-time" collections;
- disengaging services from the technologies (i.e., making certain that the same service could be provided on a range of technological platforms);
- promoting user self-sufficiency;

- integrating and coordinating electronic information regardless of format;
- engaging in knowledge management;
- unbundling electronic information to meet specific user information needs;
- moving from ownership orientation to access perspective; and
- thinking in terms of "value-added" services rather than providing only the current "basic services."

But, one person commented: "Don't dump the existing library anytime soon." What will occur is an evolutionary development of incorporating electronic resources and services over time.

In reconceptualizing the library, one person mentioned that we want to be careful *not* to automate the buggy whip. The implication here is an important one. Some aspects of the traditional library simply should not be reworked for life in an electronic context. The key question is how to determine which of the existing library information services are buggy whips?

Some raised the issue of "librarian bashing" and the inability of librarians to make changes to be effective in the networked environment. The degree to which librarians perform certain activities and have certain responsibilities is linked to library missions and responsibilities. Some libraries had innovative missions and activities and thus, were more likely to have innovative librarians. The concept of a library, as we know it now, could be a strong inhibitor to reconceptualizing the library for the future networked environment.

One participant noted that currently, the library is a collection of materials and services waiting to be used. The evolving model might be more of a demand-based approach where the library can take more of a customized stance in meeting individual information needs. The example given was one where the library could respond to a particular information need and provide unique services, say, by combining or editing a range of information from the network for an individual.

A second notion of this new model is a move toward *delivery* of information rather than pointing to where the information might reside. The networked environment encourages users to expect information delivery, and the library must be able to compete in this environment. Moreover, delivery will be much more feasible given remote access and users being able (and expecting) remote interaction with information providers.

The implications from such a model are significant. One participant commented that "core collections," except, perhaps for undergraduates, may become a thing of the past since unique and customized "collections" can be developed electronically. This perspective reinforces the "just-in-time" collections notion and recognizes
the ease with which customized collections can be developed electronically.

While there was agreement on the need to reconceptualize
the library, the participants found it very difficult to articulate what
reconceptualization meant, factors that might be used to proceed
with reconceptualization, or models to help think this out.

Moving to the Virtual, Digital Library

The virtual electronic library is a vision of a full-service, one-
stop information supermarket. Transparent to the user, the virtual
library is a collection of libraries, information services, and
resources that are scattered around the country and the world. An
"intelligent front end" is accessed electronically by users which then
directs and connects them to the information services or resources
needed—regardless of where those services and resources might
reside. These resources might be digitized traditional print materials, interactive videos, multimedia, software, specialized databases,
and even other human beings!

The term "virtual" is used because the library is everywhere,
yet nowhere. It has every type of information resources and services
imaginable, but they are all located in different locations and
remote from the user. The virtual library is a growing, changing set
of information resources and services that are beyond the control
of a single central planning unit; it is logically coherent, but physically disparate.

One cannot, however, simply overlay the new electronic information services, products, and responsibilities on the traditional
library structure. One person commented that in many cases it simply may be a matter of "religious" conversion. That is, the librarian
simply has to believe that there is a need to reconceptualize the
library and then do something. If the perception is that there is no
need to reconceptualize the library, then it cannot be done no
matter what.

An example of an area where overlay simply would not work
was electronic collection development. Are library school graduates
or seasoned practitioners prepared to do electronic information

resources collection development? How might that be done? What are the principles and practices for collection development of electronic information resources? There was some sense that reconceptualizing the notion of traditional services for the electronic environment would be needed but simply taking what we know about them and "digitizing" them would not work in this new setting.

In terms of moving to a reconceptualized digital library, one participant noted that a couple of key disciplines must be examined to see how, exactly, they are conducting research and carrying on scholarly communication within the networked context. He believed that generally this process includes little contact with libraries. Nonetheless, such a study could shed light on how the library might change if it is to be an active participant in a networked environment.

What occurred in some discussions about the development of electronic services was development of *technical* infrastructures. Technical infrastructure development is *not* the same as access and services development within an electronic library. There seems to be an imbalance between the attention being given to "wiring" the library for the electronic environment and developing a useful approach for designing access and services *within* this environment. The assumption appears to be that the services and access will evolve as the infrastructure is developed—"first, get the infrastructure in place." This may be a very dangerous assumption.

No sense of urgency was expressed about moving to the virtual library, the networked environment, or to Internet services on campus. Movement would occur as appropriate; there was no sense that others (CARL, OCLC, Freenets, etc.) were going to "steal" library users or that the library was in a competitive posture vis-à-vis these other providers. While this sense is a traditional library view of information provision (i.e., the library has no competitors, but rather a captive market), one wonders if another key aspect of the reconceptualized academic library is a competitive posture—both within the institution and externally with other information providers. Such a posture may be necessary for the academic library to survive and flourish in the future.

Survival of Libraries in the Networked Environment

One must be careful in generalizing about how well academic libraries will or will not survive in the electronic networked environment. Some libraries will survive and flourish, and others may not. An important consideration is determining what factors are important predictors for library survival. Models for survival may depend on:

- the attitudes, skills, and resources of the library;
- the nature of the clientele served by the library and their information needs;
- the degree to which the library can provide electronic services of interest and need to its clientele;
- the institutional setting, organization, and cultural climates within the university; and
- the geographic setting of the library (which affects the nature of the clientele).

There was some agreement that the notion of different libraries positioning themselves for selected service niches would be critical. An appropriate approach might be for libraries to identify clientele and service niches and position themselves accordingly. One librarian pointed out, however, that such a perspective "flew in the face of providing services for everyone."

The notion of positioning, however, in this context requires additional clarification. Models need to be developed of typologies and factors that might predict greater or lesser success in the networked environment given particular institutional settings.

There was a split opinion as to whether it was "too late" for the library to make the appropriate changes to flourish in the electronic networked environment. Again, the sense was that it is very difficult to generalize. One participant noted that in the last two years significant "improvements" on the part of librarians had been noted in terms of their comfort level with the networks, coping with the costs, and better capability in dealing with the communication technology. Another disagreed and noted that the librarians he knew were best described as "anal-retentive" and were unlikely to make any changes to accommodate the networked environment.

Generalization about how libraries might evolve over the next five to ten years would be extremely difficult. There was, however, a sense that a "Darwinian" perspective might hold true. Some consternation arose over this idea of "the fittest would survive." This scenario works well with the niche perspective discussed earlier. Libraries that could identify a niche service and were proactive, gathered resources, and such, would survive in a Darwinian view of the world.

But what about those libraries that did not know enough to know what they needed to ask? Some participants noted places that even after being exposed to the issues and provided information about the network, they still thought moving to the networked environment was not necessary in "their" setting. Didn't the government, or society, have a responsibility to help them? Some missionary zeal evidenced itself as one participant said that "if they do not know what they need to do, then we need to tell them!" Much discussion on this point occurred. Some scenarios on the issue of evolution were:

- *Library reconceptualization:* Libraries have a revolutionary change of roles and responsibilities and get into "value-added electronic information services," which at the moment, we are not quite sure what these are.
- *Library Darwinism:* The fittest libraries would survive and would carve out a niche in which they would provide key and important "library" services.
- *Incremental change and development:* There was some sense that libraries cannot afford to be on the "bleeding edge" of development, and incremental (just behind the curve) was the best libraries could do; however, some thought that incremental change would be too little too late.
- *No change:* In this scenario, libraries continued doing pretty much what it is they do and either (1) they died because of local or national competition, or (2) they continued providing traditional services to traditional clientele groups—but only a small number of libraries would be needed in the latter case.

There was some sense, however, that libraries had yet to "seize the high ground" in identifying and providing new and innovative electronic services and preferred to "moan and groan about the situation."

One person commented that maybe it was unrealistic to expect libraries to evolve into something that they could not become. There are too many historical traditions and myopic attitudes. Further, there could be a need for libraries as we know them today in the future (although fewer of them). There might always be a need for some place to provide "basic academic reference resources," or reserve room readings, for example. New "entities" might evolve that were neither libraries, networks, brokers, and so on. What that might be is, at this time, unclear.

Some librarians were avid about the need to rethink how we are going to define the library community in the networked environment. Currently, the library community is defined primarily in terms of a geographic setting, and within that setting by other qualifiers. The geographic typology allows us to provide certain types of services that are especially useful for meeting some information needs (e.g., the Cleveland Freenet). Community-based information in this context is what contributes to much of the Freenet's success.

But other approaches are available for defining (and targeting) communities. For example, local and distant remote users might be defined by disciplines, occupations, information needs, nations, or other criteria. The electronic networked environment allows the library to redefine significantly its "community" outside of locally geographic boundaries. How will the library do this? Or will the library care about targeting communities outside its immediate local geographic setting? Once again we need to develop models and typologies to explore how to define the notion of electronic "communities."

There was some agreement, however, about the critical success factors that would be needed for the library to move successfully into the networked environment:

- educated faculty, students, administrators, librarians, and network managers;
- administrative support (moral and financial);
- coordinated responsibilities and roles among institutional computing services, libraries, academic departments, and networks;
- ongoing research and development efforts;
- dedicated proponents and spokespersons for campuswide networking initiatives;
- up-to-date technological infrastructure;
- effective partnerships within the institution and with stakeholders outside the institution;
- user-based system design, development, and implementation; and
- a comprehensive strategic plan.

Ensuring that these critical success factors are in place will provide a number of challenges for most academic libraries.

Need for Further Research

In light of the broad range of topics covered, participants described what research might be needed to better understand the role of libraries in a networked environment. One person commented that higher education was just now getting up to speed in this area and really had not had time to think about what key types of research would be needed. The following were proposed directly or indirectly:

- Strengthening/defining the regionals networks. What constitutes a healthy and effective mid-level network? What criteria could be used to determine overall "health" of a regional? What types of services and activities should be strengthened in a regional context?

- What are teachers, professors, users of specific types actually doing with the network now? What tasks are they doing on the network to solve what types of problems?

- How do researchers conduct research and scholarly communication with the network? What tasks do they use the network for and to what degree does network use improve or limit their effectiveness? Given these patterns of use, what services and products might libraries develop to assist electronic researchers?

- How might libraries amortize the costs of network services development? For example, it was pointed out that every high school in the nation teaches American history. What specific learning modules and Internet-based services could be provided that would have the greatest impact and usefulness for all these potential users? This model could be transferred to other settings as well.

- What might be some basic, intermediate, and advanced instructional modules that might be used for the library for staff, students, faculty, and administrators to understand how to access and use the Internet/NREN?

- What are the staff skills that will be needed by librarians to operate the virtual library, and how will librarians (current and entering) obtain those skills?

- What new service and organizational models might be envisioned as a means of developing the virtual library? What are the strengths and weaknesses of these models. How might the more promising ones be implemented?

- What indicators and performance measures are appropriate to determine the success of the library in the networked environment? What data would be needed to justify to university administrators the importance of the library in this new environment?

This list is not intended to be comprehensive—only illustrative of the concerns for additional research to be conducted related to the role of the academic library in the networked environment.

Overall, there was some sense that diversity of experimentation was needed, but unfortunately, there were few resources available to support such research. One possible approach would be for ARL or CNI to organize research efforts. Another approach would be for a consortium of academic and research libraries to identify an agenda of key research topics of wide general interest. Members of the consortium could pay an annual membership fee that would go to support research on those topics seen as most important. Another approach is that the Federal government should support pilot projects and research and development efforts related to establishing virtual libraries. Regardless of the approach, a range of research initiatives will be needed to help the academic library successfully transition into the networked environment.

ADDRESSING THE CHALLENGE

It is interesting to compare the discussion of the issues raised in the focus group sessions to those identified and ranked from a survey distributed to academic librarians. Appendix A describes the method for developing, distributing, and collecting data from the survey. The appendix also includes a copy of the actual survey used. Briefly, however, a selection of academic librarians were asked to assess nineteen key issues related to the role of libraries in the Internet/NREN. The survey resulted in 153 useable responses which are summarized in Table 3-1.

The issues are listed in rank order from those assessed as most to least important. There was near concensus (95% agreement) among the academic librarians that networks will enhance access to information and provide new opportunities for libraries. This will, however, demand new skills for library staff. The survey respondents also reflected a strong sentiment that libraries should be a point of access to network resources (91% agreement), but there was less certainty about what information the library might contribute to the network.

TABLE 3-1. Academic Librarians' Rankings of Networking Issues (N=153)

STATEMENT	AGREE		DISAGREE		NEUTRAL	
	RANK	N (%)	RANK	N (%)	RANK	N (%)
NREN will enhance access to information	1	146 (95)	18.5	0 (0)	17.5	7 (5)
NREN will provide new opportunities for libraries	2	144 (95)	18.5	0 (0)	15.5	8 (5)
NREN will require new skills for library staff	3	143 (95)	17	1 (1)	17.5	7(4)
NREN connection should be available for all libraries	4	139 (91)	13	5 (3)	15.5	8 (5)
Users have limited knowledge of what's available on networks	5	136 (89)	12	6 (4)	14	10 (7)
Libraries should provide access to NREN resources	6	135 (91)	16	2 (1)	12	12 (8)
Libranans should organize NREN resources	7	131 (86)	14.5	4 (3)	11	17 (11)
Libraries will contribute info. resources to NREN	8	121 (80)	14.5	4 (3)	8.5	26 (17)
Libranans should provide network training to patrons	9	116 (76)	11	12 (8)	10	24 (16)
Librarians have limited knowledge of what's available on networks	10	113 (75)	9	33 (22)	19	4 (3)
Technical barriers limit effective use of networks	11	103 (68)	10	23 (15)	8.5	26 (17)
Libraries will require substantial increases in resources	12	78 (51)	8	41 (27)	5.5	33 (22)
NREN will primarily be used by patrons without librarian assistance	13	71 (47)	7	45 (30)	4	35 (23)
NREN will primarily be used by librarians to assist patrons	14.5	31 (27)	3	87 (58)	7	32 (21)
In-person services offered by librarians will not be necessary for patrons using NREN	14.5	31 (21)	4	84 (57)	5.5	33 (22)
Few info. resources are available on networks to make their use worthwhile	16	22 (14)	1	117 (77)	13	13 (9)
NREN info. resources not different than other library resources	17	21 (14)	2	90 (60)	3	40 (26)
Libraries will be bypassed by NREN	18	19 (13)	5	79 (53)	2	52 (34)
NREN resources will be too expensive for most libraries	19	14 (9)	6	58 (38)	1	80(53)

The survey respondents also expressed uncertainty about the role of librarians, and for that matter libraries, in the evolving networked environment. Only 21 percent thought that NREN will require librarians as intermediaries, and 58 percent responded neutrally. There was a similar response to the need for in-person services for people using the Internet/NREN.

Finally, approximately 66 percent of the respondents were either neutral or agreed that libraries will be by-passed by the Internet/NREN. Such uncertainty about the future roles of libraries and librarians will have to addressed, and the roles and services of libraries in the networked environment will need to be developed and clarified if the academic library is to inhabit a central place in the emerging electronic networked environment.

To a large degree, the responses to the survey (shown in Table 3-1) mirror the concerns and discussions from the focus group sessions. Moreover, it is interesting to compare the responses from the academic librarians to responses from public librarians regarding these issues. In chapter 4, the public librarian assessment of these issues is presented. Public librarians, for example, agreed with the statement "librarians have limited knowledge of what's available on networks" much more frequently than academic librarians.

Both the survey and focus group sessions with academic librarians demonstrated their overall belief in the benefits of the library moving into the virtual, electronic, networked environment. These included:

- increased access to a broader range of instructional support resources;
- better able to leverage local and remote information resources for instruction, research, and service;
- competitive advantage over other institutions in terms of recruiting top quality faculty, students, and staff;
- increased research productivity;
- increased instructional effectiveness;
- better educated students to cope with the coming electronic environment (both personally and professionally); and
- efficiencies in the administration of institutional resources.

While many of the possible benefits can be hypothesized, it is still unclear how the academic library will move from its current traditional base to a reconceptualized one to support activities in the electronic environment.

But the discussions also suggested that faculty and students increasingly are relying on networked information resources and services; some of which shortcut, replace, or extend traditional library services and products. There are a range of potential services and products that the library might provide to researchers in an electronic networked environment. But, it is unclear whether some libraries will have the vision and resources to provide these services and products.

Equally unclear are the claims of significant increases in productivity, enhanced national competitiveness, and that "everyone" can be a better scientist, researcher, student, or educator as a result of being "networked." Such claims will need longitudinal research with well-developed and defined performance measures if they are to be supported.

Moveover, aspects of a virtual electronic library are still evolving. Researchers increasingly rely on remote information resources from a range of different settings. But, much research is yet to be done on a broad range of topics and issues related to what the virtual library is and how it will affect academic libraries. Clearly, however, existing academic libraries will have to make significant and non-trivial changes to be successful in the electronic networked environment.

Many of the librarians believed that the technical problems and issues associated with the design and operation of the academic networked environment may be easier to resolve than the organizational, social, and behavioral issues. Moreover, academic institutions must rethink their roles, services, and their responsibilities in a networked information environment. The manner in which academic libraries respond to this evolving environment might make libraries either obsolete or absolutely essential in the provision of information services.

The academic community as a whole, as well as individual libraries and computing services, must develop new visions; define new roles and responsibilities; affect national, state, and local policy making; and implement successfully a strategic plan to become active participants in the electronic networked information environment.

Academic units involved in the provision of information resources and services *must* better coordinate and plan for the development and provision of information services. Academic facilities will require a significant "face-lift" and a carefully leveraged modern information infrastructure deployment to take advantage of networked information resources.

Academic administrators and library directors must provide leadership in recognizing the importance of the evolving networked environment, retooling the faculty and library staff to take advantage of this environment, and providing incentives and rewards for those individuals and units that innovate and exploit the networked resources for improved research, instruction, and service. With these perspectives in mind, the academic library could move into cyberspace and be instrumental participants in the networked environment.

Many of the issues and concerns affecting academic libraries, as discussed in these first three chapters, are similar to those affecting other types of libraries. Thus, it may be important for the academic library community to work together with other types of libraries to resolve a number of issues that they all will have to confront (e.g., copyright, connectivity, privacy, costing networked services, etc.). The following chapters discuss these issues in other types of library situations and suggest that indeed, many of the issues related to moving into the networked environment cut equally across the various types of libraries.

4

Public Libraries and the Internet/NREN: New Challenges, New Opportunities

At the recent White House Conference on Library and Information Services (WHCLIS), futurist Clement Bezold offered possible scenarios for the future of the public library: libraries fade away, libraries in cyberspace, and post-industrial libraries in the search for a more just society (Bezold, 1991). While clearly there are other possible scenarios, the question of how public libraries will evolve in the electronic networked environment remains a largely unaddressed and unanswered question. In the age of electronic communications, will the public library survive? Or will it be killed by technology? With fiber optic networks that can deliver library materials directly to the user from computerized data banks, is there any need for the library function? (Wicklein, 1983, p. 2)

These questions have been considered for some time, but have gained in importance as Wicklein's predicted future becomes reality for today's public library. How will the opportunities and challenges posed by newly emerging networked information resources and services be integrated into the traditional areas of public library activity? How should public librarians use the developing electronic networks to assist public libraries in this new environment?

Simply stated, the problem is that public libraries are likely to be the most neglected by national electronic network planners. Yet public libraries have the potential to generate some of the most innovative educational uses of the network for the widest range of individuals (Isenstein, 1992). Public libraries, however, may have difficulty adapting to the new electronic networks. Early planning and needs assessment can increase the integration of networked resources and services into public library practice.

This chapter provides findings from the aspect of the overall research study as it pertains to public libraries. (See Appendix A for a complete description of the research methodology.) The focus of this part of the research was on an exploration of key issues and possible roles for the public library in the evolving networked environment. Overall, the study suggests that:

- There is much work to be done in increasing the awareness in the public library community about the importance and significance of national electronic networking and the development of the National Research and Education Network (NREN).
- Network planners, policy-makers, and public libraries have yet to understand fully, form opinions, or influence public policy on a range of issues affecting the public library's involvement in the networked environment.
- Specific roles, services, and activities for the public library in the networked environment have yet to be identified.
- There are a range of opportunities for public libraries to lead and develop creative and innovative information services over the evolving national high-speed networks.

If the public library community is to thrive and prosper in a national electronic networked environment, many issues remain to be addressed and resolved. This study is a first step in identifying those issues and suggesting possible recommendations for dealing with them. It encourages the public library community to take action, now!

As part of the data-collection activities, the study team administered a national survey to public library leaders. (Appendix A gives the details about the survey, the survey instrument, and the demographics of respondents.) The survey instrument's primary purpose was to obtain respondents' assessments of the relative importance of key issues that had been identified from a literature review, two exploratory interviews with expert librarians very knowledgeable about Internet/NREN developments, and focus group sessions. The issue statements concerned both the current networked environment and its use by libraries, and the evolving NREN environment.

Table 4-1 presents the public librarians assessment of nineteen key issues in rank order from most to least important. Appendix A includes a copy of the survey instrument and the complete wording used for the issues in Table 4-1. Overall, the public library leaders surveyed were quite positive that the NREN would provide new opportunities for libraries (ranked 1 in agreement). They believed that it would enhance access to information (ranked 3.5), that libraries should provide access to NREN resources (ranked 7), and that librarians should organize NREN resources (ranked 8.5). They also agreed that librarians currently have limited knowledge of networking (ranked 2) and that NREN will require new skills for library staff (ranked 6).

Table 4-1 also suggests some mixed assessments regarding key issues. For example, 72 percent of the respondents agreed to or

TABLE 4-1. Public Librarians' Rankings of Networking Issues (N=120)

STATEMENT	AGREE		DISAGREE		NEUTRAL	
	RANK	N (%)	RANK	N (%)	RANK	N (%)
NREN will provide new opportunities for libraries	1	110 (94)	18	0 (0)	19	7 (6)
Librarians have limited knowledge of what's available on networks	2	109 (92)	12	4 (3)	18	5 (4)
Users have limited knowledge of what's available on networks	3.5	105 (89)	14	3 (3)	17	10 (8)
NREN will enhance access to information	3.5	105 (89)	18	0 (0)	14.5	13 (11)
NREN connection should be available for all libraries	5	104 (88)	16	2 (2)	16	12 (10)
NREN will require new skills for library staff	6	102 (86)	14	3 (3)	14.5	13 (11)
Libraries should provide access to NREN resources	7	96 (81)	18	0 (0)	12	22 (19)
Librarians should organize NREN resources	8.5	84 (73)	11	6 (5)	11	25 (22)
Libraries will contribute info. resources to NREN	8.5	84 (73)	14	3 (3)	10	30 (25)
Librarians should provide network training to patrons	10	71 (62)	9.5	13 (11)	9	31 (27)
Technical barriers limit effective use of networks	11	68 (58)	9.5	13 (11)	4	36 (31)
Libraries will require substantial increases in resources	12	64 (55)	8	19 (16)	6.5	34 (29)
NREN will be primarily used by librarians to assist patrons	13	63 (54)	7	21 (18)	8	33 (28)
NREN services will be too expensive for most libraries	14	31 (27)	6	33 (28)	1	53 (45)
Libraries will be bypassed by NREN	15	24 (21)	5	48 (41)	3	44 (38)
NREN info. resources not different than other library resources	16	15 (13)	3	67 (57)	5	35 (30)
NREN will primarily be used by patrons without librarian assistance	17	12 (10)	2	70 (60)	6.5	34 (29)
Few info. resources are available on networks to make their use worthwhile	18	6 (5)	4	66 (56)	2	45 (39)
In-person services offered by librarians will not be necessary for patrons using NREN	19	5 (4)	1	90 (79)	13	20 (17)

neutrally assessed the issue, NREN services will be too expensive for most libraries and 59 percent of the respondents agreed to or neutrally assessed the issue that libraries will be by-passed by the NREN. In short, the public librarian assessment of the key issues listed in Table 4-1 suggests a number of underlying concerns and problems that may serve as barriers in the public library community's access to and use of the evolving networked environment.

Some public library leaders, librarians, state libraries, and government officials, however, are moving to address these issues. Indeed, the findings from the site visit at the North Carolina state library suggest some possible solutions to the issues identified in this report. A concerted effort among all the stakeholders will be necessary, however, if the public library community is to respond successfully to the challenges and opportunities of the networked environment.

BACKGROUND

On December 9, 1991, President Bush signed into law the High Performance Computing Act of 1991. In addition to mandating research and development related to high-performance computing, the act authorized the establishment of the NREN and became Public Law 102-194. The process by which the bill was introduced, debated, revised, and reintroduced, was the subject of three tortuous years of hearings and lobbying. But the bill did become law (McClure et al., 1991).

The act will dramatically upgrade and expand the existing information resources and services available on the existing Internet network. Lynch and Preston (1990, pp. 280–281) describe the Internet as follows:

> In effect, then, the Internet includes hundreds of institutional or corporate local area networks (some of which contain thousands of computers), a series of NSF [National Science Foundation] regional networks, the NSF backbone (which is the primary transcontinental traffic path), MILNET [military], and a range of other agency-specific or experimental networks. The Internet provides connectivity among perhaps half a million computers and over a million people, most of them within the research and higher education community. The system is also linked internationally to networks in Europe, Japan, and Australia. Electronic mail can flow between the Internet, BIT-NET [a popular cooperative research and education network], and commercial services such as CompuServe and MCI MAIL,

further increasing the scope of communications available to the Internet user community.

The Internet, in turn, can be viewed as a prototype for the U.S. Federally funded NREN, as established by P.L. 102-194. The legislation calls for:

- establishing a Federal high-performance computing program in which science agencies and national libraries will fund and conduct research, and develop technologies and resources, appropriate for the NREN;
- mandating the creation of the NREN—to link more than 1,000 Federal and industrial laboratories, educational institutions, libraries, and other facilities — over the next five years;
- promoting the development of a number of electronic information resources and services on the NREN, such as directories of users and databases, electronic journals and books, access to computerized research facilities, tools and databases, access to commercial information resources and services, and user support and training;
- providing for improved dissemination of Federal agency data and electronic information; and
- providing users with appropriate access to high-performance computing systems, electronic information resources, other research facilities, and libraries [authors emphasis]. The network shall provide access to the extent practicable, to electronic information resources maintained by libraries [authors emphasis], research facilities, publishers, and affiliated organizations [section 102b].

Then-Senator Albert Gore described the NREN as an information superhighway. Senator Ernest Hollings, a key supporter of the legislation, suggested that the NREN could become the most powerful teaching tool ever built (Hollings, 1990, p. S18114). The Bush administration budgeted $803 million for this initiative for the 1993 fiscal year (Office of Science and Technology Policy, 1992, p. 28).

A new generation of electronic networking is poised to begin. The possible network applications range from electronic mail, listservs, file transfers, remote access to computing, electronic reference services, and uses just beginning to be contemplated by library community. As we move into the next generation of the Internet/NREN, other network uses become not only possible but a competitive necessity. Brett (1992) and LaQuey and Ryer (1993) provide additional background information on the Internet and NREN.

The High Performance Computing Act that establishes the NREN says little about the role of libraries in the evolving network. While there is some mention of libraries, in general, the library community will have to continue to force its way into the planning for the national network (McClure, 1992). Librarians will need to demonstrate roles and services that they can provide to enhance the network and convince policy-makers that libraries will be important, indeed, essential, participants. For more information, see Polly's "Surfing the Internet" (1992) and *Library Perspectives on the NREN* (Parkhurst, 1990).

Historically, public libraries, despite limited funding, have been innovative participants in the development and use of the educational components of electronic networks. Examples include:

- The use of telefacsimile for document delivery and communication (Jensen et al., 1988); videotext and teletext (Appleman, 1984; Pollard, 1983), including OCLC's Project 2000; cable television services (Chepesiuk, 1985); community satellite dishes (Amdursky, 1985); distance learning (Burge et al., 1989); rural library—college links (Vasey, 1989); and improved service to the physically handicapped (Jahoda and Needham, 1980).
- Community databases (Ahtola, 1989), including emergency services (Magrath and Dowlin, Spring 1987), events calendar, government agency directories and access, career services and travel information (Malyshev, 1988; Dowlin, 1984); electronic bulletin boards (Dewey, 1984; Dewey et al., 1985; LaRue, 1986); and electronic mail (Kemper, 1988).

Westin and Finger (1991) found that, increasingly, the public library is recognizing the importance of using new information technologies in information services provision. The Internet/NREN offers a new setting for the development of library services and the provision of network-based information resources, some of which are only now being imagined.

Will the mission of public library service remain the same, such that library resources be equally available to all citizens of the community, and that the collections attempt to represent the widest possible number of viewpoints (Dowlin, 1984, p. 24)? Will the library function remain the same, an institution guided by trained intelligence that serves as an editor and consultant...for the public concerning the information it needs (Wicklein, 1983, p. 7)? Will this function be one that we in the general public must, for the most part, delegate, if we are to make sense out of the vast amount of material available to us (Wicklein, 1983, p. 8)?

Public libraries may find that their role in the community may change significantly as a result of access to the NREN. In previous work on planning, McClure et al., (1987) developed eight service roles from which public libraries might choose to meet community needs: community activities center, community information center, formal education support center, independent learning center, popular materials library, preschooler's door-to-learning, reference library, and research center. New visions, service roles, and approaches to strategic planning will be needed as a result of the evolving Internet/NREN environment.

In serving their communities, public libraries have historically worked in close partnership with government on all levels. How will this relationship change with the advent of electronic networks? A recent study, however, found that key players in the Federal government have given little attention to how the library community could be involved [in the NREN] (McClure et. al., 1990, p. 30).

The 1990 study went on to suggest that the library community, in general, and public libraries, in particular, have no clear sense of their role in the Internet/NREN environment. The proposed Internet/NREN will present great challenges and opportunities for libraries. But, it is unclear how the public library will make use of the Internet/NREN.

SITE VISIT FINDINGS

The site visit's purpose was to identify and describe the evolution and current state of development and use of electronic networks by the state library of North Carolina and the libraries it serves. The site visit provided a detailed description of how these libraries came to their current situation and what they are planning over the next several years, so that other libraries can benefit from their experiences. A description of the site visit methodology is included in Appendix A.

The site was chosen because of its known involvement in network development, its progressive reputation, and the recommendations by participants in earlier phases of the project. The North Carolina Information Network (NCIN) met the study team's criteria of (1) a large-scale networking development effort that included a number of different types of libraries, (2) being recognized as an innovative leader in the application of networking services to public libraries, and (3) indicating an interest in meeting with members of the study team regarding the development of the project.

One objective of the site visit was to learn more about how library leadership got involved, how it influenced the North Carolina library community's vision and initiatives in this area, and how, organizationally, the state library positioned itself to play such a central role. The findings from the site visit, when compared with the results of previous data-gathering efforts, would add credibility to overall study results. The following sections provide a summary of key issues and topics related to the success of the North Carolina approach to developing a state-wide network. Numerous factors, events, people, and opportunities combined to bring the network into reality, and participants at the site visit painted an intriguing picture of how one state is successfully moving from the traditional to an electronic model of library and information services.

The North Carolina state library has a mandate to be an information distribution system and resource center for state government and the people of North Carolina. The state governor's conferences of 1978 and 1991 endorsed the idea of continued network development by the state library. To that end, Governor James Martin announced the formation of the North Carolina Information Network (NCIN) at a press conference on October 2, 1986.

NCIN provides a link between widespread sources of information and local libraries of all types, using the latest telecommunications technologies, with the additional responsibility of providing a variety of information to North Carolina libraries as quickly as possible at the lowest possible cost. As of January 1992, approximately 400 North Carolina libraries were connected to NCIN with more added daily. Library Services and Construction Act, Title I and III, funds financed the network.

Information services available through the NCIN include:

- North Carolina Online Union Catalog (13 million titles), NC Online List of Serials (begun in March 1988; as of November 1991, 40,000 records from twenty-three libraries had been entered), the state library's catalog (using Dynix software on a Prime minicomputer), Audio-Visual Catalog of the State Library, Manuscript and Archives Reference System, interlibrary loan (within the state and via SOLINETs SOLINE to ten southeastern states), and OCLCs EPIC. At present there are eighty-one full or associate OCLC members and 247 selective users.

- Internet and the various University of North Carolina campus-wide information services via UNCs X.25 telecommunications network called LINC NET. Similar connections exist to CCNET a network of the state's fifty-eight community colleges.
- A large and growing range of bulletin boards (at present there are fourteen, updated twice a week) and databases (three at present with seven more slated for September 1992) including: Calendar of Library Events, NCADMIN (state government job vacancies), NCKIDS (for children's and young adult librarians), NCDATA (current statistics from the state data center), LINC-Log Into North Carolina (statistics data accessed with FOCUS software), NCBUS (Automated Purchasing Directory of state government contracts, bids, and business opportunities started in June 1987), NCLSCA (LSCA funding opportunities, regulations and news) and IRSS (Institute for Research in Social Science opinion poll data).
- Electronic mail.
- Extensive training, technical support, OCLC tape loading, document delivery via fax (the state library has supplied at least one fax machine to most libraries), and retrospective conversion assistance (eight clerks are adding 18,000 records per month at of cost of 15 cents per record for public libraries—a popular service, there is a two-year waiting list to join).
- State personnel office job announcements, state administrative codes, state proposed contracts and bids, selected state bills made available on the day they are introduced, list of members of state boards and commissions, and Federal and state census and economic data.

A minimum required software/hardware configuration consists of a DOS-compatible microcomputer, modem (1200 baud minimum), committed voice grade telephone line, printer, and communications and word processor software. No membership fee is charged; users are billed for cost recovery or subsidized by LSCA funding.

Nontraditional Perspective of Libraries and Information Services

State library officials perceived networking in a context of opportunity, competition, and markets. One state library official noted that:

- libraries cannot afford to ignore the competition from other information services providers;
- networking provides an opportunity to serve previously neglected rural communities that are currently underserved or not served at all;
- networked information services are a wise investment of the state's assets; and
- educational applications abound in a networked environment that otherwise would not be available.

Respondents suggested that for libraries to survive, they are going to have to find the right market niche for the kind of information they provide. They will also have to move into new areas and drop certain areas of traditional service, or else atrophy will result. As one person commented: "Peddling books is not going to do it anymore."

The state librarian suggested that the state library's market will include the distribution of government-generated data, service to local governments, and repackaging of a wide range of information on a local level. A sizable population that will want customized services which the large companies will not necessarily be able to provide, and the skills of local libraries will be crucial in providing such services. The state librarian added: "It is not inconceivable that public libraries will become regional outlets for information products of the commercial sector, and that's OK."

There was strong commitment to the centrality of public institutions. State library officials believed that public information institutions like the state library, public libraries, public universities, community colleges, and their libraries should worry about missing a historic opportunity that electronic networks provide. That opportunity is to move some of the third-world counties in the United States into the twenty-first century. The state library can focus its efforts on reducing the gulf between the information rich and poor. If public information institutions do not step in, do not appropriately organize and translate information, today's information have-nots will continue to be unable to compete tomorrow. This finding echoed some of the focus group and survey results.

Migration from INWATS to Internet

For the state library, the end of the toll-free, INWATS telephone service became a test case for how to move a previously popular service from one medium (the telephone) onto another (the network). The lessons that the state library learned included:

- There was a need to provide an array of carrots and sticks which were flexible and tailored to local conditions, yet were fair to all and maximizing limited state resources.
- There should be no charge for either belonging to the network or training. Charges arise when services were used; the intent is to ensure that everyone starts as equals. As a result, the poorest library can belong and be trained before it obtains funding to actually use network services.
- Another key was to charge fees only for tangible services on a pay-as-you-go basis.
- In making the transition, you cannot just dump it on them saying, "good luck, work it out." This two- to three-year transition process allows the state library to work out the bugs, warns the librarians of the change, and builds word-of-mouth support.
- Recognize the need to provide training, and where necessary, equipment to make the new service a viable option for users of the old services.
- Only force the process when encouraging is not enough. As time went on, in the introductory phase, peer pressure also became a powerful motivator to change. Some found that they were the only one in the state or the region who was not connected or using a network service.
- A clear statement of proposed activities, a clear migration path, and a clear cut-off date were critical. "When you say you are going to do something, do it."

These decisions affect not only the present but also
how subsequent pronouncements will be regarded.

The state library has had a history of encouraging libraries to
change, and libraries were prepared to move with the state library
into the new network environment.

The process and critical incidents necessary to connect the
state's libraries were not always smooth. One of the state library
consultants remarked:

One of the things you [the researcher] need to walk away with
is that we forced a number of libraries to get on the net. They
did not all go willingly or immediately see the wisdom of getting connected.

The results of the process, however, seemed worth the risks
because:

- It caused many local libraries to develop a local reference collection and some trained capacity locally to
  answer reference questions.
- It challenged many libraries to confront the issue of
  automating their libraries. Once a microcomputer
  went into the library it was easy to demonstrate reasons for using it.
- Learning about network services (e.g., OCLC)
  sparked local librarians' interest in other network services. Some became converts, some even fanatics.

For the state library, the benefits from moving from the INWATS
to the Internet were immediate. For example, a reduction in
telecommunications costs resulted as programs were moved onto
the state library's server. But most importantly, the state library
developed, initiated, and implemented the process successfully—
and those on the network are beginning to see tangible evidence
of benefits and improvements as a result of participating on the
network.

OCLC Partnership

The decision of the state library to participate in OCLC's
Group Access Plan (GAC) and OCLC's assistance in a massive tape
load of North Carolina, non-OCLC libraries holdings (1 million

plus records), were critical to the success of the network. OCLC provided a:

- brand name known to libraries;
- proven system;
- quality product;
- level of comfort to librarians by allowing libraries that could not afford to be full OCLC members some access to the database;
- inducement to participating libraries to purchase the hardware and software to use OCLC's services as well as obtain a PC, modem, or telephone line, which many libraries did not have;
- credibility with and involvement by the academic library community;
- basis for broadened support among different types of libraries: corporate, health science, and Federal (e.g., National Oceanic and Atmospheric Administration, Environmental Protection Agency, Army Corp of Engineers, and military bases); and
- range of unanticipated partnerships across institutions that might not normally talk with each other (e.g., some libraries with the corporate sector).

The OCLC connection helped the evolving network overcome the initial product resistance. Now, almost every library in the state has a PC, modem, and telephone. Of all the possible OCLC users in the state, only two turned the OCLC GAC idea down. One was going through a corporate buyout. The other was a school system "that didn't grasp why we were trying to do this." Library directors who were once uncomfortable with OCLC involvement of any type are by-passing partial membership and becoming full members.

Future prospects are bright for additional partnerships between the state library and OCLC for new projects. A number of questions and issues remain, however, regarding the involvement and usefulness of SOLINET in the network. It is unclear how the regional bibliographic networks should evolve and the degree to which they are ready, or have a vision, to participate in a national networked environment. The state library felt that there is a role for SOLINET in the 1990s, but it will need to develop new services and products if it is to survive and flourish in the future.

The Network as a Testbed for New Product Development

A key element in the NCIN's success was the state library's efforts to create new partnerships providing innovative information resources available over the network. This involved defining inter-agency agreements to mount agencies' information resources onto the network. Examples of possible information resources already mounted or soon-to-be cooperatively mounted on the network include:

- digital library of the state's history;
- state's administrative code, job line, and purchase, and bidding contracts;
- course offerings from state colleges;
- full text of the state library association's professional journal;
- full text of bills as they are introduced in the General Assembly.

In addition, the state library has cooperative agreements with Nebraska and is exploring agreements with some Canadian provinces and an East European country to provide unique information resources. All these projects are cooperative ventures among people representing institutions that are like-minded, geographically dispersed, and not afraid to make mistakes.

A near-term challenge is to distribute information resources around the state (rather than mount them all on the state library's machine) so that demand can be shared. As users gain skills and knowledge of a particular resource, the library has found that they want additional services.

In developing new information resources and service for the network, several common themes emerged. Each venture has:

- practical, needed outcomes central to users other than libraries;
- support from the participating organization's upper administration;
- demonstrable credibility in the project's concept, particularly when technology is to be applied in a new area;
- demonstrable impact, such as improvements of an operation, quality of life, or improved education opportunities;

- recognition of the importance of users and how the project would be used rather than simply a transmission of facts or information without regard for their use;
- no geographical limit in access or partnerships
- Implementation before other competitors recognize the projects significance—the sense of "getting there first"; and
- partnerships between different agencies and organizations operating in a context of trust, shared credit, and awareness of each other's mission.

These key elements have helped shape the state library's success in the development of the NCIN.

Fostering State Agency Relationships

A cornerstone to the success of the state library and the development of the network has been its relationships with other units of state (and county) government. The state librarian, with the support of his immediate supervisor, the Secretary of Cultural Resources, actively fostered partnerships with other state agencies. The approach suggests that the state library, through the network and its contacts with public libraries, offers a neutral distribution mechanism for government information. Participating libraries are located throughout the state, even in geographically isolated areas.

The approach has met with slow but steadily increasing success. Public librarians, more than the public they represent, have to be sold on this role for their library. Some librarians view their job as "assisting children to read and adults to relax." Other librarians considered the provision of government information for public discussion and business decision making as a new role. On the other hand, providing state government information has been immensely popular with the public, particularly the business community and local governments—both of whom play important funding roles.

State agencies also had to be educated. Since some had minimum knowledge concerning breadth and depth of publicly available government information. There was minimum awareness of how this information could assist an agency in activities such as regulation, monitoring for compliance, and for planning. State agencies have been reluctant to understand their role and stake in disseminating tax-supported information products to the taxpayers.

In tight economic times, with government struggling to prove its worth, information dissemination has assumed new prominence. State agencies have needed to be educated about the important role public libraries play in a community. These libraries' presence in virtually every corner of North Carolina has been an important selling point for the network. The provision of taxpayer-supported, state-produced information is an important growth area for the network in North Carolina.

Key People, Empowered To Make Mistakes as Well as Succeed

A major factor in the success of the network has been the importance of key people, appropriately placed, trusted, and supported. Moreover, such individuals were clearly visible. One state library official noted: "We had to move from being a backup public library to being a high-tech corporate special library." A key was pinpointing people within the organization who had talent. As an example, the present network coordinator has spent twenty-five successful years as a children's librarian. State network leaders especially sought staff with business and non-traditional backgrounds (i.e., with career experience other than librarianship).

The state librarian pointed out that there were many talented people in the state library who had not previously been able to utilize their skills. Once given the opportunity, these librarians demonstrated tremendous business, information, organizational, interpersonal, and community knowledge skills. Especially underutilized were culturally diverse librarians, who have demonstrated incredible talent and skills in developing the network.

A key ingredient has been a certain flexibility rather than a specified set of credentials. The presence of a nurturing environment was essential. Staff acquired many self-taught skills and applied innovative approaches to problem solving in an environment that allowed experimentation, necessary mistakes and learning, and growth. One person commented:

> Librarians are involved in the most volatile industry today, information technology. There are new equipment, software, and management ideas being introduced frequently. Yet, we plan as if managers will never make mistakes and fire those that do. It may very well be that the manager who has made a mistake has learned something invaluable to the organization. We will commit millions of dollars for equipment yet spend next to nothing in funds for experimentation and training in the new information technologies.

The state library has created an environment in which experimentation and learning from mistakes are the dominant organizational culture. The staff did not hesitate to volunteer information to the researcher about their implementation errors. This was done in the hope that somewhere, someone else would avoid the same mistake. Dreaming big and taking risks were an important subtext in every discussion. Often the remarks were tinged with a kind of aftershock felt when people unaccustomed to leadership have seized an opportunity and been successful.

The Federal Relationship

In addressing the Federal role, the Library Services and Construction Act (LSCA) was critical to the success of the network. LSCA funds supported the network development process, according to the state librarian. Moreover, LSCA funds provided the critical seed money to move new information technology out to all corners of the state despite the "antiquated language in the law which has not kept pace with the technology."

On the other hand, there was some concern about Federal agency involvement and participation in the state's plans. State library officials thought that too often involvement of Federal agencies with the states is an attempt to generate revenue and keep the Federal agencies appropriations up rather than meet recognized state needs. In addition, too often Federal involvement means Federally subsidized competitors coming into North Carolina syphoning away possible funding for projects.

The common perspective was that all the materials in the national libraries are information assets paid for by the taxpayers; "we own it." These resources should be made accessible to the public; "give us access to the holdings that are going to help us develop our states." The state library believes that the national libraries need to become more serious about the economic development, education, and community development business than they have been. They need to better think about fees and fee structures, and to realize that charging fees at the Federal level has a ripple effect. In essence, it gives license to all the libraries down the line to tack on fees as well.

North Carolina state library officials recommended the need to involve state agencies and planners early in the process of creating new information service initiatives to ensure that what is developed meets a real need. The overall sense was of a Federal government out of touch. They felt strongly about having to pay again for taxpayer-supported information, particularly when that information was being used by people who cannot afford to pay. The state librarian suggested that the national libraries should begin to look at the state libraries as their local distribution mechanism. In general, better planning, coordination, and cooperation between the Federal agencies and the states are desperately needed to provide improved information services and resources to the public.

Importance of Vision

The need for a vision was a recurring theme. In describing successful network leaders in North Carolina, the network coordinator remarked: "They look not only for their immediate time but for tomorrow." Libraries in North Carolina are no longer (if they ever were) just places for books. Rather than be places of any one thing, libraries of the future will be places for a variety of services, and those services will not be the same at every library. A rural library director noted:

> We are at a crossroads between books and electronic information, and we will probably be here for several years The printed word was a revelation way back when. People today need information, and they need it now. That is where I see networks helping out; getting the information that people need to them faster, even in the hills of rural North Carolina.

The vision of networking in North Carolina is multifaceted and ongoing. Indeed, ideas and vision development seemed to be the order of the day.

One compelling vision of the networked library of the future is the public information authority. A project beginning in North Carolina in September 1992 represents one emerging vision of how the public library might be reconceptualized. The purpose of the authority is to provide information to anyone in the community in order to promote community, economic, and business development. Some of the unique features include:

- the public information authority will be based in the public library;
- an organization structure similar to a transportation authority or water and sewer authority; and
- widespread backing from state government, the state library, the General Assembly, county government,

community colleges and universities, local public
libraries, and the business community.

The authority will provide a set of basic services and will work with
communities and their members to customize the services into
locally useful products. The idea is to build the information and
network services into the local culture. Whatever vision emerges, it
will need to capitalize on existing library strengths and traditions.

There is a conscious attempt underway to sell the network as a
distribution mechanism for state government information both
within government and to its citizens. Two projects about to be
placed on the network include: (1) the State Administrative Code
and (2) a list of memberships on state boards and commissions.
Two projects under development are (1) to put a satellite dish on
every public library, and (2) the development of a wide area information system (WAIS) for state government documents (for information on WAIS, see Kahle, et al., 1992). These initiatives build on
existing projects with the secretary of administration, personnel
department, and the state's data center. Underlying all these efforts
are several assumptions:

- The public library is the best place in the community
  to make this information available.
- Government agencies will see the advantage of making their information available over the network to the
  library community.
- Politicians will not allow the resulting increased public
  scrutiny of government activities to limit network
  efforts.
- The information will be used, and better information
  results in better and more productive citizens.

There is much excitement surrounding the development of the
network in North Carolina. The role of the public library is changing, networked information services and resources are widely accessible, and the innovative and non-traditional activities of the state
library and the public library are successfully meeting a range of
user information needs.

KEY ISSUES AND FINDINGS
The following key issues and findings that affect the development
of public libraries in the networked environment are based on the

literature review, interviews, focus group sessions, survey results, and the site visit. The issues and findings do not constitute a comprehensive list; rather, they summarize the most significant results of the data-collection activities.

General Enthusiasm for National Networking

Public librarians are enthusiastic about national networking as represented in the literature or in speeches they have heard. Nonetheless, they raise concerns about what, specifically, national networking has to offer the public library. For example, one person commented that she never has time to just sit in her office and use any system for any period of time without interruptions; "How would I have the time to do networking on top of all my other job responsibilities?" While the concept of the NREN and remote access to information looks intriguing and may have the potential to change significantly public librarianship, what national electronic networking actually is remains vague to most public librarians.

Awareness

Many of the participants commented on the limited awareness of networking issues that public librarians typically had. They doubted if the vast majority of public librarians knew about the NREN, what it was, how it worked, and the information resources/services that it carried. They thought that public library literature has given inadequate attention to NREN issues. One person commented that she thought it had only to do with research and academe. She did not realize that other applications might be useful for public libraries.

Librarians noted that little discussion of the NREN or national networking topics and issues occurred in their local libraries or library association meetings. They rarely discussed such issues among themselves (although one said they certainly would be now after having participated in a focus group session). Librarians felt that the profession, as a whole, had little awareness of the key issues or topics related to the NREN and national networking.

Risks Associated with NREN Involvement

Some participants mentioned the risk-taking aspect of utilizing unproven new technologies and wondered if the "train had left the station or had it not yet arrived?" As one director described the situation, she wanted to be out front in the use of new technologies, but safe enough that they would not soon change under her leadership. There was general agreement that by themselves public libraries did not have the resources to take on such risks associated with developing the uses and applications of networking. They needed someone else to develop, implement, and test applications *first*. "There is no slack in current public library budgets to try something just because it may be a good idea."

An interesting aspect of this issue was the consensus on the need for public sector entrepreneurial perspectives in the public library. When asked who, exactly, should be taking these risks, they felt that someone in public librarianship should, and probably someone in the public sector because it was unlikely that others in the private or Federal government sectors would assume such a responsibility. There was general agreement that it was a very difficult time to be taking technology risks given the existing economic climate for many public libraries.

Barriers to Network Use

The group of barriers mitigating against the development of networking in public libraries includes: limited knowledge about the Internet, inadequate equipment, and limited staff knowledge in the use of computers and telecommunications; confusing and contradictory information about how to connect to the network; no "systems" people to implement the network in their libraries; and no time to commit to such activities. In addition, some public librarians were unconvinced that there was public library information useful to them via the Internet. They recognized that the network user should have a range of skills and knowledge, especially in commands and systems protocols, which they did not have and were unlikely to get in the near future.

There also was the perception that the organization of information and resources on the network was a mess. This was seen as a serious barrier in their effective use of the Internet: "How can I use the information if I don't know what's out there or can't locate it?" On the other hand, one focus group participant commented in response: "Organizing information on the NREN is our responsibility, we can do this."

A number of responses showed special concern about how public librarians would be re-educated to meet the challenges of operating in the networked environment. All agreed that libraries hosting a network connection had to do a better job of developing continuing education programs, that professional associations had to support such efforts (perhaps with post-MLS certification requirements), and that sabbaticals or other support for public librarians to leave the job situation to be re-educated were needed.

Connecting to the Internet

Although mentioned in the context of a barrier, issues of how exactly one gets connected to the Internet, how that connection is made available throughout the library system, and the costs associated with this connection process were raised repeatedly. Public librarians want a step-by-step listing of what specifically they have to do in order to get connected and use the Internet. They want to know what the connection costs are. They want to know who is best to contact to get the connection. And, they want to know *now!* Such information is not available to most public librarians.

In a number of different conversations with librarians in different parts of the country, the theme of poor technical information and instructions for connecting with the Internet/NREN was consistent. One respondent commented that she had talked to her local bibliographic network, a regional network, a private vendor, and OCLC about how to get connected. In each instance she received conflicting information and wide-ranging estimates of the time, expenses, and level of effort that would be needed to connect to the national network. As shown in the North Carolina example, solving this issue has been an important contribution by the state library.

Access to Networked Information

Some respondents thought that having public access terminals to the network in the public library would be a good idea. By doing so, the library protects those with less resources and network literacy and becomes an electronic safety net to access the Internet. There was general consensus that the public had a right to the network and it would be good for the public library to be an intermediary to provide this access. There were differing opinions, however, about the increasing use of home modems to access either the library or the Internet directly.

One focus group participant, however, immediately recognized that direct access to the NREN without going through the library might be a significant threat to the public library: "If all this information is available directly to patrons and they do not have to come to the library to get it, why will they support the public library?" When additional discussion on this topic occurred, it was clear that a number of librarians, for the first time, began to consider the Internet/NREN as a threat rather than an opportunity for public libraries.

Public Libraries and the Freenets

The Cleveland Freenet began in 1986, and since that time has grown in size and impact. The Cleveland Freenet is the nation's first, completely free, open-access, community computer system. The range of local information resources available via the Freenet is extensive. In addition to local information resources, a broad range of general reference and referral information is also available on this electronic network. The Cleveland Freenet is accessible via the Internet and a number of other communities are now developing Freenets.[1]

Freenets did not evolve from public libraries, yet many of the services and activities provided over Freenets are clearly traditional types of information services except they are delivered electronically over a network. Some participants noted that the development of Freenets is a good example of new forms of competition to the public library. If libraries are not able, or willing, to become involved in community-based networks, other agencies will. In some instances, the local library has been part of the Freenet, in others, this is not the case.

A key issue for the public library community is how can the library be an active player in the development and planning of Freenets and not simply be an observer? Might the Freenet replace traditional library services with electronic delivery of information directly to the home? Or, might the library enhance its services through active involvement and participation in a Freenet? A number of study participants believed that the public library community would be well advised to become involved and knowledgeable about Freenet services and identify strategies to work with Freenetters in developing new and innovative library services.

Public Library Information and Services on the Internet

Public librarians wanted to know exactly what there is on the Internet that might be useful to them *now*. When the investigators listed a number of typical information services and resources currently available, they clearly were unimpressed. The sense was that Internet services and resources needed to be developed and designed specifically for the public library community. They suggested that real down-to-earth information services and products would be necessary if John Q. Public was to use the public library to access the Internet. The kinds of services they suggested were:

- full-text, color children's books on the network;
- practical listservs, such as RECIPES-L, AUTOREPAIR-L, HOMEWORK TIPS-L, or CRAFTS-L;
- community-based information services in health care, community activities, and unique local resources;
- Job-net;
- dissemination and access services linked directly to the responsibilities of local governmental units in the city or county;
- remote access to library reference and referral services
- files such as adult fiction reviews, reference question stumpers, and local genealogical data, etc.;
- support for local schools and specific instructional and curricular activities; and
- making government databases accessible to the public via the Internet rather than having to go through existing vendors (see McClure et al., 1992).

One focus group participant provided the researchers with additional ideas about services and resources for a national public library database (PLD) (Newhard, 1992). The PLD would:

- be tailored to traditional users of public library services but in a new electronic medium;
- contain local library resources presently kept on index cards in shoeboxes on reference librarian desks: sources like indexes to local newspapers, local histories, local travel, and information about local government;
- contribute to establishing a national professional identity for public librarians; and
- provide a vehicle for experimenting with new, innovative, electronic information services.

For many study participants, contemplating a network of this scope was difficult to imagine.

Overall, it was difficult for some librarians to describe specific types of public library services that could be offered using the network. As one person commented: "We are real concrete people, what exactly does this network look like and how can I use it? Until I figure out how I can use it, I can't visualize it."

Role of Professional Associations and State Libraries

One person commented that a national professional association board of directors had recently discussed the role of the public library in the Internet/NREN but not much had come from it. She attributed this to the fact that the network was too vague to understand at this point. A public library branch manager pointed out that the people who knew most about the network were likely to be junior staff and not the library directors or members of the professional association boards. Some librarians were especially knowledgeable about networking, but least likely to be represented at professional associations. Thus, she was concerned that change would occur very slowly since the people with the most power know the least about what needed to be done to exploit the network.

There was wide agreement that if ever there was a time for state libraries to take a leadership stance in the use of the Internet for public libraries, it is now. A majority believed that the locus for coordination of statewide diffusion of public library use of the NREN should be the state libraries and that they need to coordinate that effort with other state and local governmental units. There was also agreement that it is unlikely that a number of the state libraries were up to the challenge given the financial difficulties many states are experiencing.

Committing Resources for Network Access/Use

Participants made it clear that they all had tight budgets and now was a very difficult time to allocate resources to support a new initiative such as access to the NREN. Support was all the more problematic since nobody really knew how much access would cost and what exactly the benefits might be for the library and the community. In fact, the sense was that *until* a better understanding of what the costs were and what benefits would be obtained (for both the library and its patrons), resources would *not* be committed to this initiative. Some librarians suggested that it would be extremely useful to develop models or typologies of possible costs for the public library to get involved in the NREN at a range of levels of effort and services provision.

The North Carolina example, as well as others identified by the researchers, suggests that finances may not be the major stumbling block to establishing access to the NREN. The state librarian likes to remark that the North Carolina Information Network was started by $750 charged to an employee credit card. First, establishing access to networked services requires a reconceptualization of what the public library might become in the electronic environment. Second, funding for public library networked information services is likely to require reallocation of existing resources (from traditional services) to electronic services—since there is little likelihood of obtaining new monies. Third, with careful and creative partnerships the financial burden becomes manageable. Addressing these three concerns is essential for public libraries wishing to move toward involvement in the networked environment.

Getting Involved

The librarians offered a number of specific recommendations for how the public library community could become a player in the access to and provision of networked information services:

- develop a model Internet-connected public library and show others what can be done and what the library can do with Internet-based information services;
- develop arrangements where public libraries with unique resources in one location make those resources available to other libraries via the Internet;
- educate state library and professional association leaders to the key issues and likely solutions regarding public library use of the network;
- initiate a massive program to increase the awareness of public librarians regarding this issue and then start a re-education program nation-wide to increase their networking skills and knowledge; and
- demonstrate to local governing bodies what access to the Internet might do for them locally.

Interestingly, a number of these recommendations have already been implemented in the North Carolina networking efforts.

Overall, the public librarians were very interested in becoming networked and they wanted to be part of the NREN. Moreover, they saw a potential to provide information services to target groups that might not otherwise have access to electronic information. However, they did not know what to do to get started, how to start up the connections, what to do once they got the connections, and how to convince their funding bodies that reallocation of resources to networked activities was worth it.

RECOMMENDATIONS

Identifying key issues is essential to understand the context for taking action. Clearly, a range of actions are needed. Based on these findings and issues, a number of recommendations can be offered to assist the public library community's move into the evolving networked environment. These recommendations include:

- identifying good examples of networking initiatives and projects;
- developing a comprehensive educational program;
- establishing leadership for networking policies and initiatives;
- clarifying connection confusion;
- developing models for network involvement;
- coordinating OCLC, regional, and national network initiatives;
- reconceptualizing provision of information services;
- revising the planning and role-setting manual (McClure, et al., 1987);
- improving access to local, state, and Federal information; and
- conducting additional research.

The following sections provide details of these recommendations.

Identify Good Examples of Networking Initiatives and Projects

An ongoing theme in the discussions was the need for some "good examples of good examples" for using the networked environment in a public library. More than once people asked why we did not have a videotape of using the network in a public library context rather than an academic library context—as had been done with the "Beyond the Walls" videotape (NYSERNet, 1991). The unsaid implication was there probably really isn't much you can do with the network in a public setting, is there?

The site visit to North Carolina demonstrates that there are good examples of networking development. Other interesting developments are occurring with Freenets, networking in Colorado, NYSERNet's New Connections Program, the California State Packet Radio Project, and public library involvement in the Internet via M-Link in the state of Michigan. Although these examples, and others, are evolving, many public librarians are unaware of their existence. Therefore, there is a need for a national clearinghouse to disseminate innovative ideas related to public library networking. A service similar to AskERIC (see chapter 5) but tailored to public libraries could be a useful part of a solution.

In short, a concrete set of examples of what to do with the NREN in a public library context must be developed. This set of examples might come from producing a videotape, or it might be in developing a showcase public library in its use of networking that others can see in a hands-on context. For many public librarians, something concrete and real was needed for them to appreciate the use and applications of the NREN.

Develop a Comprehensive Educational Program

Assuming that we can resolve the awareness problem and increase public librarians' knowledge about the importance of networking issues, there are still massive re-education problems to be addressed. Public librarians recognized the need for re-education, but they had a range of problems and fears regarding the process. A program of educational opportunities related to the Internet/NREN needs to be developed with cooperation among libraries, professional associations, library schools, network providers, and Federal and state governments. Indeed, using the network itself for distance education and Internet training is a viable strategy. Additionally, mechanisms for providing incentives and rewards for librarians to participate in such programs are essential.

Establish Leadership for Networking Policies and Initiatives

Currently, there is a leadership void in addressing the role of the public library in a nationally networked environment. There must be leadership in the profession to develop applications and uses of the Internet for public libraries. This must become a key issue for public librarians, the Public Library Association (PLA), the Coalition for Networked Information (CNI), OCLC, and the state libraries. Some librarians may recognize the importance of the NREN but may not know what to do in *their* libraries. As shown in the site visit to North Carolina, direct and innovative leadership by a state library can make a significant difference in moving the public library community into the Internet environment.

Who will come forward to provide the leadership necessary to connect public libraries to the Internet and show public librarians how to use it to meet community information needs? One participant worried: "Are we up to this challenge? I haven't recovered from the preceding challenges I have had to deal with on this job!" The leadership issue and the mounting need within the public library community to deal with national networking issues must be addressed.

Clarify Connection Confusion

There is currently great confusion about how, exactly, a public library can get connected to the Internet. Apparently, there are very few vendors that are concentrating on the public library market. Public libraries do not know who to go to for information regarding connection, costs, applications, and training. Commercial vendors must engage in networking partnerships with public libraries.

Part of the confusion stems from the apparent local nature of connecting to the Internet/NREN. The way in which a library in Georgia might get connected could vary considerably from how a library in California might get connected. This variance stems from the ease of access to regional or mid-level networks, the type of cables available to the library for connection, and the support that the local regional (or other) provider might be able to offer. This confusion adds to the "mysterious" nature of how the public library might connect to and use the Internet.

Develop Models for Network Involvement

Public libraries need a set of possible models for how they might get involved in the Internet, what costs might be associated with what models, and what types of services and benefits might be realized from a particular model. Factors to consider in the development of such models include:

- size of the library;
- organizational structure of the library and how it reports to its governing body;
- nature of the library clientele and the range of services to be provided;
- level of effort that can be committed by the library to networking;
- Staff knowledge and interest in Internet/NREN services/involvement; and
- existing technology infrastructure.

Different levels of effort may be associated with the various models. This would allow the public library some flexibility in how it might develop its network participation. The study suggests that one model of networked involvement will not fit all library situations. Additional thought and research must be given to dealing with this problem as a means of providing guidance and suggestions to the public library community.

Coordinate OCLC, Regional, and National Network Initiatives

The involvement of OCLC in the development of national networking points to the importance of cooperation and coordination among national and regional networks, especially in the context of developing networking services via the NREN. The development of the mid-level regional networks (e.g., SURANet, NYSERNet, etc.) may replace, support, expand, or eliminate services of OCLC as well as those of the regional bibliographic utilities (e.g., SOLINET, AMIGOS, etc.). The impact of the National Science Foundation (NSF) supported regional mid-level networks on OCLC and its regional networks is, at present, unclear. Equally unclear is the degree to which OCLC has affected or participates in national NREN policy-making bodies such as the NSF, or advisory committees such as that for the Federal Networking Committee (FNC).

Currently, OCLC has made a commitment to be involved in the NREN. The president and chief executive officer of OCLC stated: "Despite whatever rumors you might have heard, there has never been any question that we would link to the Internet and the NREN" (Smith, 1992, p. 3). The specifics of that commitment, however, were not known until later in 1992 when the OCLC Users Council's Committee on Networking Issues submitted a report on Internet access and advanced linking options, and OCLC issued a white paper on its policies with respect to linking to the Internet and the NREN. (For an overview of OCLC's involvement with Internet and NREN activities until this time, see Hyatt 1992, pp. 16–17.)

OCLC and the regional bibliographic utilities must identify and implement new and innovative information services accessible via the NREN. The apparent strategy of simply taking existing traditional services and making them NREN-based is inadequate to assist the library community in reconceptualizing itself for an electronic networked environment. OCLC will need to develop carefully designed plans for enhancing the usefulness of the NREN and providing seamless gateways between itself and other NREN information services and products. To the degree possible, OCLC may wish to engage in cooperative ventures with the mid-level regional networks, state library agencies, and commercial vendors in the provision of innovative information resources and services.

Findings from the study, however, are clear regarding this topic. There is too much confusion over which network entity (be that OCLC, AMIGOS, a CERFNet, a local/remote academic institution, government agencies, commercial vendors, and others) is developing what services and products for the library community. There is too little interest in gateways and intelligent front ends to provide seamless connections to the network, and there is a diffused and oftentimes contradictory level of effort among these entities. OCLC (or some other network entity) should try to coordinate these efforts, and coordinate them in light of meeting end-user information needs as opposed to library needs.

Reconceptualize Provision of Information Services

There is a need to rethink the manner in which libraries develop and provide services in the networked environment. As suggested in Figure 4-1, libraries are most familiar developing services for walk-in users. But increasingly, libraries will need to develop services for local remote users (e.g., those within the community who access the library electronically) and distant remote users (e.g., those that access the library electronically from outside the immediate service area). How should such services be developed, implemented, and evaluated?

The planning and evaluation implications of Figure 4-1 are to consider carefully the information needs of these three distinct

Target Audience	Information Needs	Possible Library Services To Meet These Needs	Library Requirements	Performance Indicators
Walk-in Users				
Local Remote Users				
Distant Remote Users				

Figure 4-1. Reconceptualizing services for the networked environment.

target audiences, identify and develop possible library services to meet these needs, describe the resources and requirements that will be needed in order to provide those services, and then develop performance indicators to assess the degree to which these services do, in fact, meet user information needs. Clearly, subgroups can be identified within each of the target groups listed in Figure 4-1. The point, however, is to (1) begin considering remote access to libraries as a key factor in the design of information services and (2) fill in the cells in Figure 4-1 for individual libraries.

An important implication of library services provision in an electronic networked environment is the development of a market- or demand-based approach. In an electronic networked environment, users can select those electronic library services of greatest quality or of most importance, regardless of the physical location of the library. Thus, by default, those libraries providing higher quality or more appropriate networked services will be those in demand and used most. Users may no longer be loyal to their local library when they have a broad range of electronic information services available from other libraries or even non-library providers.

Currently, the library is focused on the provision of services to walk-ins and traditional outreach programs. We will need to expand that attention to a broader audience of remote users who access the library electronically. Figure 4-1 is intended only as one possible approach to begin reassessing the process by which the library provides information services to its users. Certainly there are other approaches to be considered as well. The Freenet model offers guidance on how such services might be designed. The library community, however, must begin to plan for and evaluate the provision of information services to remote users.

Revise the Planning and Role Setting Manual

The need to rethink service provision in the networked environment suggests that the roles identified in the *Planning and Role Setting for Public Libraries* manual (McClure et al., 1987) could be a serious inhibitor to developing the electronic networked public library. The roles in the manual are very traditional and do not address activities associated with electronic provision of information resources. Moreover, many public librarians (including those who participated in the focus groups) have used this manual and recommended (among other things) that service roles such as the Electronic Networked Public Library should be developed and added to the acceptable list of public library roles to encourage libraries to plan for participating in the networked environment.

A range of new service roles and assistance in developing vision statements for public libraries in the networked information age are needed. Strategies for developing vision statements and assisting public librarians to design their own service roles (rather than selecting from the eight included in the manual) would provide some flexibility in planning for the networked environment. This approach would encourage public libraries to be more innovative and creative.

Another serious limitation of *Planning and Role Setting for Public Libraries* is its inattention to technology planning, in general, and planning for the networked environment, in particular. There is a discontinuity in the manual between planning for services and planning for the technological infrastructure needed to support those services. Public librarians need to better coordinate technology planning with services and service role planning. The manual needs to be revised to link technology planning with services planning and to encourage public library planners to plan for technology development and implementation as well as services.

Improve Access to Local, State, and Federal Information

The High Performance Computing Act, P.L. 102-194, encourages Federal agencies to disseminate information electronically over the Internet. Similar legislation is needed at the state and local levels to increase citizen access to government information. The mounting of local, state, and Federal information on file servers accessible over the Internet could be a most important advance for improving access to government information. Public libraries have a traditional and natural role in serving as the intermediary to provide such access—except now it needs to be done via the network.

A recent report (McClure et al., 1992) recommends that the Federal government develop a policy framework that will encourage Federal agencies to make their databases and information inventory/locator systems searchable over the Internet. North Carolina has a similar project underway to provide access to state information. Public libraries should take the lead in (1) serving as the intermediaries for citizens to access electronic government information, and (2) designing strategies to mount local government information, legislation, meeting information and summaries, and so on., on file servers that can be accessible over the NREN. Part of the success of the Freenets results from providing community access to government information that would not otherwise be available.

Conduct Additional Research

One objective of exploratory research is to develop propositions and identify research topics requiring additional attention. In effect, each of the above recommendations suggests propositions and topics for further research. However, the study team sees the following topics as especially important:

- *Development of an NREN awareness and education program.* Research efforts need to be directed at determining what specific strategies would have the greatest impact to increase the public library community's awareness of networking topics and how best to develop and implement a national education program for practicing public librarians on the importance, uses, and applications of national networking. For one example, see NYSERNet (1991).

- *Economics of electronic networking.* To date, there has been virtually no effort to identify the range of costs associated with national networking (from the library's point of view) and impacts of these costs for developing the networked public library. Moreover, a number of economic models that could assist public library managers to better plan for and implement the electronic networked public library might be developed (see Grycz, 1992).
- *Identifying community information needs to be met by networking.* Clearly, some community information needs can, and should, be met by traditional public library services. But what community information needs can be met with electronic networked information services? How might we reconceptualize public library services in an electronic networked environment along the lines suggested in Figure 4-1?
- *Public library networked information services.* What specific networked information services should be developed for, and by, the public library community, what are the costs related to developing these services for a networked environment, and how can these networked information services be assessed?
- *Affecting public policy decision making.* To date, the public library community has not been involved in public policy debates that resulted in the creation of the NREN, the Federal agenda setting of priorities and funding to support NREN development, and ensuring that the public library is a key player and stakeholder in NREN developments. Strategies for insuring public library involvement and mechanisms to encourage public library participation in public policy relating to Internet/NREN decision making is essential.
- *Sorting out roles and responsibilities of other key stakeholders.* From the public library perspective, it is unclear which organizations are responsible for what kind of networked information services and technical support. Potential key stakeholders that could affect public library networked development are the regional bibliographic utilities (e.g., AMIGOS, SOLINET), the regional mid-level networks (e.g., SURANet and NYSERNet), OCLC, Department of Education library

programs, state libraries, library vendors (e.g., Gaylord, Inc.), and commercial networks (e.g., Advanced Network Services [ANS]). How might these organizations best support public library involvement in national networking?

- *Assessing public library organizational structures.* The public library's organizational structure has changed little over the years. Indeed, this structure may limit the adoption and application of new information technologies such as the NREN. What organizational structures might be designed to enhance access to and use of the network and encourage organizational cultures to take risks and be innovative?

- *Clearinghouse for public library NREN information.* This study identified a number of good examples of public library networked initiatives. However, the knowledge gained from these initiatives, as well as a host of other general information about the NREN, is not easily available to the public library community at large. Research should identify specific information needed for inclusion in such a clearinghouse, to obtain and organize that information, to design the database, and to disseminate that information to the public library community.

Clearly, other topics for further research exist. These are seen as especially important by the study team.

A worrisome view heard in some of the focus group sessions was that the public library's role in the NREN would evolve over time. Given the recent past history of public library involvement in the NREN, this view is a dangerous one. To date, few national network planners and government officials have been concerned about libraries in the NREN. Roles for the library community in the NREN will evolve only with a concerted research and development program that addresses these and other key topics.

THE ROLE OF PUBLIC LIBRARIES IN THE NATIONAL NETWORK

There are two critical factors needed for greater public library involvement in the Internet/NREN: developing vision and taking action. That action may focus on the development of a strategic plan for new services and better use of the new networked technologies (DeKalb County Public Library, 1992), on experimentation with an Internet connection (as currently being done at the

Liverpool public library, Liverpool, New York), or on the development of services appropriate for network delivery (such as that done by the North Carolina state library). An action-oriented stance toward using the NREN is essential.

The model for taking action by the North Carolina state library is especially instructive. There appeared to be an ongoing, interactive loop among vision development, planning, experimentation, implementation, and evaluation. Some activities could not be planned completely in advance, so some plan as you go occurred. But what did not occur, was paralysis by analysis. This model of taking action is encouraged when staff have the opportunity to learn from their mistakes and keep moving forward.

Second, there is a need for imaginative and creative vision of the public library in the networked information age. A vision statement is a description of a possible future state or set of functions for the library. Vision statement development requires librarians to make explicit their assumptions about the future and to envision a future state of the organization in light of these assumptions and in light of assumptions, organizational goals, and resources.

A primary purpose of vision statement development is to define and describe visions of what the library might be in the future networked environment. In terms of strategic planning, the library can develop a range of possible visions, identify those that are most important and that would benefit the library and its clientele the most, and then take appropriate steps to ensure that the vision evolves as defined. As such, a vision statement provides a target for which the library can strive and a vision of what it would like to become. It also identifies the resources that will be needed. This can, and should be done even if the target is moving. Currently, there is little vision of what the public library might be in the nationally networked environment.

A key notion of vision is the idea of taking responsibility for the development of a library's future and not letting that future occur by happenstance. For the public library community to take charge of its future, attention must first be given to:

- developing national spokespersons for articulating the role and responsibilities of public libraries in the Internet/NREN environment;
- affecting national policies on how the Internet/NREN will be funded, used, and integrated into the public library community; and

- increasing, exponentially, the awareness of and knowledge about the Internet/NREN in the public library community.

Once these activities are begun, the more difficult work of actually getting connected to the network, developing information services and resources, and integrating these services into the community must be accomplished.

There are numerous scenarios for public libraries as the NREN environment evolves. One might be that the public library, by default, simply ignores the electronic networked environment. In this category some public libraries may continue to exist by providing high-demand traditional services—but they may find it increasingly difficult to obtain community support for the library as the world becomes increasingly electronic. In such cases, the public library dies a slow and painful death. In this scenario, the public library may increasingly service the disenfranchised while others with knowledge of electronic information services will find non-public library solutions to resolving their information needs.

Another scenario is that the public library develops a plan for transition into the electronic networked environment from its current traditional environment. While embracing and exploiting networked information services and resources, the library also maintains the high visibility and high-demand traditional services. The library, however, reallocates resources from its collections and less visible services to support their involvement in the network. All services will be more client-centered and demand-based, and the library will consciously seek opportunities to deliver electronically new types of information resources and services.

In this scenario, the public library develops and delivers services over the NREN, provides for public access to the NREN, and competes successfully against other information providers. In its networked role, the library serves as a central point of contact as an electronic navigator and intermediary in linking individuals to electronic information resources—regardless of type or physical location. The public library in this second scenario will define a future for itself in the NREN and develop a strategic plan to ensure its successful participation as an information provider in the networked environment.

Different types of public libraries in different settings are likely to evolve differently in the NREN environment. In addition, as Dowlin correctly points out (1991, p. 320–321):

> Librarians also need to make some changes in terms of our own perceptions of staff. We will have to move from being pointers and retrievers to facilitators and organizers . . . and from the concept of banking [archiving] to connectedness. . . . Essentially, this is moving from the just-in-case collection syndrome to just-in-time information delivery.

The fabric of our society continues to change as a result of the evolution of national networking and the NREN. The library community, in general, and the public library community, more specifically, must change as well.

The evolving role for the public library in the networked environment can incorporate the traditional safety net role ensuring that all citizens have access to the network. The library's role, however, should also expand into an electronic navigator and intermediary, provider of electronic information to remote users, coordinator of local community electronic information resources, and switching station for electronic information resources and services. These roles must be created and visions for these roles are needed now. Immediate public library involvement in the design and structure of the Internet/NREN will ensure that the public library is a key player and stakeholder in the evolving national networked information society.

NOTES

1. For further information with Freenets, review the video, "If It Plays in Peoria," which describes Freenetting and is available (along with other information about Freenets) from The National Public Telecomputing Network, Box 1987, Cleveland, OH, 44106.

REFERENCES

Ahtola, A. Anneli. (Fall, 1989). In-house databases: An opportunity for progressive libraries. *RQ* 29 (1): 36–47.

Amdursky, Saul J. (November 15, 1985). Dishing it out: Satellite services in public libraries. *Library Journal* 110 (19): 49–51.

Appleman, Merrie. (1984). Videotext: Options for libraries. Report Number Five of the Electronic Text Report Series. San Diego, CA: San Diego State University, Center for Communications, 1984. Available from ERIC, ED 259722.

Bezold, Clement. (1991). Libraries in the 21st century: Alternative futures for the great debate. Paper presented at the White House Conference on Libraries and Information Services, July 12, 1991, Washington, DC.

Brett, George H., ed. (Spring, 1992). Accessing information on the Internet. *Electronic Networking: Research, Applications and Policy* [special issue], 2(1).

Burge, Elizabeth J., et al. (1989). Interactive libraries: Dimensions of interdependence. Paper presented at the International Council for Distance Education Conference (Cambridge, England, September 19–22, 1989). Available from ERIC, ED311907 (see also ED311902).

Chepesiuk, Ron. (May, 1985). Information around the clock: Atlanta's channel 16. *Wilson Library Bulletin* 59 (9): 597–599.

DeKalb County Public Library. (1992). Focus on the future: A five-year plan for DeKalb County Public Library. Decatur, GA: DeKalb County Library System [available from the Library, Administration Office, 215 Sycamore Street, Decatur, GA 30030].

Dewey, Patrick R. (Spring, 1984). The electronic bulletin board arrives at the public library: The North-Pulaski library prototype. *Library Hi Tech* 1 (4), 13–17.

Dewey, Patrick R., et al. (November/December, 1985). Library use of electronic bulletin board systems. *Library Software Review* 4 (6): 351–361.

Dowlin, Kenneth E. (1984). *Electronic Library*. NY: Neal-Schuman.

Dowlin, Kenneth E. (December, 1991). Public libraries in 2001. *Information Technology and Libraries* 10: 317–320.

Grycz, Czeslaw Jan, ed. (1992). Economic models for networked information. *Serials Review* 18 (nos. 1–2) [special issue].

Hollings, Senator Ernest. (October 24, 1990). Congressional debate on the National High Performance Computing bill. Congressional Record: S18114.

Hyatt, Shirley. (May/June 1992). New era in telecommunications gives libraries new options. *OCLC Newsletter*, 15–20.

Isenstein, Laura. (Summer, 1992). Public libraries and national electronic networks: The time to act is now. *Electronic Networking: Research, Applications, and Policy* 2: 2–5.

Jahoda, Gerald, and Needham, William L. (1980). The current state of public library service to physically handicapped persons. Final Report. Tallahassee, FL: Florida State University, School of Library Science. Available from ERIC, ED313051.

Jensen, Jan, et al. (1988). A.S.A.P. (As Soon As Possible): A multitype library fax consortium. Denver, CO: Jefferson County School District R-1, 1988. Available from ERIC, ED 319389.

Kahle, Brewster, Morris, Harry, Davis, Franklin, Tiene, Kevin, Hart, Clare, and Palmer, Robin. (Spring, 1992). Wide area information servers: An executive information system for unstructured files. *Electronic Networking: Research, Applications, and Policy* 2: 59–68.

Kemper, Marlyn. (November, 1988). Emerging technologies: A roadmap for librarians. *School Library Journal* 35 (3): 36–41.

LaQuey, Tracy and Ryer, Jeanne. (1993). *The Internet Companion: A Beginner's Guide to Global Networking.* Reading, MA: Addison-Wesley.

LaRue, James. (June, 1986). Sending them a message: Electronic bulletin boards. *Wilson Library Bulletin* 60(10): 30–33.

Lynch, Clifford A. and Preston, Celia M. (1990). Internet access to information resources. In Martha E. Williams ed., *Annual Review of Information Science and Technology*, vol. 25. New York: Elsevier, pp. 263–312.

Magrath, Lynn L. and Dowlin, Kenneth E. (Spring 1987). The potential for development of a clearinghouse for emergency information in the public library. *Special Libraries* 78(2): 131–135.

Malyshev, Nina Alexis. (1988). Concept and reality: Managing Pikes Peak library district's community resource and information system. *Reference Services Review* 16(4): 7–12.

McClure, Charles R. (Spring, 1992). The High Performance Computing Act of 1991: Moving forward. *Electronic Networking: Research, Applications, and Policy* 2: 2–9 [note: this source includes a copy of the High Performance Computing Act, P.L. 102–194].

McClure, Charles R., Owens, Amy, Zweizig, Douglas L., Lynch, Mary Jo, and Van House, Nancy A. (1987). *Planning and Role Setting for Public Libraries: A Manual of Operations and Procedures.* Chicago: American Library Association.

McClure, Charles R., Bishop, Ann P., Doty, Phillip, and Rosenbaum, Howard. (1991). *The National Research and Education Network (NREN): Research and Policy Perspectives.* Norwood, NJ: Ablex.

McClure, Charles R., Bishop, Ann, Doty, Philip, and Rosenbaum, Howard. (1990). Realizing the promise of the NREN: Social and behavioral considerations. In Carol Parkhurst, ed., *Library Perspectives on the NREN.* Chicago: American Library Association.

McClure, Charles R., Ryan, Joe, Moen, William E., Babcock, Wally, and Wheeler, Terry. (1992). *Identification and Analysis of Federal Information Inventory/Locator Systems.* Syracuse, NY: Syracuse University, School of Information Studies.

Newhard, Robert. (1992). Personal correspondence to Charles R. McClure, February 2, 1992.

NYSERNet. (1991). Beyond the walls: The world of networked Information: An instructional workshop package. Syracuse, NY: NYSERNet, Inc. [111 College Place, Rm. 3–211, Syracuse, NY 13244].

NYSERNet. (1992). New user's guide to useful and unique resources on the Internet. Syracuse, NY: NYSERNet, Inc. [111 College Place, Rm. 3–211, Syracuse, NY 13244].

Office of Science and Technology Policy. Federal Coordination Council for Science, Engineering, and Technology. Committee on Physical, Mathematical, and Engineering Sciences. (1992). Grand challenges: High performance computing and communications. Washington, DC: National Science Foundation.

Parkhurst, ed. (1990). *Library Perspectives on NREN.* Chicago: American Library Association, Library and Information Technology Association.

Pollard, Richard. (1983). Videotext in libraries: An assessment of the British experience and directions for the future. Paper presented at the Mid-year Meeting of the American Society of Information Science (Lexington, KY, May 22–25, 1983). Available from ERIC, ED237093.

Polly, Jean Armour. (June, 1992). Surfing the Internet: An introduction. *Wilson Library Bulletin* 66: 38–42.

Smith, K. Wayne. (May/June, 1992). Toward the emerging digital, broadband, global community. *OCLC Newsletter.* 3.

Vasey, Bill. (1989). The intermountain community learning information services project: A participant's view. *Rural Libraries* 9(2): 105–107.

Westin, Alan F. and Finger, Anne L. (1991). Using the public library in the computer age: Present patterns, future possibilities. Chicago: American Library Association.

Wicklein, John. (September 20, 1983). Will the new technologies kill the public library? Keynote speech at the LITA conference: Information and Technology: At the Crossroads. Baltimore, MD. Available from ERIC, ED237115.

The Internet and Library Media Programs: The Technology Is Now!

Michael Eisenberg and Peter Milbury

The Internet is one of the most exciting and promising of all technological developments for providing information services and resources for education. Although initially intended to serve higher education and research institutions, the Internet is quickly proving to be an essential tool for K–12 education. For the first time in history, K–12 schools have the means to access a powerful set of real-world resources previously available only to higher education and business. Furthermore, many school library media professionals are taking the lead in fulfilling the promise of electronic networking in the K–12 environment.

This chapter offers insights into how library media specialists are using the Internet right now to meet the information needs of students, teachers, administrators, and others in K–12 settings. Even though network access is just beginning to be available to elementary and secondary schools, library media specialists across the country are already implementing an impressive number and range of network applications. Many of these applications are explored in this chapter through specific examples of Internet use by library media specialists and their clients. These examples were provided by subscribers to LM_NET, the global electronic discussion group (listserv) on the Internet for the school library media field through responses to an electronic survey in January 1993.[1]

In addition to this exploration of current use, the chapter investigates the key concerns and issues related to future use. Networking is widely recognized as the key technological innovation of the 1990s. Recent government announcements (Clinton and Gore, 1993) extol and emphasize the crucial role of networking in economic development, access to government information, and education at all levels. Networking has the potential to affect every aspect of teaching and learning, and library media professionals must be prepared to rethink services and approaches in light of network capabilities.

Before turning to the specifics of network applications, it is valuable to establish the baseline regarding the current role of library media programs in schools. Today's library media specialists fulfill highly active and widespread responsibilities. Library media specialists are central players in K–12 education, and it is important to understand the full scope of their involvement before considering the full impact and significance of networking technology on library media programs and schools.

LIBRARY MEDIA PROGRAMS: MISSION AND FUNCTIONS

Information Power (American Association of School Librarians, Association for Educational Communications and Technology, 1988), the national guidelines for library media programs, champions an ambitious service mission for the library media program: "to ensure that students . . . are effective users of . . . information." Library media specialists accomplish this mission through three related roles:

- As *information specialists*, they provide information services and expertise.
- As *teachers*, they provide appropriate information skills instruction to students.
- As *instructional consultants*, they provide guidance in the integration of information resources, technologies, and skills into the curriculum.

In fulfilling these roles, library media specialists meet both the immediate and the future needs of students. Immediate needs are met by information services and future needs by integrated information skills instruction (Eisenberg and Berkowitz, 1988).

Offering information services goes far beyond merely providing resources. Library media specialists consult with teachers on the use of information and resources in classroom instruction, offer formal and informal reading guidance activities, and work individually with students and teachers to resolve their information problems. In addition, they design information services to meet the specific needs of individuals, classes, and the curriculum.

Library media specialists also teach essential information literacy skills. Ensuring that students are effective users of information requires a carefully constructed program that helps them learn to:

- define information tasks and problems;
- develop information seeking strategies;
- locate and access information;
- use information;
- synthesize and apply information to specific tasks; and
- evaluate their own effectiveness and efficiency.

These fundamental information problem-solving skills (Eisenberg and Berkowitz, 1990) are the foundation of most modern library media instructional programs. Library media professionals recognize that students learn these skills best when instruction is tied to real information needs. A basic principle of library media practice is integrating information skills instruction with classroom instruction in the subject areas. When they use information for assignments, projects, homework, or personal reasons, students improve their own information literacy skills.

TECHNOLOGY AND LIBRARY MEDIA PROGRAMS

The explosive growth of technology affects every type and aspect of information work. Teaching and learning are particularly affected because education is fundamentally information-based. Today information is offered in a variety of electronic formats, and computer systems are widely used to retrieve, manipulate, repackage, and present information.

Library media specialists are extremely active in using technology to provide information services and information skills instruction. Specific applications include:

- *Access to collections.* Online catalogs and bibliographic databases offer improved access to and availability of resources within library media centers and beyond.
- *Direct information services.* Information is made directly available to students and staff through full-text electronic encyclopedias, newspapers, and reference works.
- *Access to technology.* Public computer, printer, and multimedia production workstations in media centers provide personal productivity tools for students and staff.
- *Instruction.* Computerized instructional programs and electronic resources are integrated with classroom curriculum, assignments, and information problem solving.
- *Library media management.* Library media specialists use computer systems for circulation, distribution, budget,

and collection management to improve the management of resources and facilities.

Computer networking—from local area networks (LANs) to the Internet/NREN—offers a whole new range of opportunities to expand each of these applications. School library media specialists are quick to recognize how networking can provide multiple access points to electronic resources, connectivity over large distances, and links to systems and services previously unavailable. They are eagerly embracing networking capabilities, making practical applications in their own programs, and considering the more long-range potential.

The remainder of this chapter focuses on aspects of current uses of the Internet as well as future potential. The discussion begins with LM_NET, the previously mentioned electronic discussion group (see Appendix C), since it has quickly become the center of networking activity for library media specialists. The chapter then moves to a detailed explanation of networking capabilities through specific examples of network use in each of the five application areas noted above.[2] The chapter concludes by considering the impact of networking on library media programs and key future concerns and issues for its effective use by library media programs in K–12 education.

LM_NET: THE SCHOOL LIBRARY MEDIA NETWORK[3]

One of the most popular and immediate uses of the Internet by persons newly connected is to extend their electronic mail interactions by joining one or more electronic discussion groups (listservs). LM_NET: The School Library Media Network is one of seventy-four such library-related discussion groups available as of January 1993 (Bailey, 1993), but it is the only discussion group that specifically targets the school library media community.

LM_NET is comanaged by Michael Eisenberg (Professor, School of Information Studies and Director ERIC Clearinghouse on Information and Technology, Syracuse University) and Peter Milbury (Librarian, Pleasant Valley Senior High School, Chico, California). It was launched in June 1992 with forty-two members and grew steadily over the summer with word spreading through workshops, word of mouth, postings to various library- or education-related listserv discussion groups and through brief articles in newsletters and journals. A dozen of the members met at roundtable discussion during the Annual Convention of the American Library Association in July 1992.

By September 1992 there were 250 LM_NET members and 400 by the year's end. Increased awareness and publicity have accelerated growth even more. As of April 1993 there were over 700 members, and about 100 new members join each month.

LM_NETTERS come from a very wide geographic area including Arizona, California, Florida, Indiana, Iowa, Massachusetts, Minnesota, Missouri, New Hampshire, New Jersey, New York, North Carolina, Pennsylvania, Tennessee, Washington, and Wisconsin. There are also a number of Canadian members, and one subscriber each from Belgium, Finland, Germany, and New Zealand.

The originators intended LM_NET to help library media professionals make better use of the services and resources of the Internet and to help them fulfill library media functions. Instructions to new subscribers state:

> Conversation on LM_NET should focus on the topics of interest to the school library media community, including the latest on school library media services, operations, and activities. It is a list for practitioners helping practitioners, sharing ideas, solving problems, telling each other about new publications and upcoming conferences, asking for assistance or information, and linking schools through their library media centers.
>
> The LM_NET listserv is open to *all* school library media specialists—worldwide—and people involved with the school library media field. It is not for general library media specialists or educators. We want to keep the activity and discussion focused on school library media. But, the listserv can be used by library media people for many different things—to ask for input, share ideas and information, link programs that are geographically remote, make contacts, etc. (Eisenberg and Milbury, 1992)

Members use LM_NET for just these kinds of things. Examples of recent use include: questions about applications of new technology to the library; planning for get-togethers at regional and national conferences; assistance to students, teachers, and staff; and administration of library media centers. These and other uses are explored in more detail in the next section.

INTERNET USE BY LIBRARY MEDIA PROFESSIONALS

The open response "electronic interview" of LM_NET members conducted in January 1993 solicited information about what prompted members to use the Internet and how they made use of the resources and communications opportunities it offers. Of the 424 total LM_NET members at that time, forty-two (10%) responded.

In response to the question, "How did you get involved in the Internet?", most answered in terms of their point of access, such as a network or university. Almost half of the respondents, 20 of 42 responding (48%), were introduced through their state network. Texas' Tenet is the largest of these, offering accounts to all K–12 educators in the state. The local or regional university was the next most frequent (28%) source of information and connectivity to the Internet, followed by local site or district (14%), college instructional program (5%), and commercial or other type of service (5%). Two professionals indicated that they had been exposed to computer communications through FrEdMail or FidoNet, while two others indicated experiences with commercial services which served to stimulate their curiosity or interest in the Internet.

Interview responses were often quite elaborate and indicated an enthusiasm and gratitude for the account or access. They also frequently indicated a number of influences on their search for the Internet connection. The following are some typical responses:

- "I got involved when the University of New Hampshire offered a pilot group of K–12 educators the opportunity for an account on a vax plus a one-day workshop on how to get around on the nets. . . . The program has now expanded to over seventy educators. . . . About a dozen of us are liberrians!"
- "I got drawn into the Internet through the Texas program, Tenet. I explored Tenet out of curiosity and, quite frankly, because it only cost $5 a year to receive an account."
- "I got involved in Internet about fourteen months ago because I am a member of the Massachusetts Telecomputing Coalition and because I was lucky enough to have no charge access to it through a Massachusetts service called the Massachusetts LearnPike (satellite distant learning system). . . ."
- "I originally used Fred-Mail as my online introduction to the world in 1990. My first big connection was to network our English-speaking Spanish class with an Argentine Spanish-speaking English class. We were so excited! Then, Dr. Frank Church, California State Department of Education, invited me to a workshop of

some selected school library media types to introduce them to what was then called Technology Resources In Education (TRIE). . . . From TRIE we were able to connect to the Internet, where the whole world opened up to me. I was born again!"

Once connected, library media specialists are quick to use the Internet for the full range of applications of technology. For example, when LM_NET members were asked, "What use do you make of Internet resources in your job as a librarian," respondents listed an impressive and wide variety of uses including:

- to communicate with colleagues;
- as a reference tool answering questions of others;
- to search remote libraries for bibliographic data;
- to teach or demonstrate computer telecommunications skills;
- for curriculum/classroom support activities;
- to participate in listserv discussion groups;
- to obtain software from remote sites;
- to obtain text files or information from remote sites; and
- to obtain data for cataloging functions.

These and other uses of the Internet can be categorized according to the five applications of technology in library media programs noted earlier.

Access to Collections

When first introduced to the Internet, school library media specialists find a structure and resources designed for universities and research institutions. Access systems are developed for a very specific clientele and generally require a high level of sophistication. At first glance these resources and systems might seem only marginally useful to K–12 schools. But school library media specialists, fulfilling their information specialist roles, found Internet-based online catalogs, bibliographic databases, and distant computer communications capabilities highly useful.

One of the library media professional's first uses of the Internet is to access online library catalogs. Connecting to a local college or university or to a major research institution [e.g., the

University of California's Melvyl catalog or the Colorado Alliance of Research Libraries' (CARL) Public Access Catalog] can serve a number of information needs. In the current era of scarce budgetary resources, for example, many school library media specialists are not able to afford regular updates of *Books In Print*, a major resource for new book purchases. An online subject search of Melvyl, CARL, or any of the hundreds of online catalogs now available through the Internet, provides basic bibliographic data including the complex MARC records needed for electronic card catalogs.

Internet-accessible online catalogs are also useful for schools that have special programs and relationships (including borrowing privileges) with local colleges or universities. Sometimes, the local institution's catalog is available through the network. If not, students and staff can search other catalogs to identify potentially useful resources before visiting the local university. And even if there is no local college or university, school library media specialists can still find needed materials, then use interlibrary loan to fill requests.

Another valuable access tool for school library media specialists is the ERIC bibliographic database.[4] ERIC is the largest and most widely used educational database in the world. ERIC provides bibliographic information and abstracts for journal articles, research papers, conference proceedings, government reports, and a range of state and local school curriculum and policy documents. While an extremely valuable resource, ERIC is not generally available in most library media centers. But ERIC *is* available through the Internet, which allows any user to log on, through the telnet function, to Auburn University or Syracuse's SUINFO service.

Direct Information Services

Full-text databases, which are available through telnet, Gopher, and/or WAIS to universities, government agencies, and other organizations, are an even more important resource than access to online catalogs. These full-text resources are often developed along topical lines and include the Cleveland Freenet's posting of Supreme Court Decisions, the University of Michigan's Weather Underground national weather information service, Project Gutenberg's extensive collection of electronic books, Dartmouth University's Shakespeare and Dante databases, and California's Automated Trade Library Service. Uses of these and other information sources are limited only by the imagination of library media specialists, teachers and students. For example:

- School library media specialists across the country can provide their social studies teachers and students with U.S. Supreme Court decisions within minutes of their announcement through the Cleveland Freenet. This extensive database contains the complete text of the decisions, both concurring and dissenting. Never before in the history of social science education have K–12 clients had such immediate access to primary source materials.

- School library media specialists are making effective use of the large amount of science resources on the Internet. One of the most popular resource sites is NASA Spacelink, a service designed for the K–12 educational community offering a wealth of information derived from space research as well as about the space program. Library media specialists help their students and teachers find NASA information on subjects from aeronautics and air flow control to composite materials and storms. NASA's impressive shuttle graphics are also available for downloading. One library media specialist makes this information available to the students through an electronic bulletin board. Another introduced science teachers to NASA and assisted them in ordering educational materials from the extensive online listings of NASA Educational Services.

- With the assistance of their school library media specialists, classes have easy access to extensive U.S. State Department economic reports on a large number of foreign countries such as those posted on California's Automated Trade Library Service. Created to serve California's vital agribusiness community in its efforts to expand foreign trade, the economic reports provide wide-ranging economic and demographic data and state-of-the-art "snapshots" of most of the world's countries. Combined with Internet full-text access to the CIA World Factbook and the World Bank's economic database, teachers can engage students in realistic, data-rich simulations and problem-solving experiences about foreign affairs and commerce.

- Library media specialists can provide teachers with direct access to information about the latest concerns and issues in education. In addition to the basic ERIC database mentioned above, over 1,000 ERIC digests are available full-text, electronically. The digests report on a variety of current education topics and are available through Internet electronic bulletin boards such as the University of North Carolina's LaUNChpad bulletin board, and through more sophisticated retrieval systems such as Gopher and WAIS. ERIC supplies information that helps school library media specialists to fulfill their roles as information specialists and instructional consultants.

• Library media specialists and other educators can also contact a new educational research information service on the Internet: AskERIC. Accessible to anyone with e-mail capabilities who is involved in K–12 education, AskERIC seeks to provide question-answering, help, and referral services. Drawing on the extensive resources of the ERIC system, AskERIC responds within forty-eight working hours. Although AskERIC is a relatively new pilot project, library media specialists have already proven to be key players in ensuring effective use by teachers and administrators.[5]

These examples of direct access to full-text information clearly demonstrate the power of the Internet to extend information availability beyond the walls of the individual school library media center. Existing information resources are frequently updated, and new ones are added every day. There is also continual development of Gopher, WAIS, and other tools to improve the ability of users to search and retrieve full-text information on the Internet.

Open Access to Technology

In their responses to the electronic interview, many LM_NET members reported that they are sharing Internet services and access with their students, teachers, and administrators. In fact, since few teachers have their own hardware/software or accounts, the only connection many have to the Internet is often through the library media program. Library media specialists make it possible for varying levels of open access to teachers and students. They also provide training—on Internet capabilities, basic commands, as well as more complex Internet uses.

Providing educators and students with some form of connection to the Internet through the library media program is an important first step towards the ultimate goal of ubiquitous access for all educators and students. Interestingly, teachers often value the filtering service that library media specialists can provide since many teachers are tied up in classes for the major part of the day, and they just do not have the time (or in some cases the skills) to search the Internet themselves. Library media specialists help target access to Internet resources and services that are most relevant to the needs of users. For example, one library media specialist noted:

> The major use right now is printing out [conversations from discussion group] lists for various students and teachers. We have a teacher receiving the military history list, the mystery list, a teacher with lupus receiving the immune list, a student from Serbia receiving Croatian News and Bosnet; students using those and other E–Europe- and CIS-related lists from social studies reports.

Often, library media specialists are the first professionals in their schools to make use of the Internet. In some cases, they have had to struggle with administrators who do not understand the tremendous potential of this new technology. One way to overcome any opposition is to assume responsibility for introducing the Internet to faculty and students and also to provide necessary training. Of the twenty-one respondents who answered the question, "Have you taught/introduced the Internet to students and/or faculty," seventeen (81%) answered yes, and another three (14%) said they planned to do so in the near future.

Here are some typical direct access activities reported by library media specialists who are LM_NET members:

- "All teachers have been inserviced on all technology in the learning resources center. One (English) is helping me write Internet curriculum, two teachers (Math and Science) are coming in to learn more on their prep periods. . . . It is a slow process!"
- "As I discover each new resource [many thanks for (information on LM_NET about) Fineart Forum, for example], I connect it to one of our staff and use the "carrot" to get them interested in an account. So far I have worked with a Middle School social studies

teacher to think about revising her "Country Report" to take advantage of CIA Country info and teach online research skills to students next fall."

- "I have been telling teachers and administrators about the Internet but very few have found time during the school day to spend time working or trying. In fact, I do most of *my* Internet work at home in the evenings. One idea that has helped is to buy modems for teacher and student check-out. I have checked out modems and had a few more interested people."
- "I have introduced Internet by way of printouts. I have just about convinced my administration that we really must have telecommunications at school or be left behind all of those schools who already have it."
- "In May I am scheduled to give our school board an introduction to the Internet—at least this way they will have some understanding of its power—and indeed, this is *the most* important/exciting professional tool that I have seen in all my many (and I do mean many) years in education."

This last comment conveys the overwhelming enthusiasm and significance that library media specialists have for the Internet. They view "spreading the word" about the Internet and providing access to be major library media functions. This is totally consistent with the overall library media objective of providing open access to the full range of information resources, systems, and services.

Instructional Applications

The prior discussion points to the important role that school library media specialists play in early uses of the Internet by classroom teachers and students. But once access is established, the crucial issue is involvement in curriculum and instruction. LM_NET library media specialists are active in all of the major K–12 Internet projects that seek to link classrooms together, regionally, nationally, and globally. The following examples provide clear evidence of the value of the Internet in the learning process:

- "Internet activities are limited only by imagination and by the fact that at this time I am the only soul in my school district (let alone my school) with an Internet account. Still, our students have been corresponding in French and Latin to students in Bologna, Italy. A student doing a paper on Clinton and his health care proposals went into SENDIT to pull up the full text of his speeches. Students reading Walkabout were able to correspond with someone in Australia. A class studying the former Soviet Union and now CIS has access to current information via the Radio Free Europe list. I am putting those messages on disk for students to search. I hope to involve one or two teachers in the Newsday project—a wonderful project."

- "I gather useful and copyright-free (or freely distributed, permission-granted) materials, such as the Radio Free Europe/Radio Liberty material . . . and mount them on our file server for student, faculty, and community use . . . I match teachers with likely sounding telecommunications programs and perform the resulting exchange of files."

- "Although we have not yet had a great impact on the total school program, we have been able to integrate some of the Internet sources into the curriculum, especially in economics and social science classes. They are using the CNN Newsroom Guides, and did use the Campaign '92 position papers and press releases we obtained via FTP. Our science classes also used the information obtained from NASA Spacelink. Since our high school has 3,000 students and 200 teachers, it is sometimes difficult to communicate. Many of our teachers need to learn telecomputing skills. I have offered to show them, but they barely have time to accomplish the requirements of their departmental curricula. I guess we really need more inservice time for these things."

This last example is typical of many LM_NET respondents who may not realize just how influential they are in bringing the cutting edge of technology into their schools. Yes, it will take time to expand to the entire school, however it is clear that this library media specialist is directly affecting the use of information resources in curriculum and instruction. The students in the economics, social science, and science classes benefit from having up-to-date, in-depth resources that directly meet their curriculum needs.

Library Media Management

While management applications may not be the first priority for Internet use, school library media specialists use the Internet, especially their LM_NET discussion group, as a valuable management tool. The Internet provides a vehicle for resource sharing, but even more importantly, for information-sharing about library media management. The LM_NET archives are filled with questions and responses about every possible topic including:

- recommendations for local area networks (LANs), electronic resources, and catalog, circulation, and integrated systems;
- approaches to inventory, circulation and distribution, scheduling, fund-raising, and facilities design;
- ways of designing and delivering information services and skills instruction;
- suggestions for print, CD-ROM, and online resources for reading promotion, reference and information service, and curriculum support; and
- discussions of roles and responsibilities of library media programs and professionals.

One of the current realities of library media specialist work is professional isolation. Although teachers are sometimes isolated from each other due to classroom demands, they generally can find colleagues "right next door" who share similar common concerns and interests. For school library media specialists this is frequently not the case. Most are the only library media professional in their school, and there are few opportunities to interact with library media specialists in other buildings or districts.

Networking, however, breaks down isolation. When hundreds of library media specialists with a broad range of experiences are available for consultation through an Internet discussion group such as LM_NET, making administrative decisions is no longer a solitary act. Speaking about the value of interacting with other professionals through the Internet, LM_NET library media specialists noted:

- "It's a way to keep in touch with what's going on. It provides interaction among school library media specialists. That's what I'm interested in, not public libraries, private libraries, and so on, but *school libraries.*

I wish I had this available ten years ago when I automated my library. I wouldn't have felt so much pressure about making the 'right' decisions. I could have turned to you folks for help."

- "LM_NET is essential. I think many library media specialists do not have colleagues with whom they can discuss issues of interest. We are teachers in one of our roles, but we have so many more dimensions to our jobs that we need to talk with other LMS. I have gained access to many great resources through LM_NET. I am president of my state organization and have been recommending use of LM_NET and AskERIC to everyone I meet."

- "We are in the process of building a new library. I have been able to make better decisions (and back them up) because of the information I have received through the Internet."

- "As library media specialists, we are horribly isolated . . . I check this list daily, and have never failed to learn something worthwhile, or be pointed to a new resource, funding, or continuing education opportunity."

The Internet makes it possible for library media specialists to have access to each other as well as to documents, files, and databases. Sharing expertise and information about management concerns over great distances is one of the most powerful capabilities of the Internet. And these examples of information sharing are just the beginning. Over time, we are likely to see formal and informal group interactions for cooperative planning, resources sharing, purchasing, and decision making.

THE IMPACT OF INTERNET USE ON SCHOOL LIBRARY PROGRAMS AND SERVICES

One of the rewarding side-benefits of technology innovation for school library media programs can be increased visibility and awareness. Technology improves the profile of the library media program and calls attention to its importance to the school. The Internet is a critical advance for communication and information access. By bringing the Internet into the school, the library media program assumes a central role in educational change and reform. Often, this draws support, encouragement, as well as improved status to both the library media professional and the program.

Respondents to the LM_NET interview provide a glimpse into the impact of Internet use in library media programs. Of the forty-two respondents, twenty-nine answered the question, "What impact has your use of the Internet had on the role or status of your library media program?" Almost all were very enthusiastic, with 23(80%) reporting that their role or status had improved, and another 4 (14%) were uncertain but hopeful that their Internet use would soon have an impact. One person mentioned that he had received several honors and recognition awards at the state, regional, and local level due to his technology and Internet innovations. Only 2 respondents (6%) felt that there was no impact.

Some of the responses reflect how use of the Internet has directly affected their programs and services, along with revitalizing their own careers. For example:

- "The Internet has completely changed how I view my job (of twenty years) and our library media program. Our library is no longer bounded by four walls and a dwindling budget. We are no longer resource-poor. I feel connected to the world. Gone is the old feeling of isolation. I see my relationships with students and teachers changing in that I have a world of resources to offer them and new ways to get at it. I see that I will allocate the budget differently."
- "There are few full time teacher-library media specialists in our district. Last year the administration considered having me teach one social studies class which, of course, would mean I was not available for students in the library. The coordinators from English, social studies, French, and technology went to administration saying that they wanted me full time in the library. It worked and I am full time in the library. I think my involvement with extending teachers and students beyond the walls of the building was instrumental."
- "I am now perceived as the person to go to for the answers. . . ."
- ". . . as site-based decision making is implemented, participants are coming to me more for suggestions since technology is also targeted as a need."
- "I know that even the small of amount of use we have made so far has really added depth to our program resources. Our school system is in the midst of systemic

> change, training, design, and implementation. . . . The
> access to the Internet really allows our system to apply
> the Information Power standards about breaking down
> the walls of the school library."

Internet use directly contributes to fulfilling the information specialist, teacher, and instructional consultant roles outlined in *Information Power* (American Association of School Librarians and Association for Educational Communications and Technology, 1988), the national guidelines for library media programs. Networking and related technological innovations provide specific capabilities that improve the ability of library media specialists to deliver services and instruction. Equally important, bringing these technologies into the library media program also results in a change in perception and status that affords library media specialists the opportunity to move to center stage in K–12 education.

A VIEW TO THE FUTURE: CONCERNS AND OPPORTUNITIES

The Internet offers a special promise for K–12 education and library media programs. For the first time in the history of school library services, K–12 schools have a means of accessing a powerful set of real-world resources previously available only to higher education. The Internet also offers the means for library media specialists, teachers, and students to learn and work cooperatively sharing expertise and experiences.

Many school library media specialists are taking the lead in bringing electronic networking to their schools. These library media specialists recognize that Internet involvement adds to the status and value of school library media programs in addition to directly contributing to the accomplishment of the library media program's mission. Although they are relatively small in actual numbers as compared to the general teacher population, school library media professionals are relatively numerous in adopting the Internet as an important innovation to the K–12 school setting.

Some school library media specialists, like some teachers, tend to see most new developments as "add-ons" to their current programs. They complain about not being able to carry out basic tasks such as building and maintaining collections and circulating materials. Others, however, quickly recognize that embracing technology offers unique opportunities to move to center stage in education, as well as to effect fundamental changes in how library media professionals fulfill their services and instructional roles.

Electronic networking is not just another "take-it-or-leave-it" option for resources and services. It is a crucial and integral tool in the modern, technology-based library and information center and in education in general.

There are, of course, serious issues facing the implementation of networking in library media programs and schools. To LM_NET members, who undoubtedly include some of the heaviest Internet users among school library media specialists, the overwhelming concerns are financial. LM_NET members lament that many states do not mandate school library media services, let alone professional staff to manage such programs. Over the past decade, most schools, especially at the elementary level, have suffered heavy cuts in library media programs; some programs have even been abolished. At the very best, budgets have been held to prior years' levels. Job security is often threatened, and critical clerical support has been lost. If highly trained professionals are always busy checking books in and out, they have little time to introduce new technology. Library media programs that have survived the past decade often had to sacrifice other parts of their programs in order to add computers and have access to telecommunications.

A library that cannot afford to buy books will seldom buy a high-speed modem, or pay long-distance telephone charges, even to a free service. Therefore, the primary roadblock hindering Internet/NREN use in schools is the infrastructure. Federal and state funds must be allocated to provide links to the network, and this should include support for modems and communications software. Implementation of the proposals outlined by President Clinton and Vice-President Gore would have a profound impact on the application of wide area networks in K–12 education. For example, they call for expanding access to the Internet and NREN to K–12 schools, including providing support for equipment to connect local networks in these institutions to the network (Clinton and Gore, 1993). Connecting all K–12 schools is an essential first step.

Free or inexpensive access results in immediate use of networking capabilities by library media specialists in learning and teaching. For example, currently the most frequent LM_NET activity occurs in Texas, New York, and California, states which provide some form of supported networks to their teachers. When access is provided, library media specialists quickly get involved. In California, the most prolific users of the free K–12 network are the school library media specialists, who use the network far out of proportion to their numbers in the school population.

Even after physical Internet access is available, however, other major impediments to a seamless Internet access exist. Very little local support or training is currently available to school library media specialists and teachers. Since it is often the school library media professionals who introduce and support technological innovations in the school, local support and training is extremely important if the national goal to bring schools online is taken seriously.

Frequent training seminars, intensives, and workshops targeted to school library media specialists are needed. These should be sponsored by district, regional, or county school systems, as well as by the network providers themselves. Funds need to be earmarked for school library media specialists to hire substitutes and attend these training sessions. Funding for local and regional mentors or trainers is necessary. Local technical support for the installation and maintenance of LANs must also be available, if access is to be spread throughout the school site. Thus, training and support for training is a second major concern.

Another concern of school library media specialists is the matter of coordinated access and use. Library media specialists have been working hard to bring online catalogs, CD-ROM periodical indexes, full-text encyclopedias and other reference resources, as well as interactive multimedia, and other technologies into their library media centers. Gradually they have been achieving the goals of integrating these systems—linking various resources through a common network and making them available on any library workstation. Some programs are already expanding this access to classrooms throughout the building or even allowing students to dial up from home. How will Internet/NREN resources and services be integrated with these existing systems? The challenge is to present a unified, coordinated system to users. That will require front end and interface development and an analysis of when and how to use Internet/NREN capabilities in relation to local systems.

Addressing the three concerns described above—infrastructure, training, and coordinated technological implementation—will go far to making Internet/NREN access and use a possibility. Truly effective implementation, however, will hinge on one additional key concern: full integration with the library media program and classroom curriculum.

A central theme of all modern library media programs is the link between information resources/services and the school's curriculum and instructional programs. All library media specialists are charged with teaching essential information literacy skills that go beyond locating and accessing resources. They also know that all information skills instruction must be tied to the needs of students. The best way to accomplish this is to fully integrate skills instruction with the overall information skills instruction program and the classroom curriculum.

The same mandate for integration holds true for Internet/NREN services and instruction. While the Internet presents a whole new range of resources and services opportunities, instruction in Internet/NREN capabilities and commands cannot be taught in isolation. Rather, instruction must be grounded in two contexts: the information problem-solving process and the classroom curriculum. Networking has a specific purpose when viewed as part of the information problem-solving process (e.g., as an information seeking strategy, to locate and access information, to present and communicate results). In addition, Internet instruction only makes sense when it relates directly to the curriculum and the real needs of students. Therefore, effective use of networking in schools requires library media specialists to rethink and revise their existing information skills and services functions and curriculum integration in terms of the capabilities offered by the Internet/NREN.

Many library media specialists are already working hard to bring the Internet/NREN into their schools. They recognize the need to develop an organized, coordinated program of resources, services, and instruction that makes full use of existing and developing networking capabilities. They also understand the importance of targeting the program to the real curriculum needs of students and teachers. The challenge on every level—Federal, state, and local—is to provide the funding, expertise, and vision to bring the Internet/NREN into every K–12 school through its library media program with the proper training, support, and personnel.

NOTES

1. Full information on LM_NET, including how to become a subscriber, is provided in Appendix C.
2. The authors are indebted to LM_NET members who participated in the January 1993 electronic interview on LM_NET for their contributions to this section.
3. See Appendix C for more detailed information about LM_NET.
4. See Appendix D for information on how to access ERIC through the Internet.
5. See Appendix E for more information on AskERIC.

REFERENCES

American Association of School Librarians and Association for Educational Communications and Technology. *Information Power: Guidelines for School Library Media Programs.* Chicago, IL: American Library Association, 1988.

ATI-NET, California's Automated Trade Library Service (includes the Automated Trade Library Service) Available: TELNET CATI.CSUFRESNO.EDU or 129.8.100.15. Log-on: public.

Bailey, Charles <libpacs@uhupvm1.BITNET> "Library-Oriented Lists and Electronic Serials," posted to PACS-L on 1-12-93. (Public-Access Computer Systems Forum). Houston: University of Houston. Available: Subscribe: e-mail: LIST-SERV@UHUPVM1.BITNET Message: SUBSCRIBE PACS-L (your name). Notebook files of previous messages are kept by listserv@uhupvm1.BITNET Message: index pacs-l.

CARL, The Colorado Alliance of Research Libraries, Public Access Catalog. Available: TELNET PAC.CARL.ORG or 192.54.81.128. No log-on required.

CIA World Factbook. Available: TELNET INFO.RUTGERS.EDU or 128.6.26.25. No log-on required, located in the Library/Reference submenu.

Cleveland Freenet. Available: TELNET: FREENET-IN-A-CWRU.EDU or FREENET-IN-B-CWRU.EDU. Log-on instructions supplied after connecting.

Clinton, Bill J. and Gore, Albert Jr. "Technology for America's Economic Growth, A New Direction to Build Economic Strength," February 22, 1993.

Dartmouth University's Dante databases Available: TELNET: ELEAZAR.DARTMOUTH.EDU or 129.170.16.2. Log-on: ddpdemo.

Dartmouth University's Shakespeare Plays and Poems databases Available: TELNET LIB.DARTMOUTH.EDU or 129.170.16.11 Login: select shakespeare play or select shakespeare poems.

Eisenberg, Michael B. and Berkowitz, Robert E. *Curriculum Initiative: An Agenda and Strategy for School Library Media Programs.* Norwood, NJ: Ablex 1988.

Eisenberg, Michael B. and Berkowitz, Robert E. *Information Problem-Solving: The Big Six Skills Approach to Library & Information Skills Instruction.* Norwood, NJ: Ablex 1990.

Eisenberg, Michael, and Milbury, Peter G. (Co-owners) (1992-). LM_NET: World-Wide Discussion Group for School Library

Media Professionals). New York: Syracuse University. Available:
Subscribe: e-mail: PMILBUR@EIS.CALSTATE.EDU Message:
ADD LM_NET (your address) (your name). Archives of previ-
ous messages are posted to the ERIC/IR Gopher
<ERICIR.SYR.EDU Port 70>.

ERIC Clearinghouse on Information and Technology <ERIC@ERI-
CIR.SYR.EDU> (1992–). ERIC Digests. Syracuse, NY: ERIC/IR.
Available: GOPHER ERICIR.SYR.EDU Port 70.

Gopher. Available TELNET CONSULTANT.MICRO.UMN.EDU or
134.84.132.4. Log-on: gopher.

LM_NET: Introduction. Available: GOPHER ERICIR.SYR.EDU Port
70. Posted in the submenu LM_NET/README.

MELVYL, The Electronic Union Catalog of the University of
California. Available: TELNET MELVYL.UCOP.EDU or
192.35.222.222. No log-on required.

NASA Spacelink, A Space-Related Informational Database.
Available: TELNET SPACELINKMSFC.NASA.GOV or
192.149.89.61. Log-on instructions provided after connecting.

Project Gutenberg's extensive collection of electronic books.
Available: FTP: MRCNEXT.CSO.UIUC.EDU or 128.174.201.12
DIRECTORY: pub/etext.

University of Michigan's Weather Underground (national weather
information service,) TELNET: DOWNWIND.SPRL.U
MICH.EDU 3000 or 141.212.196.177. No log-on required.

University of North Carolina's LaUNChpad Bulletin Board.
Available TELNET LAUNCHPAD.UNC.EDU or 152.2.22.80.
Log-on: launch.

WAIS, Wide Area Information Server. Available TELNET
QUAKE.THINK.COM or 192.31.181.1. Log-on: wais.

6

Special Librarians and the NREN

Hope N. Tillman and Sharyn J. Ladner

Special librarians must have access to networked information via the National Research and Educational Network (NREN). They need to participate in its development in order to provide information to their clients and to remain current as information professionals. In the Summer of 1992, only a small number of special librarians were actively communicating and using information resources on the Internet, and most were affiliated in some way with an academic institution.[1] There are several reasons why special librarians do not have access to the Internet, including difficulty in gaining access because of historical NSFNET rules concerning commercial traffic, lack of funding to become connected, lack of technical knowledge, restrictive institutional policies, or simply lack of awareness of Internet resources. Unless they, in some way, get involved in the planning of the NREN, special librarians—particularly those in the corporate environment—will not be able to voice their concerns about network restrictions, nor will they be able to contribute their expertise in electronic information management to the NREN planning process.

This chapter demonstrates why the NREN is an important—if not critical—resource for special librarians. It discusses their barriers to entry, identifies policy issues affecting special library use of the NREN, and delineates specific areas of expertise that special librarians can contribute to NREN development. The chapter draws on findings from a 1991 study of special librarians' use of the Internet[2], supplemented by interviews with special librarians conducted in 1992, and relevant literature to identify key issues affecting special librarians in their use of the Internet today and the NREN tomorrow.

CHARACTERISTICS OF SPECIAL LIBRARIANSHIP

Special librarians are a diverse group of information professionals with differing resources and needs. They not only hold advanced degrees in library or information science but are also specialists in one or more subject areas, often with post-graduate training in science, business, or law. In his textbook, *Special Libraries and Information Centers: An Introductory Text* (1991, p. 2), Ellis Mount defines special librarianship as library and/or information service geared to meet the needs of specialized users or specialized situations, independent of organizational structure, whether they are in "information organizations sponsored by private companies, government agencies, not-for-profit organizations, or professional associations" or in "specialty units in public and academic libraries."

Special librarians emphasize service to users, which consists of providing information directly to users, rather than teaching them how to find it themselves (Taylor, 1985). Hill (1985) observes that special librarians, especially those in corporations, tend to be closer to their users than other types of librarians. This knowledge of the user enables them to anticipate user needs and provide customized service (Cveljo, 1985). Corporate librarians also provide value-added services such as analysis and evaluation of competitors. In addition, they have different security requirements because of the existence of confidential or proprietary materials in their collections (Cveljo, 1985).

Special libraries in industry differ from special libraries in academe. They are smaller and share many of the characteristics of small libraries, such as small staff and limited time spent in technical services functions like original cataloging (Hill, 1985). Industrial libraries have more specialized collections than academic libraries, and even though small, within their specialty these collections are also more comprehensive, often including obscure journals and grey literature such as pamphlets, preprints, and technical reports (Mount, 1985).

Traditionally, special librarians in academic institutions have placed higher priorities on collection development and control than those in industry. Industrial librarians, on the other hand, emphasize access to information over collection management and stress current awareness functions more than their academic counterparts (Ladner, 1991; Taylor, 1985).

Finally, special libraries are more economically driven than academic or public libraries. Because they are part of a larger organization, usually in the for-profit sector, managers of special libraries must justify major expenditures, including capital projects, to a management which often does not understand library operations and needs (Ladner, 1990; Hill, 1985). Because they share and support organizational goals and objectives, special librarians tend to take on the coloration of their organizations. For this reason, observed the members of the National Commission on Libraries and Information Science/Special Libraries Association (NCLIS/SLA) Task Force on the Role of the Special Library in Nationwide Networks and Cooperative Programs (1984), special librarians are less likely to join with others to discuss library-related issues or participate in the development of policies affecting libraries and information centers.

RESEARCH ON SPECIAL LIBRARIANS AND THE INTERNET

In July 1991, special librarians who were currently using the Internet were asked to participate in an exploratory study of Internet use.[3] The purpose of the study was to:

- describe how special librarians who have access to the Internet (or BITNET) use these networks and how they pay for access;
- identify training needs and protocols;
- determine what advantages or opportunities these networks provide for special librarians; and
- identify barriers to access or other disadvantages for special librarians.

Study participants were self-selected Internet users who responded to an announcement posted on nine computer conferences and published in *SpeciaList*, the monthly newsletter of the Special Libraries Association (SLA).[4] Participants completed two electronic questionnaires distributed via the Internet during the summer of 1991. These questionnaires included open-ended questions concerning Internet use and training, "major advantage or opportunity" and "major disadvantage or barrier" for special librarians, and "most interesting or memorable experience" on the Internet.[5] Table 6-1 shows the type of library affiliation of the fifty-four participants in the study reported here and their subject focus.

Of the nineteen non-academic librarians who participated in the study:

- five are from for-profit corporations in the computer industry;
- six work for the U.S. Federal government, in agency libraries, the national libraries, and national laboratories;

Table 6-1. Characteristics of Survey Participants (N=54)

Subject Emphasis	Percent
Science-technology	58%
Medical	11
General, multiple subjects	11
Law	6
Maps	6
Business	4
Other subjects	4
Type of Library	
Academic	65
Government, public agency	15
Corporate	9
Not-for-profit organization	9
Other, non-library	2

- four work in not-for-profit research institutions in the United States;
- one manages a government-funded agency library in Europe;
- one works in a state agricultural extension library;
- one works for a scientific abstracting service; and
- one works for a research institute in South America.

Responses to the open-ended question, "Briefly describe your use of BITNET or the Internet," were divided into six categories of network use, based on the constant comparative method (Mellon, 1990). Table 6-2 lists these categories for academic and non-academic special librarians. The table also demonstrates that survey respondents in and outside of academe do not differ in their use of the Internet.[6]

WHY THE NREN IS IMPORTANT TO SPECIAL LIBRARIANS

There are three major reasons why the NREN will be an important resource for special librarians.

- It will enhance communication with colleagues and clients.

Table 6-2. Use of BITNET/Internet by Type of Special Library

Use*	Academic (35)	Other (19)	Total (54)	z**
Work-related communication, e-mail	91%	95%	93%	-0.575
Electronic forums, bulletin boards, e-journals	66	53	61	0.930
Searching remote databases	34	47	39	-0.930
File transfer, data exchange	34	42	37	-0.577
Research and publication	26	16	22	0.892
Personal communication, leisure activities	9	16	11	-0.722

*Multiple responses possible; percents do not total 100.

**Z-scores were used to test for differences between academic and non-academic librarians for each category of Internet use. Z-scores are standardized to the normal curve so that a z-score of 1.96 has a probability of .05 and a z-score of 2.57 a probability of .01 that the observed values occurred by chance.

- It will provide access to information not available anywhere else.
- It will decrease the time required to obtain information.

Through these enhancements to information service, the NREN has the potential to enable special librarians to transform both their environment and their role within the organization. This change is already occurring in a few pioneering special libraries that have integrated the Internet into their work environment.

Communicating with Colleagues and Clients

As information professionals, special librarians need electronic networks for contact with their fellow librarians as well as for access to networked information (Hodgson, 1992). Frequently, special librarians are isolated from others because of their specialization or because of the small size of their operation. Corporate downsizing and the concomitant elimination of middle management positions have resulted in the reduction in size of many industrial libraries, if not their outright elimination in some cases. Yet the globalization of industry and separation of colleagues makes the potential of networking electronically even more critical. Special librarians also need to acquire information quickly for their clientele. One of the major differences between a corporate and academic library is the degree of urgency with which the information must usually be obtained in the corporate environment (Wiggins, 1985; Taylor, 1985).

Enhancing communication with colleagues is a major need that will be fulfilled by the NREN. When asked to describe the "major advantage or opportunity" for special librarians in using the Internet, 93 percent of the respondents mentioned some aspect of electronic communication with colleagues. Special librarians in this regard are no different from other electronic network users. The value of the electronic mail function of the Internet (or its precursors) has been observed by researchers who studied other user groups (see, for example, Hiltz and Turoff, 1978; Sproull and Kiesler, 1991; Doty et al., 1990). As Kapor and Berman (1992, p. 203) report, "Time and time again, from the Arpanet to Prodigy, people have surprised network planners with their eagerness to exchange mail." Looking to the future, Doty and his colleagues (1990, p. 285) conclude that the NREN "will eliminate the . . . isolation of scholars at small and remote institutions, [and] encourage collaboration. . . ." It will do the same for special librarians, by reducing geographical distance and feelings of isolation from colleagues and instilling a sense of collegiality and connectedness with other library professionals.

Meeting User Needs

Special librarians also use the Internet for client service, where the speed and ease of electronic mail expedites reference service, interlibrary loan transactions, and information delivery.

For example, a corporate librarian in the study reported that she used the Internet to obtain quick copyright permission from Finland and contacted someone about ordering a report. The following remarks from an astronomy librarian in a not-for-profit organization, in fact, sum up the advantages of using the Internet for client service:

> Hardly a day passes that I don't contact a colleague with a reference query or be contacted by one. The ability to give my patrons almost instant answers to obscure questions is terrific.

Participating in Internet/BITNET discussion groups (commonly called "lists" or forums) is another way special librarians obtain information quickly for their clientele. Often questions posted on subject-oriented lists, such as MEDLIB-L or BUSLIB-L, are answered within a few hours of posting (Ladner and Tillman, 1993, pp.47–48). And much of the information obtained through the lists is often not available anywhere else. As one of the survey respondents, a librarian in a Federal science agency, stated:

> Librarians serving education, research, and sci/tech clienteles cannot ignore this revolutionary development in communications and information flow . . . user reference questions very often can only be answered via information services established on the networks, or by appealing to discussion group participants.

Corporate librarians are much heavier users of commercial, online databases than their academic counterparts (Bell, 1990; Willard and Morrison, 1988). Once access to these services through the Internet becomes commonplace, will corporate library Internet use shift away from this communication function, or will the Internet simply be seen as another telecommunications network? Predictively, both uses will take place: the communications component will continue to be perceived as a vital and valuable resource in and of itself, but at the same time the Internet will be increasingly used to access remote databases.

Special librarians can better meet client information needs by incorporating network information resources into their services. They can enhance the networking they already do by using e-mail to find information from a larger number of colleagues in a timely fashion. Cisler (1990, p.47) reports that at Apple Computer, "There are mail links between AppleLink and the Internet, so that Apple engineers can send requests to the library any way they wish." At Apple, as in most corporate libraries, "the library and its users place a premium on the speed of delivery of the information and its relevance to the researcher," including extensive use of electronic mail.

Value-Added Information Service

One of the most important services offered by special librarians to their clientele is value-added information. Matarazzo and Prusak (1990) found that corporate executives considered the "quality of information" to be the most important criterion for evaluating corporate libraries. Likewise, Taylor (1985), in a study of value-added processes in libraries, observed that special libraries, in order to prosper in times of economic uncertainty, must have a "reputation for quality, relevance, and indispensability" (p. 94).

Value-added service differentiates special librarians from academic librarians, who have traditionally viewed their role as instructors in locating information, rather than as information managers, analyzers, or intermediaries. Prusak and Matarazzo (1990) consider these functions to be critical for corporate library success. Corporate librarians must be able to offer an array of value-added services in order to maintain their status as key players in the company's future. Otherwise, Prusak and Matarazzo warn, the corporate library will cease to exist.

How will NREN affect value-added information service? Kahle (1991) believes corporate librarians will rise within the corporation, both in visibility and impact, as they shift their roles from online searchers and report writers to information consultants and instructors. As commercial online systems become more "executive friendly," both Kahle (1991) and Prusak and Matarazzo (1990) predict that end-user searching will supplant mediated searching, but not replace forward-thinking corporate librarians. These librarians will emerge as information consultants and guides, providing both value-added services as well as making internal and external databases available to others within the organization. A combination of Internet-accessible and commercial systems will probably be used to maximize access, maintain currency, and achieve relevance in information delivery. In this scenario, mode of access is a function of user need—the end-user does not care whether the data is available through a gateway to the Internet from a commercial source or internally from a company database of regional sales reports. The user wants accurate and relevant information delivered immediately. The location or format of the source is irrelevant.

This merger of internal and external information is already common practice in some special libraries serving multinational corporations. For example, the international, decentralized information network at Xerox Corporation links LAN-based information available at local installations with system-wide networks which, in turn, are linked to external information available through remote database and resource-sharing networks such as CLASS, the British Lending Library, universities everywhere, and other research organizations joined by ARPANET (Lavendel, 1988, p. 38). Other examples include the delivery of DIALOG search results directly to users' internal e-mail accounts via the Internet at Sematech (Denton, 1992) and ISCLine, a menu-driven, networked system providing access to internal corporate databases and external information sources, developed by the Cetus Corporation library (Handman, 1991).

Transforming the Special Library

The interlocking network of local, system-wide, and international networks which Xerox had in place in 1988 is just one example of the "global" library environment that McClure et al. (1992b), describe as a key issue facing academic and public libraries as a result of Internet/NREN developments. Although McClure and his colleagues discuss the rise of market-based global libraries in which the academic or public client will select the "best" information services, regardless of location or organizational ties, the scenario can certainly be applied to the special library situation. In the future, corporate information users will not restrict themselves to information resources mediated through their corporate library. Corporate users with access to the Internet as part of their interlocking network of information resources will, in fact, be able to access these market-based, global libraries on their own.

Russel (1986, p. 6) views the traditional special library as a typical product of the industrial age, where "its function was to interface the industrial organization with the industrial research community, as seen through the industrial press, a typical library function requiring typical library skills." Russel agrees with Prusak and Matarazzo (1990) that in today's post-industrial organization the special library must change or else it will disappear.

Russel, however, sees the corporate information specialist—the special librarian—becoming increasingly important to the organization as the host organization transforms itself into a post-industrial, "informationized" entity. In order for this to happen, the information specialist of the 1990s must understand the dynamics of this structural transformation of information. The information specialist must take advantage of the technologies—represented today by the Internet and tomorrow by the NREN—and become an active participant in the informationizing of the host organization. If not, the special librarian, and the information center itself, will very likely become obsolete relics of the industrial age.

Integrating the Internet/NREN into the special library environment, however, is no simple task.

BARRIERS TO ACCESS

Barriers to Internet access for special librarians include:

- historical network regulations preventing many commercial firms from joining;
- institutional policies prohibiting access or difficulty of justifying need for accessing resources on the Internet;
- lack of technical knowledge about the Internet;
- unfriendly user interface; and
- lack of interest or concern.

The following sections outline the nature of these barriers.

Exclusion of Commercial Firms

Special librarians within academe have found it easier to gain access to the Internet and keep up with network developments than have most of their colleagues in the commercial or not-for-profit sectors (Becker, 1992). In 1992, those most likely to have access to the Internet are librarians in companies which have ties to academic institutions, are involved in government research and development, or are part of the computer industry.

Klingenstein (1992, pp. 125–126) addresses the reasons why the corporate clients who have joined the Internet so far have been largely confined to "high-tech firms whose associations with universities and government labs require network access. In many of these cases, security concerns have resulted in the network-gateway being confined to e-mail transfers." Klingenstein (1992, p. 125) enumerates four factors restricting Internet growth for the corporate sector: "current regulatory usage policies, the complexity of the networking technology, the perceived potential for security violations, and the lack of useful network-accessible services."

Institutional Policies

Special library access to the Internet may also be constrained because of their own host organization's policies. Special librarians will for the most part gain access only after their institutions have, and may, in some cases, be the ones who have to convince management of the value of Internet use if they are to gain access. Some of the reasons why there is lack of access are because the parent organization has not yet joined the Internet or is not yet providing access to the library. Top management may not understand the importance of "informationizing" the organization and the vital role of the Internet/NREN in this process. The special librarian, in this situation, must take the responsibility of providing leadership in this organizational transformation. A Federal librarian expressed this process well in responding to the survey:

> I'd say lack of access or difficult access is the major problem, but it's combined with lack of awareness about Internet resources as well. I've talked to plenty of special librarians who know about the networks and would like to participate but don't have an access point. . . . Lack of awareness about the networks is especially dangerous at the administrative levels—library directors and computer/ communications personnel who don't know about the networks or who don't see the value in them. Special librarians who are lobbying for an Internet connection have to emphasize the benefits to the *organization* as a whole instead of focusing on library-related benefits.

In this economic climate, special libraries and the services they provide are vulnerable to being contracted out. While this threat may make it more difficult for the library to be the leading force in convincing an organization to join, it may be the librarian who is the only one within the organization who sees the benefits of connecting to the Internet. If Prusak and Matarazzo (1990) are right, however, about the future of the corporate library, the special librarian has no choice but to get involved and be in the forefront of advocating for access to the network.

Lack of Technical Knowledge

Lack of technical knowledge is also a barrier for special librarians. Librarians today need to master many new technologies, especially in the area of telecommunications. Technology is changing faster than our capability of mastering it, and technostress has become a buzzword of the 1990s. Special librarians are particularly vulnerable to technostress, since they frequently work without the luxury of knowledgeable colleagues to turn to for technical help (Ladner, 1992). In addition, some special librarians are just now automating library functions, and they may be locked into proprietary electronic mail systems that are not compatible with Internet access. As one Federal librarian who participated in the study stated:

> The major barrier to optimizing use of Internet will be time constraints and keeping abreast of developments. Major issues are the accelerated pace of change on the networks and the voluminous data stores.

Thus, the need to learn about the Internet competes with the need for acquiring other technological skills.

Unfriendly Interface

Lack of technical knowledge is exacerbated by the Internet's unfriendly interface. Access to the world of the Internet is not yet user-friendly, although a growing number of organizations are seeking to provide an easier entrance, such as that provided by the menu-driven front end created by Mark Resmer of Sonoma State (Stanton and Hooper 1992, p.5) and the menu of choices upon access in the Freenet libraries (National Public Telecomputing Network, 1991, Appendix II). Kapor and Berman (1992, p.203) address the issue of an unfriendly interface as a barrier to access:

> On most Internet systems, . . . newcomers find themselves confronting what John Perry Barlow calls a "savage user interface." Messages bounce, conferencing commands are confusing, headers look like gibberish, none of it is documented, and nobody seems to care. The excitement about being part of an extended community quickly vanishes.

McClure et al. (1991) also comment on the lack of user-based systems and applications as barriers for network users. Not only can the networked systems appear difficult to maneuver within, but connectivity requires technical expertise as well. Two special librarians responding to the survey commented on this point. According to the first: "There is the feeling you need to be able to build a car to drive it. Do we need to be able to install a phone to use it? There is a lack of professional 'hooker uppers.'" The second respondent lamented about how much more difficult it is to get an Internet account than a DIALOG account.

These comments speak to the computer environment within which the corporate librarian works. Corporate librarians are more intensive users of online services than academic librarians, and they are more accustomed to easy-to-use interfaces. Corporate librarians are, in general, more skilled in searching a wide variety of electronic information sources than their academic counterpart. Their information retrieval skills are superb; their computer systems skills are underdeveloped. If the Internet is also an unknown quantity to corporate computer systems staff, this technical knowledge gap is intensified. Unlike the academic research library, which typically counts among its staff at least one systems librarian or technical expert, the special library must rely on help outside the organization. There is, indeed, a need for professional "hooker uppers" in the corporate environment.

Lack of Awareness or Concern

The final barrier is attitudinal. Conversations with special librarians at SLA meetings over the past two years indicate that many feel a lack of urgency regarding gaining access to the Internet. This feeling is more common among corporate business librarians than those in high-tech industrial environments. Barriers such as time constraints involved in learning new technologies, the existing "savage user interface," and difficulties in obtaining corporate access to the Internet contribute to this current lack of enthusiasm. Special librarians must evaluate whether the resources and connectivity afforded by the NREN will be essential to their work-life, and they must be able to justify their need for networked access to management.

Special librarians and their organizations are not going to participate in the NREN unless it is in their organizational interest to do so. What remains is for the commercial and not-for-profit institutions first to see themselves as part of this world, and second, to see the need to participate in order to remain competitive. Even though many special librarians are not yet convinced that the NREN will be an essential resource, they are actively seeking information on the NREN and Internet. Programs on the Internet have been popular at both SLA Chapter meetings and annual conferences during the last two years (Tillman, 1991; Hinnebusch, 1992).

NREN POLICY ISSUES AFFECTING SPECIAL LIBRARIANS

There are four policy issues affecting access to the NREN by special librarians:

- equal access to information and connectivity;
- cost of connecting;
- privacy and confidentiality of information; and
- copyright and intellectual property.

While these issues cut across various types of libraries, they have a particular urgency for special libraries.

Equal Access to Information and Connectivity

Some special librarians perceive the NREN solely as a research and education network for non-commercial organizations. As one survey participant remarked: "If a special librarian is at an academic institution, there should be no problem connecting, but librarians in for-profit institutions cannot participate." While this statement is no longer accurate, network connectivity has been controlled by acceptable use policies which restrict commercial usage. What is important in this librarian's statement is her perception.

Some academic librarians have stated that corporate special librarians, along with their parent organizations, should not be granted access to the Internet (or NREN), whose raison d'etre is to support research and education, or other not-for-profit, functions. Yet the "ultimate aim" of the NREN legislation is "to improve national competitiveness and the national welfare" through the development of a high-capacity electronic research and education network (Federal Coordinating Council, 1992, p. 1). Obviously, librarians in the for-profit sector must be a part of this effort to improve national competitiveness.

While some special librarians in high-tech industries will be brought into the NREN environment as their parent organizations join, many others in the commercial and non-profit sectors are finding it difficult to gain access. Attempts to attract the commercial sector to electronic networking are a recent development. Today, mid-level regionals, such as the Ohio Academic Resources Network (OARnet) and the New England Academic and Research Network (NEARnet) are addressing the needs of corporations and encouraging large organizations to join. For example, the general information packet from OARnet in April 1992 begins with the statement, "Connectivity is a Competitive Advantage," and highlights its corporate members.

The NSFNET acceptable use policy of June 1992, however, has the effect of discouraging connectivity by commercial firms:

> NSFNET backbone services are provided to support open research and education in and among U.S. research and instructional institutions, plus research arms of for-profit firms when engaged in open scholarly communication and research; use for other purposes is not acceptable.[7]

The June 1992 revision of the NSFNET Acceptable Use Policy softened the section on "Unacceptable Uses" by eliminating the phrase "use by for-profit institutions." The "Unacceptable Uses," at the time of this writing, are:

- "use for for-profit activities, unless covered by the General Principle or as a specifically acceptable use"; and
- "extensive use for private or personal business."

Even though mid-level regionals and commercial networks have developed their own acceptable use policies, they must also abide by the NSFNET Backbone Services Acceptable Use Policy for traffic they wish to send to Internet sites (Schrader and Kapor, 1992, p. 21).

In a July 1992 interview, one of the commercial Internet providers, Barry Shein, owner of the World (Software Tool and Die, Brookline, Massachusetts) commented:

> Because it makes no sense NSF has given all sorts of exceptions to specific organizations and allowed them to attach to the Internet and told them not to worry too much about AUP [Acceptable Use Policy]. . . . The rules are basically being flaunted by thousands if not millions of people every day . . . At the same time, systems like ours can't attach in this manner, we haven't been granted an indulgence by NSF and do not know what the consequences are of inadvertently violating these rules are. . . . We (World, our public access system to the

commercial portion of the Internet) have been described by
many as suffering for our honesty. The government's inconsis-
tent and unworkable policy has put us at a competitive disadvantage. It has also forced us to exclude perfectly legitimate
access to the Internet, access which should be encouraged,
such as access by librarians.[8]

Since the interview, the NSFNET granted the World's request for
full connectivity to the Internet in August 1992. The lack of enforce-
ment of the Acceptable Use Policy, however, may not affect the perception of organizations who have read the Acceptable Use Policy
and believed that they were excluded from access.

Recommendation. The National Science Foundation (NSF)
must not only continue to remove roadblocks to the use of the
NREN, but needs also to encourage widespread network access
beyond the research and education communities to include both
public and private interests. The NSFNET Acceptable Use Policy
must be further modified to welcome any firm—commercial or not-
for profit—to access Internet resources. National policies should be
put in place that would include all types of special librarians in both
the planning and implementation phases of the NREN.

Cost of Connecting

Another issue is cost of connecting to the Internet/NREN.
Today, most of the resources available through Internet fileservers
are seen as "free" in that there are no access or downloading
charges. In the future this will change, as more fee-based services
are added (Klingenstein, 1992). Melvyl, the University of California
library catalog, and the Colorado Alliance of Regional Libraries
(CARL) databases, have provided early models for charging for
resources. CARL developed UnCover, a large periodical table of
contents database, providing a document delivery service. These
resources are accessible only through the Internet.
Today, in fact, a number of vendors, including DIALOG, Dow
Jones, Mead Data Central, OCLC, and STN, provide access to their
commercial services via the Internet, and although users with organizational access to the Internet do not pay the same telecommunications charges that they would pay if accessing these systems
through Tymnet or Sprintnet, access to the databases themselves
costs money. DIALOG's Dialmail never really caught on with academic librarians as a communications vehicle simply because it cost

money to use this e-mail system. What will happen to the communications function of the Internet if, for example, users are charged every time they read an e-mail message from a computer forum?

Currently, there are different cost structures for the research and education sector as opposed to the non-research and education users in either the for-profit and not-for-profit sectors. Research and education institutions access the Internet through the mid-level regional networks. Some commercial and not-for-profit organizations also enter through the mid-level regionals located in the area of their corporate offices (LaQuey, 1990). However, corporate access may also be through Advanced Network and Services, Inc. (ANS), directly or via providers who are part of the Commercial Internet Exchange (CIX).[9]

The commercial Internet providers' fees vary widely to accommodate both individual users and organization-based access. The very low fees for access charged by vendors such as the World and NETCOM are attractive to even very small organizations. While there is currently no centralized fee schedule coordinated among all the various providers, CIX members have agreed "to exchange traffic at a fixed and equal cost set by the association" (Schrader and Kapor, 1992, p. 21). Costs are roughly comparable for access from different providers but reflect the costs of the network where the organizations enter. The needs of smaller organizations for network access are beginning to be addressed by the mid-level regionals and the commercial Internet providers, which will certainly benefit many special librarians. Organizations need detailed and specific information to determine how to connect to the Internet and what the alternative choices mean.

Recommendation. Costs of connection should be kept low in order to encourage use by both organizations and individuals. In particular, connection fees for those in the for-profit sector should be reasonable so that cost is not an insurmountable barrier blocking access.

Privacy and Confidentiality of Information

Special librarians in both the corporate and government sectors are concerned with network security and privacy issues. Marc Rotenberg (1992, p. 2) of the Computer Professionals for Social Responsibility defines security and privacy:

Security refers generally to the protection of systems, the prevention of unauthorized use, and the prevention of the deliberate denial of service. Privacy refers generally to the protection of personal information, including the restriction on secondary use, efforts to minimize collection of data, and procedures to ensure fairness in data collection.

A major concern of commercial organizations contemplating participation in the Internet is the protection of their proprietary information. For example, a corporate librarian who needs to send competitive information to another corporate office wants to ensure that such information is not intercepted and read. In the same fashion, decisions must be made within the organization about whether to allow public access to the library's catalog and other organizational data, or whether a public directory will be installed on the organization's network fileserver, providing external access to non-confidential corporate reports.

Some U.S. government agencies are also concerned about issues of national security on the Internet. The Internet has had a history of free-wheeling connectivity where access into any other network could be easily gained, as depicted in *Cyberpunk* (Hafner and Markoff, 1991) and *The Cuckoo's Egg* (Stoll, 1989). Klingenstein (1992, p. 130) reports that "the original Internet protocols were never intended to provide security and privacy; in a small network of academics and researchers, facile interoperability was more important than security."

Currently available network security mechanisms, however, enable only authorized people to communicate out from a network and ensure that the people accessing a network are approved. Continued developments in this area will be very important to the special library community. The library profession must deal with the issue of achieving "a balance between open access and privacy/security" in NREN planning (Brownrigg, 1990, p. 59).

Recommendation. Clear and adequate standards must be set for use of authentication and encryption by organizations of all sizes and types so that privacy and confidentiality of information transmitted over the NREN can be assured. The current standards are inadequate to ensure confidentiality.

Copyright and Intellectual Property

Coping with copyright compliance is a high-priority concern for special librarians, who often must take the lead within their own organizations on copyright issues. Commercial firms are more vulnerable today to infringement litigation than in the past (Schaper and Kawecki, 1991). Special librarians in for-profit corporations may not be covered under fair use guidelines (Will, 1992), especially in light of the 1992 ruling against Texaco regarding fair use copying of articles in scientific journals subscribed to by the Texaco corporate library in Beacon, New York (*American Geophysical Union v. Texaco*, 1992). They need to be certain that their use of material obtained over the NREN will not cause their institution to be confronted with an infringement law suit.

The NREN presents some formidable copyright challenges because of the ease with which material in electronic formats can be transferred and manipulated. The new technologies are making copyright compliance difficult (Flanders, 1991), and copyright law needs either to be revised or clarified specifically to include electronic publishing and distribution.

Mechanisms to pay royalties to publishers for articles selected through CARL UnCover and other fee-based document services provided by library networks will be an additional incentive for network use by special librarians. These librarians have historically used document delivery services along with interlibrary loan because of their need for fast and uncomplicated retrieval. The automatic payment of royalties is a necessary component of any document delivery service used by corporate librarians.

Recommendation. Copyright law must be clarified or revised to cover intellectual property that is created and distributed electronically in order to serve both authors' and users' needs. Special librarians must have clear guidelines for compliance when obtaining copyrighted material through the NREN. Libraries and other organizations providing access to intellectual property over the NREN must also include straightforward mechanisms for payment of royalties or related fees. Contracting with the Copyright Clearance Center and building royalties into the cost of the document being delivered are two viable mechanisms for achieving these goals.

WHAT SPECIAL LIBRARIANS CAN CONTRIBUTE TO THE NREN

Special librarians need to involve themselves in the provision of network services at the library, institutional, regional, and national level. They also need to contribute their expertise in managing electronic libraries and subject-based collections to the development of the national network. In the words of an academic science librarian who responded to the survey:

> Special librarians should get involved, and make a contribution to the organization and navigability of the Internet in their subject areas. As NREN becomes reality, the role of networks in access to information is going to grow, and we need to be part of that!

There are four areas where special librarians can contribute their expertise and unique perspective to the NREN. They can:

- create subject-specific network navigational tools and provide real-time assistance to users;
- organize and participate in subject-specific network discussion groups and provide a different voice in library-oriented network discussion groups;
- contribute to the bibliographic control of "grey literature," especially in the scientific and technology-based disciplines; and
- share their expertise in managing libraries based on a philosophy of service to users rather than control of collections.

Contributions from special librarians in these areas will improve the overall information health of the NREN.

Navigational Assistance

Because special librarians have subject expertise as well as information management skills, they can participate in subject-based computer forums where they not only help others to learn how to maneuver on the Internet, but also observe how their customers make use of the network. For example, in an electronic conference outside the Internet boundaries, newspaper librarians who participate on the CompuServe journalism forum find they frequently serve as resource persons able to help other forum members. In another example, French (1990) urges agricultural information specialists to focus their energies on user-oriented rather than library-oriented technologies and cites the Forest Service Information Network as an example of a web that links librarians, information centers, researchers, practitioners, and editors within the U.S. Forest Service.

Today, academic libraries are the major providers of library-based resources through the Internet. These resources consist primarily of online public access catalogs (OPACs) and other bibliographic databases mounted on academic libraries' computer systems and accessible to remote users through the Internet's Telnet utility. Special librarians can contribute their expertise in developing subject guides to information resources on the networks as well. Wilfred Drew, reference librarian at State University of New York-Morrisville College of Agriculture and Technology, completed a comprehensive guide to Internet resources in agriculture and made the guide itself available via anonymous FTP at several Internet sites (Drew, 1992). This guide is a good model for other subject specialists to follow.

Participation in Network Discussion Groups

Special librarians are active participants in library-oriented computer discussion groups. Participants in the study report that they use computer conferences to stay informed and connected, especially to keep abreast of library issues. Astronomy librarians, for example, are active Internet users, working alongside researchers who have long been using Internet precursors. As early as 1985, librarians in the SLA Physics-Astronomy-Math (PAM) Division investigated the use of ARPANET[10] and BITNET[11] for communication and current awareness needs (Stern, 1988). The following account from the Internet survey by an astronomy librarian in a not-for-profit research institute encapsulates why the Internet is such an important resource for members of the special library community:

> Last spring, I was to present a paper to a NASA workshop exploring the question of making the literature of astronomy available electronically. A few days before the meeting, I heard about an APS [American Physical Society] study on this topic which had not yet been published. Having only the name of the task force chairman, I was able to track him to an institution on the other side of the country, send him e-mail which he read although he was in Japan, and he then e-mailed me the entire study . . . which I ran through our system in time to reproduce and take copies to the workshop. The ease and alacrity with which we were able to accomplish this *still* boggles my mind!

The overwhelming number of academic librarians in these conferences, however, limits diversity of opinion. For example, in the Internet survey, the director of a law library cautioned:

To this point the conferences to which I have access are very largely limited to academic librarians. We run the risk of excluding our commercially related colleagues and becoming too insular.

In addition to participating in computer forums, special librarians have also organized electronic forums in subject disciplines:

- SLA-AERO is the list of the Aerospace Division of SLA.
- SLAITE-L is the list of the Information Technology Division of SLA (ITE).
- SLA-PAM (also known as PAMNET) is the oldest of the three and serves the needs of the Physics-Astronomy-Math (PAM) Division of SLA.
- SLA-TECH was started by the Technical Services Section of ITE in 1992.

These four lists were set up by special librarians active in SLA and are among the large number of computer conferences available to the wider library community.

Control of Grey Literature

In addition to providing pathfinders or guides to information available on the Internet, special librarians can assist in identifying, locating, organizing, and making available a discipline's "grey literature." Much of this bibliographically uncontrolled material is located in corporate libraries and research facilities, and not all of this material in corporate libraries is proprietary in nature. Although it may be unrealistic to expect an individual corporate librarian to take it upon herself to organize the grey literature in her subject area, this could certainly be a project for members of a subject-based professional society.

Prior to the development of commercial online databases, it was common for members of subject divisions within SLA and other professional associations to develop union lists of periodical holdings, technical standards, or technical reports. For example, the Library Services Committee of the American Gas Association was formed in 1972 to participate in information sharing among members, including the preparation of bibliographies of concern to the industry, a directory of gas industry libraries, and a union list of reference tools and services (Shirk and Davis, 1981). In a similar fashion, Chicago area technical librarians, working as a task force of the Illinois Regional Library Council, published a union list of standards and specifications in 1980 (Steinke, 1981). These activities were for the most part discontinued with the advent of commercial services like DIALOG, SDC, and BRS, which provided easy access to bibliographic databases and which supplanted the bibliographic control functions previously done by the professional library associations.

Even today, much of the technical report literature—in particular, non-proprietary reports produced by industry groups or corporate research and development labs—remains unorganized and hence unavailable to clients outside the organization. Much of this material is available in electronic format and could, therefore, be accessible through the Internet. At the very least, organizations could be identified which are repositories of such information, and special librarians could encourage these organizations to make their material available through the Internet. Apple Computer Corporation already provides this service: reports in its ALUG (Apple Library Users Group) directory can be retrieved via anonymous FTP by anyone with access to the Internet.

Certainly, these resources would not have to be free. One model is the CARL UnCover database and its full-text document delivery services through a joint venture with Ebsco Subscription Services, a for-profit corporation providing photocopies of the articles identified through an UnCover search (McKay, 1992). Such an entrepreneurial endeavor, if done solely by a profit-making corporation rather than a resource-sharing library network, might be viewed by the library community as just another example of a bunch of "rapacious capitalists" selling access to information acquired by a network of not-for-profit libraries. How does CARL's activities differ from what a for-profit service could offer? Under current NSF Acceptable Use Policy, profit-making organizations are generally prohibited from using the Internet for commercial advantage. However, NSFNET granted Ebsco the right to provide the document delivery service for CARL.[12] How will this change when the NREN comes into being? Commercial organizations are not going to make their information resources available through the Internet as a public service. Should commercial providers be treated any differently from CARL in determining what they can or cannot provide through the Internet/NREN?

Expertise in Access-Based Librarianship

A particular strength of special librarianship is its long-standing emphasis on service to users and the provision of value-added information. It is unfortunate that many members of the special library community, who for years have followed a model of access to information over development of collections, are outsiders in current philosophical discussions of the future of the library because they do not have access to Internet-resident computer forums. Today, much has been written about the shift in emphasis in academic research libraries from a philosophy of ownership of materials to that of access to information (see, for example, De Gennaro, 1989, or Veaner, 1991). This change in emphasis, although it began several years before the emergence of the Internet, has become more critical with the discovery of the Internet and its capability to make the library "virtual."

Access to information, regardless of format, medium, or location, is what is important to users of information. Special librarians have a long history of providing access-based information service and can contribute their expertise in understanding the needs of users to the NREN planning process. Their experience in searching a variety of commercial databases and proprietary systems will also be a valuable contribution to NREN development.

SPECIAL LIBRARIANS AND NREN PLANNING

Many of the individuals and groups planning the future of the NREN do not see special librarians as key players. Those in the mainstream library/information world may not have a clear understanding of the roles and activities of special librarians. Another reason for exclusion, however, may be the distrust the academic and not-for-profit sectors have of profit-making organizations. In response to the "Call for Participation" to the 1991 study of special librarians' use of the Internet, for example, an inquiry was received from an academic library director who questioned whether the survey of special librarians was a legitimate use of the Internet, since librarians in the private sector were being queried. More recently, there have been flame-oriented discussions on one of the lists (LIBREF-L) as to how "capitalistic monoliths" control the flow of information.[13]

The efforts of the library community regarding NREN planning, in fact, closely parallel the development of library resource-sharing networks twenty years ago. In early discussions of library automation and networking, the dominance of academic research libraries led to the development of "networks" such as OCLC and RLIN which focussed on bibliographic control rather than access to information (Markuson, 1985). With the exception of health science librarians involved in the development of the National Library of Medicine's Regional Library Network, special librarians were not actively involved in national or even regional network-planning activities during the 1970s and early 1980s, even though many were active participants in resource-sharing networks (NCLIS/SLA Task Force, 1984; Ladner, 1990). Decisions as to the direction that computer-based library networks would take were made independently of special librarians' needs and concerns, and special libraries were accorded second-class status in some multitype networks as a result (Robinson, 1981).

Other types of libraries—college, school, and public—were also excluded from significant participation in early network development. Today, as in the 1970s, public, school, and special libraries are in the odd position of being outsiders together, excluded from the research/education base that has comprised library involvement in the Internet to date. McClure and his colleagues (1992a, p.1) examined the role for public libraries in the evolving networked environment and urge that "the public library community take action now!" They provide a series of worthwhile recommendations which special librarians should review as well. Polly (1992) describes this potential for exclusion in terms of public libraries, but her remarks apply equally well to special librarians:

> Librarians should find the stations and get on the train rather than whine later when they find that stop has been discontinued. We need to scout the resources on the Internet and figure out which ones suit our patrons' needs, and how we can exploit technology to further the mission of the public library. . . . The policy-makers are talking on the net every day. We can only join the discussion if we're at the table.

It is time for special librarians to sit at the table as well. Robinson's (1981, p.15) comments about special librarians and the "emerging national network" are just as germane today: "Special libraries cannot afford to be left out of the policy discussions or the resource pool of the national network." Hodgson (1992) appeals to librarians to see what is in the NREN for them in an article which appeared in the SLA newsletter, *SpeciaList*, as well as in the Pittsburgh SLA Chapter *Bulletin*. The Tillman and Ladner (1992) position paper also seeks to gain special librarians' attention and convince them of this need.

SLA must take the lead in educating both policymakers and SLA members about the role which can and should be played by members of this segment of the profession. It was unfortunate that during the Spring 1992 meeting of the Coalition for Networked Information (CNI), the special library community was not represented during discussions of NREN's future. There was an emphasis on the academic/research library sector, and public libraries were part of the discussion, but the "specialized" and/or corporate viewpoints were not represented.

Robinson (1981) identified an operational problem concerning effectiveness of special libraries in national policy making which is still relevant today: special libraries are an extremely heterogeneous group, and they are small—the majority are staffed by only one or two professionals. In order to make their voices heard, special librarians are going to have to organize for institutional representation. The most appropriate vehicle for this organization is SLA. Although SLA has gone on record in support of the NREN, it must do more. SLA does not currently belong to CNI. There has not been member outcry to join the Coalition to date because so few members belong to organizations which are members of CNI. The membership fee to join CNI is a barrier for SLA, which is trying to handle member needs in a fiscally responsible manner during this period of economic austerity. Special librarians must be represented in policy-making discussions, and SLA is urged to join CNI.

Academic, public, school, and special librarians need to collaborate in developing Internet-based resources in an atmosphere of mutual respect. Special librarians have valuable expertise managing libraries that are based on models of information access and value-added service. They need to bring that expertise to network resource development efforts. Special librarians must assure that the NREN provides the information that users need in the information-based, post-industrial organization.

NOTES

1. To obtain a rough estimate of the proportion of special librarians outside of academe who subscribe to library-oriented Internet forums (computer lists), the membership lists of thirteen of these forums of interest to special librarians (BUSLIB-L, CDROMLAN, CHMINF-L, GOVDOC-L, LAWLIB, LIBADMIN, LIBRARY, LIBREF-L, MAPS-L, MEDLIB-L, PACS-L, SERI-ALST, and SLA-PAM) were reviewed. This examination revealed that fewer

than 10 percent of the subscribers to these lists had Internet addresses designated by the extensions .COM, .GOV, .MIL, .NET, or .ORG. Even though there are special librarians "piggybacking" with accounts at educational institutions, the assumption was made that all BITNET addresses and Internet addresses with an .EDU extension indicated an educational institution affiliation in this analysis.

2. A comprehensive report of this research was published by the Special Libraries Association in 1993 (Ladner and Tillman, 1993a). See also Tillman and Ladner (1992); Ladner and Tillman (1992; 1993b) for other reports.

3. The term *Internet* is used here in a broad sense to include other networks which transfer e-mail with the Internet. While respondents used Internet, BITNET, CompuServe, and MCIMail, the majority by far used Internet and BITNET. Certain functions, such as remote logon (Telnet) and file transfer protocol (FTP) are available only on the Internet and not on BITNET.

4. Announcements were posted on eight computer conferences or "listservs" available through both Internet and BITNET (BUSLIB-L, PACS-L, LIBAD-MIN, LIBREF-L, LIBRES, MAPS-L, MEDLIB-L, SLA-PAM) and one Internet-only conference (LAW-LIB). These computer forums, all library-related, were chosen because of their interest to special librarians in various subject specialties.

5. Several researchers have compared electronic forms of data collection with other methods for both quantitative and qualitative applications. Hiltz and Turoff (1978) recommended the use of electronic networks for opinion research because respondents would have the capability to write as much or as little as they wanted because they could easily adapt the space provided for open-ended questions. More recently Kiesler and Sproull evaluated the use of electronic surveys in academe (Kiesler and Sproull, 1986) and in a corporate environment (Sproull, 1986). In a comparison of electronic mail and face-to-face interviews in an e-mail usage study, Sproull concluded that e-mail "was clearly the preferred data-collection method because it produced adequate data, response rates, and willingness for further participation, with little expenditure of researcher time or effort and a high degree of convenience for respondents" (Sproull, 1986, p. 167).

6. Even though there were no differences in Internet use by type of library, only responses made by the nineteen non-academic librarians in the study were included, since this chapter focuses specifically on non-academic special librarians.

7. The NSFNET Acceptable Use Policy is available via FTP from NIC.MERIT.EDU in the directory /nsfnet/acceptable.use.policies/ nsfnet.txt and has been reprinted in the *NorthWestNet User Services Internet Resource Guide* (1992) by Jonathan Kochmer. Also in the acceptable.use.policies directory of NIC.MERIT.EDU are the acceptable use policies of the mid-level regional networks.

8. E-mail from Barry Shein to Hope N. Tillman, July 21, 1992.

9. The Commercial Internet Exchange Association, Inc. (CIX), was formed in 1991 as a non-profit trade association by UUnet Technologies,

Performance Systems International (PSInet), and General Atomics (CERFnet). CIX actively solicits membership and network connections with all commercial and non-profit U.S. national, regional, and mid-level networks, Federal and state government networks, and international network organizations. EUnet, the pan-European open systems computer network, joined CIX in April 1992 (Callanan, 1992). UUnet and CERFnet also refer to themselves as the Alternet.

10. ARPANET was created in 1969 as an experimental testbed by the Advanced Research Projects Agency of the U.S. Department of Defense to foster sharing of computer resources over a large geographic area.

11. BITNET, "Because It's Time Network," began as a network based at the City University of New York. It is now a world-wide network of academic and research organizations.

12. Ebsco received authorization from the NSFnet to use the Internet to provide database services to researchers and scholars over the Internet for the CARL UnCover Service in a letter written by Stephen S. Wolff of the National Science Foundation dated December 17, 1991 addressed to John Fitts.

13. See LIBREF-L postings from June 12 to June 22, 1992, Subject line: "Subjective opinions".

REFERENCES

American Geophysical Union et al. v. Texaco. (1992). *U.S. District Court.* LEXIS 10540; 23 U.S.P.Q.2D (BNA) 1561.

Becker, Karen A. (1992). Introducing the Internet: An international network of networks. *Business Information ALERT* 4(4): 1–5.

Bell, George. (1990). Online searching in industry versus academia: A study in partnerships. *Online* 14(5): 51–56.

Brownrigg, E. (1990). Developing the information superhighway. In C.A. Parkhurst, ed., *Library Perspectives on NREN: The National Research and Education Network.* Chicago: Library and Information Technology Association, 55–63.

Callanan, Cormac. (1992). EUnet joins CIX association. Com-Priv Forum (April 6, 1992).

Cisler, Steve. (1990). NREN for special libraries. In C.A. Parkhurst, ed., *Library Perspectives on NREN: The National Research and Education Network.* Chicago: Library and Information Technology Association, 47–48.

Cveljo, K. (1985). Information activities in selected types of U.S. scientific and technical libraries and information centers. *International Library Review* 17(4): 331–345.

De Gennaro, Richard. (1989). Technology and access in an enterprise society. *Library Journal,* 114(16), 40–43.

Denton, Barbara. (1992). E-mail delivery of search results via the Internet. *Online* 16(2): 50–53.

Doty, Philip, Bishop, Ann, and McClure, Charles R. (1990). The National Research and Education Network: an empirical study of social and behavioral issues. In *Information in the Year 2000: From Research to Applications*. Medford, NJ: Learned Information, 284–299.

Drew, Wilfred. (1992). *Not Just Cows: A Guide to Internet/BITNET Resources in Agriculture and Related Sciences*. New York: State University of New York, Morrisville College of Agriculture and Technology. Available via anonymous FTP). [Available on host hydra.uwo.edu in directory libsoft, filename agriculture_internet_guide.txt and agriculture_internet_guide.wp51.]

Federal Coordinating Council for Science Engineering, and Technology, Committee on Physical, Mathematical and Engineering Sciences. (1992). *Grand Challenges 1993: High Performance Computing and Communications, The FY 1993 U.S. Research and Development Program*. Washington, DC: National Science Foundation.

Flanders, Bruce. (1991). NREN: The big issues aren't technical. *American Libraries* 22(6): 572, 574.

French, Beverlee A. (1990). User needs and library services in agricultural sciences. *Library Trends* 38(3): 415–41.

Hafner, Katie, and Markoff, John. (1991). *Cyberpunk: Outlaws and Hackers on the Computer Frontier*. New York: Simon & Schuster.

Handman, Pamela L. (1991). One-stop shopping: A library-based corporate information system. *Online* 15(5): 39–45.

Hill, Linda L. (1985). Issues in network participation for corporate librarians. *Special Libraries* 76(1): 2–10.

Hiltz, S.R., and Turoff, M. (1978). *The Network Nation: Human Communication via Computer. Reading.* MA: Addison-Wesley.

Hinnebusch, Mark. (1992). Electronic Networking and Electronic Dissemination of Information (EDI): A Review. *Academic and Library Computing* 9(1): 1–2, 4–8.

Hodgson, Cynthia A. (1992). NREN: Why special librarians should care. *SpeciaList* 15(5): 1, 6.

Kahle, Brewster. (October, 1991). Corporate librarians and electronic publishing. *Apple Library Users Group Newsletter* 9(4): 98–99.

Kapor, Mitchell, and Berman, Jerry (1992). Building the open road: The NREN as testbed for the national public network. In Kahin, Brian, ed., *Building Information Infrastructure*. New York: McGraw-Hill, 199–217.

Kiesler, Sara, and Sproull, Lee S. (1986). Response effects in the electronic survey. *Public Opinion Quarterly* 50: 402–413.

Klingenstein, Ken. (1992). A coming of age: the design of the low-end Internet. In Kahin, Brian, ed., *Building Information Infrastructure.* New York: McGraw-Hill, 125–126.

Kochmer. Jonathan. (1992). *NorthWestNet User Services Internet Resource Guide (NUSIRG).* Bellevue, WA: NorthWestNet Academic Computing Consortium, Inc.

Ladner, Sharyn J. (1990). Networking and special libraries: Impact of technology, economics and human nature. In *IOLS '90: Proceedings of the Fifth National Conference on Integrated Online Library Systems,* May 2–3, New York, NY (pp. 129–135). Medford, NJ: Learned Information.

Ladner, Sharyn J. (1991). Effect of organizational structure on resource sharing in sci-tech libraries. *Science & Technology Libraries* 12(2): 59–83.

Ladner, Sharyn J. (1992). Resource sharing by sci-tech and business libraries: formal networking practices. *Special Libraries* 83(2): 96–112.

Ladner, Sharyn J., and Tillman, Hope N. (Fall, 1992). How special librarians really use the Internet: Summary of findings and implications for the library of the future. [Report available via anonymous ftp on host hydra.uwo.ca in directory LibSoft, file-name SPEC_LIBS.TXT and ERIC Doc. No. ED345751. This report was also reprinted in the June 1992, issue of *Canadian Library Journal* and the SLA Business and Finance Division Bulletin.]

Ladner, Sharyn J., and Tillman, Hope N. (1993a). *The Internet and Special Librarians: Use, Training and the Future.* Washington, DC: Special Librarians Association.

Ladner, Sharyn J., and Tillman, Hope N. (1993b). Using the Internet for reference. *Online* 17(1): 45–51.

LaQuey, Tracy L. (1990). *User's Directory of Computer Networks.* Bedford, MA: Digital Press.

Lavendel, Giuliana A. (1988). Xerox network: A true believer's view. *Science & Technology Libraries* 8(2): 31–39.

Markuson, Barbara E. (May 6–8, 1985). Issues in national library network development: An overview. In *Key Issues in the Networking Field Today, Network Planning Paper No. 12, Proceedings of the Library of Congress Network Advisory Committee Meeting* (pp. 9–32). Washington, DC: Network Development and MARC Standards Office, Library of Congress.

Matarazzo, James M., and Prusak, Laurence. (1990). Valuing corporate libraries: A senior management survey. *Special Libraries* 81(2): 102–110.

McClure, Charles R., Bishop, Ann, Doty, Philip, and Rosenbaum, Howard. (1991). *The National Research and Education Network (NREN): Research and Policy Perspectives.* Norwood, NJ: Ablex.

McClure, Charles R., Ryan, Joe, Lauterbach, Diana, and Moen, William E. (1992a). *Public Libraries and the INTERNET/NREN: New Challenges, New Opportunities.* Syracuse, NY: Syracuse University.

McClure, Charles R., Ryan, Joe, Moen, William E., Lauterbach, Diane, and Gratch, Bonnie. (1992b). The impact of national electronic networking on academic and public libraries: Findings, issues, and recommendations. Paper presented at the LITA Third National Conference, Denver, CO, September 15, 1992.

McKay, Sharon C. (March, 1992). The Internet: Its origins, uses and future. *At Your Service. Ebsco Newsletter* 11: 9–11.

Mellon, Constance A. (1990). *Naturalistic Inquiry for Library Science: Methods and Applications for Research, Evaluation, and Teaching.* New York: Greenwood Press.

Mount, Ellis. (1991). *Special Libraries and Information Centers: An Introductory Text.* Washington, DC: Special Libraries Association.

Mount, Ellis. (1985). *University Science and Engineering Libraries.* 2nd edition. Westport, CT: Greenwood Press.

National Commission on Libraries and Information Science/Special Libraries Association Task Force. (1984). *The Role of the Special Library in Networks and Cooperatives: Executive Summary and Recommendations.* New York: Special Libraries Association.

National Public Telecomputing Network. (1991). *The Bluebook: A Guide to the Development of Freenet Community Computer Systems.* Cleveland, OH: The National Public Telecomputing Network.

Polly, Jean A. (May 14, 1992). Why librarians need to be on the net. Public-Access Computer Systems Forum.

Prusak, Laurence, and Matarazzo, James M. (1990). Tactics for corporate library success. *Library Journal* 115(15): 45–46.

Robinson, Barbara M. (1981). The role of special libraries in the emerging national network. *Special Libraries* 72(1): 8–17.

Rotenberg, Marc. (1992). Communications privacy: Implications for network design. Proceedings of INET'92, International Networking Conference held in Kobe, Japan, June 15–18, 1992. Washington, DC: CPSR Washington Office.

Russel, Robert A. (1986). The high-tech revolution. *Special Libraries* 77(1): 1–8.

Schaper, Louise Levy, and Kawecki, Alicja T. (1991). Towards compliance: How one global corporation complies with copyright law. *Online* 15(2): 15–21.

Schrader, William, and Kapor, Mitchell. (1992). The significance and impact of the commercial Internet. *Telecommunications [North American edition]* 26(2): 17, 21.

Shirk, Virginia B., and Davis, Marc L. (1981). Gas libraries: An industry-wide network. *Science & Technology Libraries* 1(2): 15–22.

Sproull, Lee S. (1986). Using electronic mail for data collection in organizational research. *Academy of Management Journal* 29: 159–169.

Sproull, Lee, and Kiesler, Sara. (1991). Computers, networks and work. *Scientific American* 265(3): 116–127.

Stanton, Deidre E., and Hooper, Todd. (1992). The LIBS Internet access software: An overview and evaluation. *The Public Access Computer Systems Review* 3(4): 4–14.

Steinke, Cynthia A. (1981). Standards, specifications, and codes: A union list approach to resource sharing in the Chicago metropolitan area. *Science & Technology Libraries* 1(2): 75–88.

Stern, David. (1988). An alternative national electronic mail network for libraries. *Special Libraries* 79(2): 139–142.

Stoll, Clifford. (1989). *The Cuckoo's Egg: Tracking a Spy Through the Maze of Computer Espionage.* New York: Doubleday.

Taylor, Robert S. (1985). *Value-Added Processes in Information Systems.* Norwood, NJ: Ablex.

Tillman, Hope N. (1991). SLA programs cover the Internet. *B/ITE, the Bulletin of the Information Technology Division of SLA* 8(4): n.p.

Tillman, Hope N., and Ladner, Sharyn J. (1992). Special libraries and the Internet. *Special Libraries* 83(2): 127–131.

Veaner, Allen B. (1991). A united professional cadre. *Reference Librarian* 15(34): 127–130.

Wiggins, Gary. (1985). *Factors Which Influence the Choice of Document Delivery Mechanisms for Serials by Selected Scientific and Technical Special Librarians.* Bloomington, IN: Indiana University. Dissertation.

Will, Linda. (1992). The law library and adherence to the fair use doctrine. *Law Office Economics and Management* 32(4): 431–437.

Willard, Ann M., and Morrison, Patricia. (1988). The dynamic role of the information specialist: Two perspectives. *Special Libraries* 79(4): 271–276.

7

The Federal Depository Library Program and the NREN*

John H. Sulzer

What is the future of the Federal Depository Library Program (DLP) in the electronic information age? What is the National Research and Education Network (NREN)? What will it be? And, what will this mean for access to and the dissemination of government information?

These are exciting and challenging questions. Not since Gutenberg have circumstances occurred of such grand historical implication in the dissemination and use of information and knowledge. Is this an overblown metaphor? Not so much of one. We are truly standing on the brink of profound changes to our society. We are now at the technological confluence of high-capacity digital storage, very fast microprocessors, and exceedingly fast means of telecommunications and transferring data. The three legs of the technology triad are in place. We are standing on them, looking over the horizon, and trying to decide what to do next.

This chapter examines two major theses.[1] The first is that we recognize that we are speaking of potential and trying to design a grand plan for the future. At this point in our evolution, a great deal about our new information society is simply unknown. Nevertheless, it is clear that a new policy for government information must be developed that reaffirms the foundation of Chapter 19, Title 44 of the *United States Code* (*U.S.C.*). That is, the fundamental concept of wide dissemination of and open access to Federal information resources. To secure our democracy and our intellectual freedom, we need to transfer to the electronic environment those principles that have successfully guided publishing in print.

Issues of access to and dissemination of electronic information are beginning to coalesce over a broad scope of interests and

* *This writing was completed on October 14, 1992.*

among a range of diverse interest groups and stakeholders. Because of the development of the NREN, the issues that government information librarians have been debating for many years have become more prominent in the arena of government policy planning. The freedom of our society, as determined by the nature of its political and educational structure in the electronic age, will depend on the accessibility of information by and about the government and a cogent electronic information policy. This policy must be based soundly on the concept of the "public good."

Second, the development of the NREN requires the restructuring of the DLP to deal with electronic dissemination of government information. If the DLP is not only going to survive as a viable alternative for distributing government information to the public, the function for which it was intended, and the NREN is to become truly an "education" network, a diverse structure for both the DLP and the NREN is critical. The DLP must be restructured to meet the public needs and requirements of an electronic environment. The NREN will change completely the nature of the DLP as an organization for dispersing the products of government publishing. Depository libraries, if they are to be a means of free public distribution of Federal information, will need to be incorporated as partners with the Government Printing Office (GPO) and Federal agencies in a new, more cohesive system of government information dissemination and use.

Moving on to the next generation of computer networking will mean broad new horizons for information transfer, of course. However, it also will provide opportunities for government information librarians to become integral parts of the research, business, and educational communities they always have attempted to serve, and to serve the information needs of the public in a way never before possible in the history of the DLP. That is, if we do things right.

BACKGROUND

This section describes the history and purpose of the DLP and the NREN.

The Federal Depository Library Program

Title 44, Chapter 19 of the *U.S.C.* is the legislative authority for the GPO and its administration of the DLP. Among other things, it provides that:

- depository libraries will be located in each state and congressional district;
- all government publications, with certain exceptions, will be made available to depository libraries; and
- all government publications received by depository libraries will be made available for free use by the general public.

The GPO outlines the DLP as being made up of five essential components (U.S. Superintendent of Documents, 1992, May 31):

> The Federal Depository Library Program can serve its purpose of providing U.S. government information for the free use of the public only when these five elements are provided by depository libraries. Free and open access, adequate bibliographic control and [sic] maintenance, sufficient resources with which to access materials, and above all, service to the public at large, are all essential to creating a first-rate depository library system.

The community formed by the approximate 1,400 depository libraries around the country is very diverse. The DLP is made up of (in descending order of number): academic libraries at four-year institutions; public libraries; academic law libraries; academic libraries at two-year institutions; Federal agency, state court, and state libraries; and special, Federal court, and service academy libraries (U.S. Superintendent of Documents, November 15, 1992). The libraries in each of those categories fall into a range of sizes from small, very specialized libraries to large academic research libraries at major universities.

The system is further divided by levels of depository status. Most depository libraries are selective depositories. They receive from the GPO only pre-selected publications that complement their main collections, or which meet the primary needs of the public in their district. The rate of selection may range from 5 to 98 percent of what the GPO distributes (J. McClane, personal communication, May 20, 1992). In order to ensure that a comprehensive and well-preserved collection of Federal publications are available in each state, fifty-four libraries around the country are designated as regional depositories and are responsible for retaining the entire distribution of the GPO. They also provide support services to the selective depositories in their regions.

The National Research and Education Network

On December 9, 1991, the High Performance Computing Act (HPCA) became law and established the NREN, mandating the creation of a computer link among more than 1,000 Federal and industrial laboratories, educational institutions and libraries, and other public and private research facilities by 1996 (P.L. 102-194).

The last major advance in networking came in 1985, when the National Science Foundation (NSF) began funding multipurpose regional networks. Five super computer networks in combination with the regional networks and a few "mid-level" networks constituted the NSFNET (Kahin, 1991, p. 452), which is the "backbone" of the Internet in the United States, and is seen as the central component for the NREN (Adler, May 1, 1992, p. 1).

As envisioned, the NREN will build on this foundation to establish a "super highway" system for computers. This proposed high-speed network will move information between computers at the rate of about 100,000 typed pages each second (Henderson, 1990, p. 3). However, notwithstanding the immensity of this technological leap forward, it is likely to be the policy and social issues where the NREN will have its greatest impact and where development of the NREN and its use will reach a critical phase (McClure, Bishop, Doty, and Rosenbaum, 1991, pp. 31-32). On the technology side it is now primarily a question of "road-building" to construct the network infrastructure. However, the issues of policy and governance, as yet, are open and unresolved.

NETWORKING FEDERAL GOVERNMENT INFORMATION: THE KEY ISSUES

Three key issues underlie the concept of networking Federal government information. They are:

- the awareness and position of the DLP;
- legislative and regulatory policy issues; and
- depository librarians and the institutional issues.

The following sections provide an examination of each of these issues.

Awareness and Position of the DLP

The vision of what the NREN will be is only now beginning to be articulated by academicians, librarians, and government officials.

The purpose of the HPCA is to ". . . ensure the continued leadership of the United States in high-performance computing and its applications . . ." (P.L. 102–194, Sec. 3). As of now, those "applications" are open to discussion. Some of the key propositions of the law, along with the establishment of the NREN, are outlined in Figure 7-1.

The act establishes under the director of the Office of Science and Technology Policy a High-Performance Computing Advisory Committee consisting of representatives of the research, education and library communities, network providers, and industry (P.L. 102–194, Title I, Sec. 101 (b)). However, whether depository libraries will play a significant role in the development of the NREN, or even be connected to it, depends on the organization of that community, its ability to function in an electronic environment, and the ability of depository librarians to collaborate institutionally and politically with other stakeholders. P.L. 102–194 clearly expresses the need for a coalition of stakeholders to develop the NREN, and it includes libraries as a central element in that coalition. Nevertheless, stating the purpose and defining the vision are two different things. Will libraries and, along with them the DLP, be able to define their

---

- Promote the further development of an information infrastructure of databases, services, access mechanisms, and research facilities available for use through the network.

- Invest in basic research and education, and promote the inclusion of high-performance computing into educational institutions at all levels.

- Provide users with appropriate access to high-performance computing systems, electronic information resources, other research facilities, and libraries.

- To the extent that colleges, universities, and libraries cannot connect to the network with the assistance of the private sector, the National Science Foundation shall have the primary responsibility for assisting colleges, universities, and libraries to connect to the network.

Figure 7-1. Key elements of the HPCA.

role and participate in developing the NREN? Is the DLP in a position to play a significant role in NREN development?

In January 1990, the American Library Association (ALA) endorsed the concept of the NREN in a resolution stating, "Libraries linked to NREN would spread its benefits more broadly, enhance the resources to be made available over it, and increase the access to those resources." The following year, while the NREN bill was still under consideration, the Government Documents Round Table (GODORT) of ALA followed up with a white paper supporting connection to the NREN of the libraries in the DLP as the best means of ensuring public access to the vast resources in government-produced information, particularly that in electronic form (Ruhlin, Somers, and Rowe, June, 1991, p. 106).

However, depository librarians face two general difficulties. The first is that recent studies indicate the library community, in general, has only limited awareness of networking issues, and no clear sense of its role in an environment of computer networks, be it the Internet or the NREN (McClure, Ryan, Lauterbach, and Moen, 1992, pp. 18–19). Discussions among officials of the Association of Research Libraries (ARL) and the Library Information Technology Association (LITA) of ALA have pointed to a major lack in understanding about networks that exist in the library community. Even among Federal depository librarians, beyond those from select depositories which are in academic institutions now connected to the Internet, there is no broadly shared conception of what electronic networking will mean to the DLP (P. Adler, personal communication, June 3, 1992).

The second problem is that there are vastly contrasting visions of the NREN. On the one hand, there is the "techie" vision. This view foresees a "very powerful network that would connect powerful scientific computers, databases, experimental instruments, and researchers." It is an elitist view of an NREN reserved to heavy users in the science and technology community that would be dominated by the Federal government. On the other hand, is the "universal" vision, which "foresees a fiber optic into every home." This kind of NREN would be the next generation in cable TV/telephone and is envisioned as a predominantly private undertaking. Weingarten also says that (Weingarten, Spring, 1991, p. 27):

> Somewhere in between these two extremes is what one might call the true NREN vision: a network serving the public, but serving it, at least for now, through traditional public intermediary institutions such as schools, universities, libraries, and museums.

Weingarten's vision is certainly an appealing one to librarians, given the HPCA's a broad agenda for the network (McClure, Ryan, and Moen, 1992, p. 67).

The broader, public view of the NREN, however, remains to be played out in the formulation of the Federal rules and policy that will follow the HPCA. To date, a general and consistent Federal electronic information policy has not developed, in spite of a number of attempts. It is here where depository librarians have attempted to play a significant role and will need to continue to do so.

Nevertheless, their effectiveness has been limited by the demands of their primary mission as librarians and their inability to define a new structure for the DLP in a network environment. In addition, they have yet to find an effective means to articulate their vision among Federal agencies and lawmakers, among information specialists and coalitions of information users, among librarians outside the DLP, and outside of a relatively small group of librarians within the DLP.

Legislative and Regulatory Policy Issues

When government information became increasingly available in electronic format, it also became obvious that computer technology had rendered obsolete the government information policy that was outlined in the Printing Act of 1895 (28 STAT 601), the Depository Library Act of 1962 (76 STAT 532), and even the Paperwork Reduction Act (PRA) (44 USC 3501, et seq.) which was enacted in 1980. Proposed measures intended to amend these statutes center on:[2]

- redefining government publication to cover Federal agency electronic products and services;
- the role of the GPO and the DLP in the distribution of and the provision of public access to electronic government information;
- the relationship between Federal information-producing agencies and private sector publishers;
- cost recovery efforts by Federal agencies through charges to libraries and the inception of user fees;
- security of government information and its classification;
- insurance of privacy and confidentiality; and
- development of standards for the format, dissemination, and use of electronic information.

The legislative focus of the late 1980s and early 1990s has been mainly on revision of sections of Title 44 covering the Depository Library Act (44 USC 1901, et seq.), the PRA, and the Freedom of Information Act (FOIA) (5 USC 501, et seq.). These are not laws that seem to inspire wide public interest. They are little known, little understood, or even considered important outside a relatively small community of stakeholders. The paper trail around Congress and the several library associations is testimony to the intense interest the stakeholders had in updating Federal information laws. But its litter obscures the fact that revision of these laws had a narrow public appeal and did not inspire assertive congressional action.

It is the conflict among the stakeholders interested in government information issues that has destroyed efforts at legislative reform. Indeed, the sentiment expressed by an official of the Office of Technology Assessment3 is that the stakeholders must reach agreement on proposals if they are to force Congress to take action (F. Wood, personal communication, April 7, 1992). It is obvious from the experiences of the last several years, that Congress cannot serve as a mediator of disputes over information policy among the DLP, Federal agencies, the private sector, and the various public interest groups involved. If the legislation needed to provide a consistent information dissemination policy is to be written and passed, it will require the collaboration of the various stakeholders to present Congress with a compelling reason to do it.

In addition, the attempt of the Office of Management and Budget (OMB), Office of Information and Regulatory Affairs (OIRA), to establish the first broad electronic information policy through executive branch action in OMB Circular A-130 (50 FR 52730, Dec. 24, 1985), and a further effort to revise A-130 (57 FR 18296, April 29, 1992), moves the debate over the issues out of the congressional limelight and legislative process, and makes it even more difficult for depository librarians to draw attention and support to questions surrounding Federal information resources management.

The Current Trend. Initiation of the NREN and burgeoning telecommunications initiatives by the telephone and cable industry have inspired a broader base of interest in certain information policy issues. All of the topics at issue in revising the PRA and FOIA are now being revived in various permutations in regard to NREN development and the efforts of the regional or "Baby Bell" telephone companies to expand into carrying video and data transmissions as well as voice communications. The chief issues fall into the same major areas of Federal information management policy. Namely, they are security of information resources and intellectual property, the value and utility of the information, the costs of electronic information systems, and public access to and control of the information and the systems.[4]

Edwin Brownrigg, director of research at the Memex Research Institute, believes the chief NREN policy issue for libraries is developing a network that is based on service of the "public good," the same as with the development of public lands, the broadcasting spectrum, and the interstate highway system (Brownrigg, 1990, p. 60). Since the very beginning of the depository program, depository librarians have held the almost reverent belief that government information is owned by the public, that the public must have free access to it, and that libraries are the natural centers for distribution of that information and for the provision of public access. "Information-age technology should be used to advance social integration and not social stratification. The social vision of a public network matches the social vision of libraries" (Coulter, June 27, 1992). The growing debate over what the NREN will be, and how it will be used, is carrying the notion of information as a public good outside the narrow scope of the Federal depository libraries and a few associations of government information users. Development of NREN policy, therefore, now has a much greater impact than that of network construction alone.

If implementation and development of the NREN makes information policy issues the concern of a larger and more diverse constituency, this could be seen as a boon for Federal depository librarians and the DLP. For the first time, it brings the issue of the freedom of government information and the development of a system of Federal information distribution into a much wider forum. Development of the NREN and the need to define its use may finally bring about needed revision to Title 44, *U.S.C.* and the development of a consistent and modern Federal information policy. For the DLP to be effective, Title 44 must be revised to reaffirm Federal agency information distribution through the DLP and to redefine "government publication" to include electronic products such as CD-ROMs and the various online services developed by the agencies. Connecting depository libraries to the NREN will be meaningless unless the Federal agencies are connected to the other end.

Recent Legislative Action. The GPO Wide Information Network Data Online Act , or WINDO bill, (H.R. 2772), introduced in 1991 by Rep. Charles Rose (D-NC), proposed establishing the GPO as a gateway service to all Federal online databases. Congressman Rose got assistance in the Senate from the chief sponsor of the NREN legislation when Senator Albert Gore introduced S. 2813, the GPO Gateway to Government Act, as the WINDO companion bill. No doubt, Sen. Gore saw the critical relation between legislation like WINDO/Gateway and the development of the NREN. Both the Rose and Gore bills would have required the GPO to provide access through the Internet.

However, on September 22, 1992, the WINDO measures were replaced by H.R. 5983. Congressman Rose, along with Congressmen Roberts and Thomas, introduced the new bill as a compromise measure to quell the Republican opposition on the House Administration Committee. The Government Printing Office Electronic Information Access Enhancement Act of 1992, narrowed the scope of the earlier bills. It reduced the number of Federal electronic services accessible through the GPO gateway to those resources now distributed by the Superintendent of Documents. The bill did retain the requirement of the former measures that online access be provided to the DLP without charge, but it did not require the GPO to be on the Internet. Instead, the Superintendent of Documents is to conduct a two-year study to ". . . determine the feasibility of providing access to Federal electronic information through a wide range of electronic networks, including the Internet and the NREN" [H.R. 5983, Sec. 3(a)(3)]. In addition, the compromise bill added a broad definition of "Federal electronic information" to Title 44 by defining it as ". . . Federal public information stored electronically" (U.S. House. 102d Congress, 2d Session. *H.R. 5983, the Government Printing Office Electronic Information Access Enhancement Act.* Washington: Government Printing Office, 1992).[5]

Although it was more restrictive than the others, and did not mandate GPO access to many Federal online services, the success of this bill would have placed the GPO and the DLP in a better position to become NREN participants. It could have provided a platform for resolution of the other policy issues of Title 44 because it did mandate the study of Internet/NREN use, and required the Superintendent of Documents to maintain a directory of Federal electronic information [H.R. 5983, Sec. 4101 (a)(1)]. The bill, however, failed to pass Congress before the session ended. Certainly, with the incoming Clinton/Gore administration, it is not unreasonable to expect that this measure, or one similar to it, would have a very good chance of success if introduced in the 103d Congress.

Depository Librarians and the Institutional Issues

Because of their knowledge and background, Federal information librarians could be leaders in the development of the network, and the DLP could be an organizational focus for the first NREN connections to the general public and the educational system. With the renewed interest in government information issues comes their best opportunity. However, there are many difficulties depository librarians face which may restrict them to a minor role or keep them out of the picture altogether. Although the NREN development may give depository library issues wider appeal, it will not necessarily usher depository librarians and their libraries into leadership roles in the policy development.

Action to develop the NREN will mean the evolution of some form of Federal electronic information policy. Resolution of the electronic information policy issues in favor of the "public good" is critical to the future of the DLP and its users. However, it is not altogether a question of writing the proper legislation and regulations. In development of the NREN and the redevelopment of the DLP, a predominant issue is one that seems to be "an institutional problem and not a statutory problem" (V. Schreibmen and J. McDonough, personal interview, April 6, 1992).[6] Finding a position for the DLP on the NREN will not only require the action of the depository library community, but also the collaboration of the GPO, the institutions which are the homes of the depository libraries, Federal agencies, private publishers, and new coalitions of interest groups (Cornwell, et al., 1993, pp. 136–137).

This will not be an easy task for several problematic reasons.

- Depository librarians must expend a great deal of their effort just trying to wrest basic support from the GPO.
- The DLP is under administration of the GPO with depository libraries and depository librarians having little control over it, even through the Depository Library Council to the Public Printer.[7]
- Relations between the GPO, the Joint Committee on Printing (JCP), and many Federal agencies are less than cordial, often placing the DLP in the middle of opposing camps and often blocking progressive cooperative initiatives.
- The GPO has little authority to demand that Federal agencies comply with provisions of Title 44.

- Depository librarians do not have a professional organization or association that is limited to their interests.[8]
- The effectiveness of the associations' lobbying efforts has been severely hampered by their limited resources and staff in Washington.
- Volunteer energy is most often committed to defending traditional library programs and is no match for the resources of opposition lobbying groups such as the Information Industry Association (IIA).
- Depository libraries are in need of better support from their home institutions to actually become part of the NREN.
- Depository librarians do not control the budgets of their own libraries, and have only marginal influence as to how their libraries become involved in networking, the use of electronic information, and the choice of electronic services.
- Depository libraries are not a homogeneous group themselves.
- There is a wide and growing gap in capability, interests, and understanding of the electronic network environment between the smaller academic and public libraries and the large academic research depositories.
- There is a need for very extensive education and training within the depository community to even reach a common ground of understanding before a structure for the DLP in the NREN environment can be laid out in the detail.

To resolve these overriding institutional problems, depository librarians will need to become more knowledgeable, more visible, and more influential.

Further, depository librarians must be more active in working on projects that will not only develop their network knowledge and skills, and develop network resources, but also bring them into collaboration with other government information stakeholders and those interested in NREN development. They must work to close the gap between librarians and technologists and the gap between the system users and the system builders.

This is a tall order, but depository librarians must convince themselves and their administrators that this is all part of the job. In this day and age, it is as important as reference service, collection development, acquisitions, and cataloging. It should be as significant in the evaluation of performance as a librarian.

CONCEPTS FOR THE DLP IN THE NREN ENVIRONMENT

The consensus among DLP librarians seems to be that:

- Depository libraries have a great deal of potential for offering the best access to a range of government information sources and services in print and electronic format.
- Depository libraries can ensure free access on the NREN to a great number and diversity of users.
- The DLP will have to be restructured to operate in an electronic network environment.

Two primary questions are: what role could the DLP perform in the development of the NREN, and how could the DLP and depository libraries be organized to receive and disseminate electronic information in the NREN environment?

To answer these questions, one must consider:

- the barriers that depository libraries face and are likely to face when attempting to use electronic resources and the NREN;
- the trends that indicate depository libraries will be in a position to take advantage of the NREN and participate in an electronic information environment;
- the contributions that depository libraries could provide or develop as the NREN becomes operational;
- the role depository libraries can play in the actual construction of the NREN infrastructure in the United States;
- the possible scenarios by which the DLP could acquire and distribute Federal electronic information via the NREN; and
- the models by which the DLP might be reconfigured.

The multi-faceted concerns facing the DLP in the NREN can be seen in the subsequent sections.

The GPO/DLP and Transition

Is the DLP ready to be connected to the NREN? In a position paper written as an advisory document to John Merritt, chief of staff for the Joint Committee on Printing (hereinafter *The*

Librarians' Manifesto), a group of depository librarians outlined the issues on the current conditions of the GPO and DLP. They provided recommendations for a transition to a new structure that would bring the DLP into the electronic environment, and provide an improved program for distribution of paper and microforms. One primary conclusion reached by the librarians was that (Cornwell et al., 1993, p. 133):

> By any measure, the current structure of the depository library system is inadequate, inefficient, and ineffective. The introduction of electronic products and services into the program has only served to heighten existing problems. As a result, the information dissemination needs of government agencies are not being met, nor are the needs of the information-using public.

Calls for the restructuring of the DLP can be traced back in library literature for over thirty years. Aside from corrections made to the 120-year-old program in 1962, Congress was unable to accomplish any revisions in 1979 and again in the late 1980s. The GPO itself has done little else to support the program. Instead, it has expanded the DLP by adding libraries and distributing more copy. The GPO has not increased the DLP budget correspondingly, nor has it argued in Congress for better appropriations for the DLP. In 1962, Title 44 amendments nearly doubled the number of depository libraries authorized to reflect population growth. Since 1962, growth has been from 790 to almost 1,400 libraries (Hale and McAninch 1989, p. 388) and the DLP budget has actually decreased 10 percent in the last seven years.[9]

Hernon and McClure (1984, pp. 316–318) have identified a number of weaknesses in the DLP. Chief among them are:

- poorly trained staff servicing depository collections;
- substantial variations in quality of reference services;
- limited bibliographic control over documents collections;
- ineffective use of new technology;
- poor geographic distribution of depository libraries; and
- a diverse assortment of libraries with individual service goals rather than an interlocking network.

In a recent article Hernon (1992, p. 103) points out that the DLP is essentially overburdened by what it has to do now. The process of collecting government information for distribution is less effective with electronic information, the resources for the program are dwindling, and the system is dated by the electronic age.

Analysis of the data from a fall 1988 survey of ninety-three academic depository libraries which are members of the Association of Research Libraries (ARL) does "... not portray a group of libraries with sufficient resources, support, or staff trained to deal with electronic data" (Smith, 1990, p. 312). Smith points to specific weaknesses in electronic resources, reference technology, and innovation within the libraries (ibid., pp. 306–308, 310–311). Only 18 percent of the libraries used their OPAC to locate documents, only 7 percent used expert systems, and only 20 percent used electronic bulletin boards. The percentages were similarly low (under 46 percent in all cases) for libraries with equipment available to provide staff and patrons with adequate access to online services such as OCLC and RLIN, to PCs with modems, to university computation centers, and to OPACs within the libraries (ibid., 1990, p. 308).

Another problem is that 65 percent of the libraries using online bibliographic vendor services (and the 48 percent using vendor numeric files) reported passing the vendor's online and telecommunication charges on to the user (Smith, 1990, p. 301). This is a strong indication that the philosophy behind library budgets is still to pay for materials and not access to information. Given this attitude, limited budgets will likely force libraries to pass on the costs of fee-based government services.

The regional depository libraries, on which an electronic network might depend heavily under the current DLP structure, seem to be overburdened by the amount of material they are required to collect and ill-equipped to handle electronic resources (Hale and McAninch, 1989, p. 389).[10] Moreover, the growth in number of depository libraries and their geographic distribution has impacted heavily on the regional system which has grown much more slowly. This has created a wide disparity in the number of depository libraries each regional is responsible for serving (Hale and McAninch, 1989, p. 389). Inequities range from nine regionals serving 40 percent of the selective depository libraries to nine serving only 6 percent (Cornwell et al., 1993, p. 135).

In addition to deficiencies of the DLP and the institutional and political problems facing the librarians, interviews and correspondence with depository librarians and information professionals around the country identified a number of other barriers to the viability of the DLP and its connection to the NREN. Figure 7-2 illustrates the commonly acknowledged barriers.

Negative Conditions Include:

- NREN development is being driven by different concepts and sets of needs from the DLP;
- the potential of regional telephone systems creating local communications monopolies and high telecommunications costs on local networks and connections to the NREN;
- a lack of support for the DLP from agencies that are dumping raw data in CD-ROMs and online files without user software;
- networking has taken many traditional roles of libraries out of the libraries;
- absence of recognition of the NREN by GPO in its *Vision* and federal agency connections to the NREN in guidelines under OMB Circular A-130;
- lack of program support for DLP from GPO and funding from Congress, along with limited federal funding for information dissemination programs.

Negative Attitudes Include:

- electronic media presents a different level of expectation for support than many libraries can address;
- concepts of traditional library roles and functions do not foster exploitation of electronic technology;
- agency and GPO attitudes that once information is distributed, in whatever format or level of usefulness, they have fulfilled their information dissemination obligations;
- mindset that electronic information, like paper and microforms, could and should be stored in multiple locations;
- shifting attitudes among library administrators as electronic information developments illustrates to them the costs of being a depository.

Additional DLP Deficiencies Include:

- the need for continuing staff training to keep up with developments;
- little understanding of networks outside many ARL depositories and increasing gaps in service provision between small public libraries and large academic libraries ;
- the ability of depository libraries to respond to electronic information access in an environment where hardcopy resources are still critical;
- covering the costs of equipment, staff resources, and access/retrieval technology, especially in areas of galloping obsolescence;
- the GPO's lack of initiative and inability to develop viable solutions to DLP problems while depository libraries move ahead in the use of electronic resources;
- the GPO's historical lack of commitment to public services and historic disregard for maintaining and developing resources for the DLP.

Figure 7-2. Barriers to depository libraries.

Nevertheless, as seen in Figure 7-3, it is generally acknowledged that there are a number of trends and concepts becoming prevalent that may mitigate the impact of the deficiencies and barriers.

Some additional positive features of the DLP generally pointed out by the depository librarians are:

- the geographic and social distribution of the program;
- it brings together a great collection of resources in the technology, the expertise of the librarians, and a wide range of access to collections of non-government information in paper, microforms and electronic services; and
- its service ideal of providing access and training for users regardless of their social status, level of sophistication, or access to the technology.

In short, there are some opportunities for the DLP to exploit the NREN to provide enhanced or innovative new services.

Depository Libraries and NREN Development

The last point in Figure 7-3 requires further examination since depository librarians generally believe the DLP has a great deal to offer as a program that can broaden the NREN and improve its diversity. What contributions can depository libraries provide to the development of the NREN as it becomes operational? What part can depository libraries play in the actual NREN infrastructure?

Geographic and Social Distribution: "Connectivity". The development of home computer technology, more widely available telecommunications access to online government information, and information locator systems, some have argued, will obviate the need for depository libraries. But, for the foreseeable future, as we develop the NREN, major gaps in "connectivity" among different sectors in the population will pose a number of access issues. The geographic dispersal of the DLP still offers particular advantages in a network environment where there are still inadequate "on-ramps" to the interstate "electronic super highway." Depository libraries can provide the "last-mile" service connection for which the Federal government does not have the resources (Park, July 21, 1992). In addition, (Ruhlin, Somers, and Rowe, June, 1991, p. 107):

Federal depository libraries, by the nature of their geographic distribution and commitment to free access to government

- a growing interest in expanding the NREN outside STI uses and creating a truly diverse research and education oriented network;

- the likelihood that NREN development will impact on the development of programs for government information distribution;

- growth in the number of local, state, and regional networks along with more universities "wiring" their campuses and building fiber-optic backbones for campus-wide information systems (CWIS) (Lynch, 1990, p. 7);

- network managers' concern about extending "connectivity" and expanding the uses of networks[11];

- a growing number of depository librarians becoming familiar with network services and uses[12];

- there is the activity of organizations like the Coalition of Networked Information with the mission to increase network diversity and develop new uses by sponsoring collaborative projects;

- experience shows that networks tend to derive their purpose from the uses made of them ;

- those on the free use side of the network use issue argue that free access is what makes networks grow and this, in turn, inspires further study and development[13];

- depositories in smaller public libraries are expanding the use of CD-ROMs, selecting more CDs from the GPO and are revealing a higher level of technological sophistication because many are located in federal libraries and special libraries;

- an evolving trend in libraries is the recognition that libraries improve their ability to get information to users by accessing off-site sources rather than trying to upgrade increasingly inadequate collections with diminishing resources. "The term 'library without walls' has been used to describe this profound change in philosophical orientation" (Shill, March 13, 1992, p. 8).

- there is growing interest in getting electronic information into the DLP and in restructuring the program[14]; and

- collectively, depository libraries in the DLP do have a significant array of resources and the potential for providing comprehensive services over the NREN to users, federal information dissemination agencies, and private sector publishers.

Figure 7-3. Recent mitigating trends.

information, would ensure equitable access to the National
Research and Education Network for all citizens regardless of
location or access to information technologies. Because
Chapter 19 provisions of Title 44 authorize at least two depository collections per congressional district, NREN links to these
designated libraries would guarantee each member of
Congress that the constituents of his or her home district
would be "electronically enfranchised." . . . Federal depositories in both academic and public libraries would play an important role as intermediaries to individuals who cannot afford
home computers or access to the educational or commercial
networks that will ultimately form the NREN.

Geographic location offers the advantages of developing state and
local connectivity to networks already in place (P. Adler, personal
commuication, June 3, 1992), and a focal point for state and local
funding to contribute to costs of developing and connecting to the
NREN (Weingarten, Spring 1991, p. 29). Almost 40 percent of
regionals are in public, state agency, or state historical libraries
(Herman and Heisser, 1991, p. 44). Some are administered by state
governments which are applying networking technology to their
public library systems.[15]

The Although the DLP is a diverse community of libraries ranging
widely in technology resources, most of the 119 ARL libraries are in
the DLP, and many of these institutions are becoming the leaders in
developing electronic library services (Ruhlin, Somers, and Rowe,
1991, p. 107). Approximately thirty-three (60%) regional depositories
are housed in major academic libraries and nineteen (57%) of those
institutions are members of ARL (Hernon and Heisser, 1991, p. 47).

The OPACs of state libraries and large research libraries could
serve as regional or national gateways to Federal information systems on the NREN. McClure has recommended that the Federal
government develop a "distributed" government-wide informa-
tion/inventory locator system (GIILS) that would identify and provide access to government electronic sources and services regardless of the type of information or the physical location of the database (McClure, Ryan, and Moen, 1992, pp. 65–78). With a GIILS
available based on an "open protocol" network server such as a
wide area information system (WAIS), or another "client-server" system using Z39.50 communications standards,[16] "gateway" depository libraries on the NREN could provide users with seamless access
to the entire array of Federal online services from one terminal as
though they were using only one system. McClure et al., points out

that the DLP could play a very important role as an intermediary between a Federal GIILS/locator system and users by providing Internet-connected terminals (ibid., 1992, p. 74). Such approaches could "create a 'virtual' depository reaching far beyond the physical collections of even the largest regional depository libraries" (Ruhlin, Somers, and Rowe, June 1991, p. 107). In addition, networking could lead, in turn, to an increased emphasis on linkages with state-wide and regional systems through advanced telecommunication networks (ARL, Task Force on Government Information in Electronic Format, October 1987, p. 16).

The Collection of Resources: The User's Advantage. Most educators and librarians believe that providing library services on the NREN will greatly enhance its educational purpose. Depository libraries' ". . . ability to provide access to specialized databases and current research relevant to public policy is of critical importance to ongoing support of NREN . . ." (Strong, Hudson, and Jewell, 1990, p. 46). Robert Oakley, director of the Georgetown University Law Center, agrees (personal communication, June 1, 1992):

> What better resources to make available than those that are free and in the public domain? Not only are they free of costs and copyright impediments, they are those which are used by large numbers of people.[17] As a result, . . . the Depository Library Program can play a role in developing the foundation of the NREN for the delivery of actual, useful information to citizens of the United States.

Gateway depositories on an NREN driven by GIILS/WAIS technology would bring tremendous power of information access to the individual citizen. Through the depository libraries, the entire array of Federal public information could be linked. For the first time, the user would have convenient and timely access to Federal electronic services and products, and to Federal information in paper and microform. In addition, depository links to regional and state-wide information systems would make state and local government information accessible nationally. This also would provide library users with immediate access to related commercial electronic products and services available at their depositories.

Furthermore, depository librarians tend to view themselves as the human resources of the DLP. They see themselves as information professionals working in the government's information program. In their traditional role, they could serve two primary functions on the

NREN. The first is as the gatekeepers and experts in locating and accessing Federal information and developing the user interfaces and expert systems that likely will be necessary. McClure notes that depository librarians could assist users in accessing Federal locators and the information to which they point (McClure, Ryan, and Moen, 1992, p. 74).

The second role will be as the instructors to teach the public to become "electronic citizens" of the NREN democracy (V. Schreibman and J. McDonough, personal interview, April 6, 1992). They have an important role to play because, unlike the systems people putting the network together, they understand user needs.[18] "Libraries are part of the glue holding the information society together" (Vial, June 27, 1992). The educational role of libraries and librarians will enhance the "E" in the NREN.

The Service Ideal: Information Equity. Finally, DLP Librarians and their supporters argue vociferously that while the vision of the NREN as a national "information superhighway" is laudable, it should not create a nation of information "haves" and "have-nots." Income distribution in this country does not provide equality of access to education and information. That is not likely to change significantly in the near future. Many people will be able to participate in the information age only as a community (Vial, June 27, 1992).

The DLP is viewed as a "safety net" by many. This has a "Reagan-omics" connotation to it that is not entirely positive. Depository librarians may have done themselves some disservice by using this term. Nevertheless, the DLP provides an important link between the unsophisticated user, lacking the hardware and the wherewithal, to the resources on the NREN. If the Federal agencies are connected to NREN, and the current mandate under Title 44 *U.S.C.* is reaffirmed, the DLP will continue to provide free and equitable access to government information to the public.

RESTRUCTURING THE DLP FOR THE NETWORK ENVIRONMENT

Creating a new government information dissemination program that preserves the principle of free and open access for all citizens means connecting the information-producing agencies to the NREN on the one end, and connecting the DLP libraries on the other. This will mean demonstrating to Federal agencies that a networked DLP can provide them with a cost-effective means of meeting their mandate to disseminate information and their mission to provide access to their electronic data. The NREN has the potential of reducing the costs for everybody. "Increasingly, the Internet/NREN will serve as the primary electronic highway for accessing a range of public information resources. . . . the network is growing exponentially, it is becoming easier to use, and the price for connectivity . . . is decreasing" (McClure, Ryan, and Moen, 1992, p. 67). If Federal agencies adopt the Z39.50 standard for their systems, use of a GIILS and information locators on the NREN will bring lower dissemination costs to the agencies since they do not have to reconfigure their data to distribute it. It would eliminate direct telecommunications costs for the libraries and, if agency data are shared with depository libraries in exchange for service assistance to users, access charges would be avoided and user fees eliminated for depository library clients. However, this is contingent on an electronic DLP being in place.

Proposed Models for the Electronic DLP

In its white paper on NREN, GODORT proposes that the basic infrastructure for the electronic DLP is in place with the present regional system taking advantage of the various local and regional networks connected to the Internet. There are 396 academic depository libraries at institutions on Internet nodes. With proper Federal support, and a developmental plan based on a well-researched model, the electronic depository infrastructure could develop through the libraries themselves (Ruhlin, Somers, and Rowe, June 1991, p. 108). The question is how best to design that model and acquire Federal support for its operation.

In 1988, the Office of Technology Assessment (OTA), in its landmark document *Informing the Nation,* proposed three alternatives for the DLP in the electronic age (U.S. Congress, Office of Technology Assessment, October 1988, pp. 151–160). The first, was the status quo which OTA found unacceptable since it would erode and eventually destroy the purpose of the program. The second alternative was an Electronic Depository Library Program which assumed the Depository Library Program could be extended to include electronic information with GPO as the disseminating agency, each depository selecting the type and number of formats needed. Regulations would need to be promulgated that would require agencies to comply with depository law and distribute all information, "regardless of format," through the DLP. With this model, OTA introduced two important notions. The first is the development of "supra" regionals providing state-wide services to other libraries and sharing information access resources including staff time and equipment support. The second is the concept of distributing electronic products and services to selective depository libraries through agency agreements with private sector vendors (ibid., October 1988, pp. 156–157).

The third OTA alternative was a Reorganized Electronic Depository System, based on a model proposed by ARL in 1987. This alternative actually restructured the DLP, retained GPO as a distributor, and added electronic products from the agencies to the DLP as did the second alternative (U.S. Congress, Office of Technology Assessment, October 1988, pp. 158–159). The 1987 model proposed by the ARL Task Force on Government Information in Electronic Format, reconstructed the DLP on three levels of libraries rather than a system of full depository regionals and a large number of levels of selectivity (see Figure 7-4). This is the first model that introduces the concept that libraries should be included in the DLP based on the nature of the information they handle and types of access they provide, rather than the selection and storage of particular amounts of materials (ARL, Task Force on Government Information in Electronic Format, October 1987, p. 2).

In addition, it proposes that government information important to narrow segments of society, but too costly to justify tax-subsidized value-added enhancements, could be distributed to depository libraries on terms that allowed cost recovery for the libraries from the user, government agency providing the information, or a consortium of users (ARL, Task Force on Government Information in Electronic Format, October 1987, p. 22). This would also open the door for private sector involvement in the DLP.

These models, however, were based on the need to handle electronic information in the DLP, more or less, in its current configuration. They leave open the question of connecting the two-thirds of depository libraries which are not Internet libraries, and they do not address the general deficiencies in the capability of the depository libraries or the overburdened conditions of the regionals and the DLP. Therefore, they do not offer more than a framework for restructuring the DLP. Under these models, the problems of building networks for the actual dissemination of the information, or overcoming the difficulties for individual depositories in handling electronic information still remain.

A later model outlined by the GPO in its proposal *GPO/2001: Vision for a New Millennium* does not provide a prospectus for use of

Basic Services: This level of depository library would serve as an information center in which there would exist a small government document collection and a computerized gateway to electronic government information located elsewhere. The service might be focused more on self-help and on-demand levels. There would be a high cost per transaction but a small fixed cost.

Intermediate Services: This level of depository library would maintain a larger government document collection and some electronic information and gateways to other electronic information located elsewhere. This library might devise products which would work well through gateways and might invest in developing value-added approaches to the government information. The service would include more mediation and synthesis than the basic level.

Full Service: This level of depository library would contain research-level government documents and a full range of electronic information and the most sophisticated gateways to other electronic information. The depository collection would be supplemented by related, locally available databases. The level of service would include the highest levels of value-added characteristics. Software packages and other approaches would be developed to change the wholesale government information into retail government information. The cost per transaction would be low and the fixed cost high.

Figure 7-4. ARL Electronic Depository System model.

the NREN by the DLP either. As a model for restructuring the DLP to handle and disseminate electronic information it has a number of major flaws.

- *GPO/2001* makes no mention of NREN or even the use of the Internet.
- It actually calls for computer networking to be left up to the depository libraries.
- It does not approach the problem of the structure and support of the DLP in the network environment.

- It seems to keep the GPO entirely out of the national network.

In GPO's "vision" of the future, GPO dissemination will be based on three basic elements: FIND (Federal Information Directory), SEND (Satellite Electronic Network Dissemination), and INTERACT (Interactive online electronic communication system). Figure 7-5 describes these services in greater detail (U.S. Government Printing Office, 1991, *GPO/2001*, pp. 35–39)

Depository librarians see *GPO/2001* as a vision to enhance the GPO Sales Program and to transfer the actual costs of government information dissemination to the libraries. They are particularly skeptical of SEND. William Hohns, deputy public printer and

---

FIND is a comprehensive Federal INformation Directory that will be an information product and service locator system, or a universal index to all government information products and services. It will incorporate existing and developing directories.

SEND is a daily Satellite Electronic Network Dissemination system planned to fulfill GPO's responsibility to distribute electronic information products and services to depository libraries. Each receiving site would require a receiving station and a computer on which the transmission would be stored and indexed for later retrieval as needed from workstations on a local area network in the depository library. The daily transmissions would be one-time transmissions, prefixed to identify their exact category and nature, and depository libraries would have the ability to download only those transmissions or portions of transmissions they wished to select. Printouts would also be up to the libraries. For archival purposes, GPO would make backfiles available on CD-ROM.

INTERACT is an interactive, online electronic communications system would be the terrestrial network provided as a service through the GPO Sales Program, and would provide interactive on-line access to the database of products and services stored by GPO or available through GPO. There would be access charges sufficient to make the service self-sustaining, file transfer capability, and order account functions. INTERACT would not be provided to the libraries.

Figure 7-5. *GPO/2001*: The basic elements.

director of the Vision project, admits that SEND "may be awkward to achieve" and probably would be some time in developing, coming after INTERACT (W. Hohns, interview with representatives of the American Library Association, Government Documents Round Table, April 7, 1992). It would also mean that the DLP libraries would have to bear significant costs. Estimates range upward from a minimum of $97,000 per library[19] for one receiving station set-up (American Library Association, Government Documents Round Table, 1992). In addition, the *GPO/2001* raises the question: With Internet connections available, and high-speed networking on the horizon with NREN, why move to a form of dissemination that requires downloading and storage in multiple locations? (D. Aldrich, personal communication, May 19, 1992)

GPO/2001 does not consider dissemination through key network nodes. With user interface, open protocol systems like WAIS, and the development of Federal information locator systems and the prospect of a GIILS, navigating the network and retrieving needed information interactively through access points on the NREN or a GPO gateway will be much more efficient and cost effective for both the libraries and Federal agencies. Downloading and storing vast amounts of electronic information in each depository library, and then reformatting it for indexing and retrieval on a local system, just does not make sense.

An additional issue for the DLP libraries that the *GPO/2001* does not address is providing access to all formats of government information. The amount of paper and microfiche distributed by the GPO and other government agencies is going up.[20] Libraries will have to deal with that trend for sometime to come. Although a number of government publications have undergone a complete metamorphosis into digital form, more often than not, development of machine-readable text has meant an additional format to paper and microfiche. To this is added new publications in electronic form only. This means that depository libraries will continue to collect and provide access to hard copy. They also must be connected to the network or to depository libraries that can provide electronic services and connections to the NREN.

A Modified ARL Model

In *The Librarians' Manifesto*, Cornwell and his colleagues make a proposal to the JCP for restructuuuring the DLP that is based on the concepts of the 1987 ARL model and adds the idea of

Electronic Regionals. "Such libraries would have the regional obligations of maintaining and providing access to government information distributed in electronic formats only, thereby relieving existing regionals of that responsibility" (Cornwell et al., 1993, p. 136). Figure 7-6 outlines *The Librarians' Manifesto* model (ibid., 1993, p. 134).

The *Manifesto* model splits the full-service libraries responsibilities in the ARL model between the resources centers and "gateway

---

A theme that appears to run through many proposals calls for a layered system consisting of the following components.

Basic Service Centers (small public and college libraries) would receive a small percentage of "core" and "high profile" documents free of charge. They would not be subject to the check-in, retention, and disposition policies that currently govern depository libraries. Another scenario would be for these libraries to operate under a voucher system that would allow them to purchase desired items directly from GPO.

Public Access Libraries would operate much like today's selective depositories. However, they would be fewer in number and would specialize in government high-interest publications. They would not be tied to the five-year retention policy, but to a more flexible system based on the needs of their primary clientele.

Resource Centers would consist of major academic, public, and state libraries. The research centers would maintain comprehensive collections without the administrative responsibilities that currently plague regional depositories. In return, these libraries would provide document delivery service to smaller libraries in their area.

Gateway Libraries, with financial support from the federal government, would assist libraries in much the same way that is currently expected of regionals. They would provide training and support for all libraries in their region. Additionally, they would act as a "gateway" or document delivery center for electronic databases.

National Depository Library, the library of last resort, would house a comprehensive collection of government information. Working in close harmony with GPO, it would advise other libraries on operational issues affecting the DLP. Additionally, it would have reference and technical service staff available to assist libraries as needed.

Figure 7-6. The *Manifesto* model.

libraries." In addition, this model recommends establishment of a National Depository Library, or a library of last resort, that would house a comprehensive collection of government information. This library would work closely with GPO and would advise DLP libraries on operational issues affecting the program. It would have reference and technical service staff available to assist depository libraries with electronic services (Cornwell et al., 1993, p. 134).

> While this model is typical of the various alternatives that have been proposed over the years, a number of factors must be considered before any firm recommendations can be made. First, the goals and objectives of the DLP must be fully delineated and examined. Second, an analysis of the dissemination needs of Federal agencies must be conducted to ensure that a revised DLP will meet those needs. Third, the needs of the information user must be fully explored. Finally, various scenarios for the restructuring of the system must be identified and evaluated in terms of cost, benefits, efficiency, and accessibility (Cornwell et al., 1993, p. 134).

This approach is the first suggestion in many of the models for a non-GPO administrative role over the DLP.

Depository Library Networks

Based on the same ARL hierarchical concept, Hayes suggests how an actual local or regional network of depository libraries might be organized to provide gateways through nodes on the NREN. Hayes points out that a primary advantage to Federal agencies of having the DLP on the NREN would be the greatly expanded number of access points available to users of their electronic services (S. Hayes, personal communication, June 6, 1992):

> The depository libraries with their computers, offer large numbers of computer ports not available at any one Federal site. With an automatic switching system, or information locator system, users could access information regardless of where it resides. By dispersing agency electronic data to be mounted at several locations, a user could be "switched" through NREN gateways to the libraries holding the information, to GPO 'Gateways', or directly to Federal agencies as need be and as ports were available.

Hayes' suggestions for three different possible scenarios for providing electronic access and for the purpose of broadening the base of access are outlined in Figure 7-7 (S. Hayes, personal communication, June 6, 1992).

Hayes' models are based on five technical points (S. Hayes, personal communication, June 6, 1992):

- Build on the collection strengths of the library. "Just as each library does not collect all documents, an electronic depository should concentrate on that information which is best suited to its collection and mission."
- Construct regional status based on specific information rather than geographic location. Proximity to the information is unimportant given the interconnectivity and speed of the NREN. Therefore, regional status should be held by an institution capable of supporting the technology and handling the information important to its mission.
- Define standards for depository libraries in terms of hardware and software requirements, number of computer ports available, maintenance, outreach, software support, and so on.
- Designate well-equipped and staffed libraries as regional "carrier" libraries which would "carry" such agency support as storage of specific databases, user assistance, dedicated ports, Federal agency liaison, and agency-supplied software, in a manner similar to what the regionals do now in the print environment.
- Assign various libraries as "development sites" to develop network directories, indexes, and user interface software and expert systems based on their resources, needs, and capabilities.

Role of the GPO

Any one of these models not only changes the configuration of the DLP but also the role of the GPO. In recommending actual structural changes for the GPO, *The Librarians' Manifesto* suggests a staged development to changing the GPO's functions and responsibilities. The approach is to allow for more progressive and positive relationships to develop with the libraries and Federal agencies. Figure 7-8 outlines four primary roles for the GPO in developing a modern configuration (Cornwell et al., 1993, pp. 128–130).

Facilitating the transition through the stages outlined in Figure 7-8 will require additional changes that are administrative

Scenario One is the "subject-specific" or national access scenario. In this scenario, major academic depository libraries on the NREN would be designated by the GPO as being responsible for resources in particular subject areas based on the strengths of their collections, or the primary discipline orientation of their institution. The system would be national, not be bound by geographic location, and would function much the same as libraries on the Internet do now. The system would require duplication of subject coverage by enough libraries for network switches using information locator systems to find and use active and "time-specific" computer ports at the appropriate sites. Initial network access could be provided to small depositories through local and regional networks

Scenario Two is a "network model." Large institutions with earth stations could receive satellite transmissions from GPO/SEND or transfer files directly from federal agencies over the NREN for archiving and redistribution to a regional network of sister institutions. In turn, these libraries would provide access to current files through their local networks. This would save federal agencies from having to archive large backfiles and make them available online. The libraries would share retention and online access responsibilities in the same way they might under the "subject-specific" model.

Scenario Three is a "state model" with institutions in each state on the NREN sharing the responsibility for handling subject files similar to the national scenario, or particular electronic publications such as the *Congressional Record* or *Federal Register*. Each of these "electronic regionals" would service the depository libraries around them. [Under this model, the libraries within the states connected to the NREN also could be the links to state and local government information networks and freenets. Initially, they would be responsible for providing access to a GPO gateway and serve as nodes on the NREN for other depositories and local libraries without network connections much as proposed in the ALA/GODORT model.]

Figure 7-7. Scenarios for electronic access.

The role of GPO should progress through various stages as it adapts to its changing functions and responsibilities. This staged approach would allow for a progressive, more positive working relationship to develop with agencies.

Intermediary: As an intermediary, GPO would assume leadership for agency contacts, facilitate information transfer, and assure that agency service desk and user support services are aware of depository libraries and are prepared to support the librarians' calls and requests for information or advice. GPO, as coordinator, would have many advantages: agencies would begin to develop non-mandatory relationships with GPO and depository libraries for information service; it would allow GPO to develop contacts, communications links, and relationships with information providers in the individual agencies; and it would present opportunities for depository librarians to volunteer to interact with agencies thereby enlarging the pool of resources GPO may call on, without increasing GPO's payroll.

Coordinator: In this role, GPO would begin to negotiate free access to various bulletin-board–based information and agency databases for the depository libraries. GPO would negotiate a favorable telecommunications contact for the Depository Library Program. Those depositories willing and able to take advantage of these contracts would do so. In other words, GPO would coordinate depository access but *not* actually provide it directly. This stage allows agencies and some depositories to experiment and see what use, questions, and problems might arise. Based on these experiences, full access to agency databases through GPO's gateway system could be designed so that it would not overtax agency capabilities or expectations. It also presents an opportunity for depositories to communicate with agencies on software specifications needed to meet "citizen" needs and help move agencies toward a common user interface software.

Gateway: As a gateway, GPO would provide "pass-through" access to agency-based information using available agency software and search strategy. Once it becomes more familiar with agency software and record structure, GPO can then move toward developing a common user interface. The potential to encourage or to actually "gopherise" agency information available through the gateway is also a possibility during this stage. To assume a gateway to only information resident in federal agencies is to limit its potential. The gateway could extend to other entities that have mounted federal data. An agency may, for example, have contracted for database services. GPO could extend the "pass-through" concept to these contracted entities, thus providing the agency with a method of meeting depository obligation without the agency developing an in-house information facility or database.

Network Mode: Agencies in negotiation with GPO may wish to mount databases with GPO for depository and subscription access. Agencies may be willing to let GPO provide a level of access, and make referrals to GPO files or other vendors. GPO has the option to contract out this function as with securing print contracts. With known file structure and guaranteed ports, private-sector firms could then develop better interfaces.

Figure 7-8. Four primary roles of the GPO (Cornwall et al., 1993).

and operational in nature. One of the primary changes that librarians point to in their recommendations to the JCP is that the GPO must gain access to the Internet and become a network participant. The lack of a GPO connection to the Internet, as Cornwell and his colleagues point out, "underserves a significant and important segment of depository libraries," or exactly those libraries that are best prepared to lead in developing the electronic DLP. In addition, since the NREN is likely to grow from the roots of the Internet, it effectively delays or pre-empts GPO connection to the NREN.

CONCLUSION AND RECOMMENDATIONS

This section provides recommendations regarding roles for Federal agencies, the GPO, and depository libraries.

Federal Information Policy and NREN Development

A discussion of NREN principles, the role of Congress and the OMB, and collaboration within the library community follows.

NREN Principles. The NREN should be a public network, available through public service institutions, and subsidized with public funds. Governments have the obligation to provide citizen access to public information, regardless of format, and should ensure that the cost of institutional access is appropriately supported for, and by, the educational community and public service institutions such as depository libraries. Like the interstate system of highways, NREN should be a coalition of public funding at Federal, state, local, and institutional levels. There is no reason why it should not be augmented with private capital by contracting through government agencies and institutions. Nevertheless, developing the network as a "public good" requires a multilevel foundation of public funding and technical support, both governmental and institutional.

NREN development, and the network itself, can and should encourage a diversity of use and access, both public and commercial. The user should be provided with choices and the diversity to meet specialized needs. Evolution of the network will be best served by the initiatives of a wide and diverse group of individual and organizational users.

The NREN should not only be public, but also be based on open standards for telecommunications and the delivery of information. Its development must include plans for information locator systems and wide area information servers.

Finally, the NREN should be the primary means of access to government electronic information at all levels of government but particularly at the Federal level. As part of an overall electronic information policy, Congress must mandate that every Federal database of public information should be available on the NREN and NREN access should be imposed on Federal agencies. Federal agencies should be discouraged from "selling" their information systems to the highest private bidder for redistribution as a means of fulfilling their dissemination obligations or cutting the costs of information dissemination out of their budgets. To do this, Congress must ensure adequate funding for agency dissemination programs and for agency participation on the NREN. This does not prevent commercial vendors from making a profit from value-added services such as more convenient user interface software, reconfiguration of agency data, better indexing, file servers, and information locators. In other words, providing the same types of services which the private sector provides now in the hard-copy environment. Nor does it exclude the for-profit information industry from partnerships with Federal agencies, the GPO, and the DLP as means of investigating opportunities for private sector investment in and profit from the production and dissemination of government information (Cornwell et al., 1993, pp. 136–139). The point is to prevent monopolisitic partnerships from developing between individual agencies and vendors that take information owned by the public and make it too expensive or inaccessible for the public to use.

Role of Congress and the OMB. The role of Congress and the OMB is not to pander to private interests but to ensure that Federal agencies and private industry are regulated and funded in such a way as to guarantee the public nature of the NREN. Federal statutes and guidelines (primarily the HPCA, Title 44 *U.S.C.*, and OMB Circular A-130) must be amended to define clearly Federal public information in electronic form as government publications that must be available to the public at very low or no cost through public service institutions such as depository libraries. Given that, and legislation that will provide gateway services through the GPO to the network, the GPO can become more than a print shop and the DLP more than a repository for its output.

In addition, the leading networking institutions in the DLP need to be encouraged to take the lead in developing an electronic DLP network through Federal support that encourages the development of their information systems. A new depository library agreement between the libraries and the Federal government might consist of Federal funding for the development of electronic information services in the larger research depositories in exchange for their developing local and regional networks of smaller depository libraries and connections to non-Federal sources of public information. The development of the DLP should be led by the libraries and instutions that can accomplish this.

The development of local networks to bring smaller libraries and state and local government information resources into the network could start with amendments to the HPCA that will encourage Federal and state collaboration and support the development of technology and networking in libraries. Federal legislation needs to be expanded in library programs that will provide technology funding for smaller depository libraries. Library Services and Contruction Act (LSCA) funding should be expanded to support the technological development of smaller libraries that will get them connected to the NREN. This also needs to be a large part of the DLP librarians' legislative agenda.

The Library Community. There is a great deficiency of networking knowledge among librarians and a corresponding deficiency of knowledge among computer technologists regarding issues of information access and dissemination from a user perspective. Added to this is the problem of developing a cogent Federal information policy suitable for a high-performance network environment.

This situation calls for collaboration among the key organizations concerned with government information and electronic information management to develop cooperative efforts and pilot projects for building networks and disseminating information online. The Government Documents Round Table of ALA, the Federal Depository Library Council to the Public Printer, the GPO, the Federal Publishers Council, along with such organizations as ARL, the Federal Library and Information Center Committee (FLICC), the Information Industry Association, the Coalition for Networked Information (CNI)[21], and others must cooperate to bring the stakeholders together.

Although still scattered and variant, the foundation for a consortium on government information is in place. The National Commission on Libraries and Information Science (NCLIS) could provide a framework to develop networking issues within the

Federal government. A national consortium of libraries, library associations, organizations of information specialists, and private sector information providers could establish a structure for broad participation in the various aspects of NREN development.

It is high time for a new direction at NCLIS. NCLIS should develop an education program to close the librarian/technologist gap. It should educate librarians on technology issues and the changing role of libraries in the electronic environment, and educate the technologists on library and information dissemination issues in the user environment (Sulzer, July 21, 1992). ALA should be working closely with NCLIS and CNI to establish a strategic program of education to be integrated into national, regional, and state conferences and the curricula of library schools and other academic programs on information management.

The primary goal of the collaborative efforts of the library community must be to break down the "beltway insularity" that has restricted the development of effective information policy and likely will negatively affect NREN development if not changed.

Restructuring the GPO/DLP for the NREN Environment

What is needed is a model for the restructuring of the DLP and the GPO that:

- reaffirms the basic principles of the DLP;
- addresses the weaknesses of the current system;
- establishes a new order of libraries based on a network of information centers rather than geographically dispersed repositories; and
- establishes the GPO as *the* information disseminating agency for the Federal government, or expands and moves the function of the DLP into a general Federal information dissemination program outside the GPO that encompasses the primary dissemination programs of the Federal government.

Developing such a model is both necessary and possible.

Role of Depository Libraries. The librarians of the DLP base their existence on the belief in the principle of open public access to government information. If the purpose of the NREN is to create a public computer network with the widest user base, a public information dissemination system such as the DLP is a natural part of it. The NREN could provide, as one of its most important functions, the means by which the DLP and information-producing agencies could most effectively accomplish their missions.

The viability of any one of the models described above depends on how the NREN takes its form. A number of these scenarios might exist simultaneously or overlap in different ways, depending on how the NREN evolves through its connection to existing and developing networks. Any one of the models for an electronic DLP could be a phase in the transition to another. The models should be viewed in that way. In other words, a strategic plan for reconfiguring the DLP should outline immediate steps for the transition to a system of electronic distribution and be open ended with longitudinal goals covering:

- meeting the needs of a developing electronic DLP;
- research that studies the feasibility of the depository models;
- a study of developing regional, state, and local networks; and
- results of pilot programs experimenting with various electronic scenarios.

The model proposed in the *Manifesto*, combined with the Hayes concepts for library networking among the depositories, offers a good framework within which to begin immediate construction of an electronic DLP. The aspects of this model should be examined without delay by joint working groups of the GPO, DLC, GODORT, ARL, CNI, the Federal publishers and/or those agencies with information/locator systems.

The important issue is to develop a Federal information access and dissemination system that will serve the needs of public users as the NREN is constructed and evolves. The system should be based on collaborative efforts among the leading institutions of the DLP and the Federal and state governments, with due regard for the role of smaller libraries in the system. The system cannot be constructed on static organizational rules and procedures and outdated legislation.

The Smaller Depositories. Small depository libraries have three possible roles in an electronic DLP (S. Hayes, personal communication, June 6, 1992):

- These libraries may become repositories for paper and microfiche collections. The larger electronic libraries could then depend on them for hard-copy–based support or document delivery services. They could serve a role as historical collections.
- These libraries could also become the information kiosks on the electronic depository network. They would be the primary intermediaries for users and could specialize in providing remote reference services by connecting the local user to the appropriate electronic depository on the network.
- If traditional hard copy or CD-ROM resources eventually do disappear in favor of online networked resources, the library may cease to be a depository. It must have the resources to assist in electronic regionalism or provide access to networked depositories. The function would shift to libraries capable of providing the service, the same way it does right now if a library cannot provide the resources the DLP requires of it. But small depositories need to have a clearly stated role in an electronic DLP.

The impact of costs and the "electronic squeeze" in available information on depository libraries have broad implications for the DLP. This is a sentiment widely held by DLP librarians, in large and small depositories alike. Chapman (1992, p. 86) says:

> It would be particularly tragic if depository librarians permitted present interest and concern over automation to overcome their primary objective as serving as information-access facilitators to our respective constituencies regardless of their background, status, or technology sophistication.

However, this is exactly the reason for such great concern about barriers to getting electronic information into DLP and getting it connected to the NREN. Without an electronic DLP, the system will wither beyond usefulness. It is not necessarily a factor of fewer publications being available in hard-copy format. That volume is not likely to decrease radically in the near future. By the very nature of its content, certain information is better produced on paper, microform, or compact disc. The problem, therefore, is with the content of the information resource. Large datasets, scientific reports, government studies, statutes, regulations, cases, congressional materials, and so on, along with indexes are the most useful to education, business, and industry when they are available online. Libraries that cannot provide access to these resources will be relegated to the backwaters of government publishing and their users confined to very limited services. This is why it is particularly important for librarians and the Federal government to amend the LSCA to provide support for libaries to develop their technological capabilites.

It is important to begin building a comprehensive Federal/State Information Network (FSIN) as part of the diversity of access that will be required if the NREN is to serve its broadest public purpose. The GPO, small and large depository libraries, and the librarians of the DLP should be using the foundation they have to build toward the goal developing a network of government information libraries and service centers. This network could encompass government information dissemination programs such as those of the Census Bureau, National Technical Information Service, the Library of Congress, the Patent and Trademark Office, the National Library of Medicine, and major state information dissemination operations. The GPO and the DLP libraries have the opportunity to play a key role in developing a national information network of governmment agencies and libraries that would establish a comprehensive FSIN component of the NREN. Given their geographic and social distribution, the collection of resources to which they can provide access and service, and their service ideal of information equity, the DLP provides the broadest base of support for a system of access and service to the widest range of public information resources.

Role of the GPO. The reconfiguration of the DLP, and development toward a FSIN, will depend not only on statutory and regulatory revisions but also on the restructuring of the GPO, both philosophically and organizationally. The GPO is primarily the printer for Congress and a bookseller for the U.S. government. Its service to other Federal agencies is basically as a jobber selling their publications. The DLP and the dissemination of Federal information has played only a secondary role in the GPO's business. Indeed, the administrative goals and managerial objectives that guide the GPO's printing and binding for Congress and its Sales Program are not compatible with the fundamental principles of the DLP and with providing the greatest amount of access to public information resources and services. If the DLP is going to be effectively reorganized to handle electronic information, and be an effective part of the NREN, the GPO must assume a broader role as the information disseminator for the Federal government and its orientation in the administration of the DLP will have to change.

The Librarians' Manifesto calls for a number of changes that must be made by the GPO in its outlook (Cornwell et al., 1993, p. 128).

- The GPO must make a major effort to develop better relations with Federal agencies and encourage their use of the DLP.
- The GPO needs to view the depository libraries as a valuable part of its enterprise and its partner in developing its role as a disseminator of electronic information.
- The GPO needs to become much more "pro-active" in its relations with the Federal agencies and the DLP.

The GPO would need to shift its primary role from one of distribution to one of coordination. It would no longer be merely responsible for information distribution to depository libraries. Instead, it would begin managing the DLP by coordinating a new system of information access libraries and their network connections to the various information resources of the Federal and state agencies. As a first step, the GPO would act as the agent for the depository libraries with the Federal publishers and vice versa. The libraries would receive their program support from one Federal agency which would have a primary stake in library program development, and the agencies would not have to deal individually with numerous libraries in the program. This would be the first phase of establishing the FSIN.

One of the most important primary steps in the process is for the GPO to connect to the Internet. This would accomplish two things. First, once "gateway" legislation passes, the GPO would be able to provide services much more effectively. It would eliminate telecommunications charges for the depository libraries, provide all Internet users with GPO gateway services to Federal information locators and databases, and provide incentives for those depository libraries not connected to get on the network or work to develop local networks with the depositories that are connected. It would be the first step in developing a DLP connection to the NREN. Second, it would provide the ability for the GPO to communicate with its leading depository and regional libraries in a much more timely fashion and truly bring them into partnership in developing electronic dissemination programs as well as handling routine operational problems that plague the DLP and hinder its effectiveness.

McClure, Ryan, and Moen have constructed a Federal Locator Database (FLD) that identifies fifty agencies with information inventory/locator systems (1992, pp. 15, 24). Clearly, these pioneering agencies are those with which the GPO should immediately begin collaboration in developing network services for the DLP. In addition, work should begin immediately to lay the foundation of the FSIN by developing network dissemination pilot projects among these leading agencies and the depository libraries. ARL institutions and regional depositories with the technical and network capabilities should be recruited to participate.

Should the GPO be the coordinating agency for a DLP network? Perhaps not. McClure, Ryan, and Moen point out that, as a congressional agency, the GPO would have difficulty in coordinating executive agencies (1992, pp. 74 , 76). Indeed, it has had little success in getting Federal agencies to adhere to the dissemination sections of Title 44. Also, given its history of inadequate support for the DLP, one might believe that the GPO would just as soon be rid of responsibility for the program. However, let us not throw the baby out with the bath water. The GPO/DLP currently has the only foundation on which to build a system of library access to a comprehensive scope of Federal electronic resources on the NREN.

Regardless of how the NREN develops, in an age of high-speed computer networks, it will be more important than ever to maintain a system of public dissemination for public information. The idea of centralizing the administration of that system in one Federal agency is arguable, and at that, the GPO is probably not the best one. Nevertheless, the GPO/DLP currently has the best foundation to begin building a network of Federal information libraries and agencies that, in some way, consolidates or coordinates existing decentralized Federal information services.

The *Manifesto* proposes a "Library of Last Resort" that would work closely with GPO and advise DLP libraries on operational issues affecting the program (see Figure 7-6). This is an administrative role over the DLP outside the GPO. McClure, Ryan, and Moen also propose that a coordinative role over a Federal GIILS may be appropriate for a number of agencies, including the National Archives and Records Administration (NARA) or the Library of Congress (1992, p. 73). The DLP could be shifted into a new information-coordinating body in the Federal government that would function as a "national virtual library" coordinating the Library of Congress, NARA, the DLP, and various information dissemination functions such as those of the National Agriculture Library, the National Library of Medicine, the National Technical Information

Service, National Science Library, and the Patent and Trademark Office. Future NREN legislation could provide for such a new body in the Federal government that would administer FSIN development as the primary function of its mission to coordinate the dissemination of Federal information on the NREN, in cooperation with the efforts of the state governments, and through other government information services such as GPO and NTIS.

Role of Depository Librarians. The role of the DLP librarians is to ensure that:

- The basic principles and policies of the DLP are transferred into the network environment.
- Federal agencies recognize that the DLP connected to the NREN provides real opportunities for them to meet their mandated missions of disseminating public information at low cost.
- Depository libraries should be used as centers for research and development of NREN tools and services.

But, there are three challenges that depository librarians must meet if they are to take advantage of the opportunities that the NREN offers to modernizing the DLP.

- They must organize politically in partnership with other stakeholder groups.
- They must better define the role, and their vision, of depository libraries in an electronic networked environment and what role the DLP can play in the development of the NREN.
- They must take a greater initiative in working to update Title 44, *U.S.C.*, revise government information regulations, and develop new information policy statutes and regulations.

To say the very least, these are daunting challenges. However, they are challenges that can be met if depository librarians can resolve the professional and institutional problems that have plagued them.

Depository librarians will need to become more knowledgeable, more visible, and more influential. As individuals and in groups, they must work to:

- develop a more prominent role in the operation of the DLP;
- exert more influence in their professional associations or form new ones;
- assert their role in the development of policy, collections, and automation in their home institutions; and
- overcome problems related to their own diversity.

To do this, they will need to develop a strategic program of education and outreach that will develop their expertise, make them much more visible on the issues of networking, and bring them into collaboration with other stakeholders, information professionals, and Federal agencies.

The fundamentals of a strategic program should include:

- development and use of grants to provide educational programs and pilot projects on the NREN, government information, and online networking;
- development of technology and networking workshops in the depository libraries, individual user communities, and among colleagues outside the DLP;
- development of research projects studying the DLP and networking that will provide empirical data on the use, costs, services, resources, and general capabilities and needs of the depository system;
- development of network tools such as indexes, directories, and user interface/expert systems;
- development of a much better interface between practicing professionals in the DLP and the library schools to integrate networking issues and practice into the curricula;
- development of educational programs and instruction on network tools such as client servers like WAIS, GOPHER, ARCHIE, and so on;
- development of collaboration among the technologists of their home institutions, local and state government agencies, and the Federal agencies developing information systems/servers; and
- collaboration with NCLIS, CNI, library schools, state library associations, the Chief Officers of State Library Agencies (COSLA) and other associations of public information professionals.

As the largest professional organization of depository librarians, GODORT could perform a key role in outlining and implementing this strategic program. It has the organizational structure that provides the opportunity for individual depository librarians to get involved as a group and to collaborate with other stakeholders in policy development and technical configuration of a government information network. GODORT should revise its organizational structure of Federal, state, and local, and international documents task forces in favor of a structure based on operational groups in education, technology services, and government information policy. In addition, it must insist that, with regard to government information issues, it be the coordinative body among all other units of ALA, advisory to ALA Council, and the association's channel to the GPO, JCP, Federal and state agencies, and other partner associations and organizations concerned with government information.

Depository librarians also should form a new association of government information librarians and professionals concerned with the operation of depository libraries and the GPO/DLP. The framework for doing this exists within GODORT, the Federal Depository Library Conference of the GPO, and the strong network that is forming around the hub of GOVDOC-L, an Internet-based discussion group. The Patent and Trademark Depository Library Association provides a fine model of a cooperative effort between libarians and Federal agency officials to operate and manage a depository library program.

Above all, depository librarians must involve the administrators of their libraries in the process. Their professional work outside the "documents section" is as much a part of the job of a "documents" librarian nowadays as are reference service, cataloging, and collection development.

Are these solutions idealistic? Yes, but it is idealism and not ideology that has kept the DLP alive and vibrant in the libraries, and will provide a framework for the future. Twelve years of ideology in Washington has accomplished little in advancing our system of education and sharing of knowledge. When you look around inside the Washington, D.C., beltway now, you wonder why so much is going on and nothing is happening. The "political setting" must no longer be allowed to distract us from our mission. It is clear and cogent vision that will determine, ultimately, whether the NREN will be a "public good" and whether the DLP will be a part of it.

NOTES

1. Although the author takes full and sole responsibility for this chapter, he acknowledges a great deal of gracious assistance with it by friends and colleagues from whose ideas he borrowed liberally and, most often, indiscriminately. They are in alphabetical order: Prudence Adler, Assistant Executive Director, Federal Relations and Information Policy, Association of Research Libraries; Duncan Aldrich, Documents Librarian, University of Nevada Libraries, Reno; Gary Cornwell, Documents Librarian, University of Florida Libraries; Stephen Hayes, Documents Librarian, University of Notre Dame; Brian Kahin, Director, Information Infrastructure Project, Science, Technology, and Public Policy Program, John F. Kennedy School of Government, Harvard University; Sally Kalin, Chief, Computer Based Resources and Services Program, The Pennsylvania State University Libraries; Ridley Kessler, Documents Librarian and Regional Depository Librarian, University of North Carolina Library; Joseph McClane, Chief, Records Control Branch [formerly Chief Inspector, Library Programs Service], U.S. Government Printing Office; James McDonough, Coeditor, *Electronic Public Information News*; Robert Oakley, Director, Georgetown University School of Law Library; Paul Peters, Director and Founder of the Coalition for Networked Information; Vigdor Schreibman, coeditor, *Electronic Public Information News*; Hal Shill, director, Heindel Library, The Pennsylvania State University, Harrisburg; and Fred B. Wood, Senior Associate, Office of Technology Assessment, U.S. Congress. With apologies for any manner in which the author may have misrepresented their thoughts, he thanks them, one and all, for their professional and collegial generosity (The author, October 14, 1992).

2. Chief among these measures were: the Government Printing Office Improvement Act of 1990 (H.R. 3849), which covered revisions to printing and publishing at the GPO, procurement of printing and other information products and services, distribution and sale of public documents, and the distribution and use of electronic products and services in the DLP; the Federal Information Resources Management Act of 1989 (S. 1742), which primarily attempted to reauthorize and amend the PRA by including in its purpose the concept of information resources management (IRM), would have changed the definitions of government information, outlined the authority and functions of OIRA, provided guidelines for information dissemination, and described Federal agency responsibilities [for an analysis of these bills see: Wood, F. (1990). Office of Technology Assessment Perspectives on Current U.S. Federal Information Issues. *Government Publications Review*, 17(4), 281-300); and U.S. House. 101st Congress, 2d Session. H. R. 3695, The Paperwork Reduction and Federal Information Resources Management Act of 1990. Washington: Government Printing Office, 1990.

3. Fred Wood was director for the OTA project that resulted in the study *Informing the Nation: Federal Information Dissemination in an Electronic Age*, the first comprehensive document outlining electronic information issues and

the basis for many of the concepts written into legislation to modernize the DLP, particularly in H.R. 3849.

4. On July 20 and 21, 1992, the National Commission on Library and Information Science (NCLIS) sponsored an open forum on "Library and Information Services Roles in the National Research and Education Network." Nineteen speakers presented positional statements on the issues of: effective mechanisms for providing NREN operation and maintenance funds; the future operation and evolution of NREN; how commercial users and services could be integrated into the NREN; how to protect copyrights and intellectual property; and policy to ensure the security of NREN resources and to protect the privacy of network users. The speakers represented all major library associations, library schools, state government agencies, regional and local network services, publishers, higher education consortia, technical research centers, computer systems developers, and those concerned with social responsibility in computing. Transcripts of the forum and copies of the *Report to the Office of Science and Technology Policy on Library and Information Services' Roles in the National Research and Education Network* (1992, November 13), Washington, DC: National Commission on Library and Information Science, are available from the Office of the Commissioner, NCLIS.

5. The GPO WINDO Act (H.R. 2772) was introduced on June 26, 1991. The act would have established online access for the public through a network gateway service maintained in the GPO. The WINDO was envisioned to be a single-account way to gain access to and query Federal online databases. Its purpose was to make it convenient for the public to obtain low-cost access to government information. The DLP would have had free access to the WINDO. The GPO Gateway to Government Act (S. 2813) was introduced on June 4, 1992. It also would have provided free access to the DLP. Both bills provided that the service would be available through the Internet. However, the Senate bill provided $3 million for implementing the gateway. On September 22, 1992, Congressmen Rose, Thomas, and Roberts introduced the Government Printing Office Electronic Information Access Enhancement Act of 1992 (H.R. 5983). It transformed the WINDO/Gateway measures into a bipartisan initiative, but watered down the other two measures by dropping the requirement that the GPO gateway be available on the Internet and limiting the services provided through the gateway to electronic versions of the publications now distributed by the Superintendent of Documents. In the stress to get a bill passed before the conclusion of the 102d Congress, Congressman Rose saw fit to compromise with the Republican members of the House Committee on Administration who had been under pressure from the Information Industry Association to kill the first two bills (Love, September 23, 1992). The Administration Committee unanimously approved H.R. 5983 on September 23, 1992, and the bill was passed in the House on September 29. However, an annonymous last minute hold on H.R. 5983 prevented a vote in the Senate before the end of the 102d Congress.

6. Vigdor Schreibman and James McDonough are coeditors of *Electronic Public Information News* which began publication in October 1991, and, to date, is probably the only newsletter on government issues that is non-aligned and not published by a stakeholder organization.

7. Since the reorganization of the Depository Library Council in 1991, depository librarians have less voice on the council. The number of practicing depository librarians has been reduced under the new structure through the appointments of the Public Printer. Council no longer advises the Public Printer in the form of resolutions and recommendations. The role of the council has, essentially, changed to that of a deliberative body only. Under the new rules, it is no longer to be concerned with anything determined by the GPO to be "operational" in nature. This was one reason the group of depository librarians chose to offer its manifesto to the JCP.

8. Depository librarians are divided among various interest groups within ALA, the American Association of Law Libraries (AALL), and the Special Libraries Association (SLA), all of which represent diverse communities of libraries. The Association of Research Libraries, the primary institutional organization which encompasses predominantly academic depository libraries, must serve a diverse range of interests also. It is very difficult for depository librarians to collaborate with their colleagues across associational lines and to develop concerted action by their own professional associations. Organizational policies which restrict roundtables from representing ALA outside of the association, for example, have hindered the effectiveness of the depository librarians within GODORT in their participation with Congress, the Federal agencies, and other professional organizations. It has been very difficult for depository librarians to get an association as large and diverse as ALA to focus on government information issues. For all its seeming power in numbers and intellectual resources, ALA has been mainly reactive to legislative and regulatory action, with no new initiatives or proposals of its own, and has not committed much of its educational resources to carrying the message on Federal information policy issues outside the confines of its own conferences. This is another area in which the issues developing over the implementation of the NREN may serve as a catalyst for change.

9. Growth in the DLP is an expansion of about 134 percent in the years 1962 through 1989 (Hale and McAninch, 1989, p. 389). In the years between FY 1985 and FY 1993, total congressional appropriations for the DLP have dropped nearly 10 percent from $28,868,000 to 26,327,000, touching a low of $24,214,000 in FY 1990. Given a 4 percent annual rate of inflation, the appropriations should have gone up to approximately $39.5 million in FY 1993 (Mawdsley, January 29, 1992, p. 1007). It has been estimated that the expenditures of the depository libraries on the program is far outrunning the budget provided by GPO. In 1989, thirty-eight regional and forty-five selective depositories alone were spending $20,456,427. The GPO's budget for distribution to depositories totaled only $19,905,000 in FY 1990 (Mawdsley, February 7, 1991, p. 940).

10. The annual cost per regional library to provide the required services and maintenance of its Federal document collection is approximately $500,000, making the total cost for all regional services greater than $25.5 million. That is equal to the total GPO budget for the entire DLP (Cornwell et al., 1993, p. 135).

11. NSFNET has just published a new "Acceptable Use Policy" which provides very broad standards for network use outlawing only for-profit activities or "extensive use for private or personal business" (Adler, May 1, 1992, p. 2).

12. In a little over two years, the documents discussion list GovDoc-L has grown to over 500 subscribers and transmits between ten to fifteen messages a day, particularly on the development of CD-ROM interface software, CD networking, file transfer, and government information and DLP issues and problems. There are over 500 depository libraries at network sites and thirty of the fifty-three regionals are at network sites (Kovacs, 1990, p.419). Most are now using the Internet. In addition, there is growing activity in adding GPO records to OPACs as evidenced by the amount of discussion on GovDoc-L, the number of workshops sponsored by ALA and state associations, and the "sold-out" nature of the workshops on loading GPO MARC tapes.

13. Libraries have been in the forefront, connecting and offering network access to their OPACs, for example. Critical developments on Internet have come about as the result of "grass-roots" projects such as the Internet Access Software developed by Mark Resmer at Sanoma State University and based on the Internet Directory data compiled by Art St. George at the University of New Mexico. Network developments best take place, as Paul Peters states, "as a result of people controlling their own world."

14. The Depository Library Council has been reorganized by Public Printer to concentrate on policy and developmental issues; the GPO has published *GPO/2001: Vision for a New Millennium*, launching a planning and development process to make it an electronic publisher; and the GPO sponsored its first Depository Library Conference in April 1992, which was heavily attended, indicating a level of interest which has not recently been attracted by the library associations. The Depository Library Council examined issues relating to the reconfiguration of the DLP at its fall 1992 meeting.

15. The New York State library and NYSERNET are working to develop electronic libraries (Schubert, 1992, July 20). The state of Maryland plans to provide Internet access for all its academic higher education libraries and school media centers by 1994 (Travillian, July 20, 1992). North Carolina plans to connect 90 percent of its libraries to the Internet by the end of 1992 (McGinn, July 21, 1992). Other systems, such as New Mexico TechNet, are also networking Internet libraries, academic research centers, and state government agencies (Sulzer, 1992, pp. 231–233).

16. A WAIS, or wide area information system, is a public domain interactive system that will inventory the databases available on a network and automatically connect a user with the computer where needed information resides. By using Z39.50 communications protocol, a WAIS is transparent

to a user because it connects the user to the needed system and allows operation of that system with the command language of the user's local computer. Z39.50 is a standard library communications protocol developed by the National Information Standards Organization (NISO). It translates the language of a "guest" computer into that of the "host" computer on the network. The user of the guest computer issues commands and sees the results in the standards of his or her home computer even though he or she may be actually using a computer miles away running on a completely different operating system. For a detailed explanation of WAIS see, Kahle, B., and Medlar, A. (1991). An Information System for Corporate Users: Wide Area Information Servers. *Online*, September, pp. 56–60; also, Kahle, B. (1992). Wide Area Information Servers [Available via anonymous FTP: /pub/wais/wais-discussion/wais-overview.txt@ quake.think.com, or WAIS server wais-discussion-archive.src]; also Wide Area Information Server Concepts: Thinking Machines Technical Report TMC-202 [Available via anonymous FTP; /pub/wais/doc/wais-concepts.txt@quake.think.com, or WAIS server wais-doc.src]. For information on Z39.50, see National Information Standards Organization. (1992). *American National Standard Z39.50, Information Retrieval Service Definition and Protocol Specification for Library Applications.* New Brunswick, NJ: Transaction Publications.

17. The GPO estimates that over 167,000 persons use depository libraries weekly (U.S. Government Printing Office, 1991, *Annual Report*, p. 29).

18. Academic librarians in particular are leading in the development of information literacy skills through a wide range of instructional programs and expert systems that teach students and general library users how to identify and access electronic resources. These skills are easily transferable to an NREN environment. They will train the users of the future.

19. The $97,000 price tag is based on the following estimates: satellite dish = $2,000; SPARC workstation = $7,000 to $12,000 or DOS 586 workstation =$3,000 to $6,000; disc storage for 500,000 pages of text = $4,000 (one primary disc and one backup); software: SPARC = $50,000 to $75,000 (BRS full-text software) or NeXT - NeXT Librarian (free with hardware) and DOS (difficult question as to what existing software would be functional); additional workstations for end use = $5,000 to $20,000 (assumes five to twenty DOS 386 workstations at about $1,000 each); LAN arrangements for additional workstations = $1,000+; staff = $25,000 to $100,000 (minimum assumes one-half FTE); and the minimum above totals $97,000 (one one-half FTE, one workstation with five substations); each increment of 100 libraries nears $1 million (assuming some are more than minimal); annual operation once equipment is in place equals a minimum of approximately $30,000 to $40,000; each increment of 100 libraries equals a minimum of $3 million (American Library Association, Government Documents Roundtable, 1992).

20. In 1991, the GPO distributed over 27.2 million copies of 57,700 printed titles. In addition, 549,000 maps and 1.8 million Department of Energy microfiche (about 47,900 publications) were distributed bringing the total

to about 29.6 million copies and about 105,600 items distributed (U.S. Government Printing Office, 1991, *Annual Report*, 1991, p. 29).

21. The CNI is made up of the Association of Research Libraries, EDUCOM (an association of higher education information technologists), and CAUSE (an association devoted to using information technology to improve business operation primarily in higher education). CNI was founded in 1990, to assist its members in addressing questions of networking by spanning the bounds of librarianship and technology. The objective of the coalition is to provide a framework in which its members and others can develop cooperative networking projects and research that will enrich the information environment rather than the technological infrastructure (Schreibman, February 28, 1992, p. 28). This concept provides a niche for depository libraries and librarians. It is an opportunity for them to fulfill their mission of outreach by developing new tools for access and retrieval of government information and projects to network depositories on local levels for specific purposes. Opportunities like this to develop cooperative projects that would contribute to the development of the NREN could ensure depository libraries a connection by putting them in roles of leadership. However, the CNI was only established for three years with an extension to six. Therefore, it is encumbent on more permanent institutions to continue this initiative.

REFERENCES

Adler, P. (May 1, 1992). NSFNET management issues. *ARL: A Bimonthly Newsletter of Research Library Issues and Actions*, 1–3.

American Library Association/Government Documents Roundtable, Ad Hoc Committee on GPO/2001.(1992). *Comments/Questions/Observations on GPO's Vision: GODORT Ad Hoc Committee on GPO/2001.* Unpublished working document prepared for an interview on April 7, 1992, with the U.S. Deputy Public Printer William Hohns.

ARL, Task Force on Government Information in Electronic Format. (October 1987). *Technology and U.S. Government Information Policies: Catalysts for New Partnerships.* (Report). Washington, DC: Association of Research Libraries.

Brownrigg, E. (1990). Developing the information superhighway. In C. A. Parkhurst, ed., *Library Perspectives on the NREN.* Chicago: American Library Association, 55–63.

Chapman, B. (1992). Willing to provide but unable to support: The dilemma of smaller depositories in an electronic era. *Government Information Quarterly* 9(1): 81–87.

Cornwell, G., D. Aldrich, T. Andersen, S. Hayes, R. Kessler, J. Sulzer, and S. Tulis (1993). Problems and issues affecting the U.S.

Depository Library Program and the GPO: The librarians' manifesto. *Government Publications Review* 20(2): 121–140.

Coulter, S. A. (June 27, 1992). Presentation as Area Vice President for Regional Affairs, Pacific Bell. In Committee on Legislation, *Libraries and the Baby Bell Battle: Information Update.* Annual conference of the American Library Association, San Francisco. (Transcript available from ALA.)

Hale, B. and S. McAninch (1989). The Plight of the U.S. government regional depository libraries in the 1980s: Life in a pressure cooker. *Government Publications Review* 16(4): 387–395.

Henderson, C. (1990). National Research and Education Network legislation S. 1067 and H.R. 3131: Background and status as of June 6, 1990. In C. A. Parkhurst, ed., *Library Perspectives on the NREN.* Chicago: American Library Association, 3–6.

Hernon, P. (1992). Discussion forum: Superintendent of Documents operates an outdated vacuum cleaner. *Government Information Quarterly* 9(2): 99-105.

Hernon, P. and D. C. Heisser (1991). GPO regional depositories. *Reference Librarian* 32, 43–55.

Hernon, P. and C. R. McClure (1984). *Public Access to Government Information: Issues, Trends, and Strategies.* Norwood, NJ: Ablex Publishing Corporation.

Kahin, B. (1991). Information policy and the Internet: Toward a public information infrastructure in the United States. *Government Publications Review* 18(5): 451–472.

Kovacs, D. (1990). GOVDOC-L: An online intellectual community of documents librarians and other individuals concerned with access to government information. *Government Publications Review* 17(5): 411–420.

Love, J. (September 23, 1992). HR 5983, Legislation to provide online access to Federal information; Successor to Gateway/WINDO Bills. Electronic mail on D. Kovacs (Moderator, DKOVACS@KENT,EDU) GOVDOC-L: *Discussion of Government Documents Issues.* GOVDOC-L@PSUVM.BITNET.

Lynch, C. A. (1990). Linking library automation systems in the Internet: Functional requirements, planning, and policy issues. *Library Hi Tech* 28: 7–18.

Lynch, C. A. (1991). The development of electronic publishing and digital library collections on NREN. *Electronic Networking: Research, Applications, and Policy* 1(2): 6–21.

Mawdsley, K. F. (January 29, 1992). Library of Congress and Government Printing Office Budget. In U.S. Congress, House,

Committee on Appropriations, Subcommittee on Legislative Appropriations, *Legislative Branch Appropriations for 1993, Part 2* (Hearings, 1992, January 23, 27–30, pp. 987–1011). (U.S. Doc. Y4.Ap6/1:L52/993/pt.2.) Washington, D.C.: U.S. Government Printing Office.

Mawdsley, K. F. (February 7, 1992). FY 1992 Appropriations for the Government Printing Office. In U.S. Congress, House, Committee on Appropriations, Subcommittee on legislative Appropriations, *Legislative Branch Appropriations for 1992: FY '81 Supplemental Request and FY '92 Legislative Branch Appropriation Request.* (Hearings, 1992, February 4–7, March 7, pp. 924–955). (U.S. Doc. Y4.Ap6/1:L52/992/ pt. 2.) Washington, D.C.: U.S. Government Printing Office.

McClure, C. R., A. Bishop, P. Doty, and H. Rosenbaum (1991). *National Research and Education Network (NREN): Research and Policy Perspectives.* Norwood, NJ: Ablex Publishing Corporation.

McClure, C. R., J. Ryan, D. Lauterbach, and W. E. Moen (1992). *Public Libraries and the Internet/NREN:New Challenges, New Opportunities.* Syracuse, NY: Syracuse University, School of Information Studies.

McClure, C. R., J. Ryan, and W. Moen (1992). *Identifying and Describing Federal Information Inventory/Locator Systems: Design for Networked-Based Locators: Final Report.* Vol. I. Syracuse, NY: Syracuse University, School of Information Studies.

McGinn, H. (July 21, 1992). Testimony of the State Librarian, North Carolina, President of the Chief Officers of State Library Agencies. In the National Commmission on Library and Information Science, *Open Forum on Library and Information Services' Roles in the National Research and Education Network (NREN).* Washington, D.C. (Transcript available from NCLIS).

Park, B. (July 21, 1992). Testimony for GEAC Computers. In the National Commmission on Library and Information Science, *Open Forum on Library and Information Services' Roles in the National Research and Education Network (NREN).*Washington, D.C. (Transcript available from NCLIS.)

Ruhlin, M., H. Somers, and J. Rowe (June 1991). National Research and Education Network and the Federal Depository Library Program: A position paper for the American Library Association/Government Documents Roundtable–Federal Documents Task Force. *Documents to the People,* 106–109.

Schreibman, V. (February 28, 1992). [Interview with Paul Peters, president of the Coalition for Networked Information]. *Electronic Public Information News,* 28–29.

Schubert, J. (July 20, 1992). Testimony as the State Librarian and Assistant Commissioner for Libraries, State of New York. In the National Commmission on Library and Information Science, *Open Forum on Library and Information Services' Roles in the National Research and Education Network (NREN).* Washington, D.C. (Transcript available from NCLIS.)

Shill, H. (March 13, 1992). An NTIS concept paper. Unpublished manuscript, The Pennsylvania State University Libraries, Penn State Harrisburg.

Smith, D. (1990). Depository libraries in the 1990s: Whither or wither depositories? *Government Publications Review,* 17(4): 301–324.

Strong, G., K. Hudson and J. Jewell (1990). Electronic networking for California state and public libraries. In C. A. Parkhurst, ed., *Library Perspectives on the NREN.* Chicago: American Library Association, 45–46.

Sulzer, J. (July 21, 1992). Testimony for the American Library Association/Government Documents Roundtable. In the National Commmission on Library and Information Science, *Open Forum on Library and Information Services' Roles in the National Research and Education Network (NREN).* Washington, D.C. (Transcript available from NCLIS.)

Sulzer, J. (1992). Regional, State, and Local News. *Government Publications Review* 19(2): 231–237.

Travillian, M. (July 20, 1992). Testimony for the Maryland State Department of Education. In the National Commmission on Library and Information Science, *Open Forum on Library and Information Services' Roles in the National Research and Education Network (NREN).* Washington, D.C. (Transcript available from NCLIS.)

U.S. Congress. 102nd Congress. (December 9, 1991). *High-Performance Computing Act of 1991.* Public Law 102-194. U.S. Code, 105 Stat. 1594.

U.S. Congress, Office of Technology Assessment. (1988, October). *Informing the Nation: Federal Information Dissemination in an Electronic Age.* (U.S. Doc. Y3.T22/2:2IN3/9). Washington, D.C: U.S. Government Printing Office.

U.S. GPO Annual Report (1991). (U.S. Doc.GP1.1:991). Washington, D.C.: U.S. Government Printing Office.

U.S. GPO/2001: Vision for a New Millennium (1991). (U.S. Doc. GP1.2:V82). Washington, D.C.: U.S. Government Printing Office.

U.S. Superintendent of Documents. (May 31, 1992). *Administrative Notes: Newsletter of the Federal Depository Library Program,* 1.

U.S. Superintendent of Documents. (November 15, 1992). *Administrative Notes: Newsletter of the Federal Depository Library Program,* 4–5.

Vial, D. (June 27, 1992). Presentation for the Alliance for Public Technology. In Committee on Legislation, *Libraries and the Baby Bell Battle: Information Update.* Annual conference of The American Library Association, San Francisco. (Transcript available from ALA.)

Weingarten, F. (Spring 1991). Five steps to NREN enlightenment. *EDUCOM Review,* 26–30.

Wood, F. (1990). Office of Technology Assessment perspectives on current U.S. Federal information issues. *Government Publications Review* 17(4): 281–300.

8

NREN and Library Education

Christinger Tomer

In December 1991, President Bush signed the High Performance Computing Act of 1991 into law. The passage of this act culminated almost five years of efforts to establish the statutory basis for a national, high-speed computer network devoted to research and education.

Since the bill's enactment, Congress, the Executive Branch, and policymakers from science, industry, and education have been engaged in the crucial business of identifying the most appropriate architecture for this network and how it will be funded and managed. Meanwhile, there has been a growing interest throughout the educational system in exploring ways in which the National Research and Education Network (NREN) might enhance education and help to alleviate the financial problems that afflict so many schools.

The NREN is of special interest to librarians and library educators because the NREN and its affiliate networks are expected to change the way in which libraries and librarians function. As Paul Evan Peters of the Coalition for Networked Information has noted, libraries in the research and educational communities are already "forming partnerships among themselves and with other interested parties to undertake projects that develop and test alternative models of the new system of information access and delivery in a manner that both shares costs and risks and produces results that are generalizable with or at least transferable to the circumstances of other libraries" (Peters, 1992).

Today, many specific aspects of coming to grips with the NREN environment cannot be addressed in a wholly adequate way. This is not only because the NREN does not yet exist, but also because the extraordinarily dynamic quality of networked environments makes it almost impossible to see beyond the short term with any clarity. So, there is a good chance that the reality of the NREN will be much different, perhaps much better than the network we can imagine today, and that the librarians who work on the NREN will play roles different and broader and more dynamic than the librarians of today.

Diane Callahan contends that if professional librarians expect to play this sort of role, negotiating "a bridge which has technology at one end and the user at the other," they must know enough about information technologies to evaluate hardware and software in terms of functionality and offer recommendations for improvement within the framework of what is technologically feasible. In this regard, Callahan has suggested that:

> Librarians, operating in an increasingly computer-dominated electronic information environment, can no longer be content to merely provide access, organization, storage, and retrieval for information in various formats. The librarian must assume a proactive role in the diffusion of these technological innovations.This is the role of the 'change agent,' defined by [E.M.] Rogers as the individual who 'influences clients' innovation decisions in a direction deemed desirable by a change agency.' (Callahan, 1991, p. 13)

This chapter is based on the presumption that the NREN environment will change the way libraries and librarians serve readers, and that in this new environment professionalism will necessarily entail a much higher level of technical knowledge. It also presumes that to meet this new standard for professionalism, graduate programs in library science will be obliged to redefine their approach to information technologies in structural, curricular, and pedagogical terms.

This chapter addresses the question of how library educators should respond to the challenges of the new environment that the NREN will spawn. More specifically, it examines issues relating to the development of appropriate learning environments and curricular frameworks, in which prospective librarians may be educated for work in the NREN environment and on other wide area networks (WANs). Finally, it suggests a series of specific means by which library educators can prepare both their programs and their students for the coming of the NREN.

NREN AND THE PROSPECTS FOR A NEW LIBRARY ENVIRONMENT

Networks operating at multigigabit speeds will enable librarians to move information from its source to the point of demand almost at will. From the perspective of users with connections to this network, the network will be the library. Their view of what is available to them will no longer be defined by the books housed in a particular building, but by the connections that their institution has made with other institutions and organizations across the network.

The demands on the librarian's skills will be considerable, perhaps far greater than today. As always, the librarian will need to be aware of and know how to use local holdings and resources. In this new environment, however, the librarian will also have to know how to locate, access, and effectively import resources from thousands of points across the NREN.

There is a widespread feeling that the NREN will breed a new environment in which librarians will flourish.[1] There are a few librarians who view the prospects of library practice in this setting with apprehension, but most librarians and library educators who have offered opinions on the subject view the NREN as an opportunity to renew librarianship as both art and profession.

Most librarians appear to believe that because of continuing advances in computing and telecommunications, librarianship is entering a new era of remarkable opportunities for collaboration, cooperation, and resource sharing. They view WANs as "ecological" in their likely effect on library services, meaning that networks such as the Internet and the NREN will bring about fundamental changes in the ways that people generate, distribute, and use information (Perkins, 1992; Postman, 1992).

THE NEED FOR CHANGE AND INNOVATION IN LIBRARY EDUCATION

No less important is the sense that as the NREN changes librarianship, library education must change accordingly to maintain its relevance and vitality. As Richard Budd (Budd, 1992, p. 44) noted recently, "Few tools are changing more rapidly than those of the information professional."

Budd suggests that library schools are not responsive enough to changes in information technology or the information infrastructure—"[T]he schools of library studies are in a chronically poor state of mental health," suffering from a "lack of strong identity and lack of confidence evidenced by a good deal of indecisiveness accompanied by a low-risk profile. . . ." He concludes that the survival of many programs may depend on the extent to which they adapt their curricula to new technologies and information environments (Budd, 1992, ibid).[2]

Yet, Budd may understate the severity of the problem. Today, most library science programs appear to lack the resources or the collective will to respond appropriately to the challenges set forth by the NREN legislation. Few programs have developed a technological infrastructure broad enough or powerful enough to support the development and implementation of necessary curricula. Moreover, the vast majority of the faculty associated with graduate programs in library science lack the technical competence to participate meaningfully in efforts to modernize their programs. As a result, it is difficult for many programs to mount more than a few technically oriented courses, integrate new technologies into traditional courses such as reference or cataloging, or establish the basis for the modernization of curricula. Nor is it surprising that library educators are moving with neither appropriate dispatch nor sufficient vigor.

Looking ahead to the NREN era, the primary challenge for many library schools will be survival. For at least a few schools, there will be the more important, more interesting challenge of adapting and reconciling more traditional views of information service with the possibilities of new technologies, of integrating technics with a traditional commitment to the public interest. This integration may prove to be, as Allucquere Rosanne Stone (Stone, 1991, p. 111) has written, "part of a range of innovative solutions to the drive for sociality—a drive that can be frequently thwarted by the geographical and cultural realities . . . increasingly structured according to the needs of powerful economic interests rather than in ways that encourage and facilitate habitation and social interaction. . . ."

THE PROBLEM OF TECHNOLOGY IN LIBRARY EDUCATION

One of the reasons why library education is not well prepared to educate librarians capable of working successfully in networked environments is that the field has been in turmoil. In the last dozen years or so, some of the field's oldest, most prestigious programs have been closed, several other important programs have had their futures subjected to intense scrutiny by parent universities, and it seems likely that within the current decade the futures of several other programs now thought to be safe and stable will be questioned. A variety of factors has contributed to this situation, but there is ample evidence to suggest that a critical area of failure for these programs was the lack of adequate curricula leading to the development of information technology-based skills (McClure and Hert, 1991).

Ironically, in the last dozen years or so many graduate programs in library education, including several programs that were closed, have worked to innovate by integrating applications of information technologies into their curricula. In the process, it has become clear that where the issue of information technologies is concerned, library educators are of at least two minds.

The basic division is clear. Most library educators believe that graduates must know how to use certain information technologies, such as online databases, but there are many educators who believe that librarians do not need to understand the technical underpinnings of the systems they use. They contend that it is not necessary for students to acquire technical knowledge beyond that which is necessary to operate the appropriate devices and systems, and the courses they offer reflect this conviction.

Library educators of the school favoring more extensive technical grounding generally argue that if professional librarians are expected to function as problem-solvers and innovators, a detailed understanding of the information technologies used by libraries is essential. They believe that the MLS degree is not merely preparation for an entry-level professional position, but also the intellectual foundation for a career as a problem-solver and decision-maker in a library, media center, archive, or other type of information service. They might insist, for example, that students enrolled in a school library program should learn to navigate the Internet and use its resources, although only a few schools in the K–12 environment currently have access to the Internet, because a working knowledge of this environment is extensible and virtually certain to be useful for most school librarians in the near term.[3]

TRAINING VERSUS EDUCATION

The development of information technology-based skills in library education, however, has tended to follow what might be called the "driver's education" model. In driver's education, students learn how to control and maneuver an automobile well enough to pass a test. They are taught almost nothing about the functional characteristics of the automobile. As a result, most of them know little or nothing about how the functional characteristics of an automobile affect their ability to control the vehicle. The emphasis is almost exclusively on developing an ability to control the vehicle in conformity with certain statutory requirements.

In library education, prospective librarians generally learn how to operate systems and applications at a level of competence akin to that achieved by the person who graduates from a class in driver's education. The flaw in accepting this low level of technical competence as the de facto professional standard is manifest most obviously in situations where librarians are called on to remedy a malfunction or expand creatively on the basic capabilities of a system or application. Lacking a specific knowledge of how systems work or how applications relate to operating systems, librarians educated in this manner are often unable to solve operational problems or extend functionality.

Library educators have long been concerned with the distinction between "training" and "educating" students. Their shared conviction is that training people how to use various systems without an examination of the ideas and standards on which the systems are based is ultimately insufficient. Therefore, in many programs, students learn about both the rules of cataloging and the principles associated with the organization of information.

However, this distinction has not migrated as successfully to the area of information technologies, in large part, because the faculty members who control curricular reform are often the least knowledgeable in technological matters, but also because the prevailing format for library education leaves little or no room to expand on technological themes. As a result, much as library educators may decry "training," most programs offer little more than training in the area of information technology.

The current situation is strongly at odds with what we expect to be the requirements for successful professional practice in the high-technology environment of the NREN. Budd (Budd, 1992, p. 47) suggests, "Library schools need to be much more open to experimentation and more concerned with new and developing systems." But, most library schools approach these matters on a highly limited basis, because they lack the commitment or the resources to do more.

Like many other observers, Budd (Budd, 1992, p. 44) contends that radical change is necessary, and that "one thing is certain: we cannot simply do better what we have been doing all along." The problem is that while most observers see the need for fundamental change in library education, particularly where information technologies are concerned, virtually none of them have yet to go beyond generalities in recommending what library schools ought to do in this regard.

WHAT LIBRARY SCHOOLS NEED TO DO

If library schools intend to make changes of the nature suggested by Budd and others, these schools must work in three related areas. Specifically, they will need to:

- re-examine their basic stance regarding information technologies;
- decide what students need to know, how they will be taught and how they will learn; and
- build an infrastructure for learning that transcends the mere provision of equipment and connections.

The following sections examine each of these new changes.

A New View of Information Technologies

First of all, library educators need to achieve a more coherent view of information technologies in relation to library practice and library education. As Wallace and Boyce (Wallace and Boyce, 1987, p. 159) have noted, "The field is inherently dependent on technology and must respond to new developments or risk becoming obsolete as a profession." While most library educators presumably agree with the idea that librarianship is by nature reliant on technology of one kind or another, at many library schools the study of information technology and its relevant applications remains an area of learning largely subordinate to more traditional core areas, such as classification and cataloging, reference, and collection development. As a result, the transformation necessary must begin with a philosophical commitment based on a recognition of the fundamental importance of information technologies. In addition, it must include an acceptance of the fact that conveying the knowledge and skills librarians need will require a substantial, well-organized curriculum.

What Students Need To Learn and How To Educate Them

In order to educate students about the emerging technologies and how to use them, a new curricula must be built. In addition, librarians must be trained to be network navigators.

Building New Curricula. Building appropriate curricula based on this view of information technologies will take time, effort, and negotiation. Most library schools do not have the human or physical resources to do so. And, in the absence of a consensus within the library profession about how to integrate or exploit new information technologies, library educators will be hard-pressed to formulate curricular models capable of satisfying the field's operational requirements. In the interim, library educators will be well served to look to the Internet for guidance as to how they should design forward-looking curricula.

Today, most Internet users work on what has been labeled the "low-end" Internet (Klingenstein, 1992). This segment of the Internet is characterized by three basic services: remote log-on, electronic-mail, and file transfer services. It also offers netnews, a small but growing number of electronic journals; access to the online catalogs of several hundred research libraries, along with the more extensive library services offered by OCLC, RLIN (Research Libraries Information Network), and CARL (Colorado Alliance of Research Libraries); and a growing array of databases, archives, and services connected to the network by virtue of their location at universities or government-supported research facilities.

Commercial traffic on the Internet is growing, too. Advanced Network and Services (ANS), the consortium that manages the National Science Foundation (NSF) backbone, has been authorized to offer commercial services via the Internet. As a result, many commercial database services, including DIALOG and Lexis/Nexis, are now accessible. Some private services, such as AT&T Mail, MCI Mail, and CompuServe Mail, have gateways to the Internet.

The low-end Internet is not a hospitable environment. The array of databases and services available across the network have not been mounted on a structured basis. User interfaces are generally primitive, query standards are commonly absent, and end-user support is minimal.

The expectation is that in the next decade first the low-end Internet and then the NREN will support a range of new services, including multimedia mail; widely distributed file systems; hypertext-like navigational tools for use on both local and wide area networks with easy-to-learn, easy-to-implement command sequences; hypermedia databases; intelligent agents that can take a natural language string and transform it into a search of distributed digital libraries (the so-called "knowbot"); real-time, multimedia conferencing; interoperable data description protocols; and interactive, online mechanisms for user education and training (Gould, 1990) (Lederberg and Uncapher, 1989).[4] In the interim, however, users will be required navigate in the unfriendly environment of the low-end Internet.

To function successfully in this environment, librarians will need to have a knowledge of one of the higher level programming languages. They will also need to understand the basic properties and functions of operating systems, information technology standards and other aspects of interoperability, and various computer and network architectures.

Librarians working in highly networked environments will require an extensive knowledge of electronic document processing. Today, users on the Internet confront a variety of document formats, ranging from ASCII to PostScript to TeX. In the near future, as learned societies and commercial publishers have established mechanisms for the electronic distribution of their publications across WANs, electronic publishing will grow dramatically, and so, too, will the number of formats with which librarians and users must cope.[5]

Educating Network Navigators. In the meantime, perhaps the most productive way to work toward the development of a curriculum that will provide for the education of librarians prepared to work in the NREN environment is to build courses that consider in detail the underpinnings of WANs and the properties of the first generation of network-based applications, such as WAIS, the Internet Gopher, multimedia mail, and Archie.

A course aimed at preparing librarians to be network navigators should include the following topics and might be organized in the following way:

1. A brief history of the development of WANs
   - Origins of ARPANET
   - BITNET
   - NSFNET and the Internet
   - The need for NREN and its anticipated effects on wide area networking

2. Telecommunications and networking standards
   - TCP/IP suite and related applications
   - OSI Reference Model; GOSIP
   - RFC 822 (and other Internet standards relevant to electronic mail)
   - X.400 and X.500 standards for directories
   - Z39.50: Information Retrieval Service Definition and Protocol
   - Specification for Library Applications
   - Z39.58: Common Command Language

3. Network architectures and topologies
   - LAN topologies and operating systems
   - Packet-switched networks, including X.25 networks
   - Distributed file systems (including NFS and AFS)

4. Electronic mail
   - Mail transport agents
   - Mail user agents/enhanced mail user agents
   - Interactive mail management
   - POP mail
   - Multimedia mail

5. Remote log-on procedures, terminal emulation

6. File transfer; anonymous FTP servers

7. Computer-mediated conferences
   - Listservers
   - USENET groups
   - Bulletin board services
   - Freenets (public-access community information systems)

8. Network-specific applications
   - WAIS (wide area information systems)
   - Internet Gopher
   - WWW (World Wide Web)
   - Archie

The goal of such a course should be to prepare students to navigate WANs on behalf of clients in search of relevant information resources and services. Another basic aim should be to familiarize students with the operational basis on which the Internet was established and now provides services.

The key issue in wide area networking is interoperability. In the establishment of WANs, interoperability, which is the ability to connect different types of computers or exchange services through "store-and-forward" technologies like electronic mail, relies primarily on standardized addressing and data transmission and a series of other protocols. Consequently, achieving an understanding of wide area networking requires familiarity with the complex technical issues underlying the interoperability of systems linked across a network. Courses concerned with networking must be devoted in substantial part to examining the importance of interoperability and the nature and purpose of the various standards that make interoperability possible. In addition, special emphasis must be placed on the open standards that have been critical to the development of the Internet and will presumably be of equally great value in the development of the NREN. And, because the heart of networking on the low-end Internet is made up of electronic mail, remote log-on, and file transfer—and, to a lesser extent, on information retrieval and distributed file services—the courses should also focus to a significant extent on these areas of activity.

The courses should devote special attention to the new generation of network-specific applications that rely on client/server architectures to expand networking capabilities because these applications represent the first generation of software applications written specifically to support the delivery of information services across broadband WANs. Their characteristics suggest directions for the succeeding generations of software that librarians will need to use and understand in order to function effectively in the NREN environment. The Internet is already a highly distributed system—a metacomputer, of sorts—and interprocess communications mechanisms such as Unix sockets or remote procedure calls are used to expand the capabilities of the network through specific enhancements, today most notably as distributed file systems and client/server implementations. The most promising of these efforts from the perspective of library and information services is the WAIS protocol. The basic idea underlying the WAIS protocol, which is an extension of the 1988 Z39.50: Information Retrieval Service Definition and Protocol Specification for Library Applications, is that in the client/server relationship, the client can formulate a search strategy on a local machine and then carry out the search in terms of a series of databases arrayed across a network.[6,7]

A popular view of the future is that the software tools developed to navigate across the NREN will bear a striking functional resemblance to the hypertext and hypertext-like systems in fashion today.[8] Two experimental applications that carry out aspects of this vision across the Internet are the University of Minnesota's Gopher and the so-called "World Wide Web."

The Gopher system, which has been constructed in general compliance with several existing protocols and standards, including TCP/IP (Transmission Control Protocol/Internet Protocol), consists of a client connecting to a server and sending the server a line of text (which may be blank) via TCP/IP. The server responds with a block of text and closes the connection. The simplicity of the protocol is based on the common need to implement servers and clients for slower, smaller desktop computers that will operate quickly and efficiently.

Under the Gopher system, the clients are navigational tools that enable users to move through servers and files on servers. The servers are interconnected. Once the Gopher client has connected to a Gopher server, the user can browse through information on any additional Gopher servers that are connected to the first server. The server presents and the client displays information as lists of items. Items can be files, directories containing other directories or files, or access to searching capabilities on index servers.10

Another prototypical application in the same category is the World Wide Web (WWW). The WWW is a project aimed at merging the basic ideas of TCP/IP networking, information retrieval, and hypertext as a basis for retrieving documents on machines arrayed across a WAN. The derived system uses the Standard Generalized Mark-up Language (SGML) as the basis for a document structure that can forge functional links to file on most Internet-accessible services.

Designed by staff at the European Particle Physics Laboratory and intended originally for a community of high-energy physicists, the WWW has attracted broader attention owing to its potential for facilitating user support, resource discovery, and collaboration. At this point, its intended uses include access to general reference sources, such as dictionaries and encyclopedias, centralized publishing, collaboration in authorship and/or design, and news services.[10]

Other areas of current network activity that seem pertinent to a course on network navigation include the new applications that enhance electronic mail and file transfer. As several surveys have suggested, much of the Internet's growth as a utility, and much of its utility for librarians, can be attributed to electronic mail (Ladner and Tillman, 1992). Looking ahead, the development and implementation of mail systems based on MIME, the Internet's new standard for multimedia, multipurpose mail, will enhance the utility of electronic mail by providing fax-like capabilities, as well as enabling users, in large part, to transmit encapsulated references to resources under the management of WWW, WAIS, and Gopher systems.[11]

Concerning file transfer, it has been clear for some time that anonymous FTP servers are among the Internet's most valuable resources. For example, the Archie client that runs on top of the X Window interface is a client/server application developed at McGill University and extended to a series of other sites in North America, Australia, and Europe (Emtage, 1991). It supports access to databases that list and index the files mounted on more than one thousand anonymous FTP servers available across the

Internet. (The significance of the version of Archie that runs on top of the X Window system is that it integrates resource discovery and file retrieval, combining the search features of the basic client with an implementation of the FTP software. As a result, a user can search the Archie database, locate a relevant file, and then copy the file within the framework of the same application.)

In terms of course readings, a publication like Ed Krol's *The Whole Internet: User's Guide & Catalog* (1992), might be used as a basic text. Additional readings might also include works of more general interest, like Clifford Stoll's *The Cuckoo's Egg* (1989) or Katie Hafner and John Markoff's *Cyberpunk* (1991). But most of the material that students would be expected to read and master could be delivered via the Internet, through electronic mail or access to various file servers. For example, students might be required to locate, retrieve, and read documents such as the Internet standard on electronic mail (RFC 822), Charles Hedrick's introduction to TCP/IP, John Chew's guide to internetwork mail, Brian O'Neill's tips on using FTP, the array of documents concerning WAIS that has been made available across the Internet by Thinking Machines, Nathaniel Borenstein's various writings on extending basic Internet mail, and so on.

Assignments for a basic course on network navigation might include: (1) downloading and installing a series of client applications, (e.g., an Archie client, a Gopher client, or a WAIS client); (2) creating menu-driven access to network resources through shell programming or a similar device; (3) appraising a series of remote library and library-oriented resources; (4) investigating relevant listserver-based groups and other computer-mediated conferences; (5) testing navigational systems like the Internet Gopher at both the technical and service levels; and (6) examining how standards for interoperability are implemented and how the quality of implementation varies.

Building Areas of Specialization Related to Networking. When Scott Deerwester (Deerwester, 1986, p. 8) suggested several years ago that there are four levels of "automation skills" necessary in libraries, he differentiated between the general librarian, who needs to be computer literate and understand the role of information technology in the setting of library services, and "the librarian with technical responsibilities," who has the knowledge and skill to apply information technologies to library processes. It may be argued, however, that because of the growing use of computers in libraries, the distinction is no longer valid, that the class of the general librarian who needs merely to be acquainted with technological matters has been or is about to be obliterated by the ubiquity of the computer, and that now the aim of a basic library science program should be to prepare "the librarian with technical responsibilities." Viewed from that perspective, a course on network navigation is only the beginning, the necessary first step in addressing the requirements of an environment in which WANs are a basic aspect of the information transfer process.

In view of such circumstances, library schools must take at least several steps that go well beyond the establishment of a basic course on network navigation. First, the faculty of library schools must set prerequisites in the area of information technology at a level high enough to permit the elimination of the largely descriptive survey courses that commonly introduce students to library automation. Raising standards for matriculation in this area should advance the level of instruction at the Master's level to a substantially higher level than is attained at present by enabling the faculty to offer more useful, more rigorous courses. Ideally, students entering MLS programs would matriculate with a knowledge of an important programming language, demonstrated competence in the use of a series of basic applications, including text editing and word processing, spreadsheets, and telecommunications software, and a background in logic and statistics.

It may not be realistic to propose that library schools can institute general prerequisites of this nature immediately. Yet it is probably at least as unrealistic to imagine that schools failing to elevate their admission standards in this area can survive in the long run. Failure to establish meaningful prerequisites in the area of computing will perpetuate the conditions that currently place unacceptable limits on the extent and scope of the technology segment of most MLS curricula.

Second, library schools must look at the technological components of their core curricula to ensure that every student develops a familiarity with basic aspects of information technology and its application to library processes and services. This examination of the core curriculum must also aim at guaranteeing that when students enter the elective phase of an MLS program, they are qualified to undertake advanced, rigorous courses in related areas such as data processing, programming, database management systems, intelligent networking, and so on.

Third, library schools must support specialization in library automation and related areas such as electronic publishing, systems administration, network management, and electronic library services. This support should take at least two forms: tracks of specialization within the framework of the MLS program; and establishment of advanced certificate programs. In either instance, the tracks should consist of upper-level courses in library science, information science, computer science, and telecommunications.

The goal of these tracks will be to prepare what Deerwester (Deerwester, 1986, p.8) referred to as "the technical expert with library responsibilities." As McLain, Wallace, and Heim (McLain, Wallace, and Heim, 1990, p. 8) have noted, this librarian should have a comparatively "deeper understanding of computers and software, and of what can be accomplished with each. . . ."

A key element in transforming this sense of purpose into meaningful reality will be determining what it means for librarians to have a "deeper understanding of computers and software," and by extension, what students enrolled in these specialized tracks ought to know by the conclusion of their studies. A key difference between what is needed now and what has been proposed in the past is that many proposals—including the curriculum for library automation specialists proposed by McLain, Wallace, and Heim, which is, in fairness, typical of how library science faculty have approached the problem of technology education for at least a couple of decades—treat programming as an elective, not a requirement. To be blunt, this aspect of such proposals makes no sense. Understanding computers entails a knowledge and understanding of the programming languages that are used to create operating systems and develop applications. If librarians are to understand computers and their applications, they must understand both programming as a process and programming languages.

Consequently, programs that propose to educate library automation specialists should have relatively extensive prerequisites in the area of programming. The argument that students capable of meeting such standards will be inclined to gravitate to other professional areas where career opportunities and income potential are greater is clearly not without merit, but it is also clear that if librarians expect to maintain their traditional roles in a technology-intensive environment, then at least some librarians will have to achieve a high level of competence in areas like programming, systems administration, interface design, and so on.

An information technology/library automation track within the framework of an extended MLS or advanced certificate program might include courses on the following topics:

- advanced cataloging;
- computer and operation system architectures;
- data processing;
- document processing;
- human factors in information processing;
- information storage and retrieval;
- information technology standards;
- library cooperation and networking;
- local and wide-area networking;
- management of library automation;
- relational database management systems;
- systems analysis and design; and
- telecommunications and data communications.

A program of specialized study would presumably incorporate eight to ten of the courses noted above, with specific courses selected on the basis of academic interests or professional goals. The aim would be to produce graduates who are familiar with the technologies that are used to automate libraries and other information services. Graduates, "technical experts with library responsibilities," would be prepared to initiate the automation of library services or the administration and maintenance of exiting systems. They would be capable of establishing and maintaining LAN access to a CD-ROM service. They would be able to provide technical leadership in connecting a consortium of public libraries and public schools to the Internet.

Building a New Learning Environment. Building a new learning environment is of critical importance. Students must be able to work with what might be termed "near leading edge" equipment, and faculty with appropriate research interests should have access to even more sophisticated facilities. Of equal importance, library educators must understand and accept the fact that in this area change will remain relentless.

Most library schools have inadequate computing facilities.[12] And, although the costs of many types of computers and peripheral devices continue to drop at remarkable rates, building a technological base appropriate for teaching and research remains a costly proposition. Those costs will seem especially high for the schools that have neglected this aspect of their operation.

Costs notwithstanding, many schools will find it necessary to create new computing laboratories or expand existing facilities to ensure that students and faculty have access to appropriate and sufficient equipment and facilities. Schools will also need to devise strategic plans for the continuing development of computing resources. University administrators must be made to realize that substantial and state-of-the-art computing facilities are as necessary to today's library programs as they are to computer science departments. Library programs might also pursue closer arrangements with technology vendors as a means of acquiring needed equipment at lower prices.

The speed with which technology changes means that the school that outfitted a laboratory this year with machines using 32-bit CISC microprocessors may need to replace those machines within the next two years to ensure that the technology supporting teaching and research is up to date. Owing to this problem alone, administrators charged with the responsibility of making, obtaining the support for, and then carrying out plans for systematically upgrading computing facilities face a formidable task.

Public Service as a Component of Educating Network Navigators. However, having well-equipped laboratories is a necessary but not a sufficient condition for success in technologically oriented education. What library schools must create is an environment in which students can learn through relevant experiences. One way in which library schools can provide students with experiences relevant to subsequent work in the NREN environment, and contribute to the commonweal in the process, is to form an association with an organization such as the National Public Telecomputing Network (NPTN). Or they might mount a Gopher server with Internet access. (The establishment of a Gopher server is an option not necessarily exclusive of the Freenet option. Given the architecture of the two systems, it would be possible for a Freenet system to provide access to a local Gopher server or the entire array of Gopher servers currently operating across the Internet.)

The NPTN is a non-profit organization established in 1989 by Thomas Grundner.[13] It has three basic objectives:

- to establish public-access community computer systems throughout the United States and then the world;

- to link all Freenet systems together through a common, non-commercial communications network akin to National Public Radio or the Public Broadcasting System. (Each new Freenet is an affiliate of NPTN, providing intersystem electronic mail and a wide range of information and news features to be produced and distributed by NPTN and its affiliates.);
- "to serve as a resource to governmental entities, corporations, and individuals in the formation of [new] policies and directions" in public-access information services and telecommunications (Cleveland Freenet, 1989).

The connection between either a Freenet service or a Gopher server and library education is a simple one. Library schools must devise means of furnishing students with direct, substantive experience in the operation of electronic information services, and they must also establish sites for ongoing research concerning the various issues—technical, operational, social, cognitive, ethical, and economic—raised by proposals to create and build on a "national electronic information infrastructure."

Affiliating library schools with community- and/or network-oriented information systems provides educators and students with:

- a learning laboratory that provides an educational experience in the operation of network information systems akin to that furnished by a college radio or television station;
- a testbed for research and development, with special emphasis on the further development of electronic library systems and electronically delivered community and social services;
- a resource for distance education, offering teachers, librarians, and archivists continuing education, and professional updates, via telecomputing links;
- a platform for electronic publications concerning community affairs, education, and related services; and
- a community service/information resource operating in cooperation with major public and academic libraries and other information service agencies, particularly those in the region adjacent to the school.

It seems certain that community computer networks of some type will have an effect on the social and cultural life of the next century akin to the one that public libraries have had in this century. By affiliating themselves with public-access telecomputing systems now, library schools will be able to play an important role in shaping the future of community-oriented library and information services. In the short term, students can get "hands-on" experience through operating, maintaining, and, hopefully, improving networked information services. In terms of research, whether the issue is the design of an interface or an electronic publication, the development of file integrity standards for electronically distributed documentation, or the use of expert systems in managing reference and interlibrary loan requests, a public-access computing system operating with a library school would offer the opportunity to investigate such issues and work toward solutions that increase access to, and the usefulness of, libraries and other information systems.

In terms of professional education, operating an electronic information service as a direct extension of graduate programs in library science represents a unique opportunity to reintegrate professional education and practical experience, and to reinvent the professional apprenticeship in a form that will be relevant well into the next century.

CHALLENGES AND BARRIERS

Whether the aim is the short-term goal of creating a course for network navigators or the more ambitious goal of creating an extended curriculum for specialization in the area of library automation, library schools face a formidable challenge in preparing for the NREN. The tasks ahead are great, in large part, because library schools do not deal well with the issues of technology or technological change. One of the main reasons for this difficulty is that the faculties of many library schools possess little or no expertise in the area of information technology.

The Issue of Technically Competent Faculty

This lack of expertise is another area in which library schools have no choice but to change. Library schools cannot continue to offer instructors for basic subjects such as reference and cataloging who know little or nothing about online database services, CD-ROM indexes and reference tools, OCLC, Z39.50, or OPACS. Nor can library schools continue to foster the view that computers are a fad, or worse yet, a conspiracy aimed at debasing cultural standards.

To change this state of affairs, library schools must begin by adding to their faculties men and women with expertise in both library science, as it is more traditionally defined, and information technology. Ironically, candidates with these competencies are scarce, because even now few of the doctoral programs in library or information science attract such students or support their development.

Another possibility is that of retraining current faculty. It seems a sensible idea at first glance, but for library schools that are top-heavy with tenured faculty, change induced by efforts to retrain senior faculty members may be painful and perhaps not fast enough to guarantee long-term survival. A large part of the problem is that the academic reward system, the system for promotion and tenure, does not provide sufficient incentives for senior faculty to "retool," and there are few signs to suggest that this system of incentives and rewards will change any time soon.

A short-term solution espoused by some administrators is to form a partnership between computer science and library and information science, such as that pursued at Long Island University (Woodsworth, 1992). However, this solution overlooks the fact that the problem has not been the lack of likely partners, but an inability on the part of library educators to specify what it is that they want their prospective academic partners to teach students of library science about computing, networking, information retrieval, library automation, and so on. Moreover, surrendering some of the instructional responsibility to another department alleviates the immediate problem of who will teach certain courses, but it does not address the more important issues of what constitutes technological competence for librarians or how it is achieved in library education.

Defining Technical Competence

As library schools attempt to build curricula that look forward to the NREN, library educators need to ask not if technological competence is going to be a principal basis for defining professional competence, but what it means to be a technically competent librarian in a highly networked environment. Given Richard Budd's grim view of library education and its responses to technological progress, the task of defining what constitutes technological competence could be the most important question now before library schools. Perhaps more to the point, answers to the question of what constitutes technological competence are likely to play a large role in determining how successful many MLS programs are in the next five to ten years.

Models based on the view that cultivating professional competence is a continuous process seem most likely to succeed. In this setting, technological competence may be defined as the ability to deal effectively with prevailing technologies and the assimilation of new ones. Acquiring the necessary knowledge and skills is a process of more or less continuous education, formal and informal.

Herbert White has argued, sensibly, that library education should address basic competencies, and that in defining basic competencies, library educators must talk "about the difference between education and training, between what is brought to the first job, what is learned on the first job, and what must be (not just can be) learned later through formal and informal job and educational experiences" (White, 1989). In the context of information technology, library schools would teach the principles, concepts, and systems, whereas the first employer would provide training for the applications in use. Beyond that, the professional librarian would use other resources, including continuing education, to expand his or her knowledge and skills.[14]

Key Issues in Revising the Technology Curriculum

One of the many areas in which library schools must wrestle with difficult problems is in the extent to which their programs can accommodate structural change. Today, it is unusual if a student in a one-year MLS program devotes more than nine semester hours of course work to the study of information technologies, and it would be even more unusual if this set of courses did not include at least one that was basically descriptive in nature. The clear implication for programs that propose to incorporate both a specialized curriculum for information technology and a more traditional library science curriculum into a single program is the expansion of the program to a four-term or two-year format.

The ongoing debate about whether the graduate library education programs accredited by the American Library Association should expand to a two-year format entails some complicated social and economic issues, but there is little doubt that if men and women who direct graduate library programs propose to establish a high degree of technological competence as a basic goal of their efforts, then programs must be expanded to provide the time and curricular "space" necessary for the development of a systematic view of the relevant technologies. In the short term, it may be feasible to offer a couple of courses on networking and network navigation and forego the painful business of revising a program's basic structures. In the long term, however, library school faculties that try to reconcile the requirements of technological competence with the limitations of a thirty-six–credit hour MLS program are destined to put their students and themselves at professional risk.

Another important issue straddling the line between the philosophical and the pedagogical is that of curricular integration. It is essential for professional education to cast relevant technologies in the context of their applications. In librarianship, the value of a technology's application is derived from its effect on service to the user, and issues relating to the desirability of a technology cannot be fully appreciated if study of the application is divorced from consideration of the setting in which it is to be used. At many library schools, however, the issue of information technology is addressed separate from the more traditional curriculum, thus limiting its integration into courses dealing with basic library functions such as cataloging and reference. As a result, many library schools' students come away with a disjointed view of the field that is fraught with uncertainties about the relationship between means—technology—and ends—service to library patrons.

There seems to be a widely held but largely unspoken conviction that this problem will diminish, as younger, more recently educated faculty members lobby to change the content of basic curricula by increasing the emphasis on the use of information technologies, particularly in courses that deal with the conduct of basic professional tasks such as reference and cataloging.[15] However, integrating new materials into a basic curriculum is not an easy task, in large part, because younger faculty members do not often control the process of curricular revision. So, it may not be provident for library educators to presume that this sort of integration will take place merely because newer, younger faculty members have gained influence.

Another problem is the attitudes of students toward technology. At an informal meeting of library school faculty convened at the January 1992 ALISE conference in San Antonio, a discussion of prospects for implementing courses concerning networking focused to a significant degree on the negative attitude of many current students toward computers and related technologies. This attitude was considered to be among the deterrents to more rapid progress by students in the area of information technology.

Should library educators worry about the attitudes of students toward information technology? The answer is yes and no. No, because although student attitudes are important, the curriculum of any program reflects the faculty's best judgments in regard to what is and what will be relevant. If the faculty is well-informed and competent, the attitudes of students about the relevance or usefulness of curricular content are comparatively unimportant, because students are not usually qualified to make specific judgments about programmatic goals or more general issues of curricular content. (On the other hand, library schools find themselves in the increasingly odd position of having faculty who teach students who know more about the technologies that are changing the field than the faculty members do.) Yes, because high-minded discourse notwithstanding, there may be no library school in this country that can afford to ignore a situation that might cause enrollment to drop. So, while faculty must set a high standard in all areas of library education, they should also be sensitive and responsive to student concerns in areas producing substantial resistance to change.

WILL THE LIBRARY SCIENCE COMMUNITY MEET THE CHALLENGE?

If one accepts the idea that the survival of many library schools will depend on how well they adapt to the NREN environment, then there is more reason for pessimism than optimism at this point. After more than a decade of loss and uncertainty and intense scrutiny, library education is in disarray, and on many occasions issues of technology and modernization and faculty competencies seem only to exacerbate this sense of disorder.

Owing mainly to the absence of a strong theoretical base for the field, library science curricula at the Master's level tend to be disjointed, if not incoherent. Doctoral studies are even weaker.

Recruitment strategies aimed at increasing the diversity and quality of library schools students often fail. In particular, library schools continue to experience difficulty in recruiting students with backgrounds in science, technology, or business. The economic return offered to graduates by the library profession continues to be low, and this low return on personal investment makes the field unattractive to many talented students in these and other areas. In the midst of such serious problems, there is, too, the expectation that the financial basis for higher education will continue to diminish. Specifically, government funding for higher education is more likely to shrink than grow in the next few years, as problems spawned by the Federal deficit and a diminishing economic position continue to reduce public investment in higher education. The pressure that this trend places on colleges and universities suggests that library schools are not likely to be successful in securing from parent institutions the assistance required to bring their programs up to date. Competition for resources, already fierce within many colleges and universities, is likely to escalate markedly, and programs not at the heart of a school's mission are unlikely to get the levels of support that they desire.

It is not clear how library schools will secure the money they need to modernize their facilities, but it is clear that to do so they will need to be aggressive and imaginative. The successful course of action may include a greater emphasis on funded research (with special emphasis on collaborative research involving investigators from other disciplines), development of contract services to local and regional consortia, consulting, more continuing education programs and courses, and developing the role of the library school within the parent institution through service courses and other initiatives that may bring the library school additional revenues and higher status.

On a positive note, the NREN can serve not only as an object of study but, of course, as a means of study. By the time the NREN is a reality, global networks will be a standard resource of library education, serving as a gigantic database and a far-flung learning laboratory. Schools will be able to share expertise and information resources with relative ease. For example, it will be feasible to offer live, multimedia courses across the network, which means that the range of courses available to students will not be limited to those offered locally, but will include courses originating at other institutions and offered by instructors not otherwise available.

The power of the NREN and its infrastructure will enable library educators to bridge the gap between professional practice and professional education, to put educators and students in regular contact with practitioners in ways that have not been practical since library education left the public libraries for the groves of academe. In effect, computer-mediated conferences like PACS-L are already bridging the gap to a laudable degree, but in the NREN environment the abstraction of education from professional practice could be all but eliminated, given wide-area networking's capacity to redefine relationships in space and time.

In the end, however, the real issue is whether library educators possess the imagination, the adaptability, and the nerve to meet the challenges implicit in the NREN. If the powers-that-be within U.S. librarianship are prepared to meet the challenges of NREN, if they are prepared to change and restructure the educational basis of the profession to prepare for this new environment, then librarians, archivists, and information specialists may find themselves in a position to assume the sort of roles that Daniel Bell envisioned for them in *The Coming of Post-Industrial Society*. On the other hand, if the library establishment is not prepared to respond with sufficient boldness and breadth of imagination, the role of librarians in the new information environment may prove to be that of functionaries, as opposed to that of decision-makers or problem-solvers.

NOTES

1. Twenty years ago, sociologist Daniel Bell suggested that one of the more important characteristics of post-industrial economies would be a markedly greater emphasis on the production, codification, and dissemination of information, and that this emphasis would have the effect of increasing the status of the workers charged with the communication and management of useful information (Bell, 1973). Since then, information professionals have watched closely for signs that Bell's predictions would be fulfilled. Today, it seems unlikely that high-speed networks such as the NREN will lead directly to the sort of socioeconomic structures that Bell envisioned, but it does seem reasonable to imagine that in the sprawling information environment that we expect the NREN to engender, librarians and information specialists and information scientists will enjoy a new, higher standing among the professions. An examination of postings to computer-mediated conferences, such as PACS-L (the Public Access Computer Systems Forum), suggest that high expectations are common among librarians.

2. In many ways practicing librarians are much better prepared to work in this new environment than the library educators who supply the field with new generations of practitioners. Practitioners established the operational basis for widely distributed electronic services through the creation of the MARC record more than twenty years ago, and then, a decade later, it was practitioners who launched the initiatives that resulted in several hundred online public-access catalogs being connected to the Internet (Brownrigg, 1990). By comparison, the contributions of library educators in this area have been modest.

   However, there are signs that important changes may be on the horizon. For example, in April 1992 Anne Woodsworth, dean of the Palmer School of Library and Information Science at Long Island University, conducted a survey via the VISIONS listserver. (The VISIONS listserver is a computer-mediated conference "dedicated to charting the future of librarians" and supporting the activities of the Strategic Visions Steering Committee, a group organized by Susan K. Martin of Georgetown

University.) The purpose of the survey was to gather opinions from leading librarians about how the Palmer School might revise its curriculum. In addressing the issue of an ideal program's basic elements, the respondents placed considerable emphasis on information technology, suggesting courses on topics such as information system design, electronic publishing, network navigation, and concepts relating to the notion of virtual libraries.

Another encouraging development is the special course on community information systems that was offered in May 1992 by Ronald D. Doctor of the University of Alabama's School of Library Science. The course was designed to introduce students to computerized community information systems. It covered needs assessment, policy, economics, structure, operation, and evaluation of community information systems, while also examining access and social equity issues, available services, and issues relating to the design of community information systems.

3. Readers are encouraged to examine the July 30, 1992 posting to the School Library Media and Network Communications listserver (LM_NET@SUVM), by Kathy Burnett, a faculty member of Rutgers University's Department of Library and Information Science. Burnett, who teaches courses concerning multimedia and emerging technologies to school media specialists, outlines her vision of what a school media center ought to look like five years from now. Burnett contends that "we are headed for a major paradigm shift in the way that we look at, access, use, and disseminate information," and that " . . . [a]t the heart of this shift will be computer networks, electronic publishing (including instantaneous electronic home delivery) and—if we wake up in time and secure a role for ourselves—libraries." In particular, she believes that "the heart of the [school] media center of the future will be an OPAC." In her view, the OPAC will be accessible from the media center's local area network (LAN) and through a school-wide network supporting dial-up access. In turn, the LAN will support full access to the Internet.

4. The notion of knowbots is the brainchild of Vinton Cerf, vice president, Corporation for National Research Initiatives. In Cerf's view of the digital library system of the future, knowbots will be small, self-contained programs that move through networks, take up residence in different machines, and carry out algorithms or searches of relevant databases. The knowbots will be capable of communicating with each other, translating requests into specific formats, executing searches, and then, if necessary, incorporating the results of the search into a modified subsequent search.

5. Understanding the operational requirements of various formats and the effect that they are likely to have on the content and use of documents will be key issues in the delivery of information services. Librarians working in the NREN environment will find it necessary to be familiar with applications that can process documents "on the fly." For example, the HTTP protocol developed as a basis for the World Wide Web can support the retrieval of a document from a server in one form and its conversion to a format compatible with the operational capabilities of the client machine. Similarly, members of the team that developed the Internet Gopher system are engaged in

a project aimed at endowing the next major revision of their system with such interpretative capabilities. Consequently, it is reasonable to imagine that in five years this sort of capability will be a standard feature of client applications.

6. The WAIS system is an attempt to automate what librarians call the "reference interview." Traditionally, a reader presents the reference librarian with a question, and the reference librarian then asks a few background questions, the answers to which enable the librarian to identify appropriate sources and select a set of potentially relevant articles, reports, or references. The reader subsequently sorts through the selected materials to find the most pertinent documents, in the process redefining relevance based on the contents of the documents in the set retrieved by the reference librarian, and revising the terms of the follow-up search, if one is necessary. In the WAIS scheme, the client is the user interface. The server does the indexing and retrieval of documents, and the protocol is used to transmit the queries and responses. The client application translates a query into the WAIS protocol, and transmits it over a network to a server. The server receives the transmission, translates the received packet into its own query language, and searches for documents satisfying the query. The list of relevant documents is then encoded in the protocol, and transmitted back to the client. The client decodes the response, and displays the results. The documents can then be retrieved from the server.

7. The principal value of WAIS is as an instrument for information retrieval, but WAIS may also be highly relevant in the context of planning for the future of library education. If WAIS is prototypical of the information retrieval instruments that are likely to be in use on the NREN, then librarians must understand the basis of such applications to use them effectively. But it also seems reasonable to presume that librarians will need to be familiar with a variety of related topics, including the structure and use of various networking protocols, remote procedure calls, indexing, search algorithms, resource control, and file caching.

8. It is an oddly uninspired view that the software in use five to ten years from now would be so much like the software in use today. Yet the notion may not be far off the mark, since efforts to simplify end-user computing by taking complex applications and reducing them to push-button sequences may be expected to continue for a long time.

9. Unlike WAIS, which is a search-and-retrieval instrument, Gopher is designed to act mainly as a distributed document delivery system. The Gopher protocol was designed to resemble a file system because file systems are good models for locating documents and services. The Gopher client software presents users with a hierarchy of items and directories. In fact, the items are files and services mounted on machines arrayed across the network (Alberti, et al., 1992).

10. At the operational level, the WWW consists of tagged documents, links, and a browser. The web consists of hypertext documents, real or virtual, that contain links to other documents, or specific segments of documents. Making a web involves writing SGML files that index the relevant data or

documents and set pointers capable of activating a link between the browser and the relevant file. In the WWW system, a customized version of SGML, the Hypertext Mark-up Language (HTML), is used write the web's indexing files. An operational advantage of the WWW system is its adaptability. The browser can access remote file systems by means of existing protocols, for example, FTP (file transfer protocol), NNTP (Network News Transfer Protocol), or via HTTP (the Hypertext Transfer protocol), and it is designed to retrieve, convert, and display many format types, ranging from text files to rich text formats such as PostScript, TeX, DVI, and Microsoft RTF.

11. MIME (formally, the Multipurpose Internet Mail Extensions) extends the basic Internet standard for electronic mail, RFC 822, by offering a simple, standardized means of representing and encoding a variety of media types, including textual data represented in non-ASCII character sets, for transmission via Internet mail. The importance of MIME is that it addresses the issue of format standards within the framework of an open standard (RFC 822), such standards being the key to interoperation among various multimedia mail systems (Borenstein, 1992). The potential use of multimedia mail in library services is great. For example, with the capabilities standardized by MIME, a user in Pittsburgh requesting a specific sound recording from a library in New Orleans could receive a copy of the recording requested via electronic mail, where the best that could happen today under most circumstances is that a librarian in New Orleans could advise the user in Pittsburgh as to the location of the recording and the means by which it could be borrowed. Or, as noted above, a multimedia mail system based on MIME could also create and transport messages that included embedded links to data or documents mounted on various servers. As a result, a message of this type concerned with the study of Shakespeare's sonnets could include embedded links to the sonnets themselves, to appropriate references in network-accessible online catalogs, full-text commentaries, digital facsimiles of original source materials from the Folger Library or a library in England, or recordings of readings of the sonnets. In the last instance, the recipient of the message might be presented with an array of choices based on the identity of the reader, so that a preference for readings by, say, Sir John Gielgud, could be exercised by merely activating the appropriate link conveyed by the mail message.

12. There are some notable exceptions. For example, there are the computing resources provided of the University of Pittsburgh's School of Library and Information Science, which may be viewed as a "high-end" model. The computing laboratories that support teaching and research at Pittsburgh include a Sun 6/670 server, a cluster of Sun 3/150 and SPARC workstations, a Silicon Graphics Indigo graphics workstation, a PC lab outfitted with twenty 80486 personal computers linked by a Novell NetWare LAN, and a Macintosh lab that includes two Quadra 700 and ten IIsi model computers. (There is also a separate laboratory supporting the university's program in telecommunications, and, beginning in 1993,

students in telecommunications have had access to TERN, the Telecommunications Education and Research Network, which is an educational consortium dedicated to providing faculty and students experimental access to a high-speed telecommunications network.) In addition, every machine has direct access to the Internet and an array of local services, including network-based printing services, library services, netnews, and electronic mail.

13. According to Grundner:

> The concept behind NPTN is to establish a national network of community computer systems similar to National Public Radio, or the Public Broadcasting System. Affiliates will come from either NPTN established community computer systems, or by soliciting existing non-profit community systems to join NPTN. These systems will be able to receive very high-quality network feeds (called "cybercasts") from NPTN, as well as intra-system electronic mail and other services (Cleveland Freenet, 1989).

14. In a similar vein, the recent Syracuse report on the potential relationship between public libraries and the national networks recommends the development of a comprehensive educational program involving libraries, professional associations, library schools, network providers, and government agencies (McClure, et al., 1992).

15. In the case of cataloging, the downsizing of OPAC systems to take advantage of workstation-level technology and RISC processors is likely to increase the use of computers in an area of library education where the use of computers and telecommunication links is already considerable. In the case of reference services, there is growing interest in electronic capabilities, including the so-called "virtual library" and the transformation of the reference literature into machine-readable formats. So, the need for equipment and facilities, including connections, is likely to grow progressively and dramatically during the next decade or so. How library schools respond to these needs will determine how well prepared they are to translate the NREN's services into lessons of value to their students.

REFERENCES

Alberti, Bob, et al. (1992). *The Internet Gopher Protocol: A Distributed Document Search and Retrieval Protocol.* Minneapolis: University of Minnesota Microcomputer and Workstation Networks Center.

Bell, Daniel (1973). *The Coming of Post-Industrial Society: A Venture in Social Forecasting.* New York: Basic Books.

Borenstein, Nathaniel S. (1992). *Internet Multimedia Mail with MIME: Emerging Standards for Interoperability.* Morristown, NJ: Bellcore.

Brownrigg, Edwin (1990). Developing the information superhighway. In C. A. Parkhurst, ed., *Library Perspectives on NREN*. Chicago: LITA.

Budd, Richard W. (1992). A new library school of thought. *Library Journal* 117: 44–47.

Callahan, Diane R. (1991). The librarian as change agent in the diffusion of technological innovation. *The Electronic Library* 9: 13–15.

Cleveland Freenet, Cleveland Freenet State of the system message, 1989.

Deerwester, Scott (1986). Teaching about Computers and Technology. *Bulletin of the American Society for Information Science* 12: 8.

Gould, Stephen B. (1990). An intellectual utility for science and technology: the National Research and Education Network. *Government Information Quarterly* 7: 416.

Hafner, Katie, and Markoff, John (1991). *Cyberpunk: Outlaws and Hackers on the Computer Frontier*. New York: Simon and Schuster.

Klingenstein, Ken (1992). A coming of age: the design of the low-end Internet. In B. Kahin, ed., *Building Information Infrastructure: Issues in the Development of the National Research and Education Network*. New York: McGraw-Hill, 119–143.

Krol, Ed (1992). *The Whole Internet: User's Guide and Catalog*. Sebastopol, CA: O'Reilly & Associates.

Ladner, Sharyn J. and Tillman, Hope N. (1992). How special librarians really use the Internet. Unpublished paper distributed via PACS-L, LIBREF-L, BUSLIB-L, MEDLIB-L, LIBRES, LIBADMIN, PAMnet, MAPS-L, and LAW-LIB.

McClure, Charles R., Ryan, Joe, Lauterbach, Diane, and Moen, William E. (1992). *Public Libraries and the INTERNET/NREN: New Challenges, New Opportunities*. Syracuse, NY: School of Information Studies, Syracuse University.

McClure, Charles R., and Hert, Carol A. (1991). Specialization in Library/Information Science Education: Issues, Scenarios, and the Need for Action. Presented at the Conference on Specialization in Library/Information Science Education, Ann Arbor, Michigan, November 6–8, 1991.

McLain, John P., Wallace, Danny P., and Heim, Kathleen M. (1990). Educating for automation: can the library schools do the job? *Journal of Library Administration* 13: 7–20.

Perkins, Michael J. (1992). Librarians and the Internet. Message posted to *PACS-L*.

Peters, Paul Evan (1992). Perceptions of the National Networked Information Environment. *EDUCOM Review* 27: 22–23.

Postman, Neil (1992). *Technopoly: The Surrender of Culture to Technology.* New York: Knopf.

Stone, Allucquere Rosanne (1991). Will the real body please stand up? boundary stories about virtual cultures. In Michael Benedikt, ed., *Cyberspace: First Steps.* Cambridge, MA: MIT Press, 80–118.

Stoll, Clifford (1989). *The Cuckoo's Egg: Tracking a Spy Through the Maze of Computer Espionage.* New York: Simon and Schuster.

Toward a national collaboratory: report of an invitational workshop. (1989). Edited by Joshua Lederberg and Keith Uncapher. Washington: National Science Foundation.

Wallace, Danny P., and Boyce, Bert R. (1987). Computer technology and interdisciplinary efforts: a discussion and model program. *Journal of Education for Library and Information Science* 27: 158.

White, Herbert (1989). *Defining Basic Competencies. From Librarians and the Awakening from Innocence.* Boston: G.K. Hall. (Originally published in American Libraries 14, September 1983: 519–525).

Woodsworth, Anne (1992). Re: Library School Students. Message posted to the VISIONS Listserver.

9

Who Will Pay? What Will It Cost?: Libraries and the Economics of Networked Information

John R. Garrett

Where's the wisdom we have lost in knowledge?
Where's the knowledge we have lost in information?
—T.S. Eliot

There is a shared vision of the new information world. It is a world of ubiquitous, reasonably priced digital information in any and all media, available to everyone from a desktop (or palmtop) computer, that is as predictable, ordinary, and universal as a toaster.

While the basic outlines of this vision of a national digital library system are shared among the key stakeholders—including creators, rightsholders, technologists, database providers, librarians, and end-users—the plebian details of when, how, who pays, and who benefits are much less clear. Key questions to be addressed include:

- Where is networked information now?
- What are the roles and views of the key stakeholders?
- What is a national system of networked digital information likely to cost?
- How are prices for digital information established?
- What are the implications for libraries?

This chapter investigates the details of these questions and provides the context to begin answering them.

WHERE IS NETWORKED INFORMATION NOW?

In composing this chapter, a combination of old, new, and bootstrap technologies were used. I consulted my computer files of related e-mail messages, which had been culled from personal communications and the six or seven bulletin boards which I frequent. I bulldozed through six linear feet or so of journal articles, informal papers, conference reports, and my own publications, looking for useful quotes, pointers toward new ideas, and counter arguments. Finally, I sorted this blizzard of paper into appropriate piles, rethought my initial ideas, and started to write.

Many use the networks in similar ways. How useful are they? What purposes do they serve? First, the good news.

The Internet continues its dramatic growth. Message traffic is currently increasing at a rate of about 15 percent per month, which means that it doubles every eight months. As of January 1992, at least 727,000 host computers were connected to the Internet (Lottor, 1992, p.4). Since Merit began managing the NSFNET in 1988, network capacity has expanded more than 700 times, and the number of network connections has grown by a factor of twenty-six. (Merit/NSFNET Information Services, 1992, p.12). In February 1992, packets on the NSFNET reached 13.4 billion (Merit/NSFNET Information Services, 1992, p. 16).

The online information business has grown in recent years. Between 1975 and 1991, the number of databases has increased by a factor of twenty-five, producers by a factor of twelve, and vendors by a factor of nine (Williams, 1992, p. 1). The number of searches has increased in similar fashion, from 800,000 in 1974 to 34,500,000 in 1990. And, in the information center and library sector of the business, revenues to online vendors over the same period have expanded from $40 to $690 million, with 88 percent going to three vendors—Mead, West, and DIALOG (Williams, 1992, p. 3).

There are also a number of projects around the country building and implementing full-text, networked digital libraries in a variety of settings and disciplines. At Cornell University alone, for example, experiments are underway involving journal literature in chemistry and, in a separate test, materials science; digital preservation of rare and endangered books; digitally compiled anthologies for classroom use; enhancing user interfaces; and multiuniversity distribution of technical reports. Among the more dramatic efforts overseas is President Mitterand's project to digitize major portions of the collection of the new Bibliotheque de France project, which is budgeted at around $1 billion per year for the next several years.

There is good news in the library world as well. As compiled in an electronic mail message on the Interpersonal Computing and Technology bulletin board (IPCT-L) by Katy Silberger:

- There are more libraries (100,000 +) in the United States than there are McDonalds.
- More children participate in library summer reading programs (700,000 +/-) than in Little League baseball.
- More than 14.2 million students, faculty, and public use college and university libraries each week—more than the number watching the top-rated TV network.
- Libraries save business leaders, scientists, and engineers an estimated $19 billion a year in information resources.

Also, "more than 60 percent of U.S. citizens visit the library at least once each year, and 40 percent use it every month." Good news, right? Expanding Internet use, expanding business in networked information, experiments everywhere, everyone using the library.

But on the other hand,

- The pencil business is orders of magnitude larger than all online information combined.
- There are extended debates on bulletin boards and at conferences about whether e-mail really benefits research and teaching, or is just a feel-good toy for an elite group who are unwilling to pay their way, and think the Internet is free.
- Many of us are drowning in a sea of undigested, undigestible electronic information. We're nostalgic for the piles of paper lining our window sills—the piles are still there, but we never have time to riffle through them anymore.
- Publishers and other rightsholders fear for their traditional print revenue stream due to illicit electronic exchange of information, which could, in their view, dilute the quality and quantity of new intellectual works, and the availability of older ones.
- There are abiding concerns, from rightsholders, distributors, and users that government support for the costs of the network will lead inevitably to government control.
- Librarians are uncertain about their profession in the new information world (see, for example, Strategic Visions Steering Committee, 1991), and even question whether there will be any meaningful role for librarians at all.

- It is difficult to cost out networked information.
- It is harder to price it.
- It is harder still to figure out how to pay for it.

Compared to these issues (and the list could go on and on) solving the technical problems will be a piece of cake...or fiber.

WHAT ARE THE ROLES AND VIEWS OF THE KEY STAKEHOLDERS?

Some years ago, I began an address to a group of librarians with the following comment: "Contrary to popular belief, librarians and publishers do have one thing in common. Each sees the other as a bunch of blood-sucking leeches."

We have come a long way since then . . . haven't we? In the several communities which depend on the creation and dissemination of new, written intellectual works, there is a growing recognition of interdependence, and a shared commitment to find consensual solutions to common concerns. According to a recent article (D.L. Wilson, 1992b, p. A23):

> In recent months, however, many of the leaders of the copy-right-reform movement have come up with alternatives to revising the law. To make the current system workable, they hope to develop new forms of contractual arrangements, new entities that act as intermediaries between buyers and sellers of information, and new technologies.

Stakeholders: Economics of Libraries and Librarians

For many libraries, the cost of critical information seems to increase in direct proportion to budget shrinkage; electronic storage and dissemination promise to reduce storage and shelving expenses, but long-term information costs are uncertain, as are (it seems) standards and consistent supply. Equally important, many librarians are questioning their traditional roles, as users explore computer-assisted methods for identifying and locating information themselves.

In the academic world (Dougherty and Hughes, 1992, p. 5):

> Universities are also faced with grim financial realities, and many officials believe that universities have entered a long-term period of tightly constrained economic resources. The demand for campuses to invest in diverse electronic formats and the equipment necessary to use them has come at the very

time when costs of traditional library materials are rising at unprecedented rates. The critical question is, how can universities, libraries, and computing centers respond to create new and more effective information environments in this period of fiscal restraint?

Dougherty and Hughes, and others, propose a reconsideration of the traditional separation of budgets and operations among libraries, computer centers, and other related university or corporate operations. In their view, library budgets—based on facilities, personnel, and print-based materials—are simply not sufficient to provide for the costs of identifying, acquiring, storing, accessing, and disseminating digital information.

The need for linkages among organizational entities with responsibility for digital information extends far beyond budgets. In an increasingly complex environment, responding to end-user requirements for digital information requires close and carefully planned linkages between the information itself, wherever it is lodged, and the systems and equipment which store and carry it.

Creating these linkages in a competitive resource environment will require leadership at all levels of the institution. It is particularly important for presidents, provosts, and deans to recognize that old structures may no longer suffice, and to lead the effort to build and test new ones.

These new linkages will not arise on their own. Clearly, librarians must convince their institutional leadership that old models no longer suffice. To do so, librarianship itself must be transformed. One ad hoc group, the Strategic Visions Steering Committee, has outlined a professional vision for librarians which includes the objective to establish librarianship as a world-class profession by (Strategic Visions Steering Committee, 1991):

- designing and delivering information that users need at the point and moment of need;
- maintaining a client-based orientation (not facility-based, i.e., affirm that libraries are services, not merely places) and developing the "virtual library" concept:
- identifying and collaborating with strategic partners and allies in information delivery; and
- taking responsibility for information policy development, information technology application, environmental awareness, and risk-taking in making strategic choices in the information arena.

But for now, public, corporate, and academic librarians must deal with dramatically declining institutional resources and must forecast further declines in the future. Some acquisitions budgets are being cut by 25 to 30 percent a year. At the University of Massachusetts, for instance, the library has tried bake sales and candy wrapper redemption in an attempt to find meager additional funds. At a recent conference, librarian and publisher participants suggested considering "crop rotation" for libraries within a library system, so that each library would, once every several years, stop acquiring new materials for a year and use the money for training and infrastructure development. Proposals like this demonstrate the depth of concern about library support throughout the entwined author, publisher, librarian system, and the need for new vehicles to fund digital information and the infrastructure it requires.

As librarians contemplate the future digital library world, four issues predominate:

- What will information cost?
- Where will the money come from?
- How can information access be assured for "have-nots?"
- What will librarians do?

Finding answers to these questions is essential.

Stakeholders: The Role of Publishers in a Digital World

As publishers, other rightsholders, and database providers contemplate the evolving digital library world, five issues predominate:

- How will access be controlled and integrity of the individual work be assured?
- How will revenues from existing works be maintained as digital information access expands?
- How should costs and prices be established?
- How will intellectual property rights be protected?
- What will publishers do?

Some librarians, and others, argue that "a handful of European, for-profit publishers have charged extraordinarily high prices to generate large profits, expand existing journals, take over the publication of not-for-profit journals, and create new publications" (Bennett and Matheson, 1992). Publishers, on the other hand, believe that their business is under siege, threatened by users who want publisher-owned information without paying for it,[1] and by emerging digital access to information, which seems to endanger existing revenues without clear promise of new ones.

Underlying these debates are divergent assumptions about the nature of the information and business world that the several parties inhabit. Publishers and database providers like to see information as a business, not fundamentally unlike any other: the publisher's job is to provide the information their customers want, when and how they want it, at the price which generates optimal short and longer term revenues. Steeped in a public library/free information tradition, some librarians—at least in public—look to information as a public good, which should be provided to all who seek it, without regard to their ability to pay. And both publishers and librarians worry about narrowing access to information as a result of increasing costs: librarians because they may be unable to provide services to all users, publishers because their potential markets will narrow as potential new customers are turned away by price.

Scholarly publishers also emphasize that they are caught in the crossfire between the demands of academics for more peer-reviewed outlets for their work, with each new journal or book mandating a high unit cost due to limited circulation, the complaints of librarians who face budget reductions, and increased information demand from their patrons. As Peter Lyman of the University of Southern California points out in a recent article, "there may well be a conflict of interest between the faculty and the library, which is masked by the conflict between the library and the publishers" (Lyman, 1992, p. 99).

Publishers are also concerned that electronic systems offer new opportunities for illicit, unauthorized use. Even if libraries and others pay to access information electronically, can rightsholders be assured that dissemination will be limited to authorized users and uses? If dissemination can be controlled, can publishers assure authors that the integrity of their work will be maintained? And if assurances were provided, in the face of rapid technological advances, what would the assurances be worth?

Despite these concerns, major scientific and technical publishers, whether for-profit or not, are experimenting with providing journal and book information online (Wilson, 1992, p. 9). Some publishers, like McGraw-Hill and Simon & Schuster (Weyr, 1992), have made electronic information the centerpiece of their corporate strategy; others, including the Association for Computing Machinery (ACM) are building long-range programs to integrate, electronically, all phases of the information acquisition, editing, peer review, and delivery process.

This response by publishers, in part, results from the growing recognition that the scholarly and technical information landscape is changing rapidly. Information exchange in science and technology, has in the past been controlled largely by the painstaking process of selecting, reviewing, editing, and publishing scholarly journals. Electronic networks provide new alternatives to scholars in all disciplines, especially those in periods of rapid change; increasingly, they are replacing the journal as the primary vehicle for exchanging information concerning new developments.

In physics, for instance (Gould and Pearce, 1991, p. 7):

> Probably the most important and heavily used current awareness resources for physicists are electronic networks such as BITNET. These networks allow physicists to keep in constant communication with each other worldwide, reducing the time this takes from weeks to days or even hours. . . . The explosive growth in this type of information implies a more casual approach to the acquisition of information and may ultimately pose a threat to the orderly reporting and maintenance of the records of research results.

Increasing quantities of electronic and print information also raise a web of user-related issues, like overload, technoxiety (anxiety which results from an overexposure to technologies' potential assets, and limited time and ability to make use of them), and infophobia (the feeling that if one more item enters the brain, it will begin bubbling over). These issues are fundamental to publishers. The deep structure of print-based journals and books—segmented into chapter or articles, accompanied by orderly bibliographic and citation data, preceded by abstracts—defines how users expect to find information, and how they are expected to use it. The journal and book assume a leisurely sequence of exploration, from bibliography and citations to abstract to article or chapter, with most readers actually reading articles or chapters from beginning to end. Many publishers and librarians understand that is not always the case, but the book and journal paradigm binds all parties to these assumptions and constrains alternative uses.

A recent study, conducted by Eric Almquist of Decision Research Corporation, and commissioned by The Faxon Institute for Advanced Studies, provides interesting insights into these traditional assumptions (Almquist, 1991). The study looked at "information acquisition and usage behavior of scientific professionals" (Almquist, 1991, p. 1) in chemistry, genetics, and computer science. Respondents identified source, access, and value of a set of "information encounters," which were then analyzed along several dimensions. In addition, participants were asked several more general questions about their information-acquiring behavior.

Some interesting results from this study are: the percentage of information needed to do the job well which is actually read was reported as 51 percent by researchers under age thirty, 42 percent by researchers aged thirty through forty-nine, and 37 percent by researchers over fifty.

The more you know, the more you know you do not know? Or is this a product of greater specialization of younger researchers? Or have older researchers given up?

Other results were that online database usage also differed according to the seniority of the researcher. Online databases were personally accessed by 52 percent of junior researchers, 54 percent of mid-level researchers, and 40 percent of senior researchers.

Content sources used for the information encounters look fairly traditional; for example:

- journals, 39 percent;
- colleagues and associates, 34 percent;
- books, 25 percent;
- online databases, 7 percent; and
- current contents, 6 percent.

But the frequency of use for the following items for one does not look fairly traditional:

- electronic mail, 14.7 times/week;
- personal library, 9.7;
- in-person discussions, 7.7;
- library, 2.8; and
- online databases, 2.6.

A related question asked how comfortable participants were with their level of reading of work-related information. In general, the higher the percentage of needed information which participants read, the higher the level of comfort. But respondents also agreed with both statements: "I am confident I have most of the information I need to do my job" and "I think I should be doing more to keep up."

Perhaps most important for authors and publishers, most respondents confirmed that they "rarely read an entire book" or "an entire article" (Almquist, 1992, p. 41).

What does this data tell us about information and the scholarly enterprise? First, many professionals, in the immortal words of *Alice in Wonderland*'s Red Queen, are running as fast as they can just to stay in the same place. Second, the traditional methods of acquiring information—journals, books, written information from colleagues—are too time consuming and slow footed in rapidly changing, information-rich fields. Third, the basic units of scholarly information—the book and the article—are often probed and discarded, rather than read and experienced in their entirety.

Upside down, every problem is an opportunity. These fundamental changes in the art and business of creating and disseminating information create significant new opportunities for all stakeholders. Publishers are learning that gatekeeping and quality control are more important in electronic media than in print. They are also finding new markets for their information, both from individuals and organizations they have not known how to reach before, and from current users—libraries and end-users—who may be willing to buy snippets, as long as they do not have to pay for the whole bolt of cloth. Librarians, after decades of dodging stereotypes, may discover that the friendly information escort is more in demand than ever, as sources and options proliferate. And database providers (who may be publishers or librarians) will thrive if they can successfully address the concerns of all parties while generating revenues in one direction and information in the other. The opportunities are there: they require creativity and cooperation.

Stakeholders: Technologists and Technology

Compared to the social, professional, and financial problems in the transition to computer-mediated information, the technical issues seem relatively straightforward. If the richness and variety of images, sound, and motion are to be incorporated into networked information, higher speeds and larger bandwidths will be required. Second, standards are needed for defining and identifying units of information; naming and locating users, authors, and rightsholders; identifying authorization and payment requirements; building and maintaining communications protocols among networks and machines; and ensuring user, data, and system security. Third, rapid improvement in search, retrieval, and selection engines are necessary, if we are to make full use of selecting among enormous quantities of information and avoid exacerbating infophobia.

A detailed review of the status of current technical research in these areas is outside the scope of this chapter. The Corporation for National Research Initiatives (CNRI) is working with universities, government, and private research organizations to test gigabit transmission speeds and determine what applications require these speeds, as well as building digital libraries, and exploring key issues like copyright. Many organizations are working on standards and protocols, and the evolving experiments with electronic distribution of scientific and technical information, mentioned earlier, test solutions to critical naming, protocol, and rights issues. And there are exciting developments in searching and retrieval for both ASCII and bit-mapped databases; CNRI's Knowbot® programs provide a useful paradigm for addressing these questions, and CNRI continues to apply knowbot technology in a variety of information environments.

One topic does require further discussion: automating rights and permissions management. Traditionally, rights and permissions departments in publishing companies have dealt mostly with requests from other publishers to include a chart, illustration, extended quotation, or other material in a printed work. Typically, responding to these requests has required researching the relevant contracts granting rights from the author or other rightsholder, negotiating a fee, and executing a new agreement for the proposed use. This labor-intensive process has been adequate for print publishing. Now, however, rights and permissions departments in major publishing houses receive a steadily increasing flow of requests from faculty, copy shops, document suppliers, and individuals for a plethora of other uses, including the creation of anthologies, entry into databases, delivery via fax, storage in computer files, and the like. But while demand is escalating, the publisher's manual procedures have not changed. The system is already beginning to gasp. Automation, soon, will be required to keep it from choking, and choking progress toward digital libraries at the same time.

Digital libraries will require more authorizations, and more payments, to more users and rightsholders than have ever been contemplated in the existing system. Automation raises a number of difficult issues for all parties, but particularly for publishers and other rightsholders: agreement on protocols and systems will be required. Individual, case-by-case decision making may have to be supplemented by publisher-set criteria covering general categories encompassing large numbers of individual requests. But the benefits to all parties greatly outweigh the risks, since it is difficult even to contemplate a national digital library network without automated rights and permissions management.

One observer noted recently, "the basic dichotomy is one of networks as technology-driven information highway systems v. networks as value-driven collaborative organisms of individuals and institutions" (Brown, 1991, p. 8). The value-driven model implies fundamental transformations in the ways that information is prepared, structured, and transmitted, and technology applied. Who will pay for these changes?

WHAT IS A NATIONAL SYSTEM OF NETWORKED DIGITAL INFORMATION LIKELY TO COST?

In order to understand the economics of building and maintaining a networked national digital information system, key topics need to be discussed in detail: (1) cost of system components and (2) cost of information.

Cost of System Components

To date, analyses of the cost of building digital libraries and disseminating information to end-users have been general rather than concrete. While there have been several attempts to construct economic models of digital libraries, none has been adopted or even widely discussed among the various stakeholders. Rather than reviewing abstract models, this discussion focuses on what little is known about likely actual costs, recognizing that, as in any nascent market, the data are necessarily tentative and incomplete. Indeed (Garrett, 1990, p. 34):

> No one, in my view, has thought through carefully enough who is going to pay for the NREN and how prices will be established. In the print world, publishers have learned over the years to estimate the value of their information. This value is built out of a complicated set of calculations involving, among other factors, cost and an estimate of the size and value of the potential market. All of these calculations need to be rethought in an electronic information world. There is, of course, some experience in these directions through DIALOG,

Bibliographic Retrieval Service, and other information providers, but it is not comprehensive or broad based enough to respond to all of the needs of a fully articulated system.

The most ambitious attempt so far to estimate the cost of a national digital library system was generated at Carnegie Mellon University, where the Information Networking Institute class of 1990, under advisors Marvin Sirbu and Paul Zahray, spent a year preparing a "Development Plan for an Electronic Library System" (Information Networking Institute Class of 1990, 1990). Their report looked at a wide range of implementation issues, including architecture, user interfaces, security and naming, transport, retrieval, and storage. It also included an extensive discussion of cost modeling and pricing and an estimate of market test costs (a little over $5,000,000 for delivering one publisher's journals and indexes to one set of library end-users, with no additional hardware for users included).

The study also looked at costs attached to a national system, although it recognized, for instance, that "estimating the hardware and storage costs of a nationwide electronic library system falls something short of a science, as there are far too many unknowns for which to account" (p. 189). Using various use and cost estimates, the authors calculate that at about $25 per user per month, the initial investment would be paid back in seven to nine years, not including costs of infrastructure, hardware, software, and so forth. The report concludes (p. 213–214):

> After analysis of the financial figures, several key observations can be made. First and foremost is that an ELS [Electronic Library System] can be an independent, financially viable system, which has the potential for significant return on investment. Second and equally important is that the basic assumptions are sound and will not affect the overall system's financial viability if any of these assumptions varied within a reasonable amount of their assumed levels.

But this "financially viable system" needs to be considered in light of other factors.

A review of economic issues underlying one key component of a national information infrastructure—an element not included in the Carnegie Mellon analysis—has recently been presented by Bruce L. Egan, in his new book *Information Superhighways: The Economics of Advanced Public Communications Networks* (Egan, 1992).

Egan looks primarily at the costs involved in creating a national network of fiber-optic linkages to each organization and home. Assessing the likely role of cable companies, Egan concluded, "There is simply no business case for fiber-to-the-home (FTTH) in net present value (NPV) terms until a very broad increase in customer demand occurs for real-time, two-way, interactive broadband services" (p. 103).

In contrast, however, Egan believes that telephone companies "could support an aggressive FTTH strategy due to their favorable capital structure and cash flow from regulated operations" (p. 103). But he estimates the national costs of FTTH at $3,100 per subscriber, for a total pricetag for fiber-to-the-home, nationally, of about $310,000,000,000 (that's billions)![2] And this only includes the fiber connections, without any money for computers, software, support, or information!

FTTH would potentially make full-scale high-speed, broadband service available to everyone. But for libraries, fiber-to-the-curb (FTTC—a hybrid fiber-copper configuration) may be sufficient, since libraries with FTTC could take full advantage of high-speed links. Egan estimates the cost of a national FTTC network at $1,000 to $1,500 per subscriber, much less than FTTH but still requiring well over $100 billion (p. 113).

The National Research and Education Network (NREN) initiative provides the most important national forum for continuing discussions of the issues involved in building universal electronic access to information.[3] But the recently passed NREN legislation provides little or no new money for building these networks, or for providing for have-not institutions or individuals. And, despite Egan's optimism, even the $310 billion (or even $100 billion) pricetag is daunting for the phone companies, too.

At least for the next few years, projects to build and disseminate digital libraries are likely to involve specialized scientific and technical information and partnering among publishers, database producers, and users, rather than trying to supply all users with all the information they might want or need. For these experiments to flourish, the parties require a better understanding of what networked information should cost, how to price it, and how to pay for it.

Cost of Information

The previous discussion demonstrates how difficult it is to estimate what it will cost to design and build a national electronic information infrastructure. But what about the information it will carry? More specifically, what will happen to the cost of scientific and technical articles and books if they are made available via networked computers?

Some in the library community have assumed—or perhaps hoped—that the cost of accessing articles, journals, and books would decline if they were made available through distributed digital libraries. As one expert has pointed out, in an electronic mail message (Weibel, 1992):

> The change in the nature of publishing, from object-based, paper ownership to content-based, electronic access will force us to understand that information flow is not inexpensive now, nor will it be in the future. . . . Don't expect free electronic journals—those that are free now are only so because their real costs are buried in someone's budget, and that someone does not think of themselves as a publisher. The great unanswered question is not whether electronic publishing will prevail but how the transition will occur and how monies which now support a flow of paper will be redirected to support a flow of electrons. In both streams, however, someone will pay for editing, for selection, for cataloging, and for the systems necessary to support access, whether they are shelves or computer networks. In the long run, digital systems will probably reduce these costs below what they are for production of paper journals, and this factor alone will force us into the electronic domain.

That is, without including infrastructure or network operation costs in these calculations. Put them in, at or near Carnegie Mellon/Egan's estimates, and the conclusion might be different.

The Carnegie Mellon study and other analyses (Lesk, 1992) point out that print publishing as a business faces very high first-copy costs, with the unit costs declining substantially as more copies are printed and sold. This is because most of the expense of producing scientific and technical books and journals rests in building and managing the publishing enterprise and publishing organization, working with authors, acquiring manuscripts, advertising, managing peer review, editing, printing, distribution, billing, rights management, collection, and other front-end and overhead expenses. But as long as publishers can reasonably predict how many copies of a particular journal or book they are likely to sell, they can set a price for the item, create, print, and distribute it.

The situation is different in electronic publishing. Front-end costs are significantly higher than they are for print, since the publisher—or a database producer as an intermediary—must perform the editorial tasks listed above as well as designing and building a structured database, laboriously constructing indexes and computer-readable linkages to citations, abstracts (if available), and the article or book itself. According to one database producer, these costs make it counter-productive to budget for electronic journals using traditional publisher profit and loss models, since they make it look impossible ever to break even in electronic publishing.

But there is money to be made in electronic publishing: the reason, of course, is that the incremental costs of print publishing—paper, printing, binding, warehousing, distribution, and the like—largely disappear in the electronic environment. But ultimately, as Lesk points out, "We simply do not know enough about how users will employ electronic journals to make reliable pricing decisions" (Lesk, 1992, p. 3).

In deciding whether to publish electronically and what to charge, publishers of academic books and journals must worry about whether electronic versions will cannibalize their print versions, which are their most important revenue source. This issue is further complicated by legitimate publisher concerns, cited earlier, about unauthorized redistribution of electronically accessed information. These pressures may cause publishers to consider establishing a high price differential between their print and electronic versions.

Also, too much exposure to hype about the wonderful world of electronic information may lead to price inflation, as publishers try to estimate and price the added value to customers that will result from electronic availability. All of these factors tend to result in higher charges for electronically provided scientific and technical information, outweighing the potential savings in paper, print, and warehousing.

But other forces push in the opposite direction. Desktop scanners are increasingly available and reliable; transmission speeds on the networks constantly increase; even long articles can reasonably be transmitted at modem speeds of 7200 or 9600 baud.

Also, several major current or would-be database vendors have already initiated or announced programs to provide journal articles on demand, usually via fax.[4] Some university and public libraries, pressured by declining budgets and increasing information prices, have announced fee-based document delivery programs, with or without benefit of authorizations from rightsholders. Therefore, even if academic publishers want to avoid electronic publication, they may have little choice but to dip a toe gingerly into the digital waters.

HOW ARE PRICES FOR DIGITAL INFORMATION ESTABLISHED?

How are publishers and intermediary information providers likely to set prices for their information? Traditionally, database publishers price by first determining the pre-tax profit margin which is desired, calculating the initial and incremental costs of publication, estimating the total market-by-market segment, and establishing a pricing model and price that will yield the margin. Print publishers seeking to price print and electronic versions must look, in addition, at the costs and desired profit margin for each product (e.g., print, microform, online, CD-ROM, floppies, multimedia, etc.) and establish a pricing model and price for each (Elias and Unruh, 1991).

Publishers must also think about whether they want to encourage their clients to migrate from print to one or another electronic format (hence pricing their electronic versions attractively, and easing access) or discourage migration (through high prices and tight restrictions on authorized uses).[5] Finally, print publishers—whether for-profit, not-for-profit, or universities—must project sufficient revenues to cope with potential unauthorized uses, including costs of possible litigation, and price accordingly.

Models and Strategies

Once you know how much money the database needs to make, how do you set a price for your users? Publishers and database providers consider alternative pricing models before selecting one which most adequately satisfies the requirements and conditions outlined above. The models bear profound implications for the growth and development of digital libraries and for the capacity of librarians and other users to acquire digitized material. Therefore, they merit discussion in depth.

Traditionally, prices for access to online information have been based on a definition of critical use events in each transaction, with a price derived for each relevant use event. This system takes advantage of the computer's talent for counting and recording any data available to it, and transactional pricing has been the foundation for the online information business. But while there has been significant growth in the volume of online information, it remains a relatively narrow niche in the information universe. Of equal concern to current and potential stakeholders is the domination of three providers (DIALOG, Mead, and West) and one professional area (law). Therefore, in the last few years, alternative methods of pricing online information have been explored, resulting in the adoption, by several providers, of alternative pricing methods.

Transactional Pricing

This has been the standard model for selling access to end-users to the large national databases, such as DIALOG and Lexis/Nexis. DIALOG, Lexis/Nexis, and their colleagues act as intermediaries between the owners of the intellectual property contained in the databases and users. Generally, the databases are leased by the owner or publisher to the intermediary, who then prices access to the users following the transactional frameworks outlined below (Elias and Unruh, 1991, p. 84).

Usually, transactional charges include one or more of the following elements: connect-time charges, record viewing charges, record downloading charges, record transmission charges, and record printing charges. These elements may be combined in the price structure: one recently developed pricing model for forty hours of use and 1,200 prints per month generated equivalent income for $90 per connect-hour and 80 cents per item, on the one hand, and for $10 per connect-hour and $3.50 per item viewed, on the other (Sreebny, 1992). These are not just theoretical models (Spigai, 1991, p. 53):

> CAS (Chemical Abstracts Service) recently set forth its novel plan to move away from connect-hour pricing for its online databases and toward 'search term' pricing—that is, the more complex the query is, the more the search costs. . . . CAS believes that this pricing formula will 'relate the return to the database producer more closely to the value delivered to the customer and open up the possibility of mixing databases of various database producers, with each producer receiving fair payment for the use of [its] data.'

Another new model is being offered by the OCLC's FirstSearch program. It is really a transactional system which looks like a fixed-price license: user organizations buy searches in large blocks, rather than paying for them one at a time. Institutions do not need to be quite as concerned about large numbers of inefficient searches, and costs are somewhat more predictable (at least up to the level of searches purchased).

Database providers constantly balance their pricing factors to respond to user expectations and concerns, generate additional users and uses, and maximize revenues. Publishers and owners of intellectual property also want to maximize use, but they must consider the potential for cannibalization and misuse—and CAS' dream of "mixing databases" could easily be another publisher's copyright nightmare!

Transactional pricing schemes raise salient concerns for librarians and other users. First, the long-term transactional cost of database access is inherently unpredictable, and additional personnel or software may be required to protect against abusive individual users or budget overruns. Second, it is very difficult to compare the prices of one database with another, if they use (as they almost certainly do) different pricing formulae.

One recent article points out that "online pricing is too complex, too confusing, and too volatile. Two main problems are identified: (1) as searchers learn of techniques and technologies to save money, vendors and producers 'move to protect their income,' and (2) it is difficult to estimate online search costs in advance and just as difficult to determine the final billable cost after the search is completed but before billing" (Spigai, 1991, p. 57, quoting Garman, 1988, p. 6–7).

Third, what is the actual value of the information to users? Is it best described by the amount of time users connect to the database? Or is CAS' new formula, based on search difficulty, a better paradigm? What if you are looking for patents, and find that your invention is unique? There is one search, and no hits, but the information might be extremely valuable. Are more searches, and more hits, always better? Should they always cost more?

Is connect-time the right paradigm? Or is connect-time largely a factor of user skill, database size, access speed, user-friendliness of the software, searching style, and other considerations which are extraneous to the value to the user of the information? Librarians have always worried about how to define the value of any individual item in a print collection: the problem is multiplied in determining what database access is worth. Is pricing for actual value more trouble than it is worth?

The advantage of pure transactional pricing, particularly if it is based on connect-time, is that it is easy to explain and calculate, at least for the database provider. The difficulty, which becomes increasingly important in scarce money times, is that connect-time expenditures are hard to track, harder to budget for, and hardest to justify.

Fixed-Price Licensing

Prodigy was the first major database provider to offer unlimited use for a flat monthly fee. More recently, however, Prodigy has introduced added charges for heavy users of their e-mail and bulletin board services (Spigai, 1992, p. 52). Several database providers have recently announced fixed-price licenses for selected databases. For instance, UMI/Data Courier has announced a fixed-price lease program for some of its most popular abstract, index, and full-text databases, including ABI/INFORM and Business Dateline. Sociological Abstracts has an "SA Uniprice Licensing Option" that "provides a fixed-fee option to institutions that wish to offer unlimited access to their students and faculty either via onsite installation, or by working in conjunction with a licensed host system" (Sociological Abstracts, Inc., 1992).

The Research Libraries Group (RLG) and University Microfilms, Inc. (UMI), are previewing their CitaDel "citation and document delivery service." The service provides "unlimited online access to five CitaDel files: ABI/INFORM, Periodical Abstracts, Newspaper Abstracts, Ei Page One, and Current Bibliography in the History of Technology." The fixed annual fee includes unlimited searches; full-text document delivery bears an additional charge, either to the institution or end-user (Research Libraries Group, 1992).[6] Some vendors, however, are considering fixed-price licenses for database access and document delivery. Finally, the RLIN service offers individual fixed-price subscriptions for access to some, at least, of their databases.

HOW ARE FIXED-PRICE LICENSES CALCULATED?

For Prodigy, and the individual subscriptions offered by RLIN, it is simply a flat monthly or annual charge—a flat-price license. The Sociological Abstracts license fee "is determined by two variables: (1) the amount of data in the chosen package and (2) the size of the host institution based on total enrollment, plus faculty" (Sociological Abstracts, Inc., 1992). Institutions are divided into five classes, from small (up to 2,500 population) to very large (over 20,000). The fee for UMI/Data Courier's license "is priced according to the size of your institution or consortia. The license fee is determined by the number of simultaneous users accessing the database" (UMI/Data Courier, 1992, p. 2).

Simultaneous-use pricing, also known as concurrent-use licensing, is being proposed as a standard for fixed-price licensing of databases. As in the UMI/Data Courier example, the price is based on the maximum number of simultaneous users, regardless of their relationship to the licensee. Therefore, concurrent-use licensing obviates the need for the database provider to monitor whether unauthorized users are accessing the database, since the problem, if any, is solely the responsibility of the licensee. It has also been adopted as "the network pricing standard by the MMA (Microcomputer Managers Association)" (Nelson, 1992). Some will recall that the MMA led the successful struggle against copy protection in software.

There are advantages and disadvantages to fixed-price licensing. The main advantage, of course, is that costs and revenues are relatively predictable, and it permits longer term budgeting. Second, flat-price licenses (as opposed to concurrent-use licenses) remove nearly all of the restrictions on uses and users that are intrinsic in transactional pricing. Third, user organizations can easily compare prices among fixed-price licensed databases, although comparing them to transactionally priced information is daunting. Fourth, concurrent-use licenses (but not other fixed-price licenses) remove the concerns about illicit users (but not illicit uses) that are present in other pricing models.

There are also less attractive aspects to fixed-price licenses. Although of primary importance to librarians, database access charges are only one element in the total institutional cost picture for electronic information access. However it is calculated, transactional pricing brings a level of market discipline to information access which is absent in fixed-price schemes. In a fixed-price program, there is little direct incentive for the institution, or the library, to improve the efficiency of searches, limit unnecessary or useless ones, develop more efficient interfaces, or accelerate end-user training. Transactional pricing at least encourages user institutions to improve efficiency and reduce total costs of information utilization. OCLC's FirstSearch is an interesting attempt to link some of the advantages of fixed-price licensing to the search discipline of transactional pricing, and merits further review.

WHAT ARE THE IMPLICATIONS FOR LIBRARIES?

A number of divergent models of the library and librarianship have profound implications for the future of digital libraries:

- just-in-case;
- just;
- just-in-time; and
- adjust.

Traditionally, libraries have adopted a just-in-case model, acquiring materials which their patrons might want to use, guided by a combination of the librarian's professional judgment and the requests (or demands) of users. At the same time, larger libraries—at least in the candlelit past of seemingly unlimited acquisition budgets—have just acquired everything and anything which might bear on the scholarly enterprise, both to serve their patrons and to build a comprehensive, unbroken collection of materials in as many subjects and disciplines as possible. Now, for even the largest research libraries, budget constraints and storage and staff limitations require new attention to what information is needed, who needs it, and when it is needed—while also seeking to maintain the traditional role of major libraries as archives of record.

Libraries have always been Janus-faced, looking backward to the past and forward to the future. Now, budgets require librarians to focus new analytical microscopes in both directions, seeking maximum effectiveness from limited resources.

These considerations are causing librarians to add a third paradigm to the just and just-in-case models. The distributed digital library, in principle, permits libraries to provide access to just-in-time information, while choosing to maintain selected repositories of important just-in-case and just materials. In the just-in-time distributed digital library model, librarians need to know where to look for information which is not part of the collections they manage, and how to search, access, manage, control, and pay for it.

The just-in-time model has obvious economic advantages for libraries, reducing storage, cataloging, shelving, and other costs which are important parts of library budgets. Just-in-time information acquisition shifts the burdens of collecting, storing, organizing, and managing the information to others, as well as easing concerns about copyright compliance (as long as receiving libraries can be assured that the materials received are authorized by the rightsholder). It is too early to tell whether the just-in-time model will increase or reduce net costs to libraries, and ultimately to end-users. But just-in-time information costs can be readily identified by the user, should libraries choose (or be forced) to charge them back.

There are also fundamental social and cultural implications in moving toward the just-in-time library. Libraries, in this model, are a resource rather than a repository. Information passes through the library, resting only long enough, perhaps, to be reformatted, repackaged, and integrated into other packages. The effectiveness of librarians depends on how seamlessly they can manage this multilayered system to serve user needs, not only on how well they organize their own collection. These assumptions are reflected in the emphasis on creativity and risk-taking in the Stategic Visions document, and other similar calls to action.

Where just-in-time information is physically located is unimportant. What is important is creating systems that make the information easy to find, search, control, transmit, and manage. The evolving debate over the distributed, just-in-time library v. the traditional library model misses the core issue: for the foreseeable future, at least, most libraries will utilize all three—just, just-in-case, and just-in-time—models at once. The first question for library managers is, which model is most appropriate for which information, for which users, when, at what price? The second, more basic question is, will librarians lead, or will they follow?

Libraries, Money, Leadership

Where will the money come from?

- not from traditional library budgets, which are already stretched to accommodate the just and just-in-case expectations of their users;
- not from reduced costs, either from unrealistic attempts to supplant traditional publishers with untested alternative models (see, for example, Dougherty, 1992), or through savings in print and paper;
- not from government, either, except perhaps to defray some of the initial infrastructure costs, nor from investment (except in infrastructure) by large corporations, without the certainty of profit; and
- not, indeed, from anywhere except the library and user communities themselves.

The task is difficult, but not impossible. But it does require libraries and librarians to look toward new alliances, new models of leadership, new ways of thinking about information, and its costs. And it may require reassessing some cherished hopes and dreams about libraries, perhaps the very dreams that led librarians to this unique, demanding profession.

New Leadership. Librarians need to assert, more insistently than ever, the core value of information for the universities and other organizations they serve. To do so effectively, they need to understand and represent the total information management and utilization system at their institutions—not just the library portion of it. This means, for instance, knowing the organization, flow, access points, and storage of the organization's "collective memory" recorded in memos, publications, meeting notes, conference videotapes, and other media.

It also implies a much deeper allegiance to, and working relationship with, each scholarly community at those institutions where scholarship is an important generator and consumer of information. And it means transforming the library's training and orientation role into a permanent multilog about the uses (and abuses) of the full range of information which is shared in trust collectively by creators, rightsholders, librarians, and users. Finally, it means taking seriously things like titles and reporting relationships: a dean of libraries can do more than a head of the library, a provost still more—and if all information functions (including computing, for instance) are lodged in a single structure, well, then. . . .

New Alliances, New Money. The heat in the relationship between librarians and publishers is down to a simmer—and dropping fast. It is time to forge alliances with database providers and publishers to demonstrate the enhanced value of networked information, in order to reconstitute the library's portion of the total institutional investment in the information enterprise, including computers, networks, staff, governance. Projects such as Elsevier's TULIP (Wilson, 1992a) are one step toward demonstrating the practical value of these alliances: they need to be expanded, accelerated, and evaluated.

Equally important, libraries need to build new alliances within the institution itself. Several attempts are underway to persuade university presidents and provosts to allocate more support to libraries, in order to increase access to networked information (Dougherty and Hughes, 1992). Academic library managers should also consider leading the movement toward campus-wide information systems (CWIS), which will provide for institution-wide networking of information stored at the library or accessed just-in-time. CWIS development requires close collaboration among all university operations, but particularly among the library, computing center, and administration. It is essential that CWIS planning and funding include provision for information acquisition, storage, and transmission, as well as for infrastructure and equipment costs. Furthermore, with broad participation in planning and implementation, other organizational units can be expected to contribute to the cost of building a CWIS, as well as accepting cost recovery for some or all of its services.

Hopes and Dreams. The traditions of librarianship are an important part of the visions that are currently seeking to reinvigorate the profession. Among other things, those traditions encompass assuring equitable, timely, and affordable access (for more information, see Creth, 1992). In other contexts, this value has been described as assuring equitable access to information for "have-not" individuals and institutions, at a price all can afford.

The development of a national digital library system may require a reevaluation of these laudable goals, in several senses. First, except for a few major public libraries, it is difficult to conclude that the current system provides "equitable access" for those without resources, or linkages to well-endowed corporations or universities. Second, it is unlikely that digital libraries will reduce costs to end-users or to libraries and other organizations, at least over the short and mid term. Third, a publicly funded and managed digital library system—which might be able to assure more equitable access—could lead to government control of information, conflicting with values which see "access to information as essential in maintaining a democratic society" or which treasure "intellectual and academic freedom" (Creth, 1992).

There are no easy solutions to these complex dilemmas. Years ago, Seymour Sarason said that the difference between scientific problems and social problems is that scientific problems have solutions. "Solutions" to social problems always create new problems. Instead of choosing solutions, we need instead to choose which problems we prefer—the old ones or the new ones. That is, to the extent that we retain the power to choose. Or will we wait for others to choose for us?

DESIGN FOR THE FUTURE

This chapter has considered the multiple, intertwined issues surrounding libraries, economics, and networked information.

Implicit in the analysis are several major conclusions and recommendations which bear on these concerns. They include:

- Libraries and librarians must play a primary role in the development of networked digital libraries.
- Playing that role will transform the tasks librarians have traditionally performed, their professional preparation, and the way librarians have seen themselves and their profession.
- Building the library of the future will require cooperation—not vilification—among the major stakeholders in the university, database, technology, and publishing communities.
- Creating the infrastructure for a distributed information environment is an exceedingly costly and complex enterprise, requiring the skills and wisdom of all concerned parties.
- Electronic information is not intrinsically cheaper than print information. For the foreseeable future, it is likely to be more expensive.
- Information providers and users consider multiple interacting factors in determining how to price, and how to pay for, electronic access to information.
- For the short and midterm, successful libraries will continue to provide just and just-in-case services to their patrons, while adding just-in-time access to information stored at other locations.
- Libraries and librarians must lead, not follow, progress toward a national digital library system. Leading will not be easy, and may require giving up cherished views and values, as well as adopting a new view of the role and the profession.

These perspectives are based on a framework which mandates cooperation among key stakeholders and relinquishing certain traditional library practices and attitudes. Collaboration and change will be essential if librarians and publishers expect to play key roles in the new world of digital information The alternative to hanging together is, once again, hanging separately.

NOTES

1. For publishers, the increasing use of interlibrary loan for "resource sharing" in order to replace subscriptions to infrequently accessed journals is a case in point which appears to violate copyright law. The Association of American Publishers (AAP) has published a paper (1992) emphasizing the need for authorizations among libraries sharing documents electronically.
2. In a subsequent conversation, Egan raised the estimate to $360 billion, but $310 billion is close enough. New technologies, like Bell Northern Research's new semiconducter laser, may bring down these costs somewhat.
3. For a comprehensive discussion of NREN issues, see McClure, Bishop, Doty, and Rosenbaum (1991).
4. CARL's UNCOVER is the first significant effort, which was followed by a similar program from Faxon. Both claim that any articles they provide will be authorized by the rightsholder. Others, who may be less strict about copyright, are in the wings.
5. For its TULIP project, Elsevier has considered a clever pricing option. Universities who subscribe to the print version receive the electronic one at a relatively low incremental charge; those who do not subscribe to print pay more for only receiving the electronic form. A similar pricing scheme is used for the ADONIS medical information database.
6. A similar pricing scheme is used in ADONIS, where a library pays less for a document if they already subscribe to the print version.

REFERENCES

Almquist, E. (1991). *An Examination of Work-Related Information Acquisition and Usage Among Scientific, Technical and Medical Fields.* Conference Report. Westwood, MA: The Faxon Institute.

Association of American Publishers. (1992). *Statement of the Association of American Publishers on commercial and fee-based document delivery.* Washington, DC: Association of American Publishers.

Bennett, S. and Matheson, N. (May 27, 1992). Scholarly articles: valuable commodities for universities. *The Chronicle of Higher Education*, p. B1–B3.

Brown, R.C.W. (1991). Issues in Networking. In Eugene P. Trani, ed., *The Future of the Academic Library.* Urbana, IL: Occasional Papers of the Graduate School of Library and Information Science, numbers 188 and 189, pp. 7–23.

Creth, S. D. (1992). Vision and Values Documents. Developed at the *Vision/Values Session*, University of Iowa Libraries, March 18–19, 1992.

Dougherty, R. M. (June 17, 1992). A "factory" for scholarly journals. *The Chronicle of Higher Education*, B1–B3.

Dougherty, R. M. and Hughes, C. (1992). *Preferred Futures for Libraries: A Summary of Six Workshops with University Provosts and Library Directors*. Mountain View, CA: The Research Libraries Group.

Egan, B. L. (1991). *Information Superhighways: The Economics of Advanced Public Communication Networks*. Norwood, MA: Artech House.

Elias, A. and Unruh, B. (1991). *Economies of Database Production*. Report 1. Philadelphia, PA: The National Federation of Abstracting and Information Services.

Garman, N. (April 11, 1988). Online Pricing : A complex maze not for timid mice. *Database*, 6–7.

Garrett, J. (1990). The Future of the National Research and Education Network. In C. A. Parkhurst, ed., *Library Perspectives on NREN* (pp. 33–34). Chicago: Library and Information Technology Association.

Garrett, J. and Alen, J. (1992). *Toward a Copyright Management System for Digital Libraries*. Salem, MA: The Copyright Clearance Center, Inc.

Gould, C. G. and Pearce, K. (1991). *Information Needs in the Sciences: An Assessment*. Mountain View, CA: The Research Libraries Group, Inc., Program for Research Information Management.

Information Networking Institute Class of 1990 (1990). *Development Plan for an Electronic Library System: Final Report*. INI Technical Report 1990–1991. Pittsburgh, PA: Carnegie Mellon University.

Lesk, M. (1992). Pricing Electronic Information. In C. J. Grycz (Ed.), *Economic Models for Networked Information, Special Issue of Serials Review* 18 (1–2): 38–41.

Lottor, M. (April 1992). Internet Growth (1982–1991): Internet RFC #1296. Cited in *Research and Education Networking* 3 (3): 4.

Lyman, P. (1992). Can the Network Reduce the Cost of Scholarly Information? In C. J. Grycz, ed., *Economic Models for Networked Information, Special Issue of Serials Review* 18 (1–2): 98–100.

McClure, C. R., Bishop, A., Doty, P. and Rosenbaum, H. (1991). *The National Research and Education Network (NREN): Research and Policy Perspectives*. Norwood, NJ: Ablex Publishing Corporation.

Merit/NSFNET Information Services (March/April 1992). *Link Letter* 5: 1.

Nelson, M. (March 19, 1992). Electronic mail message on the PACS-L bulletin board.

Research Libraries Group (1992). Program announcement.

Silberger, K. (May 1992). Electronic mail message on the IPCT-L bulletin board, citing *College and Research Libraries News*, 326–327.

Sociological Abstracts, Inc. (1992). News Release.

Spigai, F. (1991). Information Pricing. In Martha E. Williams, ed., *Annual Review of Information Science and Technology* 26 (pp. 39–73). Medford, NJ: Learned Information, Inc.

Sreebny, O. (April 23, 1992). Electronic mail message on the PACS-L bulletin board.

Strategic Visions Steering Committee (December 19, 1991). Draft Vision Statement. Message on Visions bulletin board.

UMI/Data Courier (1992). UMI/Data Courier's Database Licensing Program.

Weibel, S. (April 2, 1992). Electronic mail message on the VPIEJ-L bulletin board.

Weyr, T. (June 1, 1992). The Wiring of Simon & Schuster. *Publishers Weekly*, 32–35.

Williams, M. E. (1992). Highlights of the Online Database Industry. In *Proceedings of the Thirteenth National Online Meeting*, pp. 1–5. Medford, NJ: Learned Information, Inc.

Wilson, D. (June 3, 1992a). Major Scholarly Publisher to Test Electronic Transmission of Journals. *The Chronicle of Higher Education*, A17, 20.

Wilson, D. (May 6, 1992b). Critics of Copyright Law Seek New Ways to Prevent Unauthorized Use of Computerized Information. *The Chronicle of Higher Education*, A23–24.

10

Towards a New Librarianship

The preceding chapters identify key issues and concerns that shape the context for the emergence of virtual libraries and a new librarianship. This chapter suggests next steps that librarians should consider as they establish the framework, then design, and implement the digital libraries of the future. Walton (1989) counsels that change will often fail if the foundation is not properly set. This chapter identifies eight critical success factors (Rockart, 1979) which should be addressed as the groundwork is laid for the new librarianship and the virtual libraries of tomorrow are built:

- thinking and acting together as a profession;
- balancing technology used with who we are, what we do, and how we do it;
- forming a professionally supported national development institute;
- training continuously for innovation and transformation;
- mediating between a networked government and an electronic citizenry;
- preserving the past while embracing the future;
- seeking new partnerships and renegotiating old agreements; and
- creating and sustaining political leadership.

This chapter discusses each factor in terms of its current *need* for attention, an *assessment* of the library community's capacity to respond, and *recommendations* for next steps.

Librarians and librarianship face a simple choice. They can be dragged kicking, screaming, and whining into a new digitally based information age or they can take the lead in making this new information environment better than the last. Three overriding and interrelated challenges link the critical success factors that will propel us into this new digitally networked age:

- *Do librarians know who they are?* Can librarians rediscover their professional roots and reinvent their core values and practices for a digital era? Can librarians disengage from their local attachments and think and act as a profession once again?
- *Do librarians know what must be built and how to get from here to there?* What aspects of the digital information process are a global, public, good? What information products and services must be tailored, customized, and bound to a local identity and need? How can the balance among technology, identity, purpose, and structure be maintained in a new digital information environment?
- *Do librarians have the will to live and thrive by competing, collaborating, and leading?* There is money to be made by electronically selling information products and services to the communities libraries have traditionally served (see, e.g., Charbuck, 1993). Is this an extraordinary new life, or a death knell for the profession?

Few are positioned as well as librarians to be leaders in national information infrastructure building in terms of training and heritage. But the key questions remain: Do librarians know who they are? Do they know what they must do? and, Do they have the nerve?

THINKING AND ACTING TOGETHER AS A PROFESSION

Librarians, as information professionals, have many dual or hybrid roles that balance local need with more general demand (Rockart and Benjamin, 1991). Librarians must provide quality information products tailored to their local community. But librarians are not hired or retained for their local talent alone. Librarians are expected to know the best practices, technologies, organizational structures, and values necessary to create that unique institution communities have historically found so useful. Librarians must look beyond their local ties while they preserve them. The first critical success factor suggested here addresses this larger role that each local librarian must play. There is a need for librarians to think and act together to continuously reaffirm and reinvent their profession.

The Need

The need to act as a profession is crucial as the national information infrastructure begins to unfold. Many stakeholders are involved in information infrastructure development, each with a point of view and a direct material interest in the outcome. There is great complexity, and shifting of positions as the form and substance of the network becomes clearer. Professionals striving together for a larger purpose can articulate a core sense of who they are in their work. This sense of identity enables librarians to distinguish opportunity from threat and friend from foe in rapidly changing circumstances. Professionals also create an inclusive governance structure to support thorough but timely decision making. This mechanism enables those called on to represent the profession to know how to act amidst uncertainty. Librarians must think and act together to agilely respond to a rapidly changing environment.

A librarian's dual identity, both local and professional, was clearly on the minds of those interviewed for Chapters 1 through 4 of this book. These chapters focused on library leaders who were early adopters of electronic networks. The objective was to find out: What was the impact of electronic networks on librarians and libraries? Invariably the respondents would answer the question by posing these questions to themselves: How will the network affect what I do? What does it mean to be a librarian in a networked environment? Probing their responses was like peeling an onion, for every layer removed, another was revealed.

Librarians had to strip away the many other roles they played, so tightly were they embedded in their local context and institutional affiliation. Peel off the faculty role here, the educator role there, the storyteller, the public servant, the manager, the accountant, or the media advisor. Pare away the strong identification with the information processes and responsibilities librarians have traditionally performed be they acquisitions, cataloger, system, reference, access services, or depository librarians. Finally, librarians had to detach themselves from historically useful media: the book, the journal article, and more recently microforms, floppies and CD-ROMs. Slowly, images of what librarians are and could be in a networked world emerged.

Robert Taylor (1968, p. 194) writing in an earlier time of change remarked with great prescience:

If libraries, at any level of service, are going to grow and evolve (and indeed exist) as integral parts of our urban technico-scientific culture, then they must know themselves. They must know themselves both as local and rather special institutions and as parts of very large, very dynamic, and very complex information and communications networks, which operate on both a formal and an informal level.

Together, profession and institution, meet local needs for specially tailored information products and services while remaining strategically tied to a larger purpose. The mid-morning story hour is tied to informing the nation. In those simple moments of fun, the young listener learns that there is an exciting world out there beyond the day-to-day and that reading is a way to learn about it. Librarians training marketing personnel in end-user computing is linked to corporate restructuring. The organization can more flexibly respond to tomorrow's challenges if the company's workforce can become computer literate today. It is not surprising then that librarians and their institutions sometimes lose their way. Librarians' dual roles, responsibilities, and challenges are often only recalled in times of change.

What became clear to the research team was how infrequently librarians had been asked what they thought about their chosen profession. Librarians rarely expressed themselves as librarians with their unique insight, responsibility, and expertise. What was equally clear was how deeply librarians thought about what it means to be a librarian and what the future holds for libraries. It is time to bring these local thoughts to professional forums. Librarians must think and act together to continuously reaffirm and reinvent their profession as they create a new information environment.

The Assessment

The challenge is not new to librarianship. Pierce Butler (1933, p. 6) on the occasion of the creation of a new library school and a new way of educating librarians in the 1930s remarked:

In the course of the new departure, librarians will win a new outlook. They will transfer their attention from process to function. They will come to strive for accurate understanding just as ardently as they now do for practical efficiency. They will temper their ideals with realistic considerations and discover standards in the nature of their elements rather than assume them as *a priori* values. They will seek for knowledge in typical phenomena instead of in particular occurrences. They will study librarianship rather than single libraries. Their enthusiasm for vocational unanimity will give way to a recognition of real differences in operative levels, but their quest they will still regard as a cooperative enterprise of the whole profession.

Butler might very well have e-mailed this message to PACS-L (Bailey, 1986) readers today but the occasion might be quite different. Perhaps the note would be written in response to a potential library school closing. Perhaps it might be in reaction to a recent article in *Forbes* (Charbuck, 1993, p. 204) which began:

It would be too much to argue that the jobs of the 152,000 librarians in the United States are in jeopardy. But it's fair to say that their jobs will change dramatically over the next two decades, courtesy of the Internet . . .

Perhaps it might be a modern-day Butler wondering if the Freenets (Grundner, 1991 and 1993) are the 1990s reconceptualization of the earlier, free, public library.

Thinking and acting together as a profession may be the toughest of the critical success factors to attain for many librarians. Freeing ourselves and our perceptions from local ties that bind so that we may achieve larger strategic purposes is not easy. One of the study respondents commented that in many cases it may simply be a matter of "religious conversion." That is, librarians may simply have to start believing that there is a need to reconceptualize themselves and their libraries and then do something about it. If the perception remains that there is no need to reconceptualize the library, then it will not be done no matter how important.

The Recommendation

At issue for librarians is our ability to change. Do we need to be led or do we want to lead? Do we have the energy? Can librarians and the organizational structures and processes which have served them and their users so well adapt and flourish in a new electronically networked world? At the heart of this effort will be a clear understanding of what librarianship means in a networked environment along with models illustrating how this understanding can be applied in local settings. To begin this process we suggest the following recommendations.

At the International and National Levels. Librarians need to arrive at a consensus concerning what librarianship means in the context of a new national information infrastructure. What values are important? What roles should librarians play? What do librarians give up by contributing to national or global virtual libraries? What do they gain? How important are the issues which have historically moved the profession in the context of an electronically networked environment? For example: How necessary is universal and free access to electronic information? Who owns digital information? Should an electronic message's source, content, and destination be private? What should be censored, by whom, for whom? Should there be limits on freedom of speech on the networks? These are really old concerns transposed to new environments. What about the new, yet to be imagined issues! Attention must be paid now to establishing a governance process that results in a product that is useful, timely, and that ensures that all are included. One scenario is outlined in Figure 10-1. The task must be approached with a sense of urgency sufficient to energize related professional organizations, avoid "turf battles," and get the job done in a timely manner.

At the Institutional Level. The process of creating the new librarianship should be an important, institution-wide, team-building event. Constructive questions with which to begin the discussion include: What are the core values that you as a librarian identify as the essential ones for the future? What are the principles that you as a librarian are willing to strike for as a professional? Do you support this assessment of libraries of the 1990s and beyond from *Genealogical Computing* (Naukam, 1993, p. 23):

> As a regular person, you are not "entitled" to free access to Internet, as you traditionally may have dealt with public libraries. This is the 1990s, folks, and the market economy is the way things are going. The free library is done and the gates of knowledge are fully open only to those with coins (or plastic cards) in their pockets.

Does equal access to electronic information matter? Is there such a thing as network literacy? Is it the same as information literacy? If so, whose job is it to provide it? How? The discussions that take place around the coffeepot need to be brought to the wider audience of professionals as together we rethink what we do.

Begin by gaining agreement from all professional library associations to devote a year to envisioning the new librarianship and the
new virtual library. This process could start by expanding and
extending an effort begun by Sue Martin and Don Bosseau at ALA
several years ago. At the same time, existing library electronic
forums (for a list see Bailey, 1993) could be invited to engage in a
similar process. This would place, in a more formal context, discussions long underway on listservs such as COMMUNET (Cavrek,
1993), LM_NET (Eisenberg and Milbury, 1992), and PACS-L
(Bailey, 1986). Finally, other organizations that have had long-
standing relationships with librarianship should be invited to
engage in the same process.

The product of these deliberations should be a set of models
which articulate what the new librarianship is and what the digital
libraries of the future should be. What are the right questions to
ask, who should be included, how to proceed, should all be left
up to the associations and their units. Circulation and exchange of
emerging issues and ideas throughout the process should be
encouraged. At the end of the ninth month, the resulting models
and statements should be collected and distributed widely among
the associations. These products should represent the professions
best sense of core issues, values, principles, practices, and guidelines which must inform electronic librarianship in this new information age. Culminate this year of discussion in a extraordinary
meeting joining all professional library associations in thoughtful
debate, negotiation, and adoption of a public declaration of inten-
tions and beliefs. The arrangements for this meeting should be discussed by representatives of all of the associations in advance. Let
this meeting conclude with the preparation of a manifesto which
captures the new librarianship in both its conflict and consensus as
we enter the digitally networked era.

Figure 10-1. One possible national and international scenario.

At the Local Level. Parent institutions, partners, and patrons
need to be prepared and proactively engaged in the redefinition
process. What will the networked librarians of the future do in the
local community? What will libraries be like in an electronic era?
Diplomatically, but assertively, parent institutions must be remind-
ed of the precedence of professional commitments and priorities
we view as a healthy practice. All local libraries are likely to need
greater autonomy and flexibility during the process of network
integration that is ahead. Preparing external administration and

governing boards now will make the transition easier. Librarians also need to gain experience with, and explore for themselves, the emerging professional strategies and ideas about bringing the new librarianship to their local communities. A reassessment of user perceptions of librarians and libraries is needed in many local communities.

How can librarians prepare themselves, and their communities for the impacts of electronic networking on libraries? The following four approaches are a start to recognizing that local success depends on local context and rapport with key stakeholders:

- Recognize that your parent institution has a problem that your profession has uniquely qualified you and your library to solve. The problem: how to prepare a community to be effective electronic communicators. Identify the likely competition to solve this problem in your environment. Develop a plan which includes their talents as copartners. Go to your administration and your potential partners with your solution. Get there first!
- At the next meeting of the upper administration say yes to that small to medium-sized, remotely information-related project that senior management wants done. You know, the one that normally goes to the data processing department, computer center, marketing, or the part-time computer hacker (in the old sense of the word).
- Identify and interact with those in your environment who you have not historically served. This can be an awkward even painful experience for some. What are their information needs? Have you and the library been overlooking something here? What do the interviews tell you about non-library user perception about librarians and libraries? Are you satisfied with their judgment?
- Organize network training sessions and relevant community-wide listservs for communicating with upper management, administration, and leaders. Use the experience gained to prepare your larger community of users.

These activities put librarians and the library in a new context and perhaps a new role, that is, taking the lead. This mirrors the newly emerging networked world, the context is new to librarians and the opportunity is there for librarians to take the lead.

For the librarian, the hope is that these actions will simulate the experience that a traveler has in a foreign land. Librarians in a new context may learn something about themselves. These activities, or something like them, should also encourage the community to change their perceptions of libraries and librarians. Library users, actual or potential, working together with librarians willing to listen, can evolve a powerful definition of what networked librarianship can be. Asking the help of those you serve, and those you do not but should, in reinventing librarianship might be very instructive, if not indeed, revolutionary!

United We Stand. The choice is as clear as it is simple. *Librarians* can choose to change what they do in a rational, consensual, and empowering manner without sacrificing core professional values. *Libraries* can change, where they do what they have historically done without losing their unique, effective, approach to information transfer. Both librarian and library influence in the network world will be greater if they can change sooner rather than later. Other professions and institutions have yet to consolidate their thoughts and positions on this new electronically networked world. This creates a window of opportunity for librarianship.

The alternative is for librarians to watch (perhaps from the unemployment line) and wait. Soon others will come along from somewhere else. They will perform what we used to do, albeit electronically. Maybe they will not do as well. But you can be sure it will be at a higher pay. Gone, of course, will be any regard for the core values librarians, over generations, have come to appreciate and respect. Do not worry, people will remember libraries. Libraries will even exist in this new phase of the information era. The library will be found about halfway down, between the blacksmith and the milliner, on the living historical museum tour!

If librarians have no core values that they are willing to fight for, it is worth finding this out sooner rather than later. Everyone, from national policymakers to students picking a career, can better plan for the next generation of the information age knowing that librarians do not matter. If, on the other hand, librarians can agree on a set of principles they are prepared to act on in the networked environment, their clear voice will make a difference amidst the babble and bewilderment of networked-induced change.

The librarians who shared their insights and experience with the study team have made up their minds. These librarians are committed to reinventing librarianship and the libraries where they work. But there is a disconnect between their innovative practice and the profession's knowledge and shaping of that innovative practice. The wider profession is not interactively sharing in the experiences these early network adopters are having, as they have them. The profession is not contributing to shaping the formative evaluation criteria used at these innovating institutions as well as learning from the summative evaluation. There is no funding requirement, no incentive for the innovator, no reward for the profession. "So what if CMU did 'it,' it doesn't apply to me." Think of it as librarianship's version of the "not invented here" syndrome. So what must be done? The first critical success factor is a change in mindset, a recognition of librarians' dual roles. Librarians need to think and act together globally as a profession learning and valuing together. At the same time, librarians need to continue to deliver locally customized information products and services.

A second needed change will emerge as librarians become reacquainted with their rich professional heritage and begin to reinvent their collective professional identity. At present, it is easier to remain an isolated island of excellence than it is for libraries to share the experience of innovative practice with the profession. There is insufficient infrastructure in place to support collective professional thought and action on an innovative project without inhibiting timely local decision making by the innovators. It should be easier for all of us in the profession to know about, invest in, constructively interact with, and learn from, "leading-edge," early adopter, library professionals, than it is today. The risks that early adopter libraries take should be shared by the profession. The electronically networked future ought to mean that an advance in a local user community is an advance for the profession as a whole. Some of the key elements in the creation of such an infrastructure are embodied in the critical success factors which follow.

BALANCING TECHNOLOGY WITH IDENTITY, PURPOSE, AND STRUCTURE

It seems self-evident that information technology drives our profession today. But must we be ruled by it? One cannot simply overlay the new electronic information services, products, and responsibilities on the traditional library structure. Paul Peters (1992, p. 58) poses the question this way:

> What benefits can be realistically achieved? We have to find a way to spend less time on wishful thinking and more time on

improving the performance of the systems and technologies that we already have. We must figure out ways to get new value out of these existing assets. We must also be ready, willing, and able to change the way we have been doing things to leverage these existing assets to get more things done faster and without a loss of quality. But the major thrust of the technical question is the pressing need to improve our ability to hold technology accountable to providing real benefits to real people.

The profession must come to terms with the role and use of new information technologies in the networked environment.

The Need

Dizard (1982, p. 12) suggests that success in our generation will depend on the degree to which we shape information technologies in accordance with human values. This critical success factor suggests that the introduction of electronic networking be used to realign the imbalance in the relationships among:

- Who we are: our personal and professional identity.
- What we do: our institutional purposes, practices, and tasks.
- How we do it: our organizational design, reward structure, and procedures.
- Information technology: the tools we use to improve these relationships.

Information technology has been very beneficial to end-users, librarians, and libraries alike. The ubiquity of cooperative electronic cataloging, online search services, CD-ROM products, and library online public access catalogs (OPACS) has established the worth of digital storage, organization, representation, and presentation. But there have also been costs.

When the study participants were asked to describe their own or their staff's experience with information technologies descriptors such as "dazed and confused," "shell-shocked," "burned-out," "bypassed," "technophobic," "technophoric," and "resistant" were common. Many respondents framed the question as: Are new information technologies, such as the electronic networks, allies or enemies? The librarians interviewed raised this issue in a number of ways:

- "Motivating my reference staff to get involved with networking will be difficult after all the CD-ROM burnout. Librarians are tired of technology-driven services. It seems like librarians have been 'rolled over' by technology instead of 'rolling with' it!"
- "My staff can't handle the pace anymore. Everything is happening so fast!"
- Librarians at well-endowed institutions asked where was the value added? Some libraries with huge investments in paper and non-digital sources of information have been slower to recognize the need for change. Yet less well-endowed libraries look to these larger libraries for leadership in the future networked world.
- A young, public library branch manager noted that change to a virtual library would be slow. "Those that know the most about exploiting networked opportunities are the newly hired with the least power."
- Librarians working with the historically underserved questioned whether information technology fostered a "level playing field" or added another inequity?
- Other librarians worried that electronic networks would end the social interaction and human contact which were prime motivators for their entry into the profession.
- A library school faculty member eager to teach a networking course told of facing students unwilling to learn about it. He wondered if library schools were attracting refugees from failed technology "experiments" elsewhere.

Librarians seemed unsure whether they had transformed their organizations using information technology or merely substituted a costly, leased, digital warehouse for slowly burning, acid paper-based, stacks.

The Assessment

The past generation of librarians have been leaders in making new information technologies work in day-to-day operations. As a result, librarians have been exposed to some of the mirages that information technologies may provoke in its users. These include technology's:

- *Imperative.* A specific technology is seen as so wondrous that it must be adopted immediately or, our peers have already adopted a specific technology and we must immediately do so as well or be left behind.
- *Lack of neutrality.* Postman (1992, p. 5) notes "that those who cultivate competence in the use of a new technology become an elite group that are granted undeserved authority and prestige by those who have no such competence." Postman (1992, p. 5) goes on to discuss Harold Innis's (1951) idea of "knowledge monopolies" which he summarizes as "those who have control over the workings of a particular technology accumulate power and inevitably form a kind of conspiracy against those who have no access to the specialized knowledge made available by the technology." See also Samarajiva and Shields (1990).
- *Narrowing of focus.* A technology's novelty or complexity focuses adopters' attention on technical requirements to the exclusion of social effects.
- *Role reversal.* A new technology is perceived as monolithic, inflexible, and invincible. This provokes two common behaviors. People think they must adapt to technology because it is not smart enough to change. People feel inadequate when compared to a technology's superior abilities. A remarkable role reversal results. Instead of tool serving human, human serves tool.
- *Experimental unpredictability.* In coping with the novelty of new information technology, the librarian fails to establish an audit trail (let alone sophisticated experimental controls). Much of information technology's effects remain unknown and not capable of manipulation as a result.
- *Automation effect.* Running does not beat walking if you arrive faster at the wrong place. Information technology misapplied may speed up information processing without noticeable improvement for users. Postman (1992, p. 6) paraphrasing Thoreau indicates the extreme: "our inventions are but improved means to an unimproved end."
- *Utopian outcomes.* New technology as provocateur of change is confused with a technology, that by its very

nature, automatically redresses old wrongs. Postman (1992, p. 4–5) notes ". . . that it is a mistake to suppose that any technological innovation has a one-sided effect. Every technology is both a burden and a blessing; not either-or, but this-and-that."

- *End to regional disparities.* It is widely assumed, without evidence, that new communications technologies will automatically reduce the inequality between urban and rural residents in terms of information access and use. Often the disparities are made worse, see for example, Gillespie and Robins (1989).

- *Costliness.* A new information technology that provides better access must always be more costly than the old, now and forever or so goes the convention in the United States. So much for the Japanese idea of kaizen which suggests "that everything—work, social, and personal life—deserves to be constantly, patiently, incrementally improved" (Feur and Lee, 1988). A standard measure of improvement is a reduction in cost for the same product over its life. For a rich exploration of this topic, see Imai (1986).

- *Wizards.* Librarians have learned self-reliance the hard way by discovering that real experts are few and far between and never there when needed. Librarians have had to learn the technology in order to appropriately apply it in the library setting. While the learning curve has been steep, the process has been empowering. Many technological wizards will offer to fulfill libraries' needs but few will deliver without extensive training in the library application environment.

Slowly, librarians as researchers and as practitioners have gained experience with information technologies and can more wisely assess a new technologies' potential and how best to achieve it.

Recently researchers have begun to free themselves from the illusions outlined here. See for example, Beckhard and Harris (1987), Schein (1987), Scott-Morton (1991), Sproull and Kiesler (1991), Walton (1989), and Zuboff (1988). They have come to see that information technology is only one of several fundamental elements in the information transfer process. These elements include technology but also the missions and operational tasks of the organization, the culture and values of the institution and the industry, and the organizational structures which permit innovation to take place. Each of these elements must be in balance, like a Calder mobile, for the change process to be effective.

The next generation of information technology will require a balanced sense of who librarians are, what they do, how they do it, and the tools they use to improve these relationships. Note the distinction between being balanced and fixed. Librarians with a balanced sense will have the necessary capacity and agility to adjust and reinvent libraries for a networked world. Librarians with a fixed sense of these relationships will be unable to adjust to the opportunities and challenges presented by the transition to a virtual library. Finally, librarians with no sense of the need for a balance between these relationships or that these relationships even exist will lack the ability to effectively choose among the opportunities and ameliorate the risks and consequences.

The Recommendation

The next major step in virtual library formation is connecting all libraries and providing meaningful reasons for them to remain connected. Well-intentioned efforts to mask the process using illusions from previous information technology implementations should be actively resisted. Thoughtful attention to all elements now known to be necessary when successfully introducing information technology will be required. This approach suggests that library connection and continued use of electronic networking should be collaboratively evolved in a timely fashion. The introduction of new network technology to form a virtual library should be one element in a balance between individual staff, organization, profession, user community, and national objectives.

Minimum recommendations for the near term include the commitment of librarians and library organizations to actively assist each other to:

- Get connected. This may take a variety of forms including legislative lobbying, educating area librarians as to the importance of getting connected, advocating for inclusion of "neighborhood" libraries in parent institution connection plans, or even funding connections for the "forgotten" libraries in your area. Electronic networks, like the telephone system, are only worthwhile if everyone is connected.

- Obtain an interface, knowledge representation software, and a set of navigation tools which meet minimum requirements for successful access based on the type of users served. Librarians belong on the software design teams designing these tools. Librarians should develop the capacity to "make" if it is needed as well as "buy" in order to obtain quality, customized network tools. The alternative is to continue to be victimized (as are our users) by what passes for interfaces and information systems today.
- Obtain free access to a minimum set of network-based information resources, perhaps selected by type of library. Free resources could motivate paying customers to invest the time to learn new ways.
- Ensure that every librarian is literate, competent, indeed a master of the information technology in use in our profession. Needed actions may include institutionalizing what were temporary responses to new technology introduction including: ongoing continuing education, a reward structure that values innovation, and interdepartmental and interlibrary planning and implementation teams. (See a later critical success factor.)
- Guarantee that every library user is offered the opportunity to become literate, competent, indeed a master of the information technology used in libraries. (See a later critical success factor.)
- Remove the fear of librarian job loss due to information technology displacement. Innovation occurs best where employees' jobs are secure. The profession should commit to finding information technology solutions which guarantee displaced workers jobs with equal or greater pay, responsibility, and intellectual challenge in the same organization.

These future states are part of a vision which can move the profession forward. But one cannot move forward if one clings, without purpose, to the past. These recommendations have costs and those costs cannot be added on to an already overburdened budget. These recommendations will require choices including dropping traditional library products and services that do not serve the user communities' present and future needs. Together these recommendations begin to address the balance among who we are, what we do, how we do it, and what role information technology should play in achieving this vision.

FORMING A PROFESSIONALLY SUPPORTED DEVELOPMENT INSTITUTE

Pretend for a moment that you have become excited about electronic networking and you want to make it a part of your organization's service offerings. You have managed to convince your organization and you have managed to get connected to the Internet . . . still no mean feat these days. You are presently contemplating how you can help make the rich potential of electronic networking a reality for yourself, your fellow staff, and for your community. Said differently, you are overlooking an abyss!

The Need

In trying to make the change to electronic networking, what you quickly discover is that there is:

- No common interface across the varieties and types of computers so that when you sit down at any terminal you are immediately at home ready to use the network.
- No supporting software which allows you to easily and intuitively begin to harness the rich potential that networking promises. There is no automatic and customizable filtering of messages and editing of extraneous material or basic indexing and retrieval capabilities (automatic or otherwise).
- No network navigation tools combining intuitive ease of use with power. It appears that users will have an even longer wait for the much heralded knowbots.
- No network organization, structure, or standards. Simply finding a correct network address is difficult if not impossible. Tapping into the rich variety of network resources already available requires modern-day shamans, treasure hunts, and other rites of passage.
- No integration of text with graphics or sound. The network, as commonly used, remains ASCII-text driven.
- No clear-cut sense of who owns what or, if that can be established, what one should pay to purchase the data. Are network transactions secure or private?

- No representative form of governance. Who is in charge of the network? Do the laws and regulations which govern other forms of communication apply here? Who will enforce the laws and how can these laws be enforced?

. . . and the list goes on. How can librarians obtain answers to these and many other difficult questions and concerns? Obviously any one of the questions above will require an item in short supply at most libraries, many dedicated hours of reflection, research, and development.

The purpose here is not to complain or malign or even vent frustration. Even casual users of the network would agree that the existing network, interfaces, support software, resources, and services represent a major triumph. The network is largely the result of part-time, voluntary efforts of herculean proportions. This has been accompanied by a modicum of investment from government promoting the public good and private sources seeking future gain. The effort to create the network is a modern-day version of what historically has made America great.

But this lack of infrastructural support does not much help committed networked librarians. They wonder how they can help make the rich potential of electronic networking a reality for themselves, their fellow staff, and for their community today? Nor is the lack of network facilities on this global data highway of any help to the new majority of the network's users. New users ask, where are the services like the library offers in the paper-based world? The days of the network pioneer as the sole inhabitants of the network frontier are passing if not over. Gone is the fairly homogenous culture, able to count on users versed in the arcane aspects of computers and telecommunications. The settlers are here! They are diverse and multicultural, and for them the network is a means, not an end in itself. Both new network user and old often feel like Edward Bear (Milne, 1926, p. 3):

> Here is Edward Bear, coming downstairs now, bump, bump, bump, on the back of his head behind Christopher Robin. It is, as far as he knows, the only way of coming downstairs, but sometimes he feels that there really is another way, if only he could stop bumping for a moment and think of it. . . .

Who is going to do the reflection, research, and development necessary to assist both the settlers and pioneers to work together to reach the network's full potential?

The Assessment

The study team explored with the respondents the options they saw for doing the research necessary to develop support services and to address the questions and concerns of the new network user. Was it the librarian's responsibility? If so, how were the tasks to be accomplished. Would future librarians serve as intermediaries between network and settlers in a manner analogous to the reference librarian mediating between the library, its OPAC, and the user? Would librarians supply the structure, organizing principles, and interfaces in roles similar to those historically played by library technical service departments? If it is not the librarian's job, whose job is it?

The librarian participants' uniform first reaction was a human one. They turned to each other in the focus groups, looked to see who was not represented, and "offered them up" for the task! Small libraries looked to the large; public libraries suggested the academic; and round it went. As the conversations deepened several trends, presented here in summary fashion, could be discerned:

- Librarians were keenly aware of the network research and development needed. Comments like "the network isn't yet ready for prime time" were regularly followed by an incisive list of issues which needed attention.
- Librarians from every type and size of library felt that there would be little support or reward from their institutions for participating in needed network research given the present organizational structure and constraints on libraries. Libraries could not afford to commit the staff.
- Librarians are close to the issues and have much to offer in terms of system design specifications. After a detailed discussion of the requirements for a network navigation tool, one librarian interviewed emphatically added: "Librarians belong on the software design teams that build these tools!"
- Librarians are aware that some libraries are doing research on networks. The study team used respondent suggestions to conduct the site visits reported on earlier in this book. But participants knew few details of the precise research being conducted and were unable to relate the research at these other sites to their own situation.

- Librarians likened the present state of network development to the early days of online, and later, end-user searching.

Eventually the idea that the traditional library vendor should be the supplier of products backed by their own research emerged in the discussions. For some this was like finding a key jig-saw puzzle piece. There was an audible sigh as if to say, "Thank goodness it's not my problem anymore!"

But for most librarians interviewed for this study their reaction to vendor-provided solutions was at best, mixed. Frequent comments concerned cost, quality, ability to customize products, responsiveness to suggestions, and slowness of vendor innovation. The researchers sensed that librarians wished for more control and influence over the products being offered by vendors as a result of research in which librarians were involved.

A key issue for librarians is the unclear return on investment for collaborating in research with vendors and lack of ownership of core business processes and products that result. Cooperating libraries built the OCLC database yet their ownership is in question. Core library functions such as providing a catalog of holdings, and more recently the library acquisition function, have been outsourced. The ability to customize these functions to local needs is not locally managed or owned. The practice of renting access to reference sources pioneered by online search services, and eagerly pursued by CD-ROM vendors, is an issue. This practice shifts the control of who has access to a significant portion of a library's collection from librarians to vendors. Librarians are professionally bound to provide equal access to all users, profit-making companies are without this constraint.

The lack of ownership of core business processes and products raises a second significant issue. The inability to own data renders impractical, if not impossible, the common library practice of investing once, up front in anticipation of its future worth and repeated use over time. This environment has contributed to librarian reluctance to participate in vendor-funded research projects in which they cannot control or effectively influence the resulting products.

The senior representatives from prominent, traditional, library vendors interviewed by the research team had a distinctly different perspective. In their view, bringing a useful product to market based on research and development was a vendor's job. As a prominent library vendor bluntly put it:

> If we had waited for the librarians to tell us what new informa-
> tion technology to introduce, we would still be doing manual
> cataloging. Vendors are defining what the marketplace needs,
> and we'll have to drag the librarians along "kicking and
> screaming."

The study team's research design was not intended to test how
widespread the views of librarians or vendors are. What is significant is that these views exist and the contrast. Equally surprising to
the study team were those who were not mentioned as candidates
for doing or funding the library research necessary to develop support services and to address the questions and concerns of the new
network user.

The study participants did not initially mention three conven-
tional sources of library research when discussing who will do the
research necessary to develop network-based libraries and librarians:

- the Federal government;
- library schools; and
- traditional funders from the non-profit sector.

The following comments are based on limited probing of the participants in this study on this issue. The researchers would welcome an
opportunity to further explore the roles that these key funding
agents could play in promoting research on network use in libraries.

The perceived lack of a Federal government role in library
research may have been related to the viewpoint of the administration (President Bush) during the period of time this study was conducted. A statement from the first Office of Science and
Technology Policy's (1992, p. 27) NREN report to Congress as
required by P.L. 102-194 (the High Performance Computing Act
mandating the creation of the NREN) summarizes the Bush administration view:

> The library community is concerned that it as a whole be inter-
> connected, and that many diverse information sources be avail-
> able at low (or no) cost. Nearly all research libraries, and sever-
> al public library systems, are already connected, but no NREN
> funding has been targeted specifically for library connectivity,
> and the magnitude of the task clearly precludes a Federal
> approach. *Achieving widespread library connectivity will depend
> inevitably on creative ideas introduced at the local level.* [emphasis
> added]

In sum, librarians feel like they are on their own. Librarians' feelings may change with recent proposals of the present administration. President Clinton proposes to provide direct support and connectivity to libraries and other sectors of society in order to "reconnect the country using telecommunications."

The case of library schools as a source of research on electronic networks is addressed, in part, in Chapter 8. Practicing librarian participants in this study clearly feel a disconnect with the profession's library schools. Comments like "out of date," "not up to the task," and "not in touch with the issues we face" were common. The library faculty interviewed noted that many of the faculty were not network literate themselves. Those faculty members that were network aware often found their peers ignorant of the issues and their students reluctant to be trained. Several faculty members noted that much of the needed network development effort might not be considered scholarly research (a key criteria in promotion and tenure decisions).

In the case of non-profit funders of library research, this author can only offer personal observations. Perhaps the lack of recognition of the non-profit sectors impact on library research can be attributed to the following factors. These comments relate to non-profit funders' efforts in the basic and applied research areas and not in their funding for capital improvements. The number of sources whose funds are primarily devoted to libraries are few. The number of grants and their size are small for any given time period. Many non-profit funding sources do not have their own publication division. Non-profits must often depend solely on the researchers to widely disseminate the results of their research. It is also quite possible that network research was a new area in which to consider funding researchers during the study period. As a result not many projects had been funded or reported to the wider library community.

The library research enterprise is a complex arena which has been discussed on several occasions (see for example McClure and Hernon, 1991). Several points particularly germane to librarians' involvement in network research and development can be highlighted from this work:

- There are a number of network-knowledgeable librarians who have made significant contributions to growth of the present network infrastructure.
- These librarians' contributions have often been made on a voluntary, part-time basis without professional

reward or recognition. There is often little incentive or reward structure from the local library.

- Finding an effective and systematic way of involving these professionals in the national development process while allowing them to retain their close working ties to their local communities should be a high priority.
- There is a large gap between librarian, vendor, and library school views of each other's roles in the research and development process.
- There is growing interest among librarians for librarian-produced and librarian-controlled research on librarian-defined issues and development problems.
- Most library research projects are designed for, and have an impact on, a local library. The profession learns little and plays little role in formative or summative evaluation of these projects. Applied research that does not generalize is doubly crippling in an environment of limited funding.

There has been very little research on how the advent of electronic networks can improve library research. Clear potential exists for establishing much more effective links between agenda setting, problem definition, researcher, funder, and the profession at large. The network itself has enabled the creation of new interorganizational partnerships, or virtual corporations (see Byrne, 1993 and Davidow and Malone, 1992), even among intense rivals with disparate interests. The idea of an electronically networked virtual organization for the purpose of stimulating the stakeholders that establish, fund, and use library research has great potential.

The Recommendation

A virtual, professionally supported, national (or even international) library research and development institute using electronic networks will not resolve the long-standing problems and issues that face our community. For example, the critical need to train library practitioners in basic research methods will remain. But a virtual library research institute can ameliorate these problems and will create a revolution in network accessibility and use of research. The institute's success would depend on experienced leadership with the ability to bring disparate interests together.

The proposed institute would depend on electronic network technology and the network community to stimulate the research and development enterprise. The institute would have the following characteristics:

- The institute would be *virtual*. This recommendation does not require a new building or physical organization. Proposed is the use of the network to better coordinate planning, leadership, ideas, resources, and result and evaluation dissemination.
- This institute would serve as a national/international focal point for library research and development. The network can create a focused electronic marketplace for turning research ideas into action and local library problems into profession-wide solutions.
- Collective virtual agenda setting. The network can provide a public forum for all the stakeholders to suggest areas that need research and problem-solving. Once several participants became interested in an idea, it could be publicly developed via the network into a proposal.
- Funding ideas: a single source for funding announcements/ideas. Stakeholders seeking funds and funders seeking researchers would have a common place to meet.
- Funding proposals: Participatory proposal development. Once a group became interested in the same idea, it could move to the proposal stage. Over time, software could be added that constructively aids the reflection process necessary for good proposal design.
- Opportunities/requirements for formative participation and evaluation. At every step in a research project, the profession and associated stakeholders would be invited, indeed required, to participate for the project to go forward.
- An organized dissemination point for library research. The need for easy and free access to research in progress and research results would be magnified by the heightened interest and participation in the research process.
- A formalized, public, feedback mechanism on the research process. The ideas described above suggest a

robust feedback process with the potential of yielding
far more rewarding results.
- The end of the isolation of the research community.
Isolated researchers and libraries could more readily
participate in the research enterprise than they do at
present.

The suggestion to create a virtual library research institute is a sketch.
Its form and substance should be determined by the library community. This institute offers the library community three opportunities.
This is a chance to reinvent the library research process in light of
our experiences with modern practice and stakeholders. This lays the
foundation for libraries to develop the capacity to "make" where necessary rather than "buy" what is available. The institute is also an
opportunity to begin the evolution of a new way of conducting
research which capitalizes on an exciting new technological environment to bring the profession, warts and all, much closer together.

TRAINING CONTINUOUSLY FOR INNOVATION AND TRANSFORMATION

The information age, with its ever-changing technology and extraordinary growth in data production, has spawned an acute interest
in the learning organization (Senge, 1990). Electronic networks
will intensify the need for an agile, network literate, workforce. The
challenge for librarians is to train themselves so that they, in turn,
can train their users.

The Need

The goal of the new information infrastructure is information-
literacy in the networked world often referred to as network literacy. An American Library Association (1989, p. 1) report notes:

> Ultimately, information-literate people are those who have
> learned how to learn. They know how to learn because they
> know how knowledge is organized, how to find information,
> and how to use information in such a way that others can learn
> from them. They are people prepared for lifelong learning,
> because they can always find the information needed for any
> task or decision at hand.

Information literacy has historically been a core function of
libraries. The critical success factor discussed here stresses the need

to translate the concept of information literacy into an electronically networked world for both librarian and library user.

There are several facets to the issue of network literacy that have been highlighted in the previous chapters, including the need to:

- systematically train librarians in effective use of the network;
- provide library professional education via the network;
- train the library user community in network use; and
- provide general and specialized education on diverse topics to library users without dependence on local knowledge and expertise.

These activities are interrelated. Critical prerequisites include those mentioned in the previous section, specifically, easy affordable, connection; common, powerful, yet intuitive interfaces and navigation tools; and, a minimum group of free, essential, and exciting information resources. The key challenges which will then need to be addressed are who will train the trainers, and will librarians be seen as the network training authority in their communities?

The Assessment

The task of training librarians in network use so that they can, in turn, train their user communities is a major undertaking. The challenge rivals that faced by earlier generations of library educators to acquaint librarians and users with OCLC, RLIN, online searching, or library OPACS. The traditional method of educating librarians has included:

- attendance at conferences;
- vendor training;
- in-house training;
- hiring newly trained professionals from library schools;
- continuing education if near to a library school; and
- a core of dedicated "fanatics."

These approaches will not be sufficient to achieve network literacy objectives in a timely manner. The use of the network to promote network literacy is another possible training mechanism but it is still in its infancy.

Librarians have been unable to keep up with the range of new thought in their field, be it prompted by information technology or new scholarship. There is a widely acknowledged gap between professional practice and research in library schools. Top-notch paraprofessionals at remote libraries are unable to continue their education due to local family and community ties. Electronic networks offer solutions to these and other related challenges. It is likely that library-related listservs (see Bailey, 1993) have already contributed much to the network-connected librarians' knowledge of the field. But much work needs to be done to formalize these efforts.

Libraries have committed substantial resources to training their user communities in literacy in a variety of information technologies. Libraries are an established diffusion path for new technological innovations. Many library users saw their first phone, phonograph, cassettes, VCRs, and microcomputers at the library. So it is not surprising that many new network users view libraries as the logical place to receive training on this latest information technology.

But it is presently unclear whether librarians will accept network literacy training as a library responsibility. Others are likely to be involved in this massive task as well. What should their roles and responsibilities be? Perhaps the job belongs to the computer center or data processing units? What role should K–12, colleges, and universities play? Maybe the training should be part of a student's education in a discipline or received by a worker in the course of being introduced to a business process? How will each of these agents coordinate their efforts with each other? How will all this be funded?

Who will retrain and reskill the displaced workers of today and tomorrow? The physically challenged continue to face barriers in access to libraries and use of printed materials. Local users are bound by the limits of their libraries' local collections and frustrated by the time delay using interlibrary loan. Yet already the network is an exciting and educational place to be. Jean Polly (1992, p. 1) describes her network explorations this way:

> Today I'll travel to Minnesota, Texas, California, Cleveland, New Zealand, Sweden, and England. I'm not frantically packing, and I won't pick up any frequent flyer mileage. In fact, I'm sipping cocoa at my Macintosh. My trips will be electronic, using the computer on my desk, communications software, a modem, and a standard phone line.
>
> I'll be using the Internet, the global network of computers and their interconnections, which lets me skip like a stone

across oceans and continents and control computers at remote sites. I haven't "visited" Antarctica yet, but it is only a matter of time before a host computer becomes available there!

Libraries have historically supported their communities by supplying information that is both entertaining as well as enriching.

Librarians, better than most professions, know the issues and the traps involved in network or information literacy. As Patricia Senn Breivik (1992, p. 9) remarks:

> Although the term "information literacy" seems to become easily associated with the scores of claims to fast educational success, the perception is misplaced. Inherent in the information literacy efforts is a down-to-earth, common sense approach to moving past mere lip service and actually preparing students for lifelong learning.

Network literacy has different requirements from its parent information literacy. Some of the most obvious differences are that users need to:

- have access to equipment which many cannot afford at present;
- overcome barriers such as computer phobia before they can begin to use the network effectively;
- cope with an admittedly unfriendly interface and a lack of network navigation aids; and
- discover useful network resources that are without fixed address or easy-to-find location. Whether the resource is another individual with a shared interest or a specialized digital library, these resources are hard to locate and their address may change without notice in today's networked world.

Will librarians take the lead in moving the rich learning environment of today's library to the virtual library of tomorrow?

Will librarians take on the task of preparing themselves and their communities for a networked future? We do not know. We do not know if librarians will train themselves to be network literate so that they can, in turn, train their communities. But we do know that the profession that acts together first will have the greatest challenge and richest reward during this next phase in the information age.

The Recommendation

At the heart of this critical success factor is the recognition by librarians and those they serve that learning is no longer peripheral, ad hoc, a luxury, or a "thing for kids." The continual and lifelong learning embodied in the information literacy concept has become "job one" for librarians. This trend is mirrored in every other profession and for the organizations and communities in which they work. Yet the library's planning, budgeting, reward structures, and other organizational designs continue to limit learning "to after hours and at your own expense." These issues need to be rethought in the context of an electronically networked environment. Electronic networks have the potential to bring employment and training opportunities to the best served as well as the most remote and least served portions of the United States and the world.

Librarians can take the lead in their communities to provide effective, workable, training solutions using a national electronic infrastructure. Key components of a network literacy plan involving librarians and their libraries include:

- A thoughtful restructuring of internal library reward structures, organizational design, and incentives. Librarians must realize that electronic technology is not a new information technology but another in a series of technologies that require a systematic, continuous, learning plan for every employee. If information technology is part of your business, continuous learning is the name of the game.
- The realization that no group, be they public or private, can meet the network literacy challenge alone. A national network literacy plan for librarians and their users is needed. The plan should include network awareness, connection, and use. A coalition of governments, library schools, universities, and vendors, led by national library associations to develop these national plans is a start. Particular attention and commitment is needed to assist librarians and users for whom a telephone is their library's most recent information technology acquisition.
- Standard interfaces, backed by easy-to-use network navigation aids will be essential to make training everyone possible. The complexity of the network aid should be no greater than that of a book in operation.

- Network resources must exist to motivate the desire for network training and use. Librarians in partnership with the entertainment industry could play a significant role in this area if they were required to produce more than entertainment and rewarded appropriately.
- The network needs a systematic organization plan for its resources. Already the duplication of resources is as immense as it is unnecessary. Access methods are unclear. Network resource selection, acquisition, and retention policies are made locally without training and without regard for their global impact. As a consequence, basic network guides need to be continuously updated to reflect changes in the location of old knowledge rather than to reflect the presence of new knowledge.
- Network literacy will require a phased approach. Once libraries are connected and librarians trained, the training of key community members can begin including teachers, elected officials, and business leaders. These groups can, in turn, train the community.

As one illustration of librarians' great depth of experience in this area, a state-wide prototype for this effort was developed in North Carolina and led by former State Librarian, Howard McGinn. This project is briefly described in Chapter 4.

A national network literacy plan is essential to promote continuous training for innovation and transformation. Perhaps the urgency to regain national competitiveness can be melded with the promise of a national electronic information infrastructure to form an enduring new covenant for our local communities. But the challenge begins with the library profession and with you. There is a harder obligation which we believe is first and primary. Librarians must ask themselves: what role do we, who have played such a critical role in fostering information literacy, wish to play in achieving network literacy for ourselves and our institutions? What should be altered in the equation that has linked government, private sector, library, and community so successfully in the past? Has the agreement been fair to librarians? Can the relationship be sustained in the electronic era? Will librarians accept less, do we want more? What will it take for librarians to be all that they can be for themselves and their community? With these questions addressed, personally and professionally, librarians can then assume the other key roles they will be called on to play in leading the effort to bring network literacy to themselves and their communities.

MEDIATE BETWEEN NETWORKED GOVERNMENT AND ELECTRONIC CITIZENRY

Citizens view their community library as an essential, sometimes the only, gathering place to obtain neutral, authoritative information about government. Libraries are where the local candidates debate. Libraries are where you get your tax forms. Libraries allow a citizen to find out about benefit eligibility. Libraries enable citizens to develop a more informed view about a current policy issue. Will the library serve as the electronic civic gathering point in a networked world or will that job be filled by others?

The Need

In the United States, there has been a somewhat sporadic, though sustained, commitment to the idea that the library is a key participant in the citizen-to-government information infrastructure of the nation. This information infrastructure consists of a series of public and private agreements among U.S. citizens and organizations to make it easier for citizens to participate in government than to remain ignorant of it. The library's role has been to select, acquire, organize, represent, store, retrieve, and present information that citizen's are likely to need.

The context for this section has been framed by Chapter 7's discussion of the Federal Depository Library Program. Additional background includes the authors' work on a Federal, government-wide, information locator system (McClure, Ryan, and Moen, 1992). A further relevant source is a recent report written in part by the authors (McClure, et al., 1992, p. 1) for the U.S. Congress, Office of Technology Assessment (OTA) entitled *Federal Information Policy and Management for Electronic Services Delivery* which sets the stage:

> American citizens are surrounded by an increasing array of technologies that are changing the way we work, shop, communicate, do business, and spend our leisure time. We have grown accustomed to automatic teller machines (ATMs), cable and interactive television, computer networks, touch screens, and a variety of technologies too numerous to list that not only process electronic information but also deliver services. We

have grown accustomed not only to these technologies but to the services, the responsiveness, and the flexibility enabled by them. For example, personal banking can be done on a twenty-four-hour basis with ATMs; organizations provide toll-free numbers for customer services. We become impatient with slow and ineffective services, with organizations that lack a customer-centered service attitude.

Many private and public sector organizations have emerged or have been reinvented that envision information technology (IT), combined with a renewed commitment to serving their clients and customers, as fundamental to their continued existence. Should not citizens expect their government, whether at the Federal, state, county, or local level, to adopt a responsive customer-centered service attitude and deploy modern telecommunications and information technology in the provision of government services?

Already a significant fraction of government information is in digital form with the trend increasing every year. According to one estimate (Bortnick, 1990), 75 percent of all Federal transactions will be handled electronically by the year 2000.

Who will provide the citizen and government with an electronic, civic space similar to the one provided by the library for so long? A summary of the major points which supply a framework for this need include:

- An informed citizenry is mandatory for the U.S. version of democracy to work.
- Libraries of all types have played a historic role in educating citizens to their roles and responsibilities in the democratic governance process and supplying government-produced information to make informed decisions.
- Both government and citizen see libraries as a neutral source, in some cases the only source, of access to the diverse range of government information.
- The Federal government is the world's largest publisher of information. These publications are paid for by the taxpayer and effective citizen access and use is essential. How will the U.S. citizen obtain effective access to and use of this information?
- The private sector has historically added value to government information for a profit.

- There has been a historic conflict over what value should be added for a profit and what value should be added for free in the provision of government information. In the United States, this issue is most frequently resolved via negotiation with the unit of government (agency) and with policy guidance of varying impact offered by the level of government (Federal, state, or local).
- The nature of the medium, the message, and even the process of governance is undergoing a radical transformation as a result of the information transfer capabilities of a ubiquitous electronic network.
- The majority of U.S. citizens of today will need training and access to equipment at minimum to take advantage of government information provided on the networks tomorrow.
- Citizens, libraries, for-profit organizations, and governments need to engage in thoughtful, coordinated, planning to achieve the rich potential for an enhanced democratic process that the electronic environment promises.

The transition to the provision of government information and services to citizens using an electronic information infrastructure has already begun. But much will need to be done by all of the stakeholders to ensure full use of the potential of network technologies.

The Assessment

The Federal government is beginning the process of reinventing what it does using a national electronic infrastructure as a service and information delivery vehicle. State and local governments have already begun this process on a limited scale. To date, there has been a notable lack of coordination among governments in their information infrastructure building. A government service and information delivery infrastructure is a large, multiyear endeavor that is just getting underway. Where we believe this process is leading is summarized in the recent OTA study (McClure, et al., 1992, preface, p. iii):

Our vision proposes that the Federal government must undertake a concerted, major effort to build a national electronic information infrastructure to serve its own internal needs and to reach its citizens. Without a national information infrastructure the Federal government will be relegated to a second-class organization operating merely at the periphery of the U. S. society in the twenty-first century. It is imperative that the Federal government plans strategically *now* for its role as a services provider in the development of the national information infrastructure.

Librarians have much to offer in this process. But governments tend to take libraries for granted and librarians find it is easy to keep the future at a distance.

Librarians have at least two important reasons to engage in the planning, research, and development of a government electronic service and information infrastructure today. Librarians need to better define their role in this infrastructure and obtain the necessary resources to mediate between government and citizen in an electronically networked environment. Librarians can have much greater influence if they are active participants in the discussions being conducted now. A second key reason is much more practical. The transition to the use of a national electronic infrastructure will be a time of confusion. As new ideas are tried, decision makers will need constant, thoughtful, feedback from all stakeholders to avoid doing inadvertent harm to them.

At present, the entire mechanism for the dissemination of Federal government information is under review. Is the Depository Library Program a good idea? What should be the role of GPO, NTIS, the National Archives, or the Library of Congress in the distribution of Federal information? What should be the relationship of government to the private sector in information provision? If librarians are not visibly present in the decision-making process, it will be their loss.

The Recommendations

Librarians have key leadership roles in mediating between a networked government and the electronic citizen. Recommendations include:

- Reappraising the historic equation that has linked government, library, and librarian so successfully to citizens in the past? Has the agreement been fair to librarians? Can the relationship be sustained in the electronic era? Will librarians accept less, do they want more?

- Prodding the government to provide to its citizens electronic information products and services using the network.
- Fully participating in negotiations between governments and the private sector on the use of government information.
- Re-examining the electronic citizen librarian's civic responsibility in an networked era. Should librarians continue to advocate for citizens rights in a digital era in such areas as access, freedom of speech, censorship, privacy, freedom of information, and intellectual property rights?
- Preparing citizens in local communities for effective use of government information and services available on the evolving electronic networks.
- Actively experimenting with government in new and innovative uses of networked technology in better serving and informing both citizen and government.
- Redefining the library's civic responsibility in a networked era. What are the libraries roles, obligations, limits? Is the library's neutral, authoritative image compromised in an electronic era?

This will be among the most challenging and exciting times for those interested in the provision of government information and electronic service delivery.

The ability of the library profession to successfully address these recommendations will be critical to citizen, government, and librarian alike in the electronically networked era. The existing national information infrastructure, these series of public and private agreements among U.S. citizens and organizations, have made it easier for citizens to learn than to remain ignorant. It is, once again, time for librarians to review and renew the national information infrastructure agreements which have been in their trust, and at the heart of a democratic society for so long.

PRESERVING THE PAST WHILE EMBRACING THE FUTURE

The volume of information being produced is outstripping our ability to store and preserve it. In the United States, books and journals have been published using high acidic paper since the mid-nineteenth century. Civilization's recorded knowledge is literally, slowly, burning up in the stacks of libraries today! The situation internationally, particularly in those countries lacking developed library infrastructures, is much worse. Recorded knowledge in these countries vanishes often within months or years. Digital information technology is the only known mechanism for meeting present and future needs for storage and preservation. When digital technology is networked in a national or international information infrastructure, many attractive solutions emerge allowing us to preserve our past while embracing the future.

The Need

Within the next generation the majority of items in present-day libraries' main circulating collections will have moved to the libraries' archival collections. That is if they have not already been destroyed by embrittlement, the result of highly acidic paper used since just before the Civil War. Said differently, the physical collection you see as you enter the door of the library today will become obsolete and irrelevant for most library users a generation from now. Library users will have migrated to a virtual library environment to meet their information needs. The good news is that for many libraries the move from the circulating to archival collections will be administrative rather than involving physically repositioning each book. But the bad news is that the switch from paper-based information technology to digital will leave all libraries facing immense problems.

Deciding What to Preserve from the Paper-based Past and How?
There are few librarians who have not been exposed to the slowly burning books issue libraries presently face. Many of the books presently housed in libraries are deteriorating due to the acid paper stock used. See for example, Sanders (1989), U.S. Congress, Office of Technology Assessment (1988), Committee on Government Operations. (1989 and Joint Committee on the Library of Congress (1992). The U.S. Congress, Committee on Government Operations (1990, p. 2) notes:

> Most paper manufactured since the mid-nineteenth century has a high acid content. Over time, the acid attacks the cellulose that makes up paper, breaking it into smaller and smaller pieces until it becomes impossible to turn the pages of a book without destroying it. Only heroic and expensive efforts can save a book that is crumbling. . . . The life-span of a 'modern' acidic paper may be only a few decades.

But the public has largely ignored this issue. The immensity of the problem and need for a coordinated response by so many stakeholders has daunted even the most committed preservationists. Will we be able to preserve the paper record stored in the nation's libraries for future generations? If so, how? Will digitally scanning these materials meet the future requirements of learners and scholars alike? What about the rest of the world's paper-based heritage?

Deciding What to Preserve from the Computer-based Present and How? A recent U.S. Congressional report (Committee on Government Operations, 1990, p. 2) provides background:

> A record remains useful only as long as the medium on which its information is stored can be read and understood. There are many examples of historical records that were preserved but became unusable because the ability to read them was lost. Ancient Egyptian hieroglyphics were undecipherable for centuries until the discovery of the Rosetta Stone in 1799. Stonehenge—a standing stone circle on Salisbury Plain in England—is now believed to have been a lunar eclipse calculator. The ability to read this "stone computer" was lost for thousand of years until the middle of this century.

Preservation of our paper-based heritage has been reduced with great effort to *merely* a problem of immense size, cost, and coordination. The problem of what to preserve from the computer-based present and how to do so has all these problems plus many technical concerns. Many of these issues are addressed in a recent article by Michelson and Rothenberg (1992).

One oft quoted example from a U.S. Congressional Committee on Government Operations report (1990, p. 3) illustrates the additional technical problems:

> The case of the 1960 U.S. Census is illustrative. The type and format of computer tapes used for census returns in the 1960s became obsolete a few years later. There are only two machines in the world that can read the original data tapes from that census. One machine is in the Smithsonian Institution and the other is in Japan.

Fortunately this specific problem has since been resolved, however, it is not unique. Some of the literature addressing these issues include: Bearman (1991), Cook (1991–1992), Dollar (1992), Higginbotham and Jackson (1992), National Historical Publications and Records Commission (1990 and 1991), and the National Academy of Public Administration (NAPA) (1989).

The Assessment

Some of the librarians' core assumptions about where they work are being challenged by the need to preserve our recorded heritage including:

- The collection is sacred. Librarians often believe that their collections provide a certain job security. To which the sharp undergraduate today might respond, "tell that to the Egyptians, or even the Mesoamericans." It might be simpler for the new "digital barbarians" to walk away from the ruins of acid-embrittled paper and reinvent things as they go along. Librarians and libraries may well be seen as irrelevant in a digital age.
- Paper lasts forever. Librarians and their users find it easier to ignore the nearly invisible problem than to confront it. "I don't care what they say, where there is no smoke there is no fire!" It is hard for everyone, even librarians, to grasp the seriousness, complexity, and consequences of a slowly burning collection even if it is happening right before their eyes.
- Going digital automatically confers protection. Digital conversion without thoughtful life-cycle inventory management is not enough. "It ain't my problem, I've converted. I'm digital. I'm all backed up and have a disaster recovery plan ready to go." The National Institute of Standards and Technology estimates magnetic tapes, carefully stored, will last about twenty years. The longevity of other electronic media and floppy disks improperly stored is much less (see NAPA 1989, p. 44–45).

These challenges to librarians' basic beliefs have provoked a core segment of the library profession not previously concerned with electronic networks to ask: *What is the library's business in a digitally networked era? Is preservation still an element?*

The use of networks connected to digital libraries offers the library community and all concerned with recorded knowledge new options. Key findings include:

- There is a fire in the library and it needs to be put out now. Significant portions of the collections of major research libraries are already in danger and to delay means certain loss.
- Digital technology combined with networking offers a realistic technological solution to the preservation issue. Digital capture and network dissemination already represent an attractive replacement for microforms (see Kenney and Personius, 1992).
- While technological barriers exist to using this technological solution, the principal barriers are social, organizational, cultural, and a lack of experience.
- Preservation will require win-win collaboration on campus and off. Librarians will be forced to collaborate with telecommunications, computer, printing services, and bookstore departments on campus to preserve the library's heritage. Libraries will be forced to work together and with the commercial sector to avoid the duplication of digitizing embrittled books and to allow access to digitally preserved materials.
- If this digital/network solution works, it will likely create demand for all materials (both old and new) to be accessible in this form. At minimum, the microform industry will need to rethink what it does. The consequences for paper-based publishers and laws such as copyright will need close scrutiny.
- These issues are not in the future. The existing stock of acidic books are literally fueling the need for the resolution of these issues and concerns today!

It is clear that the digital era has not simplified preservation problems. Instead it has offered more partial solutions.

Viewing the history of recorded knowledge through a preservation lens offers several useful and unique insights as we embrace the new network-based information era:

- Paper technology was not perfected overnight. It is likely, though hard to imagine with all the hype and expense, that we have only reached the papyrus equivalent level in our perfection of digital technologies.
- On the road from papyrus to acid-free paper we must watch for, and beware of, the digital equivalent to acid

paper. In scaling a new technology up for mass consumption, it is easy to lose sight of the technology's larger purpose and settle for the "quick fix."
- Ziman (1969) observes that the paper era "killer application" for science and technology was the journal article. This was centuries after paper was invented and decades after the printing press. Will we need to wait as long in the digital environment?

Preservation is another core function of librarianship that is coming to rely on a national information infrastructure. But if we are truly in the process of finding a substitute for paper, a successor to a process like agriculture that allowed humanity to better conquer space and time, why limit our thinking to a *national* information infrastructure?

The Recommendation

Paul Peters (1992, p. 59) poses this last question somewhat differently when he notes that in an electronically networked environment:

> . . . we must assure ourselves that what we do contributes to improving the basic conditions of human existence and that we can explore that concern by asking the human question: Why will these benefits contribute to the quality of life and the inspiration of the intellect?

We are encouraged by the Cornell/Xerox/Commission on Preservation and Access project (Kenney and Personius, 1992) which has had success with taking an embrittled collection and making it available in both digital and paper form cost effectively. While there are still technical and scaling problems to be addressed, successful projects like this and Cornell's follow-on project "Rebuilding America's Infrastructure" suggest that there is hope that we can successfully preserve our past by embracing a digital future.

Key recommendations for using electronic networks combined with digital libraries to preserve recorded knowledge include:

- A change in mindset that recognizes that solutions must be found today that will preserve our heritage for tomorrow's generations.

- Recognition that the digital/network solution has a significant preservation role to play.
- Active pursuit of public and private partnerships, on a win-win basis, both on and off campus if civilization's heritage is to be preserved. The problems are not so much technical as in coordination. Getting everyone to move in the same direction at the right time.
- Understanding that solutions will require time and thought but experience with the issues and benchmarks useful in scaling are needed now. Well-designed pilot projects can teach the library community and its partners much.
- Educating the public and key leaders to the seriousness of the problem is essential.
- Consideration should be given to the idea proposed in Dougherty and Hughes (1993, p. 18) to establish "an authoritative body assigned the responsibility for 'copies of record' for electronically published information . . ." It is not too early to establish responsibility for who will preserve what in the digital era.
- The issue of technological refreshment, ensuring that today's data will be usable on tomorrow's technology is a serious concern. But it cannot be reasonably used as a rationale for delaying the conversion from analog to digital preservation of endangered materials any longer.

Preservation of digital information will suffer the same fate as its analog counterpart unless preservation is done with an eye to continuous inventory management of the data during the entire lifecycle of information.

SEEKING NEW PARTNERSHIPS AND RENEGOTIATING OLD AGREEMENTS

If you have read this far in this book, you have the sense that we have truly entered a new stage in the information era. A range of partnerships that worked during the analog era are being called into question in the networked digital environment. These arrangements range from who should preserve recorded knowledge to where do I get next year's tax forms? As the agreements that have worked for so long to move information from author to user and back again become unfrozen, librarians have the chance to seek new partnerships and renegotiate old agreements.

The Need

An information infrastructure consists of a large number of public and private partnerships expressed in agreements. Wilson (1989 as cited in Henderson, 1990, p. 8) notes that:

> The term partnership is used to describe a working relationship that reflects a long-term commitment, a sense of mutual cooperation, shared risk and benefits, and other qualities consistent with concepts and theories of participatory decision making.

These partnerships must exist to sustain the information flow from author, through a variety of value-added processes and intermediaries like libraries, to user, and back again. Dougherty and Hughes (1993, p. 1) point out that:

> Stakeholder interdependencies will make it difficult, if not impossible, for any single group to achieve its own goals unless it can successfully establish alliances and collaborative strategies based on the intersection of its priorities with those of other stakeholders.

In mature information infrastructures, such as book publishing, most partnerships are invisible or tacit with a limited, predetermined number of agreements open to explicit negotiation.

Schein (1987) suggests that values, attitudes, and beliefs become "unfrozen" at certain points in the change process. This allows previously frozen partnerships and arrangements to be called into question. New information infrastructures go through a phase in which every partnership may become explicit and need reappraisal and renegotiation. This phase is occurring in the case of the electronic network infrastructure today.

The preceding chapters have identified and begun to describe old and new partnerships that librarians must examine in this evolving environment. Other discussions and negotiations are being carried "live" on the networks' listservs each day. The need expressed in this section is for librarians to actively and creatively explore and establish the critical partnerships and agreements that they will need to flourish in the newly dawning national information infrastructure.

The Assessment

Librarians need to be prepared to actively seek new partnerships. Old alliances may not survive in the networked era. Some of

the senior representatives of traditional library vendors believe that
the network will enable them to redefine their markets in new ways,
leaving the librarian out:

> Librarians are the greatest single obstacle to a user obtaining the
> information they need. . . . The network will allow us to market
> directly to the end-user, bypassing the librarians completely.

Other partnerships and agreements will need to be re-examined.

The study team finds merit in the assessment by Dougherty
and Hughes (1993, p. 19):

> Although organizations such as the Society of Scholarly
> Publishing and the Coalition for Networked Information have
> stimulated dialogue among librarians, publishers, and technol-
> ogists (and even a few projects), for the most part various
> groups continue to pursue their own interests independently.
> This pattern must be broken before a new era of collaboration
> can successfully develop. There is considerable overlap of inter-
> ests—and self-interest—among the stakeholder groups.

But the first principle of negotiation remains: know thyself.
Librarians' capacity to re-examine crucial relationships with old
and new partners in an electronic age will hinge on their ability to
address the critical success factors discussed earlier in this chapter:

- If librarians can begin to think and act together as a profession, they will have a firm grasp of what is central and
  what is peripheral to librarianship as they negotiate.
- If librarians can balance the tools we use with who we
  are, what we do, and how we do it, we will see opportunity where others are challenged. A critical first step is
  simply to bring on board the rest of the profession for
  whom electronic networking is more myth, if it is anything, than reality.
- If librarians form a professionally supported, virtual,
  research and development institute to share and
  extend what the profession collectively knows, they
  gain flexibility, control, and autonomy over their des-
  tiny and their dealings with others.
- If librarians continuously train themselves and their
  communities for innovation and transformation, both
  librarian and community will be able to respond to
  change more flexibly.

- If librarians define as their job the task of leading the effort to educate the new electronic citizen, they will have begun the process of identifying the relationships which will be critical to librarianship's future.

Electronic networking will create more partnerships among a greater diversity of people and communities than any previous technology. Librarians have always functioned in an interdependent world matching the needs of users with that of authors and publishers (at minimum). Librarians, more than most, know the types of information partnerships needed and how to make them work. There is a leadership role here for librarians in establishing these new relationships for themselves and their communities in the network era.

The Recommendation

Librarians have an extraordinary opportunity over the next several years to actively lead, creatively explore, and firmly establish the critical partnerships and agreements necessary to flourish in the newly dawning national information infrastructure. Recommendations include:

- Create a negotiating space. Dougherty and Hughes (1993, p. 19) note: "Agreements exist or could be negotiated on many more substantive issues than many realize; but there is very little opportunity for the key stakeholder groups to talk or work together for a sustained period."
- Define the core missions and relationships necessary for libraries to function in the networked environment.
- Understand the mission of those with whom you must relate. Librarians will need to use the market intelligence and environmental scanning skills that its online search and business librarians have perfected for others for librarianship's own gain.
- Build and maintain the necessary flexibility, alternative options, autonomy, and internal balance needed when faced with a volatile external environment.
- Collaborate. An example deserving wider emulation is the international effort to harness information to

resolve the global warming problem. See National
Research Council (1991). This effort captures the
promise of electronic networking but it will not happen accidentally.

- Coordinate. Dougherty and Hughes (1993, p. 1) suggest that "coordinating and achieving the information
future will come from regular dialog that pinpoints
areas where pilot projects can be undertaken with full
support of all who will be affected."
- Compete. There is nothing like competition to
improve internal operations and clarify missions. The
competition between bookstores and public libraries
have enriched both and should be carried over into
the networked environment. For example, electronic
cross-listing of holdings.
- Bargain. Who knows how to price network-based products? Vendors have already begun to test the waters.
Our advice: Libraries should bargain hard while there
is nothing to lose and use profession-wide economies
of scale.
- Turn the tables. Suppose the Federal government
ends entitlement programs including LSCA. Charge
the government for library-provided government services: counseling, literacy training, government form
distribution, and maintenance of inventories of government publications. As the bill for these services are
presented to the various governments, the profession
should offer to settle out of court for LSCA restora-
tion, legal fees and, say, inflation plus 10 percent!
- Walk away. Sometimes potential partners need to feel
autonomous, that they can walk away if an agreement
is not there. Libraries should mean it and have an
alternative in mind. The Internet offers a number of
intriguing possibilities for inventive, collective action.
Candidates: Price-gouging serials vendors and digital
indexes.

What are the types of new partnerships needed. The network is full
of successful working agreements. Ask Steve Cisler<sac@
apple.com>, Apple librarian, to describe the Apple Library of
Tomorrow program. In particular, ask him to describe Apple's partnership with the Zuni Middle School, Zuni, New Mexico. Together

they created a Zuni-English dictionary using HyperCard and Sound Recorder and donated Apple equipment. A Zuni BBS is now being set up for the reservation to use. Consider the range of partnerships necessary to hold most Freenets together. Explore the motivations of participants in a network listserv for shared agreements.

To strategically assess potential partnerships and then successfully negotiate agreements requires a different kind of leadership from the library community than in the past. For a good introduction to the issues, see Dougherty and Hughes (1993). Characteristics to watch for (see Henderson, 1990) are mutual benefit, sustained commitment, predisposition to partnering, shared knowledge, distinctive competencies, and trust. Savvy acquisitions librarians may be a resource. Keeping the lid on runaway serial prices have proven a trial by combat. It is not too early to begin preparations to obtain the leadership needed.

CREATING AND SUSTAINING POLITICAL LEADERSHIP

The days in which the library represents the best or the only way to satisfy the information needs of users are over (if they ever existed). Viable alternatives exist and the competition in the electronic information environment will be greater. At present, we are engaging as a nation in the process of electronic information infrastructure building. One view of an infrastructure is that it is simply a set of agreements in which we have agreed to collaborate so that we can more intensively compete in other areas. Librarians will need to be trained political leaders to negotiate the new agreements for the twenty-first century and beyond.

Electronic networks make it much easier for all participants to shift roles up and down the information value-chain. Today, authors can become their own publishers and publishers can offer library-like services directly to users. This is only the beginning. Divide and conquer is a competitor's first tactic and only the united or well-represented survive. Who is it that speaks for librarians, with what clarity of purpose, with what bargaining chips and authority? Collaborations and partnerships work best when negotiators are credible. Library negotiators will need to be clear on core competencies and values. Library political leaders need to argue from a position of strength. Librarians will need experienced, savvy, political leaders enabled to represent what we think and know, and are prepared as a profession to act on, in a competitive environment.

The Need

In each of the earlier chapters of this book, in each of the critical success factors within this chapter, the need for a cadre of trained political leaders to represent librarianship's interests in a volatile environment is clear:

- Librarians need to think and act together as a profession, but who will show the way? There are a number of library professional associations with geographic and specialty ties. Who will bind these groups together to a common vision and purpose in an electronic environment? Who will heal the divisiveness of a profession too long accustomed to doing more with less?
- Librarians need to lead their organizations to a networked future balancing the tools librarians use with who they are, what they do, and how they do it. Where will these manager/leaders be found. Who will communicate the librarians unique identity within the web of institutional alliances and arrangements?
- Librarians are in desperate need of research that makes a difference in their work and for their users. Who will direct these efforts? Who will seek the funding to develop the new and innovative solutions? Who will find the new partners in unlikely places to advance the professional research agenda? Who will coordinate the efforts of existing funders of library research so that the whole is greater than the sum of its parts?
- Librarians will need to be trained to use the network. Librarians need to keep up with the breathtaking pace of information technology innovation. Librarians will need to train their user communities. Librarians will need to find the words to express to a skeptical public a new vision that will materially change their users' lives. Who will speak those words?
- Who will be the lone voice crying out for the end of electronic censorship? Who will demand privacy in a networked world? Who will obtain access to information for those that have historically had none? Who will be the quiet but essential preservers of democracy and trainers of future electronic citizens?
- It won't be long before the popular equation will place books next to trash when it comes to enlightenment.

> Who will have courage then to stand and say, "But this is our heritage, too. It must be preserved against future need."

In all of these situations political leaders must be found to seek new partnerships and renegotiate old agreements. To articulate old values central to the profession while creating new values for a new age. Librarians have been shy when it comes to power. Yet clearly a power shift (Toffler, 1990) is underway. How will the profession create and sustain a new generation of political leadership to match the times?

The Assessment

In interviewing librarians for this project, the issue of political leadership was the most difficult or disagreeable for librarians to consider. Any assessment of the present library political leadership must begin with an acknowledgement that with next to no training and often no support, library political leaders have maintained the profession's standing against great odds and in difficult times. But any assessment must continue by noting that these efforts are no longer enough, erosion of professional standing has already begun. A new breed of library political leader will be necessary to chart new directions for a new information era. In order to accurately assess the needs of the new library political leadership in a networked environment, some analysis of the old leadership is necessary.

Comments such as the following concerning librarians as political leaders resulted from the study team's discussions with national, state, and local officials involved with electronic network development:

- Librarians are seldom seen as players in virtually any of the political arenas in which they need to participate: from NREN development caucuses to the local school board.
- "They whine and they complain then ask for inflation plus 10 percent for maintaining yesterday's ideas, then they are surprised when their budget is cut 10 percent."
- In the few cases where librarians are effective, it is as advocates for someone else's cause. Often librarians seem distracted from the core issues affecting their profession.

- Librarians rarely seek partners from within or external to the profession. Many academic libraries are seen as the last of the medieval baronies.
- Librarians rarely set the agenda. They tend to react, and in defense, that is when they show up at the bargaining table.
- To play you have to come up with solutions. Librarians are guaranteed to arrive at policy discussions with no new ideas.
- Librarians need to learn the meaning of compromise. Unwillingness to compromise in the political process is fatal.

This picture is not by accident. It is simply the result of the systematic effects of lack of training in political leadership, lack of experience in the political process, uncertain and underfunded financial support, and lack of an infrastructure which allows rapid consultation among key library constituencies.

The Recommendation

The following approaches should be considered to obtain the library political leadership necessary to build the national information infrastructure:

- Identify existing successful library political leaders and systematically capture their political expertise for transfer to newly emerging library political leaders. It is from these leaders' wisdom and experience that future training can be based and a curriculum built.
- Educate the present and next generations of library political leaders. Political leadership skills are rarely an agenda item in curricular redesign of library schools. They ought to be. ALA offers seminars to its leadership during national meetings. While primarily managerial in focus, this approach could be constructively expanded in scope and to other library organizations.
- Provide present and future generations of library political leaders with a set of guided experiences exposing them to the political process. These experiences should not be Civics 101. Instead a "hard-headed" look at the requirements for making governance

work for the profession is in order. An equally close look at the political process in corporate board rooms would be helpful.

- Support a sustained and appropriately funded political lobby. Understand how the lobbying process really works. All of the library communities' potential partners have lobbying groups. Library lobbying remains fractured, often part-time, understaffed, underfunded, and with uncertain future commitment. Let's get it together!

- Build the national information infrastructure *with* the national information infrastructure. Effective representation of the library community's views in a political process demands the capacity to assemble rapidly a credible position and marshall support for it. Electronic networks make this task possible if we, as a profession, start using our information skills *for* our profession rather than merely for our clients.

Librarians are not trained to think this way. Librarians' day-to-day professional experience does not necessarily demand political skills. So, like the burning book problem previously discussed, the need for library political leadership is easy to forget and ignore. But this critical success factor, like those previously discussed, must be successfully addressed if we are to build our place in the future digital era.

REALIZING THE NEW VISION

One way of understanding the research and ideas presented in the preceding pages is to conceive of them as a series of emerging visions of the virtual libraries and librarians of tomorrow. We do not suggest that we have somehow seen our shared future with perfect 20/20 vision. Indeed we celebrate the visions' imperfections and their incompleteness. Librarians do not need experts to tell them what to do at the moment. What has been suggested here is a framework in which librarians can begin to think and act together so that a credible and representative vision for librarianship in the twenty-first century emerges.

Something in the visions offered here must annoy, excite, and provoke you to begin the process of reconceptualizing what we do as librarians and where we do it. Something must cause you to forsake for a moment the comfort of your other roles as parts of larger institutions and processes. Something must stimulate all of us to see and give voice to our unique song as librarians. As this song becomes clear, it must be added to the swelling chorus of other singers who seek to make our next attempt at conquering space and time even more robust than the last.

Who will define what local means in a global, virtual world? Local means self-reliant. Local means our friends, neighbors, colleagues, a community. Local also means people with whom we might not always agree but with whom we share a common purpose and environment. This work reports to the library community about early research on a new, emerging, local information community with a global reach. It describes key issues and concerns that pioneering librarians are investigating as they explore, discover, and establish a new home for librarianship in this new virtual community. A hundred years ago the frontier was declared closed in the United States. A hundred years later it is time to officially open a new frontier. That new world is waiting to be created. Library communities, acting locally, can help shape that world, or we can watch while others do it for us.

REFERENCES

American Library Association. (1989). *Presidential Committee on Information Literacy Final Report.* Chicago, IL: American Library Association.

Bailey, Charles W. Jr. <LIB3@UHUPVM1.BITNET or LIB3@UHUPVM1.UH.EDU>. (Compiler). (1993). *Library-Oriented Lists and Electronic Serials.* Houston, TX: University of Houston. Available as a regular part of a PACS-L subscription or from the author.

Bailey, Charles W. Jr. <LIB3@UHUPVM1.BITNET or LIB3@UHUPVM1.UH.EDU>. (Founder). (1986). *Public Access Computer Systems Forum, PACS-L.* Houston,TX: University of Houston. Available: E-mail: LISTSERV@UHUPVM1 Message: SUBSCRIBE PACS-L First Name Last Name.

Bearman, David, ed. (1991). *Archival management of electronic records.* Pittsburgh: Archives and Museum Informatics Report No. 13.

Beckhard, Richard and Harris, Reuben T. (1987). *Organizational Transitions: Managing Complex Change.* Reading, MA: Addison-Wesley.

Bortnick, Jane. (1990, July–August). Information technology revolution. *CRS Review.* As cited in: U.S. Congress. Committee on Government Operations. (November 6, 1990). *Taking a Byte Out of History: The Archival Preservation of Federal Computer*

Records (House Report 101-978). Washington, DC: Government Printing Office.

Breivik, Patricia Senn (March, 1992). Information literacy: An agenda for lifelong learning. *AAHE Bulletin*, 6–9.

Butler, Pierce. (1933). *An Introduction to Library Science.* Chicago: University of Chicago Press.

Byrne, John A. (February 8, 1993). Virtual corporation. *Business Week*, 99–103.

Cavrek, Steve <SJC@UVMVM.UVM.EDU>. (1993). *COMMUNET.* Burlington, VT: University of Vermont. Available: E-mail: LISTSERV@UVMVM.UVM.EDU Message: SUBSCRIBE COMMUNET First Name Last Name.

Charbuck, David C. (February 15, 1993). Good-bye Dewey decimals. *Forbes*, 204–205.

Cook, Terry. (1991–1992). Easy to byte, harder to chew: The second generation of electronic records archives. *Archivaria* 33: 202–216.

Davidow, William H. and Malone, Michael S. (1992). *The Virtual Corporation: Structuring and Revitalizing the Corporation for the Twenty-first Century.* NY: HarperCollins.

Dizard, Wilson P. (1982). *The Coming Information Age: An Overview of Technology, Economics, and Politics.* New York: Longman.

Dollar, Charles. (1992). *Archival Theory and Information Technologies: The Impact of Information Technologies on Archival Principles and Methods.* Macerata, Italy: The University of Macerata.

Dougherty, Richard M. and Hughes, Carol. (1993). *Preferred Library Futures II: Charting the Paths.* Mountain View, CA: Research Libraries Group.

Eisenberg, Michael <MIKE@SUVM..SYR.EDU> and Milbury, Peter <PMILBURY@EIS.CALSTATE.EDU>. (Owners). (1992). *LM_NET.* Syracuse, NY: Syracuse University. Available: To subscribe send an e-mail message to either listowner.

Feuer, Dale and Lee, Chris. (May, 1988). The kaizen connection: How companies pick tomorrow's workers. *Training*, 23–35.

Gillespie, Andrew and Robins, Kevin. (Summer, 1989). Geographical inequalities: The spatial bias of the new communications technologies. *Journal of Communication* 39 (3).

Grundner, Tom <aa001@cleveland.freenet.edu> et al. (1993). Toward the formation of a "corporation for public cybercasting." Available: ftp: NPTN.ORG directory: PUB/CPC.

Grundner, Tom <aa001@cleveland.freenet.edu> et al. (1991 and ongoing). *Cleveland Freenet.* Available: telnet: FREENET-IN-A.CWRU.EDU <129.22.8.75 or 129.22.8.76 or 129.22.82>.

Henderson, John C. (Spring, 1990). Plugging into strategic partnerships: The critical IS connection. *Sloan Management Review*, 7–18.

Higginbotham, Barbra Buckner and Jackson, Mare E. (1992). *Advances in Preservation and Access.* Westport, CT: Meckler.

Imai, Masaaki. (1986). *Kaizen (Ky'zen), The Key to Japan's Competitive Success.* New York: McGraw-Hill.

Innis, Harold Adams. (1951). *The Bias of Communication.* Toronto: University of Toronto Press.

Kenney, Anne R. and Personius, Lynne K. (1992). *Digital Capture, Paper Facsimiles, and Network Access* (Cornell/Xerox/Commission on Preservation and Access Joint Study in Digital Preservation Report: Phase I). Ithaca, NY: Cornell University Library.

McClure, Charles R. and Hernon, Peter, eds. (1991). *Library and Information Science Research: Perspectives and Strategies for Improvement.* Norwood, NJ: Ablex.

McClure, Charles R., Ryan, Joe, Moen, William E. (Winter, 1992). Design for an Internet-based government-wide information locator system. *Electronic Networking: Research, Applications and Policy* 2 (4): 6–37. (Volume 1 of the expanded two-volume report for the U.S. Office of Management and Budget, National Archives and Records Administration, and the General Services Administration is now available from ERIC as ED 349 031).

McClure, Charles R., Wigand, Rolf, Bertot, John C., McKenna, Mary E., Moen, William E., Ryan, Joe, and Veeder, Stacy B. (December 21, 1992). *Federal Information Policy Management for Electronic Service Delivery* (Report prepared at the request of U.S. Congress, Office of Technology Assessment). Syracuse, NY: Syracuse University, School of Information Studies. (This report will be available shortly from ERIC).

Michelson, Avra and Rothenberg, Jeff. (Spring, 1992). Scholarly communication and information technology: Exploring the impact of changes in the research process on archives. *American Archivist* 55: 236–315.

Milne, A. A. (1926). *Winnie-the-Pooh.* NY: Dell Publishing.

National Academy of Public Administration (1989). *The Effects of Electronic Recordkeeping on the Historical Records of the U.S. Government.* Washington, DC: NAPA.

National Historical Publications and Records Commission. (1991). *Research Issues in Electronic Records: Report of the Working Meeting.* Washington, DC: The Commission.

National Historical Publications and Records Commission. (1990). *Electronic Records Issues: A Report to the Commission.* Washington, DC: The Commission.

National Research Council. Committee on Geophysical Data. Commission on Geosciences, Environment, and Resources. (1991). *Solving the Global Change Puzzle: A U.S. Strategy for Managing Data and Information.* Washington, DC: National Academy Press.

Naukam, Larry. (January/February/March, 1993) What Internet can do for you. *Genealogical Computing* 12 (3): 1, 22–23.

Office of Science and Technology Policy. (December, 1992). *National Research and Education Network: A Report to Congress* [DRAFT]. Washington, DC: Office of Science and Technology Policy.

Peters, Paul Evan. (1992). Networked information resources and service: Next steps on the road to the distributed digital libraries of the twenty-first century. In Sutton, Brett and Davis, Charles H., eds. *Networks, Open Access, and Virtual Libraries: Implications for the Research Library.* Urbana-Champaign, IL: Graduate School of Library and Information Science, University of Illinois.

Polly, Jean Armour. (December 15, 1992). *Surfing the Internet: An Introduction Version 2.0.* (Original appeared in June 1992, *Wilson Library Bulletin*). Available: ftp: NYSERNET.ORG or 192.77.173.2 Directory: PUB/RESOURCES/GUIDES File: SURFING.THE.INTERNET.

Postman, Neil. (1992). *Technopoly: The Surrender of Culture to Technology.* NY: Alfred A. Knopf.

Rockart, John F. (March–April, 1979). Chief executives define their own data needs. *Harvard Business Review* 57: 81-93.

Rockart, John F. and Benjamin, Robert I. (June 1991). The information technology function of the 1990s: A unique hybrid. *Center for Information Systems Research Working Paper* (CISR WP No. 225). Cambridge, MA: Sloan School of Management, Massachusetts Institute of Technology.

Samarajiva Rohan and Shields Peter. (Summer, 1990). Integration, telecommunication, and development: Power in the paradigms. *Journal of Communication* 40 (3).

Sanders, Terry. (Producer-director). (1987). *Slow Fires: On the Preservation of the Human Record.* Santa Monica, CA: American Film Foundation. [videocassette (59 min.)].

Schein, Edgar. (1987). *Process Consulting Volume 2.* Reading, MA: Addison-Wesley.

Scott-Morton, Michael, ed. (1991). *Corporation of the 1990s: Information Technology and Organizational Transformation.* NY: Oxford University Press.

Senge, Peter M. (1990). *The Fifth Discipline: The Art and Practice of the Learning Organization.* New York: Doubleday/Currency.

Sproull, Lee and Kiesler, Sara. (1991). *Connections: New Ways of Working in the Networked Organization.* Cambridge, MA: MIT Press.

Taylor, Robert S. (1968). Question-negotiation and information seeking in libraries. *College & Research Libraries* 29 (3): 178–194.

Toffler, Alvin and Heidi. (1990). *Power Shift.* NY: Bantam.

U.S. Congress. Committee on Government Operations. (November 6, 1990). *Taking a Byte Out of History: The Archival Preservation of Federal Computer Records.* (House Report 101-978). Washington, DC: Government Printing Office.

U.S. Congress. Committee on Government Operations. (March 23, 1989). *Establishing a National Policy on Permanent Papers.* Washington, DC: Government Printing Office.

U.S. Congress. Joint Committee on the Library of Congress. (1992). *Report on Progress in Implementing National Policy on Acid-Free Paper* (Senate Report 102-82). Washington, DC: Government Printing Office.

U.S. Congress. Office of Technology Assessment. (1988). *Book Preservation Technologies.* Washington, DC: Government Printing Office.

Walton, Richard E. (1989). *Up and Running: Integrating Information Technology and the Organization.* Boston: Harvard University Press.

Wilson, D. D. (March, 1989). A process model of strategic alliance formation in forms in the information technology industry. *Management in the 1990s Working Paper* (No. 89-070). Cambridge, MA: Sloan School of Management, MIT.

Ziman, John M. (1969). Information, communication, knowledge. *Nature* 224: 318–324.

Zuboff, Shoshana. (1988). *In the Age of the Smart Machine.* NY: Basic Books.

Research Study Methodology

There has been little empirical research focusing on the impacts of electronic networking on public and academic libraries. From the outset of project planning, the research team envisioned the study as an exploration of and investigation into the issues that are already confronting or anticipated by librarians as they enter the networked environment. The research team decided that a variety of data-gathering techniques would be necessary to accomplish the study's purpose, namely, to provide a description and assessment of key issues affecting public and academic libraries in the use of Internet/National Research and Education Network (NREN) information services and resources.

The exploratory investigation reported in Chapters 1 through 4 consisted of a two-phased approach: (1) obtaining descriptive information regarding public library Internet/NREN uses, futures and potential impacts, and, (2) analyzing that descriptive information in light of various policy issues. The study relied on quantitative and qualitative methods as well as a range of data-collection strategies. The following sections provide a detailed description of the study methodology used, including descriptions of the data-collection activities, data analysis, and write-up.

PURPOSE AND OBJECTIVES OF THE STUDY

The study's purpose was to provide a description and assessment of key issues affecting academic and public libraries in the use of networking technologies, and in particular the use of national electronic networks (i.e., the Internet/NREN) and networked information resources in the provision of library services. The study's objectives were to:

- identify key factors (within the library and from the larger external environment) that may affect the possible involvement of the library community in national networking and the NREN;

- identify key policy issues affecting libraries and their possible involvement in the NREN;
- propose a range of library-related responsibilities and activities that could significantly contribute to the overall success of the NREN; and
- suggest strategies and public policy initiatives by which the library community can become more effectively involved in the planning and development of the NREN and national electronic networking.

The study team expected the research results to help define a range of roles, services, and responsibilities for the library community as it becomes an "electronic intermediary." Moreover, the study offers an assessment of the policy issues and suggestions for specific strategies by which the public and academic library communities can better transition to and operate in the national electronic networking environment of the 1990s.

OVERVIEW OF METHOD

The study methodology combined qualitative and quantitative research approaches. Through a variety of exploratory data-gathering activities, the study team sought to address a number of research questions including:

- How knowledgeable is academic and public library leadership about present developments in the national electronic networks?
- What are the innovative ways that academic and public libraries *presently* use electronic networks?
- How are academic and public libraries integrating networked information resources into their organizations' service delivery?
- What new techniques are academic and public libraries employing to improve organizational productivity and effectiveness using networks?
- What service roles might be developed for academic and public libraries with the advent of the next generation of electronic networks?
- What Federal government information sources and services would academic and public libraries like to access on the Internet/NREN?

- What future network services do academic and public library leaders wish to see? Which should be adopted first?
- What barriers stand in the way of academic and public libraries in exploiting the potential of a national electronic network?
- What specific steps are academic and public libraries presently taking to position themselves to take advantage of the networked environment?
- Will we need to reconceptualize "the library" as we face the challenges posed by the new technology?
- How will academic and public libraries balance the demands for electronic and networked resources/services with the demands for paper-based and other formats of library materials?
- What is the relationship between various stakeholders in the academic and public libraries' environments in the provision of networked services and products?
- Who will be responsible in the academic and public library communities to resolve the variety of problems (from technical to policy) in the networked environment?

These questions guided the research and assisted in understanding how academic and public libraries are meeting the challenge of the networked environment.

STUDY POPULATIONS

The study focused research activities on academic and public libraries. The differences between these types of libraries suggested that separate populations should be identified. The study team also conducted focus groups with library science educators, networking leaders, and library automation vendors. The data collected from these groups informed our broader understanding of the context in which academic and public libraries exist. The following describes the populations examined for each type of library.

Public Libraries

Two key groups of participants comprised the study population:

- Public library leaders were targeted because this group is likely to be most aware and most in need of information about the Internet/NREN environment.
- Practicing public librarian middle managers with network familiarity were chosen because their knowledge base determines what is practical to accomplish today and tomorrow.

The study team also obtained additional data from other types of librarians, network managers, and state/national government officials.

Academic Libraries

There are several distinct units involved in networking activities on academic campuses. Although the focus of the research was on academic libraries, it was essential to interview and survey other stakeholders in the academic networked environment. The study population for academic libraries included:

- library administrators;
- library professional staff (public and technical services);
- systems librarians;
- campus administrators;
- academic computer center staff (including telecommunications and network services); and
- academic faculty.

The majority of participants in the study, however, was associated with the library.

DATA-GATHERING ACTIVITIES

The research project used a two-phased approach: (1) obtaining descriptive information regarding academic libraries' present and future uses of the Internet/NREN and potential impacts of these national electronic networks, and (2) analyzing that descriptive information in light of various policy issues. The overall study employed qualitative and quantitative methods in a range of data-collection strategies. These multiple data-collection techniques assisted the researchers in examining the topic from a range of perspectives and increased the likelihood of collecting valid and reliable data. The data-gathering activities for this research included:

- a wide-ranging literature analysis that helped initially to specify relevant issues and concerns;
- a national survey questionnaire administered to targeted academic and public librarians attending electronic network sessions at conferences and to a select group of public library leaders;
- focus group sessions with public, academic, and research library administrators, public services, technical services, and systems staff, and other stakeholders;
- individual interviews with academic and public library leaders and managers; and
- site visits to national leaders in academic and public library Internet/NREN developments.

Figure A-1 presents an overview of the method and data collection and reflects the evolutionary nature of the methodology. The study team responded to the emerging understanding of the issues by employing Glaser and Strauss's (1967) theoretical sampling approach, which involves conducting data collection, coding, and analysis jointly. As Figure A-1 suggests, the study consisted of four primary data-collection efforts: literature review, focus groups, a survey, and site visits.

The study team reviewed the literature at the outset of the project to help explain and explore the terrain for variables, factors, and issues. The literature review (for academic libraries reported in Chapter 1; for public libraries reported in Chapter 4) provided a list of emerging issues and guided our preliminary data collection. An ongoing monitoring of the literature informed the data analysis and our understanding throughout the project.

Focus groups are particularly useful in exploratory research to discover issues, concerns, and problems, and to generate further research questions (Krueger, 1988). This technique has been previously used, most successfully, by the researchers studying scientific communication and electronic networking (McClure, et al., 1991). Prior to conducting the focus groups, the study team interviewed library experts to provide a framework for focus group sessions. Each focus group session informed the following sessions in terms of content and emerging issues to be discussed.

The survey instrument went through a number of iterations and was pretested and revised prior to administration. The selection of issues used on the survey resulted from the literature review, the study team's previous experience and knowledge regarding this

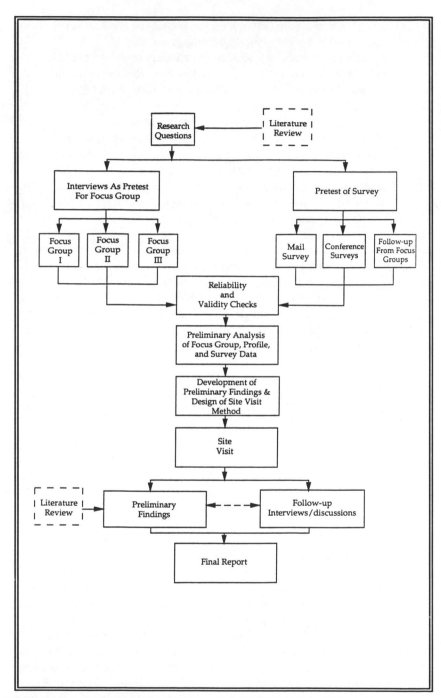

Figure A-1. Overview of method and data collection.

topic, and preliminary information from the interviews with experts. Figure A-7 is a copy of the survey instrument.

Site visits provided a focused and detailed look at how particular libraries were meeting the challenges of the electronically networked environment. The method employed for the site visits evolved from preliminary findings from the literature review, interviews, the focus groups, and the survey data. The specific topics and strategies used for data collection at the site visits could not have been developed as effectively without conducting the preliminary assessments.

The study team presented preliminary findings from the study at the May 1992 American Society for Information Science Mid-year Conference (McClure, et al., 1992a) and at the September 1992 LITA Third National Conference (McClure, et al., 1992b), both of which focused on topics of information technology, the Internet, and NREN. As a result of those presentations, study team members were able to discuss the preliminary research findings with a number of national leaders and obtain their comments and assessment of those findings. This feedback was considered in the writing of the final report.

QUALITY OF DATA

The study team closely monitored the quality of the data collected in each stage of the project. To increase the validity and reliability of the data, the study team incorporated techniques including the following:

- All instruments were pretested.
- The study team used multiple data-collection techniques. Each discussion with a group or individual included, for example, the completion of a questionnaire providing background information about the subject(s).
- Preliminary assessments and planning efforts ensured that subjects selected were appropriate, assured the subjects that the study had organizational support and permission (encouraging them to respond fully and openly), and eased the logistics of contacting and communicating with subjects in a manner that put them at ease.
- Criteria for conducting effective focus groups sessions were met:

–Subjects were asked to speak from their own experience about subjects with which they were familiar.

–The experiences discussed were firsthand and not too remote in time.

–The sessions encouraged openness, frankness, and relaxed responses, by attention to the group's "atmosphere."

–At least two members of the study team took notes during most focus group sessions and the individual interviews (except on the site visits). The study team members prepared independent summaries and analyses of each session. These summaries were then compared and integrated.

–A representative from the focus group session had the opportunity to review and comment on the written summaries to correct errors of fact.

- The study team administered similar questions to focus group participants, survey respondents, and participants at the site visit. Their responses indicated a high degree of consistency.

The combination of these steps and the multiple data-collection techniques assisted the researchers in examining the topic from a range of perspectives and increased the credibility, validity, and reliability of the data as well as the overall utility of the study's findings (Kirk and Miller, 1986).

FOCUS GROUPS

The study team conducted three focus groups sessions with public librarians, two sessions with academic librarians, one session with networking leaders, one session with library and information science school educators, and one session with library vendors. The structure and procedures were similar for all focus groups.

The literature review and individual interviews with library networking experts provided a range of issues to discuss at the sessions. The study team developed a list of questions for each focus group including common questions presented to all groups and specific questions drafted for each group. The common questions allowed the researchers to compare data gathered from all the sessions. The unique questions provided the opportunity to explore ideas and issues relevant to specific focus group participants.

For the focus groups to accomplish their objectives, it was necessary that the participants share certain characteristics. The study team developed the following criteria for selecting potential participants:

- knowledgeable about Internet-related activities, NREN development, and national networking initiatives;
- hands-on experience, to the extent practical, with Internet and national networking technologies; and
- able to articulate views, ideas, and opinions in a group setting.

In most cases, the study team contacted prospective participants requesting their participation in the study and arranged meeting places and times for the sessions. However, for several of the focus groups, a liaison onsite invited potential participants and used the criteria established by the study team for selection of participants. Each participant received a follow-up letter after the session. At each session, participants completed a profile sheet which included demographic information about the participant.

One moderator (from the study team) led the discussion for each session. In most cases, two other study team members took notes at the sessions. The discussions were not tape-recorded. Study team members prepared summaries and analyses of the focus group sessions. These transcripts and analyses provided the data on which the findings and key issues were developed for the reports included in Chapters 3 and 4. This was accomplished by naturalistic data analysis techniques as well as through a computer-assisted coding of transcripts. The study team analyzed the resulting data using the Qualog software which permits detailed analysis of textual materials gathered using qualitative research techniques (Shelly and Siebert, 1985; Shelly and Siebert,1986).

Public librarians participated in focus group sessions held at the following locations: Decatur, Georgia, October 1991; New York, New York, November 1991 (New York Library Association Conference); and San Antonio, Texas, January 1992 (ALA Midwinter Meeting). A total of twenty-four people participated in the sessions, and eighteen usable profile questionnaires resulted. Table A-1 provides a summary of the public library focus group participants based on the solicited demographic information. Eleven of the eighteen participants held administrative positions, although all functional areas of a public library were represented. All

TABLE A-1. Background Information for Public Library Focus Group Participants
••

Type of Position Held		Years of Public Library Experience		Knowledge of Networking	
Administrator	11	1–7 years	0	1= Extensive	1
Public Services	4	8–14 years	5	2=	1
Technical Services	1	15–19 years	3	3= Some	9
Consultant	1	20+ years	10	4=	6
Systems	1			5= None	1

respondents had a minimum of eight years of experience in a public library with the average experience being 18.7 years. Over half the participants had "some" to "extensive" knowledge of networking, while only one participant responded as having no experience. These data confirm that the participants for the focus groups had significant public library experience and "some" knowledge of networking issues.

Academic librarians participated in two focus groups sessions held in Troy, New York, December 1991 and San Antonio, Texas, January 1992 (ALA Mid-winter Meeting). Nineteen people participated in the focus groups. As shown in Table A-2, ten of the nineteen participants held administrative positions, although most functional areas of an academic library were represented. Only one of the participants had less than eight years of experience, and the average years experience was 19.1. Nearly 90 percent of the participants claimed that they had "some" to "extensive" knowledge of networking.

Other focus group sessions included:

- Networking leaders, New York, New York, January 1992; conducted at Electronic Networking and Publishing Conference; eleven participants.
- Library and information science educators, San Antonio, Texas, January 1992; conducted at the Association of Library and Information Science Educators Annual Meeting; eight participants.
- Library vendors, San Antonio, Texas, January 1992; conducted at the American Library Association Mid-winter Meeting; eight participants.

TABLE A-2. Background Information for Academic Library Focus Group Participants					
Type of Position Held		*Years of Public Library Experience*		*Knowledge of Networking*	
Administrator	10	1–7 years	1	1= Extensive	3
Public Services	4	8–14 years	3	2=	3
Technical Services	5	15–19 years	4	3= Some	10
		20+ years	11	4=	2
				5= None	0

A total of seventy people participated in eight focus groups conducted for this research.

SURVEY QUESTIONNAIRE

The primary purpose of the survey was to obtain respondents' assessment of the importance of a number of key issues that the study team had identified through the literature review and interviews with expert librarians knowledgeable about Internet/NREN developments. The issue statements concerned the current networking environment (i.e., the Internet) and its use by libraries as well as the evolving NREN environment.

The study team designed the survey instrument to be relatively quick to answer and to provide ease of data entry. It collected background information from the respondents such as type (and size) of library, type of position held by respondent, years of professional library experience, and respondents' networking knowledge. Given the limitations on the desired size of the instrument, other possible demographic and respondent attitude questions were not included. Respondents assessed a total of nineteen issue statements on a five-point Likert scale.

A group of seven librarians agreed to pretest the instrument. Five responded and suggested changes in wording, order of questions, and other editorial changes. The study team revised the instrument according to the changes suggested by the librarians who completed the pretest. A faculty member at Syracuse University who has expertise in research design and methods reviewed the revised version. His suggestions resulted in changes across several questions to maintain consistency. The final form of the survey instrument is presented in Figure A-7.

The study team intended to distribute the survey to a select group of library and networking leaders and a sample of current network users. The design of the instrument accommodated multiple uses and audiences since academic and public librarians as well as others received it.

Data from the survey came from three different types of administration:

- *Focus group follow-ups.* A copy of the instrument was sent along with letters of thanks to participants in the focus group session; a self-addressed, stamped envelop was provided.
- *Conference meetings.* Conferences provided an excellent opportunity to obtain input from targeted audiences. At two national library conference meetings, study team members distributed the instrument to targeted meetings where it was likely that participants had a basic knowledge and/or interest in national networking issues. Drop boxes provided at the meetings allowed respondents to leave completed forms. In addition, some completed forms arrived via the mail.
- *Public library leaders associated with PLA.* The study team obtained a list of names from the Public Library Association (PLA) who were participants on various committees or had other association assignments. The instrument was mailed to all 173 individuals on the list, and 104 responded within two weeks (60 percent response rate). Given the high response rate, no follow-up was done.

The study team used SAS, a statistical analysis program, for data entry, data analysis, and report generation. Completed questionnaires received a unique identifying number, and study team members input data. Data entry quality was reviewed by examining the SAS dataset. After data entry was completed, SAS generated a variety of descriptive statistical reports.

Public Librarian Survey Respondents

A total of 120 usable responses from public librarians resulted from distribution at national conferences, focus groups, and the mailing to public library leaders provided by the PLA. The questionnaire distributions at the two national conferences resulted in very few responses from public librarians. Thus, the vast majority of responses came from the PLA list.

Table A-3 is a summary of the demographic characteristics of survey respondents. The data suggest that respondents generally came from medium to large public libraries, held administrative or public services positions, had significant professional experience, and had limited national networking experience. This profile data of survey respondents are similar to the descriptive data for the

TABLE A-3. Demographic Characteristics of Public Librarian Survey Respondents

*Size of Library**	*Percent*
Large	42
Medium	34
Small	2
Library Systems/Consortia	15
State Library	7
Position Held	
Administration	54
Public Services	21
Technical Services	9
Library Systems	9
Other	7
Professional Experience	
10 or more years	86
9 or less years	14
National Networking Experience	
Don't use networks	55
Used less than 12 months	22
Used more than 12 months	23

* Large defined as community served > 200,000; medium= 20,001 to 200,000; small= 20,000.

focus group participants (see Table A-1). Table 4-1 in Chapter 4 summarizes and ranks public librarian responses to the nineteen issue statements

Academic Librarian Survey Respondents

A total of 153 usable responses from academic librarians resulted from distribution at national conferences and the focus group participants. Table A-4 presents a summary of the demographic characteristics of survey respondents. The data suggest that respondents generally came from medium to large academic libraries, held public services or administrative positions, had significant professional experience, and had extensive national networking experience. This profile data of survey respondents are similar to the descriptive data for the focus group participants (see Table A-2). Table 3-1 in Chapter 3 summarizes and ranks academic librarian responses to the nineteen issue statements.

TABLE A-4. Demographic Characteristics of Academic Librarian Survey Respondents

Size of Library	Percent
Large	54
Medium	40
Small	6
Position Held	
Public Services	39
Administration	32
Technical Services	16
Library Systems	11
Professional Experience	
10 or more years	78
9 or less years	22
National Networking Experience	
Don't use networks	3
Used less than 12 months	18
Used more than 12 months	79

SITE VISITS

As part of the multiple methods research design for the overall project, the site visits provided opportunities for a focused examination of how particular academic and public libraries are meeting the challenges of the electronically networked environment. Although an increasing number of innovative libraries are involved with electronic networking and networked information resources, practical considerations of budgetary and staff resources limited the study team to conducting two academic site visits (Carnegie Mellon University and the University of Southern California), and a public library site visit (North Carolina State Library). The diversity and richness of the data collected during the site visits exceeded the expectations of the investigators.

While several potential stakeholders are contributing to the development and use of the national networks and networked information sources, the study team chose as the unit of analysis the "library in the electronic networking, resources, and services environment." It was also necessary, however, to obtain a clear understanding of the broader institutional environment in which the library functions as an "electronic network player." Therefore, the researchers collected data about and from other stakeholders, such as the computing center, telecommunications unit, and other key players.

The study team derived the site visit methods and procedures from standard case study methodology, particularly as described in Yin (1989). Planning and development of the methodology consisted of three parts:

- development of an interview protocol and profile form, pre-visit planning, and background study;
- identification of data-collection methods and procedures; and
- planning for data analysis and report preparation.

Given the exploratory nature of these site visits, the study team adopted an approach that would provide an opportunity to collect comparable data across the sites. In addition, the procedure's flexibility enabled the researchers to focus on unique questions most appropriate to the site visited.

The study team conceptualized the site visit as a three-tier procedure, represented in the interview protocol by the questions and probes. While it was understood that not all the protocol themes would be present at all of the sites, their function was to provide a general outline of topics to be covered and serve as a common base for information gathering. Figure A-2 presents the questions and probes articulated by first-, second-, and third-tier concerns.

Central to a case-study method and data-collection procedure is the interview protocol. While there are several useful data collection techniques, "one of the most important sources of case study information is the interview" (Yin, 1989, p. 88). The interview protocol for the study's site visits covers eleven thematic areas with corresponding questions and probes that helped to structure the interview. The themes emerged from other data-gathering activities, particularly the literature review, the focus groups, and the analysis efforts performed earlier in the study. Figure A-3 summarizes the themes and questions agreed on by the study team.

The site visits offered opportunities to talk with the people who are (or have been) directly involved in the development of library networking activities. In general, the study team identified the stakeholders in the networking environment at the sites as:

- library administrators;
- librarians;
- library systems personnel;
- computer center administrators and key staff; and
- agency and/or institutional administrators in charge of information technology/services.

The first tier includes a general set of questions and probes to gather similar information from all sites/interviews (e.g., role of interviewee, chronology of networking, critical success factors, leadership, and organizational issues).

The second tier includes questions and probes specifically geared to the site being studied. In the case of the two academic sites, these questions and probes were very similar for data comparability (e.g., interaction between campus computing center and library, faculty and student uses of networks, etc.).

The third tier is an open-ended tier for information that presents itself at the time of the site visit. Since the study is exploratory, this level could not be specified until the site visit was in process. The questions and probes from the first and second tiers would help uncover the contents of the third tier.

Figure A-2. Three tiers of site visit procedures.

THEME 1: Description of Current Networks and Networked Resources
Questions: What electronic networks, resources, and services are provided?
What's available? For whom?
How have user populations been defined?
How are networked resources and services used? By whom?

THEME 2: Technical Description of Network Infrastructure
Question: What is the network infrastructure?

THEME 3: Chronology/Development of Network(s)
Question: What is the history of the critical events in the development of the network(s) and the use of networked information resources?

THEME 4: Organizational Relationships and Structure
Questions: What relationships or organizational mechanisms were/are employed to further the development of the network?
Who were/are the key players?
What is the governance and leadership structure for network development, operations, and use?
Who are the key players/positions that drive the network and its services?

THEME 5: Roles of Players
Questions: What were/are the specific roles of the key players?
Roles related to decision making, policy making, selection/management/organization and creation of networked resources and services.
Who takes the lead and for which initiatives/tasks (e.g., library or computing center)?

Figure A-3. Site visit themes, questions, and probes.

THEME 6: Internal Impacts
Questions: What internal effects have been experienced in the library? In ACS?
Changes in staffing, organizational structures, services
Staff training

THEME 7: External Impacts
Questions: What external effects have been experienced related to network development and use?
User support and training
Fiscal effects
Effects on faculty instructional and research/scholarly productivity

THEME 8: Policy and Planning Issues
Questions: What were/are the policy issues that involved the library? ACS?
How does network planning and policy making occur?
Is there a campus vision or goals statement related to information technologies/network development?

THEME 9: Barriers/Solutions
Question: What were/are the barriers you encountered and solutions found?

THEME 10: Future Plans and Vision
Questions: What are your plans, next steps, vision for the next five years?
What about the campus?

THEME 11: Words of Wisdom
Questions: Based on your experiences, what are the most important messages to share with others?

Figure A-3. Site visit themes, questions, and probes, *continued.*

The researchers negotiated a schedule with a contact person at the sites to maximize opportunities to talk with as many of the identified stakeholders as possible. However, given the one- to three-day timeframe for the visits and the number of stakeholders, the researchers realized it was not possible to talk directly with all those identified. In an attempt to maximize the available time at each site, the researchers planned group meetings and/or interviews along with the individual interviews. The study team targeted the following types of meetings/interviews:

- focus group interview with library managers;
- group discussion or focus group interview with a mix of library managers, computer center managers, and agency/institutional administrators; and
- individual meetings with:
    - person primarily responsible for library networking activities;
    - library director;
    - computer center director;
    - computer center liaison to library (and possibly their librarian counterpart); and
    - agency/institutional administrator responsible for information technology/services.

The study team's interview protocols guided the questions and discussion with the various staff. However, the protocols should be understood as exploratory instruments fitting the exploratory nature of the site visits. As topics and concerns arose in the interviews, the researchers used their discretion to explore and expand those topics with probes and additional questions. Flexibility and on-the-spot modifications to the structured questions were the rule more than the exception.

Other Forms of Data Collection During Site Visits

In addition to information gathered from the interviews and meetings, the study team identified other forms of data collection such as: documentary information, archival records, and direct observation. Yin (1989, p. 96) notes that the use of multiple sources of evidence is "a major strength of case study data collection." In addition to the advantage of being able to cover a broader range of historical, attitudinal, and observational issues, the primary benefit of multiple data sources is the triangulation effect.

With multiple sources of evidence, the findings and conclusions in a case study are more likely to be convincing and accurate. Yin (1989, p. 97) explains how construct validity is addressed by multiple sources of evidence, since they "essentially provide multiple measures of the same phenomenon." The study team recognized the importance of a variety of documentation including minutes of meetings, reports of events, progress and technical reports, policy and planning documents, and evaluation reports. Archival records of potential value included: records of clients served; organizational charts and budgets, and maps and charts of the networking infrastructure or information technology system components. Informal observations occured naturally throughout the site visit. In addition, more formal observations were possible during demonstrations of information technologies and on tours of facilities and resources.

Data Analysis and Reporting from Site Visits

The data analysis plan included qualitative methods of content analysis of interview transcripts, notes from observations, and documents collected. Analytic strategies included comparison and explanation-building. Making comparisons involved comparing findings from the sites to determine similar themes, patterns, and attitudes. Of course, distinct differences and unique features would be identified and contrasted to emerging patterns. Explanation-building refers to the process of attempting to explain the possible causal links about particular outcomes or findings and generating hypotheses and propositional statements that seek to elucidate a phenomenon.

The site visit reports would be both descriptive of the situation as explained by the key players, documentary and archival evidence, and direct observation, as well as analytical, since propositions would be generated from the data. These propositions would be subsequently examined in light of findings from other components of the NREN study's data pool. Therefore, the study team planned the site visit report to include:

- descriptions of networking and networked information resources development at the sites;
- data findings organized around the broad themes of the interview protocol instrument; and
- propositions derived from the findings.

The researchers reviewed and analyzed the data gathered during the site visit for information pertinent to the eleven broad themes of the case study.

Site Visit Implementation

Study team members sent initial requests for site visits to the appropriate administrative staff (e.g., the state librarian, the university librarian, the vice-president for academic affairs). One study team member coordinated the arrangement and conducted each site visit. After receiving approval for the site visits, a main point of contact at each site was named, and this person served as the coordinator for the visits. In conjunction with the contact people, the researchers worked out the general framework for a single visit and the general categories of staff to be available for discussions during the visit.

As is usually the case in applied research, events and situations arise that necessitate modifications and revisions to the methods and procedures planned. The study team chose sites that are nationally recognized leaders and innovators who receive many requests for tours and demonstrations. Staff and leaders at the sites have very full and busy schedules around which the site visits had to work. The researchers and the site coordinators attempted to accommodate the maximum number of meetings with staff possible while recognizing that a one-, two- or three-day visit would mean that some important staff would not be available, or only available for limited interaction with the researchers.

Public Library Site Visit. The purpose of the site visit was to identify and describe the evolution and current state of development and use of electronic networks by the state library of North Carolina and the libraries it serves. The site visit would provide a detailed description of how these libraries have arrived at the point where they are and what they are planning over the next several years, so that other libraries can benefit from these experiences. Chapter 4 presents the results of this site visit.

The study team selected this site because of its known involvement in network development, its progressive reputation, and the recommendations from participants in earlier phases of the research project. The North Carolina Information Network met the study team's criteria of (1) a large-scale networking development effort that included a number of different types of libraries,

(2) being recognized as an innovative leader in the application of networking services to public libraries, and (3) indicating an interest in meeting with members of the study team regarding the development of the project.

With the assistance of the state library network coordinator, the researcher arranged a series of focus groups and interviews over a three-day period in May 1992. A total of twenty-five people participated in the data-collection activities. Figure A-4 lists the staff interviewed during the site visit.

The major objective of the site visit was to learn how the state library assumed a leadership role, how it influenced the North Carolina library community's vision and initiatives in this area, and how, organizationally, it has positioned itself to play such a central role.

Academic Site Visits. The University of Southern California (USC) provided a site at which the library provides substantial leadership in campus-wide use of networking for the delivery of information. The library, through its vast traditional holdings and its new campus information service, USCInfo, has staked out a place as the focal point for information resources on campus. The Center for Scholarly Technology (CST), a collaborative project between the library and University Computing Services (UCS), the campus academic computing unit, has served as an "incubator" for the development of innovative information technologies and the exploration of the active interdependencies of the library and UCS in the networked environment. The library's leadership role and the new approaches to organizational arrangements convinced the study team that USC would be a rich source for a site visit.

- Secretary of Cultural Affairs and Deputy Administrator
- State Librarian
- Network Coordinator
- Systems Librarian
- State library consultants and section chief
- State agency officials
- Community college system administrators
- Representative library managers from all over the state

Figure A-4. North Carolina State Library site visit participants.

Carnegie Mellon University Libraries has received national prominence as an innovator and pioneer in developing an electronic library in conjunction with its Project Mercury. In addition, the unique organizational structure of the library and computing services was a major contributing reason for its selection. It was one of the first institutions to undergo a major reorganization of information technology and resources providers, placing the library and academic computing units within one division reporting to a vice-president for academic affairs.

The one- and two-day visits in April 1992 at Carnegie Mellon and USC, respectively, included interviews and discussions with library staff, computing center staff, administrators, project leaders, and others. Individual interviews provided the opportunity for in-depth discussions about the libraries' and the universities' involvement in the many aspects of the evolving networked environment. Group interviews and discussions allowed the researchers to gain an understanding through the stories, issues, and anecdotes of many individuals. Figure A-5 lists the USC respondents and their organizational units. At Carnegie Mellon, the researcher conducted interviews primarily with library staff. All interviews lasted approximately one and a half hours. Figure A-6 lists the staff interviewed during the visit. Chapter 2 reports the findings from these two site visits. Appendix B includes descriptive background information on these sites.

At USC, the researcher received permission to tape-record all sessions. Summaries of the recorded sessions served as the basis for the write-up and analysis for the site visit. Field notes from the visit supplemented the transcribed sessions. At Carnegie Mellon, field notes documented the interviews and these were later transcribed and sent to the interviewees for their review and approval. Sessions at Carnegie Mellon were not tape-recorded.

The USC primary informant provided the researcher with selected internal documents as well as published documents relating to the systems, the network, and the information resources available. A number of published reports on Carnegie Mellon and in particular its Project Mercury, supplemented information gathered during the site visit.

The site visits also included demonstrations and tours. At USC, staff presented the Online Chronicle of Higher Education Project and a tour of the Music Library. The Music Library offers users sophisticated information technology related to music such as computer stations with music software and hardware, a multimedia station, and several digital audio workstations.

- **University Library**
  University Librarian and Dean of Libraries
  Assistant University Librarian for Academic Information Services
  Assistant University Librarian for Collection Development
  Reference Librarians, Doheny Reference Center
  Head, Philosophy Library
  Head, Science and Engineering Library
  Head, Online Instructional Services, Science and Engineering Library
  Head, Access Services, Science and Engineering Library
  Head, Reference and Informational Services, Science and Engineering Library
  Head, Andrus Gerontology Library
  Head, Hancock Library for Biology and Oceanography
  Technical Services Librarian, Hancock Library for Biology and Oceanography
  Head of Cataloging

- **Center for ScholarlyTechnology**
  Acting Director and Senior Research Consultant
  Associate Director
  Head, Library Automation Development
  Systems Development Librarian
  Project Coordinator
  Director, Software Development
  Programmers
  Project Coordinator

- **University Computing Services**
  Executive Director
  Director, User Services
  Manager, User Services
  Manager, Decision and Information Systems

- **Faculty**
  Assistant Professor of Music History and Literature

Figure A-5. USC staff participants in site visit.

The researcher at Carnegie Mellon observed two demonstrations, one of the Library Information System II (LIS II), the newly implemented electronic library which was made available campus-wide in January 1992, and the second of a test database

- Coordinator of Database Searching
- Director of Library Automation/Technical Director of Project Mercury
- Acting Director of University Libraries
- Systems Librarian/Liaison between Project Mercury and library staff
- Vice-president for Academic Services

Figure A-6. Carnegie Mellon staff participants in site visit.

of bit-mapped, full-text journal articles from the fields of engineering and artificial intelligence.

The site visits to North Carolina, USC, and Carnegie Mellon University offered opportunities to explore, identify, and describe the evolution, development, and current state of electronic networking and networked information provision. The rationale for the visits was to provide a description of the libraries' use of networking technology and what they are planning for the near future so that other libraries might benefit from their experiences. According to the general structure of the site visits developed by the study team, site visit informants provided information covering the eleven broad themes.

SUMMARY AND CONCLUSION

The multiple methods used in this study have provided the researchers with a rich array of empirical evidence on which to base the analysis and the findings as reported in Chapters 1 through 4. Through a combination of data-collection activities, the study team attempted to find common themes and issues facing academic and public libraries as they participate in the evolving national networked environment. The separate data-collection activities also uncovered issues unique to academic or public libraries.

Overall, the methods employed by the study team assisted in accomplishing the study's original research goals. Qualitative research methods can be very effective in identifying key issues in exploratory studies such as this. In addition, rigorous attention to validity, reliability, and data quality added credibility to the overall results of the study.

**Assessment of Issues Related to the Impact of the
National Research and Education Network (NREN) on Libraries**

Conducted by
School of Information Studies,   Syracuse University
Principal Investigator
Dr. Charles R. McClure

We would like to know your thoughts concerning the impact on libraries of the National Research and Education Network
(NREN). Your cooperation in completing this questionnaire is greatly appreciated. By taking a few minutes of your time
to fill out the questionnaire, you will be helping us identify key issues and roles for libraries in the evolving national
networking environment. Please drop the completed questionnaire in the box near the doors on your way out. Thank you
again for your help.

For each of the questions, please mark the box that most closely fits your answer.
1. Your Employer is:
    [ ] Small Academic Library   [ ] Medium-size Academic Lib.   [ ] Large Academic Library
    [ ] Small Public Library   [ ] Medium-size Public Library   [ ] Large Public Library
    [ ] State Library Agency   [ ] Special Library   [ ] School Library
    [ ] Government Library   [ ] Independent Information Professional/Consultant
    [ ] Other, please specify: _____

2. Your Position is in what general area:
    [ ] Library public services   [ ] Library technical services
    [ ] Library administration   [ ] Library systems office
    [ ] Other, please specify: _____

3. Your years of professional library experience: _____ (years)

4. Your general use of networks is for (check all that apply):
    [ ] OCLC and/or RLIN   [ ] Listservs, BBS, Computer Forums
    [ ] Electronic Mail(Internet or Bitnet)   [ ] Telnet/Remote Login (Internet)
    [ ] File transfer (Internet or Bitnet)   [ ] Other, please specify:_____

5. Please indicate your use of currently existing national electronic networks (Internet, BITNET):
    [ ] Don't use networks
    [ ] Have used networks for less than 12 months
    [ ] Have used networks for more than 12 months

Please check the box to indicate the degree to which you agree or disagree with the following statements:

		Strongly Agree	Agree	No Opinion	Disagree	Strongly Disagree	Don't Know
6.	NREN will enhance access to information.	[ ]	[ ]	[ ]	[ ]	[ ]	[ ]
7.	NREN connection should be available for all libraries.	[ ]	[ ]	[ ]	[ ]	[ ]	[ ]
8.	NREN will provide new opportunities for libraries.	[ ]	[ ]	[ ]	[ ]	[ ]	[ ]
9.	Libraries should provide access to NREN resources.	[ ]	[ ]	[ ]	[ ]	[ ]	[ ]
10.	NREN will require new skills for library staff.	[ ]	[ ]	[ ]	[ ]	[ ]	[ ]

Figure A-7. Survey Instrument.

	Strongly Agree	Agree	No Opinion	Disagree	Strongly Disagree	Don't Know
11. Librarians should provide training to patrons about using the networks (Internet, BITNET).	[ ]	[ ]	[ ]	[ ]	[ ]	[ ]
12. Librarians should organize NREN resources (e.g., develop navigational tools, indexes, directories).	[ ]	[ ]	[ ]	[ ]	[ ]	[ ]
13. Libraries will contribute information resources (excluding OPACs) to the NREN.	[ ]	[ ]	[ ]	[ ]	[ ]	[ ]
14. NREN will primarily be used by patrons without librarian assistance.	[ ]	[ ]	[ ]	[ ]	[ ]	[ ]
15. NREN will primarily be used by librarians to assist patrons.	[ ]	[ ]	[ ]	[ ]	[ ]	[ ]
16. In-person services offered by librarians will not be necessary for patrons using the NREN.	[ ]	[ ]	[ ]	[ ]	[ ]	[ ]
17. Libraries will require substantial increases in resources to exploit the potential of the NREN.	[ ]	[ ]	[ ]	[ ]	[ ]	[ ]
18. Technical barriers exist which limit effective use of the existing networks (Internet, BITNET).	[ ]	[ ]	[ ]	[ ]	[ ]	[ ]
19. Few information resources are available on the networks (Internet, BITNET) to make their use worthwhile.	[ ]	[ ]	[ ]	[ ]	[ ]	[ ]
20. Librarians have limited knowledge of what is available on the networks (Internet, BITNET).	[ ]	[ ]	[ ]	[ ]	[ ]	[ ]
21. Users have limited knowledge of what is available on the networks (Internet, BITNET).	[ ]	[ ]	[ ]	[ ]	[ ]	[ ]
22. NREN information resources will not be different than other library resources.	[ ]	[ ]	[ ]	[ ]	[ ]	[ ]
23. NREN services will be too expensive for most libraries to use.	[ ]	[ ]	[ ]	[ ]	[ ]	[ ]
24. Libraries will be bypassed by the NREN.	[ ]	[ ]	[ ]	[ ]	[ ]	[ ]

Any additional comments?

If you don't leave the questionnaire in the box, please mail it to me; or if you would like more information, please contact me: Charles R. McClure, School of Information Studies, Sci-Tech 4-206, Syracuse University Syracuse, NY 13244   Telephone: (315) 443-2911 BITNET: CMCCLURE@SUVM.BITNET

Thank you for your help!

Figure A-7. Survey instrument, *continued.*

REFERENCES

Glaser, Barney G. and Strauss, Anselm L. (1967). *The Discovery of Grounded Theory: Strategies for Qualitative Research.* Hawthorne, NY: Aldine de Gruyter.

Kirk, J. and Miller, M. L. (1986). *Reliability and Validity in Qualitative Research.* Newbury Park, CA: Sage Publications.

Krueger, Richard A. (1988). *Focus Groups: A Practical Guide for Applied Research.* Beverly Hills. CA: Sage Publications.

McClure, Charles R., Ryan, Joe and Lauterbach, Diana. (1992a). The role of public libraries in the use of Internet/NREN information services: Preliminary findings. In *Proceedings of the American Society for Information Science 1992 Mid-Year Conference.* Medford: NJ: Learned Information.

McClure, Charles R., Ryan, Joe, Moen, William E., Lauterbach, Diana and Gratch, Bonnie. (1992b). The impact of national electronic networking on academic and public libraries: Findings, issues, and recommendations. In Thomas W. Leonhart, ed., *Information Technology: IT's for Everyone! Proceedings of the LITA Third National Conference.* Chicago, IL: American Library Association.

McClure, Charles R., Bishop. Ann P., Doty, Philip and Rosenbaum, Howard. (1991). *The National Research and Education Network (NREN): Research and Policy Perspectives.* Norwood, NJ: Ablex Publishing Corporation.

Shelly, A. L. and Siebert, E. E. (1985). *The QUALOG User's Manual.* CIS Technical Report No. CIS-85-2. Syracuse NY: Syracuse University, School of Computer and Information Science.

Shelly, A. L. and Siebert, E. E. (1986). Using logic programming to facilitate qualitative data analysis. *Qualitative Sociology* 9(2): 145–161.

Yin, Robert. (1989). *Case Study Research: Design and Methods.* Beverly Hills. CA: Sage Publications.

Carnegie Mellon University and the University of Southern California: Descriptive Information Based on Site Visit Data

Site visits to Carnegie Mellon University and the University of Southern California (USC) provided the researchers with a wealth of descriptive information. Appendix A describes the site visit methodology and the site visit themes around which researchers focused the data-collection activities. This appendix presents descriptive information about the two sites and serves as background information for the findings reported in Chapter 2.

The descriptions reflect the situation at these sites in April 1992, and the reader should be aware that both Carnegie Mellon and USC have evolved and changed in the intervening time. Some of the projects have taken new directions, and in the case of Carnegie Mellon, the arrival of a new university librarian in fall 1992 coincided with a change in the organizational arrangements between the libraries and computing services. These descriptions are a snapshot of two dynamic institutions at one point in time. They detail the evolution, development, and current use of electronic networks and networked information resources.

This appendix begins with general information about each site and then discusses their organizational structures, organizational relationships, and policy and planning groups. Following this are descriptions of the local networked environment, library networking activities, and networked resources and services. A references section points to other sources for further reading and information about these sites.

PROFILES OF TWO INNOVATORS

Carnegie Mellon University is a private research university in Pittsburgh, Pennsylvania, enrolling over 7,000 students (including more than 2,700 graduate students). It is nationally known for its strength in engineering, computer science, robotics, fine arts, and campus computing. Carnegie Mellon has been an innovator and leader in several areas related to computer science and has received numerous grants and contributions of equipment from computing/information technology companies. It collaborates with these companies on joint research and development projects and collaborates with library automation companies and other universities.

A 1985 published statement of university goals and plans incorporated the Carnegie Mellon libraries' strategic plan and vision which proposed an expanded electronic information provider role by the libraries for the campus. The document stated, "the library will be transformed into an advanced electronic information service" (Arms and Michalak, 1990, p. 254). Arms and Michalak noted that linking the libraries' plans to the university's agenda was an effective strategy that paved the way for the merger between two divisions (the libraries and computing services) into a single division called Academic Services.[1]

Carnegie Mellon libraries' networking development has centered on an effort called the Mercury Electronic Library Project (referred to throughout this report as Project Mercury). Project Mercury is developing the elements of an "electronic library" that includes relevant current information in electronic format and will make available full-text documents to scholars' workstations. It has focused on developing an advanced information retrieval system, and the library's new online system, LIS II, incorporates research and development from the project.

There is much about Carnegie Mellon's situation that is unique and not generalizable to other settings (e.g., a private institution with strength in computer sciences; a tradition of collaboration with computing and information technology companies). But Carnegie Mellon serves a useful illustration of one attempt by a medium-size library, whose collections were quite limited, to create a vision of the electronic library where, as Kibbey and Evans (1989) state, "the network is the library."

The University of Southern California (USC) is a private university located in Los Angeles, California. Approximately 25,000 students attend USC and approximately 2,000 faculty serve the instructional needs of those students. A 1986 accreditation self-study by USC identified the following two goals as high priorities necessary to support the academic community:

- the continued development of the library system; and
- the development of a new generation computing environment.

Also in 1986, the university created the position of vice-provost for academic computing. The university librarian (who has the rank of dean and vice-provost) and the vice-provost for academic computing have initiated joint projects to develop new information technology and resources. These two positions are senior members of the staff of the provost who is the chief academic officer of the university. While the library and academic computing are organizationally separate, the university librarian and the vice-provost for academic computing recognize the functional interdependence between their units (Johnson, Lyman, and Tompkins, p. 177).

In the mid-1980s, the library initiated USCInfo, the University of Southern California campus-wide information system, which makes available a range of electronic information resources including campus information, bibliographic databases, and the online catalog. The library's leadership on this project reflected an understanding by library administrators that the flow of information, not just access to computer resources, will be the primary focus of the campus network.

Organizational Structures

At USC, the library and University Computing Services (UCS) share responsibilities to serve the teaching and research needs of the academic community. USC libraries consist of Doheny Library (the central library), which is the largest campus library and eighteen specialized subject libraries spread around the campus. These subject libraries are often located near the school or department they serve.

In 1985, the library created the Division for Academic Information Services (AIS). AIS manages all automated library services, including the integrated GEAC library system. In addition, the assistant university librarian (AUL) for AIS is responsible for developing new projects related to electronic access to information. The current AUL is also the associate director at the Center for Scholarly Technology (CST).

UCS supports the academic community's research and instructional goals. The vice-provost of academic computing, to whom computing services reports, is committed to the use of information technology, particularly computers and networks, to serve the educational and research activities of faculty members. UCS facilities and services include campus-wide networks, central host systems, on-campus and remote access to high-performance computer resources, and user support services, including training, consulting, software and system documentation, and informative publications.

The CST, created in 1988, has played a pivotal role in bridging the library and computing services. According to its founding director, who is now the university librarian, the center is an "incubator," which serves as a focal point for the research and development of new applications using a range of information technologies. CST is not intended to take operational responsibilities for the applications its staff develop. Instead, it provides a point of departure to mainstream information technology into the library. The CST, through programs and services, assists "faculty in using technology and information resources for instruction and scholarship. The Center's activities include research on the use of information technology in higher education, enhancement of the information resources available through USCInfo, assistance in the development of instructional resources, and planning for the technologies that will be part of the university's new teaching library" (A Guide to USC Libraries, 1991). The director of CST reports to both the university librarian and the head of computing services and is jointly sponsored by the library and computing services. Funding and staffing come from both organizations.

Carnegie Mellon responded to the increasing interdependence of the library and computing services by merging these two units into the division of academic services in 1986. The configuration within academic services consisted of five areas whose directors all report to the vice-president of academic services:

- academic computing and media;
- university libraries;
- computing systems;
- communication networks; and
- Center for the Design of Educational Computing.

Perhaps typical of dynamic, innovative organizations, the organizational structure at Carnegie Mellon has changed since the 1986 merger, in large part, because of the needs of Project Mercury staff to be housed and work closely with the library staff. Project Mercury, while not purposefully established to act as a bridge, has evolved in a similar way to USC's CST by involving staff from both the library and computing services and encouraging collaboration.

Except perhaps for the relatively large library automation staff, which includes the Project Mercury funded positions, the libraries' organizational structure is rather typical of academic libraries.

Organizational Relationships

Carnegie Mellon places a high value on organizational relationships among and between campus units and external research organizations and computer companies. The Andrew Project, Project Mercury, and the CLARIT Project (which is the Center for Machine Translation's project for developing linguistic tools for indexing and retrieval) reflect the importance of these relationships among Carnegie Mellon's computing and networking units, campus and external research organizations, and computer companies. The relationships predate the 1986 merger of the library and computing services units and were important in making the new organizational arrangements successful.

According to Arms and Michalak (1990, p. 247):

> . . . the first major collaboration between the libraries and the computing center was in 1978 . . . when the vice-provost of information services and the director of libraries worked together to secure a grant of $210,000 from the Andrew W. Mellon Foundation to study the automation needs of middle-sized academic libraries, investigate available systems, and develop recommendations for automating.

Subsequent phases of library automation and information technology development—automating acquisitions (1981); installing the Integrated Library System (ILS) (1982–84); the development of automating serials and reserves (1983), and interlibrary loan (1983–84); the development of LIS I (1986); and most recently development and implementation of LIS II (1991–1992)—have all occurred with the active cooperation and collaboration of several other university units, most notably the computing services units. As a result of this decade of automation projects, there was a tradition of close, working relationships and experiences with the expertise and commitment among library staff, computer services technicians and specialists, computer science and other research institute faculty, and administrative leaders.

The strong and productive organizational relationships could not have developed or been sustained without the involvement of certain key players—within the university and as a result of partnerships with outside organizations and companies. The key university players for the reconceptualization of the libraries' expanded role and the vision of Project Mercury included:

- the former director of libraries and associate vice-president for academic services;
- the vice-president for academic services;
- the former university president;
- several computer science faculty and engineering faculty members;
- the librarian in charge of library automation;
- the librarian who had been in charge of electronic services; and
- certain staff in computer network services.

Currently, the Project Mercury team consists of the acting director of libraries, the director of library automation, the manager of library automation, the systems librarian, the senior research, design, and programming staff of Project Mercury, and the vice-president for academic services.

Key external organizations such as a bibliographic utility, businesses, professional associations, and foundations have provided financial support and/or equipment and research. The Andrew Mellon Foundation funded a library automation feasibility study which resulted in the original LS/2000 system. The Pew Charitable Trusts provided the major funding for Project Mercury to develop and build the second version of the electronic library and to provide access to additional electronic materials. Digital Equipment Corporation provided a major equipment grant to develop the Project Mercury software used in the distributed computing architecture necessary to accomplish the electronic library. OCLC granted a development license for its Newton software for indexing, searching, and retrieval. Apple Computer and Bell Atlantic also provided grants for specific parts of the project. Publishers and associations such as Elsevier, University Microfilms Incorporated (UMI), Institute of Electrical and Electronics Engineers (IEEE), and others provided support in the form of permission to scan journals or data to be used in the electronic library.

These collaborations between the university and external groups demonstrate the strong tradition and success of entrepreneurism and university-business-research organizational partnerships. Michalak stated in a recent interview that "Carnegie Mellon prides itself on being an aggressive, entrepreneurial institution always looking for new approaches and partnerships in research" (Heath, Spring 1991, p. 63).

USC appointed a new vice-provost for academic computing and research in 1988. This person strongly supported collaborative relationships between the library and computing services. The University Librarian also firmly believed in such a collaboration. As a result, the CST came into existence as the bridging organization and focus for establishing a more dynamic linkage between these two organizations. According to CST's founding director, CST was a strategy to formalize the interdependency between the library and computing services. For example, the library had the resources (e.g., database tapes for USCInfo) but not the technical staff to run USCInfo.

The vice-provost for academic computing also served on the university library committee during a needs assessment. He had fundamental input in the library's strategic plan. Through this experience, he formed a strategic partnership with the university librarian to develop campus information resources and delivery mechanisms. The model for these relationships focused on building collaborations and joint projects between the two organizations, not the integration of the two organization into a single reporting structure.

CST is a focal point for collaborative project teams (e.g., USCInfo and the Online Chronicle of Higher Education). Other collaborative efforts occurred on a more ad hoc basis (e.g., the Network Navigation Team). All the collaborative activities draw on interested and knowledgeable people who cross organizational boundaries, thus producing the benefits of matrix-oriented project-based activities. As one respondent suggested, the best way to achieve collaboration is through actual work on projects. The team members work together and bring the perspectives and political insights from their respective organizations. They raise ideas and select activities based, in part, on whether their organizational units will support them. Plus, respondents claimed that these working arrangements sensitized project team members to the different cultures that inform the separate organizations.

Not all attempts at developing good working relationships in the electronic information environment have been successful. Failures, according to one respondent, are as interesting as some of the successes.

Policy and Planning Groups

Planning occurs at several levels including campus-wide strategic planning, unit strategic and operations planning, and project planning occurring in the collaborative work groups. Plans may be formalized and published in a document. In other cases, the collaborative arrangements between units lead to more informal planning processes.

At USC, the collaborative projects between the library and computing services provide opportunities for cross-unit communication as well as for planning. The support of the vice-provost for academic computing has been critical in the planning and implementation of projects by the library and computing services. He supported the creation of CST, and its director affects a considerable amount of cross-planning and cross-fertilization by participating in administrative staff meetings of both organizations. Each organization could be apprised of what the other was doing and respond proactively, not merely reactively.

Within the library, there is a conscious attempt and plan to introduce and support the use of networking technologies and resources. Library management involves library staff in discussions and planning for the future—its impacts, demands, and opportunities. As one example, the AUL for information services prepared a discussion paper and circulated it among library faculty to involve them in the concerns and decisions brought about by the networked environment.

From the perspective of one respondent in a group discussion with librarians, however, planning appears at times to be a top-down activity. Higher levels of administration made a decision that USC would become an electronic campus. "The vice-provost is gung-ho in getting not only librarians but also faculty and staff to use the network—interested in pushing the use of computers and networks."

Within computing services, one respondent described the planning process as not really existing. Managers see what needs to be done and go do it. While these things may be discussed, "there is no vote." Planning, this person noted ironically, is a "good way to spend a year of one's time." In fact, several library and computing services respondents highlighted the difference in the type and value placed on planning that occurs in these two units. Computing services staff had difficulties working (initially) with library staff— the latter were more process oriented and the former were more interested in getting the job done. "Computer people tend to see the answer and it's obvious. Let's not just talk about it, but do it."

Discussions with the Network Navigation Team provided a glimpse into the flexible, entrepreneurial planning process and execution of tasks that occur within the framework of CST. This group, formed in January 1992, consists of CST staff, faculty members, librarians and computing services staff who organize and carry out educational efforts related to the use of the larger networked environment of the Internet. The members of the group see themselves as initiators, responding to perceived needs or potential needs of the academic community. The group hopes that their successful activities will be noticed by others and that these activities can be mainstreamed by other units on campus.

Because of a very entrepreneurial culture within the university—one that promotes risk-taking and independent action—the stakeholders from computing services, the library, and CST have been able to move, under the leadership of the vice-provost and the university librarian, toward a vision of the electronic, networked library. However, without a university-supported strategic plan for information resources and technology, and without the appropriate financial and staff resources to carry out the plan, such efforts as those being undertaken in 1992 may be jeopardized in the bleak budget climate.

At Carnegie Mellon, the yearly program reports Project Mercury must file with its funding agencies assist the project's planning process. Since much of Project Mercury's work involves the libraries, to a great extent it shapes the libraries' strategic planning. Of course, both Project Mercury's and the libraries' priorities and future plans shift as local situations change or unanticipated opportunities become available, but the interconnectedness of their plans remains constant. What seems to keep their goals on track, however, are the strength of their vision of the electronic library and the commitment of many dedicated staff members.

Project Mercury's research and development emphasize more than bibliographic retrieval and include areas such as image processing, natural language processing, and electronic publications. Other campus units are also directly involved with planning and taking leadership for these initiatives. For example, LIS II and Project Mercury initiatives depend heavily on the networking developments of the Communications Network division; thus all decisions related to networked information resources include key members of this staff.

An administrative group provides governance and leadership for the libraries. This group is responsible for the development and revision of the libraries' strategic plans and policy development, and includes:

- library director;
- associate director;
- director of library automation;
- department heads; and
- heads of the branch libraries.

These administrators have the primary leadership role for all activities and plans related to the libraries' online information system (LIS II) and the networked information resources made available via LIS II. The libraries take the lead for evaluating and acquiring databases for the library network, preparing documentation for LIS II and other databases, and conducting user training for the library-based systems.

A number of factors influence the planning process—organizational structure (i.e., the organizational location and reporting structure of various units), culture (i.e., the organizational values, attitudes, and beliefs of the units), and personalities (the personal chemistry for working or not working together). These libraries recognize that the various planning processes help to define the future states to which they are working as well as guide decisions at the operational and tactical levels to move effectively toward their goals. Collaborative planning between the libraries and other campus units is essential since the libraries jointly develop and deliver services and products with these units.

Development of the Local Networked Environment

Carnegie Mellon's Andrew Project marked the change from a campus-wide time-shared computing environment. During the early to mid-1980s, Carnegie Mellon created and implemented a distributed computing environment composed of three components: powerful individual workstations and personal computers, shared file server computers, and a network that links these campus components as well as connecting to national networks. The Andrew Project file system is a key component of the distributed computing environment.

Leong and Arms (1988) and Leong, (1989) describe the network in detail. The goal of the network was to provide a set of services to everyone on campus and to have the network be as transparent as possible to users. By 1988, the network had over 12,000 outlets, with at least one outlet in every room on campus and all network types (e.g., Token Ring, AppleTalk, or Ethernet) available in every room and all using the TCP/IP protocols. Network services included a network file system, access to printers, electronic mail, library information, connections to external networks, and the Cray computer at the Pittsburgh Supercomputing Center. The university network connects to all leading national networks and is one of the hubs of the NSFNET, as the jointly run Pittsburgh Supercomputing Center is housed on the Carnegie Mellon campus. According to Arms (1990, p. 37), "national networks have become an integral part of academic life," and since Carnegie Mellon has adhered to the TCP/IP protocols, a smooth integration was possible with the national networks.

Carnegie Mellon's library system, LIS II, did not, in 1992, function as a gateway to the Internet, although future plans have identified this as a goal. A systems librarian explained:

> Obviously we definitely want to access other libraries' catalogs through LIS II . . . the whole reason we're using protocols like Z39.50 is so that we can interact with other information resources. Most of our efforts so far have been aimed at the provision of local databases because this is the foundation of our system, but the next step of moving out to access remote sources is definitely in our plans.

Some of the campus networks, such as Andrew, are linked to the Internet, and observations from librarians and Andrew logs indicate that there is a great deal of Internet use by the campus community. The director of library automation cited the following uses of the Internet at Carnegie Mellon:

- bulletin boards and discussion groups;
- electronic mail;
- use of repositories of software and shareware; and
- use of specialized databases.

He commented that academic computing staff publish lists of resources in the Internet in its newsletter, but this is generally on a very ad hoc basis.

Two main campus networks exist at USC. One is the campus backbone called USCNet. USCNet is a high-speed network and supports a variety of network protocols including TCP/IP, DECNET,

XNS, AppleTalk, and IPX (Novell). USCNet connects various local area networks (LANs) as well as computers that are directly connected to the backbone. USCNet provides connectivity within the academic community and to the external networked environment via connections to BITNET and the Internet. The other campus network is an asynchronous network using a Micom data switch that provides a direct, exclusive connection between the user and the host machine, and dial-up access to campus computers. According to a respondent from computing services, future expansion of campus networks include a gigabit network infrastructure connecting the buildings and fiber distributed data interface (FDDI) configurations existing in the buildings. Wireless networks will be likely in a five- to six-year time frame.

The overall networking environment at USC has developed in somewhat of an ad hoc fashion since there is no central budget for bringing the network to each desktop. This has led to an uneven spread of network connections through the academic community. Those schools and departments that are science and technology oriented (e.g., engineering) are more likely to have made network access from the desktop a priority. Other disciplines that have less historical experience with computing or have yet to become aware of available networked resources are less likely to have direct connections to USCNet. These differences will continue, in part, because of different computational needs of various departments. The science- and technology-oriented disciplines will be easier to accommodate than the humanities. The type of textual and graphic information retrieval and the interfaces for the latter group will require more complicated processing and "computational smarts," according to a computer services respondent.

All members of the USC community can request and receive a basic e-mail account (this is free, but there is a nominal charge for the electronic mail manual which has the account application included). Basic e-mail accounts provide BITNET and Internet mail messaging functionality. Although these have been the primary means for network access, an increasing number of users are using Telnet and FTP capabilities through Unix accounts. The public terminals in the library that provide access to USCInfo do not, as of 1992, provide Telnet and FTP capabilities. This was understood to be a logical next step in using the campus network and information service in providing network access to remote resources.

While computing services has a clear mandate to develop the campus-wide network, some respondents suggested that the deans of the schools would like to see the computing budget carved up and have direct authority for computing resources. So far, the vice-provost for academic computing has successfully argued that it is more cost effective to have common services. While the central computing service will hold onto the network, it is not clear that it will hold on to all the servers. This is one of the challenges of the distributed computing environment.

Library Networking Activities

In 1985, the USC library was one of the first units on campus to install a LAN for its internal administrative uses. This provided productivity software for staff and also offered electronic mail for computers connected to the LAN. The LAN is scheduled for replacement, and the new network will provide enhanced services as well as operating on protocols for interconnection and interoperability with USCNet. The library also maintains and operates its own computer and hard-wired terminals. The library relies on a GEAC computer for all technical processing including cataloging, circulation, acquisitions, and HOMER, the online catalog.

Part of the infrastructure developed for USCInfo included a number of library satellites, units located in student activity areas around campus where networked microcomputers provided students with access for searching local information resources (e.g., the online catalog, bibliographic databases, etc.), and also productivity software (e.g., word-processing and spreadsheet applications). The library established, maintained, and operated the library satellites, thus leading the campus in exploring networked-based delivery of information. As one respondent suggested, the library satellites seemed to put a fire under computing services to examine its roles and responsibilities with distributed computing. The library satellites have since been closed as library operations, and the facilities have become the responsibility of computing services and are operated as public computer facilities.

Currently, USCInfo is available through the campus-wide network from terminals within the library and to users on computers at home, in offices, and in dormitories. USCInfo (consisting of databases, the database manager, BRS/Search Software as the search and retrieval engine) resides on an IBM 3090/200E mainframe operated and maintained by computing services.

Carnegie Mellon's original online public access catalog, the LS/2000 system, became operational in early 1984, and is still used in the library to provide local holdings information. In 1985, as part of an overall plan to increase access to information in electronic form, the libraries began using the recently acquired IBM 3083 mainframe computer as a database server, thus expanding access to every terminal and personal computer on the campus network. In fact, an existing well-developed campus-wide communications network linking an "enormous number of terminals and personal computers," facilitated planning for network access to library databases (Arms and Michalak, 1990, p. 259). Library staff acquired IBM's STAIRS retrieval system and developed a customized user interface for the new Library Information System (LIS), which became available campus-wide in March 1986. The success of this system was due to a single user interface, and according to a 1989 faculty survey, it was very popular: 76 percent of faculty reported that they used it at least once per week. (Arms, 1992).

Due, in part to, campus and library leadership visions of greatly improved access to library and remote materials, the accomplishments of the Andrew project, and the merger of library and computing units, the time was ripe in 1988 for several key players to begin to conceptualize the idea of an electronic library. The vision took shape as the Mercury Electronic Library Project (Project Mercury) which is central to current library networking activities.

Project Mercury began in earnest in the 1988/89 academic year. It is described in several publications (Evans, et al., 1989; Kibbey and Evans, 1989; Arms, 1992; Troll, Spring 1992; and Troll, 1992), so only a brief description is provided here. Funded entirely by outside grants, Project Mercury has been a multiyear effort. It is research and development oriented and has focused on (Arms and Michalak, 1990, p. 262):

> . . . the expansion of electronic resources; facilities for storage and display of full text; the development of a convenient, flexible user interface; integration with networked computer applications; the use of inexpensive distributed file servers in place of large, central mainframe computers; and the systematic enhancement of bibliographic records to improve access to information.

Its current focus is on developing an advanced information retrieval system to provide the infrastructure for further developments leading toward the realization of an electronic library (Evans, et al., 1989).

Project Mercury's collaborative research related to capturing and representing complete documents, image processing and transfer, distributed storage and retrieval, and user interface design has fed directly into the development of LIS II, which the library released campus-wide in January 1992. LIS II is "a significant milestone on the way to a functional electronic library with the capability to deliver full-text documents to users' desktops" (Troll, 1992, p. 1).

Project Mercury's architecture developed with a distributed computing environment as its foundation. Although project planners wanted Mercury to be compatible with the Andrew Project, they recognized that Andrew was dated. To compensate, Project Mercury acquired software from MIT, implemented standards-based software (e.g., Z39.50), and developed new software specifically for Mercury. The architecture of the Mercury electronic library is best understood in terms of its five components: retrieval servers, communications standards, gateway systems, user interfaces, and storage space. The architecture of LIS II is a distributed environment of clients and servers (Troll, Spring 1992, p. 91):

> The clients are the machines on people's desktops (e.g., Unix workstation, Apple Macintosh, IBM PCs, and terminals). A Motif user interface is used for Unix workstations running X.11 windows, and a terminal interface is provided for other machines. . . . The servers are workstations where the databases and retrieval software reside. LIS II divides the workload between the clients and servers. For example, the client machines construct queries, send them to the servers, and provide interactive displays of information; the server machines provide security, search, retrieval, and bulk manipulation of data. Databases are built on a VAX 6410, then moved to retrieval servers, which are DECstation 5000s. Presently LIS II uses four retrieval servers. The protocol that enables clients and servers to communicate with one another is Z39.50 layered on TCP/IP. The database-building and retrieval software is Newton, developed by OCLC. The system incorporates existing or proposed standards and is designed to be machine independent. Security is provided by the authentication system based on Kerberos.

The retrieval software, the interface, a retrieval protocol, and many networked electronic resources determine the quality of retrieval for users. The use of Z39.50 retrieval protocol will allow LIS II users to send queries to retrieval systems using the same protocol at other sites, thus making searching of remote library catalogs and other networked resource via the Internet much easier. In 1992, a project was underway to update LIS II with the 1992 version of Z39.50.

These libraries' networking activities have used existing distributed computing environments and also have been instrumental in expanding that environment to focus on the flow of information. They have initiated major projects to explore and develop the infrastructure to deliver networked information services and products.

Networked Resources and Services

USC library's campus-wide information system, USCInfo, offers users a variety of information resources from public access terminals within the library as well as via remote access from computers outside the library via USCNet. A grant from the Ahmanson Foundation to the library originally funded the development of USCInfo for a three-year period. These funds acquired the hardware, software, leased commercial databases, and the support staff to create new library programs using microcomputer technologies.

A critical planning decision, according to a respondent, was to build USCInfo from scratch, integrate the library's online catalog and the commercial databases under a single user interface, make this available via the campus network, and do this consciously and collaboratively with computing services. The CST's director acted as a bridge between the library and computing services, drawing on expertise from computing services to move USCInfo into operation. He also worked with commercial database vendors to acquire bibliographic databases. Vendors at that time had little experience with this new market for their information products. The director was able to cooperate with the vendors, arrange leasing terms for the databases, and offer the vendors a real-world testbed for their information products.

USCInfo became available in test mode in fall 1987 and operational in 1988. A detailed description of USCInfo is available in Waiblinger (1992). USCInfo includes HOMER, the library's online catalog, campus information files (e.g., a campus telephone directory), and online indexes to periodical literature. Figure B-1 lists the periodical indexes available on USCInfo as of 1992. To enable a single interface for all the databases, a global data dictionary and index exist to these locally mounted databases.

USCInfo also serves as a development platform for new information resources. A project team within CST has the responsibility for developing and enhancing USCInfo. In 1991, CST and the *Chronicle for Higher Education* embarked on a project to provide online through USCInfo the full text of the *Chronicle of Higher*

Applied Science and Technology Index	1983 to present
Art Index	1984 to present
Computer Database	1986 to present
General Science Index	1984 to present
Humanities Index	1984 to present
Magazine Index	1983 to present
Management Contents	1986 to present
MEDLINE	1980 to present
National Newspaper Index	1981 to present
PsycINFO	1984 to present
Public Affairs Information Service	1972 to present
Social Science Index	1984 to present
Trade & Industry Index	1982 to present

Figure B-1. Periodical indexes available on USCInfo (as of 1992).

Education. The goals of the project were to mount the full text of the *Chronicle* as another information resource through USCInfo and to explore the implications of offering full-text information through USCInfo. The Online Chronicle became available in fall 1991. As a research and development project, continuous enhancements are made to the Online Chronicle.

USCInfo is available only to members of the USC academic community because of database licensing restrictions. Users can download and print information gathered during their sessions on USCInfo. The system offers several options for doing this, including sending the file of information as an e-mail message to the users' computer accounts, doing a file transfer using FTP to their account, or sending the file to a printer. At the time of the site visit, access from USCInfo to remote Internet information resources was not yet implemented.

Carnegie Mellon library's LIS II functions as a common information retrieval system for the library catalog and many other databases. The electronic resources in LIS II are a growing collection of campus and commercial databases in two formats: ASCII text and bitmapped page images. Figure B-2 presents a summary of the types and examples of databases in the system.

Since some of the databases listed in Figure B-2 are licensed from commercial firms, Carnegie Mellon has carefully defined

---

Bibliographic databases of local campus information: enhanced library catalog; journal list; ArchPics, an electronic index of illustrations from architecture books in the Carnegie Mellon Collection.

Commercially produced bibliographic databases: ABI/Inform; Computer Database; INSPEC; Newspaper Abstracts; Periodical Abstracts.

Commercially produced full-text databases: Academic American Encyclopedia; American Heritage Dictionary; Business Dateline.

Other databases of local campus information: Who's Who at Carnegie Mellon.

Other commercially produced databases: Choice book reviews; Guide to Resources and Services of the Inter-University Consortium for Political and Social Research.

Figure B-2. LIS II accessible databases.

access for various user groups to protect the licensing agreements for the databases. These groups include the following:

- *Public users* are people who do not have authentication with the Kerberos system such as external users or campus users who have not applied for the Andrew System authentication, the library's LIS II's authentication system, or other departmental computer systems. This group can use all databases except those that are commercially licensed.
- *Authenticated users* can use all released databases.
- *Library staff* can see and use all of the released databases and a subset of the test databases.
- *Database testers:* can see all of the databases that have been built, both released and test databases.

The libraries' and Project Mercury's goals place a top priority on expanding the electronic resources available to users. These goals include:

- adding local campus information databases to LIS II and assisting with the creation of departmental databases of various types for LIS II;

- acquiring additional commercial bibliographic data-bases, particularly for the social science, humanities, and fine arts, as well as for numeric and statistical information (e.g., census data);
- increasing availability of full-text access to journals and technical reports via LIS II;
- providing gateways to commercial systems (e.g., DIA-LOG); and
- distributing more information about networks and networked information that are available beyond the Andrew environment.

These resources will be available over the network and projects are underway or being planned to accomplish these (Carnegie Mellon University Libraries Strategic Plan 1991–1995; Troll, 1992; Troll, Spring 1992).

In addition, new services will provide links between databases. Plans call for several types of links:

- connecting commercially licensed bibliographic data-bases and the *Choice* book reviews to local holdings information;
- linking the library catalog to the circulation system (this project has been delayed because of the need to replace LS/2000, the libraries' management system); and
- connecting several bibliographic databases to full-text databases in bitmapped page image format to provide document delivery service.

Carnegie Mellon is committed to linking enhanced retrieval systems and document delivery. Delivering electronic documents to the user's personal computer or terminal is a major objective of Project Mercury.

The January 1992 release of LIS II delivers full-text documents in ASCII format of articles from *Business Dateline* and the *Academic American Encyclopedia.* A current project with UMI involves two bibliographic databases in LIS II which are being linked to full text page image databases on CD-ROM. Users can submit electronic requests to print the full text of the articles on a designated printer in the library for pickup. In the second phase of this project, users will be able to view the full-text on personal computers that have the ability to display bitmapped page images.

Another Project Mercury initiative with Elsevier and the Institute of Electrical and Electronics Engineers involves scanning articles from selected academic journals using TIFF Group 4 Fax compression. These are stored on a retrieval server by journal name, volume, and number, and users can request and display these page images on personal computers that have the ability for such display. Moreover, the scanned images in this project are linked to bibliographic records in the INSPEC database and will be available through a serials browser. This feature uses the serials browser by which users can "select a particular journal issue and view the pages the way they would naturally navigate a printed journal" (Troll, Spring 1992, p. 95–96).

A page-image database of computer science technical reports linked to the library catalog is in process. This collaborative project with several universities creates a page-image technical report database. An indexed bibliographic database will be replicated at each university, but the full-text page images will be available across the Internet. Carnegie Mellon libraries are also pursuing licensing programs with publishers, such as Elsevier's TULIP University Licensing Program, which would provide the full text of many materials science journals.

A continuing thrust of Project Mercury is the enhancement of catalog records. Additional information is added to bibliographic records including the titles of plays in collections, individual titles of papers contained in scientific and technical conference proceedings, individually authored chapter titles of collected books, and author-supplied abstracts to Carnegie Mellon technical reports.

CONCLUDING COMMENTS

The library managers and staff at Carnegie Mellon and the University of Southern California are aware that a major transformation in library services and facilities is in the making. The descriptions point to the various arenas in which these libraries are acting. Carnegie Mellon and USC understand that it is not simply a matter of choosing the "right" technology or the "right" organizational arrangement. In the dynamic environment of networking and information provision, the "right" technology today could be the "wrong" technology tomorrow. Rather than thinking in terms of "right" and "wrong," they are building on what they have done and making plans for an uncertain future (in terms of technology, funding, etc.). In their own ways, they are planning for and creating their futures. Essential to planning and implementing is a capacity of flexibility and continous willingness to re-evaluate, re-examine, and change. In the process they have faced or are facing major issues that range from calling into question the existence of the library to deciding on the number of user interfaces they can support. Chapter 2 reports these issues and other findings based on the data collected, analysis, and an understanding of the historical and current situations of these sites as described in this appendix.

NOTES

1. In fall 1992, this organizational arrangement was restructured, and three separate units, libraries, computing services, and educational technologies now report to the provost.

REFERENCES

Arms, William F. (1992). *The Mercury Electronic Library and Library Information System II: The First Three Years.* Mercury Technical Report Series, No. 6. Pittsburgh, PA: Carnegie Mellon University.

Arms, William Y. (Fall, 1990). Reflections on Andrew. *EDUCOM Review* 25(3): 33–43.

Arms, William Y. and Michalak, Thomas J. (1990). Carnegie Mellon University. In Caroline R. Arms, ed., Campus Strategies for Libraries and Electronic Information (pp. 243–273). Bedford, MA: Digital Press.

Carnegie Mellon University Libraries Strategic Plan 1991–1995. (June, 1991).

Evans, Nancy H., Troll, Denise A., Kibbey, Mark H., Michalak, Thomas J., and Arms, William Y. (1989). *The Vision of the Electronic Library.* Mercury Technical Report Series, No. 1. Pittsburgh, PA, Carnegie Mellon University.

A Guide to the USC Libraries. (August, 1991). Los Angeles, CA: University of Southern California, USC Libraries.

Heath, Fred M. (Spring, 1992). An interview with Thomas J. Michalak. *Library Administration and Management* 6(2): 62–65.

Johnson, Margaret L., Lyman, Peter, and Tompkins, Philip. (1990). University of Southern California. In Caroline R. Arms, ed., *Campus Strategies for Libraries and Electronic Information* (pp. 176–192). Bedford, MA: Digital Press.

Kibbey, Mark and Evans, Nancy H. (Fall, 1989). The network is the library. *EDUCOM Review* 24(3): 15–20.

Leong, John. (March, 1989). Designing a campus network with management in mind. *LAN Technologies* 5(3): 42–50.

Leong, John and Arms, William F. (1988). Data communications development at Carnegie Mellon University. In Caroline R. Arms, ed., *Campus Networking Strategies* (pp. 66–89). Bedford, MA: Digital Press.

Troll, Denise A. (Spring, 1992). Information Technologies at Carnegie Mellon. *Library Administration and Management* 6(2): 91–99.

Troll, Denise A. (1992). *Library Information System II: Progress and Plans.* Mercury Technical Report Series, No. 5. Pittsburgh, PA: Carnegie Mellon University.

Troll, Denise A. (1990). *Library Information System II: Progress Report and Technical Plan.* Mercury Technical Report Series, No. 3. Pittsburgh, PA: Carnegie Mellon University.

Waiblinger, John. (1992). USCInfo. In Walt Crawford, ed., *The Online Catalog Book: Essays and Examples* (pp. 491–506). New York: G.K. Hall & Co.

LM_NET: The School Library Media Network

LM_NET is the world-wide electronic discussion group (listserv) on the Internet focusing on the school library media field.

Conversation on LM_NET encompasses topics of interest to the school library media community, including the latest on school library media services, operations, and activities. It is a listserv for practitioners helping practitioners, sharing ideas, solving problems, telling each other about new publications and upcoming conferences, asking for assistance or information, and linking schools through their library media centers.

GROWTH OF LM_NET

LM_NET started in late June 1992 with twenty subscribers. By fall over 250 had joined, and by the end of 1992, the listserv had over 400 members. As of April 1993, LM_NET had about 800 members. LM_NET is growing by over 100 new members a month and should easily surpass 1,000 by its one-year anniversary. Consequently, LM_NET has become more than just another listserv—it is truly the electronic community for those interested in the school library media field.

SUBSCRIBING TO LM_NET

LM_NET is open to anyone with Internet access who is interested in the school library media field. Subscribing to LM_NET is free— simply send an e-mail message requesting to join to Peter Milbury (PMILBUR@EIS.CALSTATE.EDU). Include your complete e-mail userid and address and full name in the request.

SENDING/RECEIVING MESSAGES

Only subscribers of LM_NET can send and receive LM_NET messages. If you are a member, just send an e-mail message as you would to anyone else with an electronic mail address (i.e., to LM_NET@SUVM.SYR.EDU).

LM_NET FEATURES

LM_NET offers a number of special features that may not be found in every listserv.

Archives

All previous LM_NET communications are available through the AskERIC Electronic Library. To access, simply type GOPHER ERICIR.SYR.EDU Port 70.

Digest

Subscribers have the option of receiving the messages posted to LM_NET one at a time, or they can be compiled into a single message received once each day. To activate this *digest* function, subscribers send a mail message to LISTSERV@SUVM.SYR.EDU with one of the following commands in the body of the message: to turn the digest on SET LM_NET DIGEST; to turn the digest off SET LM_NET MAIL.

Mentoring

LM_NET has established a mentoring program in which more experienced network users are available to novice or inexperienced subscribers who need assistance in getting acquainted with network resources. For more details contact Shelley Lochhead (s_lochhead@ NHNET.UNH.EDU).

Monitoring

LM_NET strives to be the "listserv of listservs" for library media specialists by having members volunteer to monitor other listservs and repost relevant messages to LM_NET.

Targeting

To cut down on the volume of messages but still facilitate information sharing about a specific topic, LM_NET recommends that members specifically TARGET-> their requests for information in the subject line, and later summarize responses back to the entire listserv. TARGET-> in the subject line indicates that the sender wants information about a specific topic (e.g., TARGET-> online catalogs). Anyone with information on this topic responds directly to the sender not to the LM_NET, and after a period of time, the sender posts a summary or compilation of responses back to LM_NET.

For more information about LM_NET contact: Mike Eisenberg (MIKE@ERICIR.SYR.EDU) or Peter Milbury (PMIL-BUR@EIS.CALSTATE.EDU).

Internet Access Points to ERIC

The following are two of several systems which currently provide unrestricted Internet access to ERIC resources. For general information about ERIC, contact ACCESS ERIC, 1-800-LET-ERIC or email to ACCERIC@GWUVM.GWU.EDU.

AUBURN UNIVERSITY LIBRARIES

Auburn University Libraries offer the complete ERIC database, 1966 to the latest quarter. Searchable fields include title, author, subject heading (descriptor), and keyword (Note: requires TN3270).

1. TN3270 auducacd.duc.auburn.edu (or TN3270 131.204.2.13).
2. At the opening screen, tab to Application, and enter 01.
3. At the main menu, type ERIC.
4. Follow screen instructions to search.
5. To end the session, type STOP.

Tip: The keyword search field allows use of Boolean operators, truncation, nesting, and other special search features. Type EXP K for a complete explanation.

SYRACUSE UNIVERSITY

Syracuse University offers the latest five years of the ERIC database on the SUINFO system. Searchable fields include author, title, descriptor word, descriptor phrase, and abstract.

1. Telnet acsnet.syr.edu (or 128.230.1.21).
2. At > prompt, type SUINFO.
3. At Enter Terminal Type prompt, type VT100.
4. Bypass the Userid and Password prompts with the tab key.
5. At the Command prompt, type SUINFO.

6. When prompted, type Y (yes) to continue.
7. Find ERIC through the menus (first type 1 for General Interest files, then the number corresponding to ERIC), or type ERIC to enter directly.
8. Follow screen instructions to search. (If function keys do not work, type in corresponding commands.)
9. To end the session, type LOGOFF.

Tip: Whenever MORE or HOLDING appears in the lower right corner of the screen, hit the Home or Enter key to advance, or hit ESC and then period (.) key in sequence, not together.

The AskERIC Service for K–12 Educators

The Educational Resources Information Center (ERIC) is a federally funded national information system that provides access to an extensive body of education-related resources. The ERIC Clearinghouse on Information and Technology (ERIC/IT), which sponsors AskERIC, is one of sixteen ERIC Clearinghouses nationwide which provide a variety of services, products, and resources at all education levels.

AskERIC is an Internet-based question-answering service for teachers, library media specialists, administrators, and others involved in K–12 education. The hallmark of AskERIC is the human intermediary, who interacts with the information seeker and personally selects and delivers information resources within forty-eight working hours. The benefit of the human-mediated service is that it allows AskERIC staff to determine the precise information needs of the client and to present an array of relevant resources, both from the ERIC system and from the vast resources of the Internet.

The AskERIC Electronic Library is a Gopher/FTP site of selected resources for education and general interest. Some of the contents include lesson plans, ERIC Digests, Internet guides and directories, government information, and archives of education-related listservs. The address of this site is: ericir.syr.edu (port #70). To request further instructions on how to gopher, telnet, or FTP to the AskERIC Electronic Library, send an e-mail message to AskERIC@ericir.syr.edu. Anyone involved with K–12 education can send an e-mail message to AskERIC@ericir.syr.edu.

AskERIC is an Internet development and research project funded by the U.S. Department of Education as part of the ERIC program. AskERIC is also part of a series of Internet projects at Syracuse University (the Syracuse Projects on Information Networking, SPIN) seeking to explore Internet usefulness and accessibility. The specific goals for AskERIC are to develop and study Internet-based education information services, systems, and resources that seek to meet the needs of K–12 end-users.

Through AskERIC Partnership, state networks and education agencies work cooperatively with the ERIC Clearinghouse on Information and Technology to provide the highest level AskERIC information service to large groups of educators. To discuss options, contact: Nancy Morgan, or Richard Tkachuck, AskERIC Coordinators, askeric@ericir.syr.edu; or Mike Eisenberg, Director, ERIC/IT, mike@ericir.syr.edu.

Contributors

MICHAEL EISENBERG <mike@ericir.syr.edu> is a Professor at the School of Information Studies, Syracuse University, New York, and Director of the ERIC Clearinghouse on Information Resources. Eisenberg teaches courses in library media management, curriculum concerns, information technology, and information use, reporting, and presentation. At various times he held positions as teacher, school library media specialist, and administrator (university level). He offers speeches and workshops and consults on curriculum mapping, computers and information technology, networking, library and information skills instruction, and other topics at conferences, in-service sessions, and workshops for professional organizations, school library systems, state education departments, and local school districts. Eisenberg's writings include numerous journal articles, papers, and monographs on school library media, education, and information science and technology topics including the books (with Robert Berkowitz) *Information Problem-Solving: The Big Six Skills© Approach to Library and Information Skills Instruction*, 1990 and *Curriculum Initiative: An Agenda and Strategy for Library Media Programs*, 1988. Eisenberg currently directs the AskERIC networking project and comanages the LM_NET listserv with Peter Milbury.

JOHN R. GARRETT <jgarrett@NRI.RESTON.VA.US> is director of information resources at the Corporation for National Research Initiatives. He is responsible for developing and implementing research programs to study potential uses of electronically accessible information, and for building research alliances with publishers, universities, technical and scientific organizations, and others. Garrett holds a Ph.D in cultural anthropology, and has written widely on information policy issues related to copyright, privacy, and the digital library.

SHARYN LADNER <sladner@umiami.ir.miami.edu> is assistant professor and business librarian at the Richter Library, University of Miami, Coral Gables, Florida. Active in the Special Libraries Association, she is a former chair of the Networking Committee

479

and currently serves as a director of the business and finance division. She has published papers on resource sharing and electronic networking in special libraries and with Hope Tillman has coauthored several papers and a book on electronic networking in special libraries. Prior to her academic appointment, she managed a special library in the medical device industry and worked as a project manager/analyst for a market research firm. She received her B.A. from Gettysburg College and her M.L.S. from Indiana University

CHARLES R. MCCLURE <cmcclure@suvm.acs.syr.edu> is a professor at the School of Information Studies, Syracuse University, where he teaches courses in U.S. government information management and policies, information resources management, library/information center management, and planning and evaluation of information services. He completed his doctorate in library and information services at Rutgers University. He has authored some twenty-five monographs and over 150 articles, reports, and chapters on topics related to library and information center planning, evaluation, and management, information resources management, networking, and government information. McClure's research activities have won a number of national awards from the American Library Association, the Association of Library and Information Science Education, and the American Society for Information Science. McClure is also the associate editor of *Government Information Quarterly* and is also the editor of the journal *Internet Research: Electronic Networking Applications and Policy*. As president of Information Management Consultant Services, Inc., he has consulted with a number of academic, public, and special libraries; government agencies; and corporations regarding the design, implementation, management, and evaluation of information services.

PETER MILBURY <pmilbur@eis.calstate.edu> is a librarian at Pleasant Valley High School, Chico, California. He is an active member of the California Media and Library Educators' Association, and regularly offers seminars and workshops on the use of the Internet for teachers and librarians. His writings include "Finding Free and Inexpensive Materials on Computer," *CMLEA Journal*, Fall 1992, and "LM_NET: The School Library Media Electronic Community," (with Mike Eisenberg), *Information Searcher*, Winter 1993. Other writings include interviews, poems, short fiction, and book reviews for *East West Journal*, *Macrobiotics Today*, and

Soyfoods magazine. Milbury has a B.A. in English literature, an M.A. in education, and has done advanced graduate studies in instructional design and educational technology. Milbury has worked as a high school teacher, county school curriculum and media consultant, university media resources center director/instructional designer, Upward Bound Director, university lecturer, and student teacher supervisor. Peter also worked for a leading producer of organic natural food products, creating Riz Cous, Quick Cooking Brown Rice and other rice products. He co-manages LM_NET: World-wide Discussion Group for School Library Media Professionals and is an occasional contributor to other listservs and the statewide K–12 Bulletin Board of CORE (California Online Resources for Education).

WILLIAM E. MOEN <wemoen@rodan.acs.syr.edu> is a doctoral student and research associate at the School of Information Studies, Syracuse University. In collaboration with Charles R. McClure and Joe Ryan, he has published articles and reports on Federal information policy and the use of information technology to deliver government information and services. His research interests also include information technology standards and the standards development process. He teaches courses on information technology standards and the organization of information. His recent conference publications deal with classification issues for networked information resources, and information technology standards as a component of Federal information policy. Prior to beginning doctoral studies, he worked at the Library of Congress, Network Development and MARC Standards Office. He received his M.L.S. from Louisiana State University.

JOE RYAN <joryan@suvm.acs.syr.edu> is a doctoral candidate interested in the impacts of electronic networks on information policy and management at Syracuse University's, School of Information Studies, Syracuse, New York. His previous experience includes professional assignments in public, special, and academic libraries in the United States and internationally. Most recently he served as library associate professor at the University of Vermont where he authored *First Stop: The Master Index to Subject Encyclopedias*. Ryan's recent research and publications have been in the information policy area as part of the Syracuse study team with William E. Moen and led by Charles R. McClure. Projects have been funded by OCLC, Inc., the U.S. National Archives and Records Administration, Office of Management and Budget, General Services Administration, and Office of Technology Assessment. Ryan is resource review editor for *Internet Research: Electronic Networking, Applications, and Policy.*

JOHN H. SULZER <jhs@psulias.psu.edu> is head of the general reference section of the Penn State University Libraries. Prior to moving to general reference he served fifteen years in the government documents section both as a paraprofessional and a librarian. He served as chair of the American Library Association/Government Documents Round Table (1990–91), was a Group Leader on the Statewide Committee to Develop the Federal Documents Distribution Plan for Pennsylvania (1986), a member of the National Commission on Libraries and Information Science Committee on Government Information Policy (1989–90), and is now serving on the Depository Library Council to the U.S. Public Printer.

HOPE N. TILLMAN <tillman@babson.bitnet> is director of libraries at Babson College, Babson Park, Massachusetts. She is currently chair of the Special Libraries Association Networking Committee and of the SLA Information Technology Division Networking Section. In the past two years, she has promoted Internet use for special librarians at local SLA chapter programs, as well as presenting programs at the SLA annual conferences. With Sharyn Ladner, she has coauthored several articles and a book related to electronic networking and the special library community. She received her M.L.S. from Rutgers University and her M.B.A. from Rider College.

CHRISTINGER TOMER <ct@lis.pitt.edu> is an assistant professor, Department of Library Science, School of Library and Information Science, at the University of Pittsburgh. He has also taught at Case Western Reserve University, Notre Dame College of Ohio, and Slippery Rock University of Pennsylvania. Tomer was educated at the College of Wooster and Case Western Reserve University. His research interests include distributed file systems, electronic mail systems, wide area networking, and the application of information technologies to library processes.

Index